MySQL and mSQL

MySQL and mSQL

Randy Jay Yarger, George Reese, and Tim King

O'REILLY®

Beijing · Cambridge · Farnham · Köln · Paris · Sebastopol · Taipei · Tokyo

MySQL and mSQL

by Randy Jay Yarger, George Reese, and Tim King

Copyright © 1999 O'Reilly & Associates, Inc. All rights reserved.
Printed in the United States of America.

Published by O'Reilly & Associates, Inc., 101 Morris Street, Sebastopol, CA 95472.

Editor: Andy Oram

Production Editor: Jeffrey Liggett

Editorial and Production Services: Electro-Publishing

Printing History:

> July 1999:   First Edition.

ISBN: 1-56592-434-7

Table of Contents

Preface

In the world of computing, the 1990s may rightly be called the decade of *Open Source software*. From Linux to Perl, from palmtop to mainframe, the Open Source movement has left a mark in practically every niche of technology. This impact is especially strong in the commercially neglected world of mid-range server applications commonly needed by nonprofit organizations and small businesses.

The idea of mid-range servers was fairly rare in the first few decades of the computer age. Computers were expensive items used by large institutions such as banks and universities. Enormous time-sharing servers provided the computing power for entire companies. Much of the software running on these systems was as monolithic as the servers themselves. After all, because only one computer was serving several departments—if not the whole organization—that computer had to fulfill everyone's needs.

At the other end of the spectrum was the personal computer. With the PC revolution, you could find one computer for every household instead of one computer for an entire company. While these computers were easily powerful enough to satisfy the needs of a single user, a wide gulf still existed between the capabilities—and the costs—of personal computing and corporate computing.

The area where this gulf was most apparent was in data management. Database applications for large mainframe servers included every feature possible. Because of the multipurpose nature of this software, if any odd feature was needed by a single user, it was included. Database applications that satisfied those data management needs of the individual user emerged. However, where mainframe databases were too massive for mid-range needs, personal databases were too narrow.

In the first half of the 1990s, the "lowly" personal computer had advanced to the point where it was actually more powerful than the mainframe computers of yesteryear. While hardware was no longer a barrier to mid-range computing, the lack of affordable software was. To meet the data storage needs of a nonprofit organization or small business, you needed an affordable server operating system and an affordable database management system. The introduction of cheap and powerful server operating systems like FreeBSD and Linux helped solve the operating system side of that equation.

MySQL and mSQL are two solutions that solve the database management side of the equation. They are powerful and flexible while at the same time lightweight and efficient. MySQL, in particular, packs a large feature set into a very small and fast engine. While neither database engine has anywhere near the full feature set of expensive corporate databases, they easily have enough of a feature set to meet the needs of mid-range database management.

Audience

This book is primarily for two classes of readers. The most obvious is the reader interested in using MySQL and mSQL from either a database administration perspective or from a database programmer perspective. In addition, anyone who wants to learn about relational database administration and programming without paying out the nose for a license from one of the big guys will find MySQL or mSQL an excellent starting point. If MySQL or mSQL is your starting point, then this book is your guide.

From a database administrator's perspective, we cover the basic methods of creating and managing databases and tables in MySQL and mSQL. We go beyond the simple and provide performance tuning and troubleshooting tips to help you make sure your MySQL and mSQL applications are running their best. Finally, all of the tools that come with MySQL and mSQL are covered in detail. We assume no prior knowledge of SQL or relational databases.

Database programmers will find that we have covered all of the major programming interfaces from the most popular client/server and web programming languages. When we cover the interface for a particular language, we assume that the reader has a basic grasp of the language in question. For example, in the Java™ chapter, we assume that the reader knows how to write basic Java applications and now wants to learn how to make those Java applications talk to a MySQL or mSQL database.

The immense popularity of MySQL and mSQL on the Web has made it natural to provide a focus on CGI programming with *MySQL and mSQL*. Web developers should therefore find this book useful in describing how to drive their web sites with a MySQL or mSQL database. For these chapters, very little CGI knowledge is needed, but we still assume that the reader is familiar with the basics of the programming language in question.

Purpose

At first glance, the purpose of this book seems obvious: MySQL and mSQL are two of the most popular applications offering public source code. They offer the practical advantages of Open Source software even through their licenses are a bit too restrictive for the Open Source mark. For anyone who has spent a significant amount of time learning MySQL or mSQL, the answer is a little more complex.

One of the biggest complaints about Open Source projects is almost always the lack of comprehensive and comprehensible documentation. In the case of MySQL and mSQL, however, lack of online documentation is rarely a problem.

MySQL has a wonderfully complete and free online reference manual available from the web site at *http://www.mysql.com*. This manual covers the full MySQL SQL syntax, installation, and its C API, as well as database administration and performance tuning. Similarly, mSQL has a good, if less comprehensive, online manual at *http://www.hughes.com.au*.

To make matters even more complex, MySQL and mSQL are both moving targets because of rapid development. In the case of MySQL, "moving target" is a euphemism. Thanks mainly to the efforts of Michael "Monty" Widenius, MySQL is a target moving about as fast as a freight train. So be prepared, you may find some of the information in this book either ahead of older versions or behind newer versions.

But wait! Don't put this book back on the shelf just yet. We knew about all of these issues before we tackled the task of writing this book. One major reason made a book on this topic not only justified, but essential. The worlds of MySQL and mSQL are not limited to a couple of database engines. Because of the degree to which they have been embraced by the Open Source community, MySQL and mSQL also encompass a host of tools for managing and programming applications for these databases. The purpose of this book is therefore to provide a single, definitive guide to these database engines and the world of APIs and tools used to build end-to-end database solutions. Anyways, a book is much easier to read in the bathroom or on a plane than online documentation.

Using This Book

We have divided this book into three sections. The first section covers getting started and managing a MySQL or mSQL database. The second section builds upon that foundation by demonstrating how you build applications that use your MySQL or mSQL database. Finally, we provide a full reference section to provide a resource for quickly looking up any of the APIs or tools we cover in the first two sections.

If you are a member of the audience we described earlier, you fall into one of three categories:

- MySQL users and administrators

- mSQL users and administrators

- Undecided, but definitely will be using either MySQL or mSQL

We have directed the first section of the book at database administrators. We start at a high level by addressing the question of what exactly is a database. Perhaps you have experience with databases; if so, such a discussion is certainly way too basic for you. You will still want to catch the end of Chapter 1, *Introduction to Relational Databases*, for a short introduction to MySQL and mSQL. This discussion is of particular interest to anyone who has not yet made a decision on which database to use and who wants a short overview of the two.

Chapter 2, *Database Design*, may appear at first unimportant. It is, on the contrary, one of the most important chapters of the book. Proper database design is essential for both database administrators and programmers if the goal is to build database applications that will be flexible enough to scale as application needs change. You also need a proper database design if you want your database to actually perform well.

Chapter 3, *Installation*, covers installation of both engines.

If you have chosen a particular database engine, you can skip either Chapter 4, *MySQL*, or Chapter 5, *mSQL*. Each chapter is specific to one of the two database engines and is completely irrelevant to users of the other engine. If, however, you have not yet made a decision, then these two chapters will be key to your selection process.

We close out the administrative section with a discussion of the variants of SQL presented by MySQL and mSQL. While programmers may be largely uninterested in the first section, they will find the need to occasionally refer to this section even if they are experienced SQL programmers. Anyone who has never before used SQL definitely needs to read this chapter.

The second section begins with an overview of the client/server programming model. This discussion is very high level, but it is key to understanding how the database and the application programming work together to build a solid database application. Of course, if you are experienced with client/server programming in other environments, this sort of architectural discussion may be old hat to you. The rest of the section contains chapters devoted to programming in specific languages or using specific tools. Of particular interest to web programmers will be the chapters on Perl, Java, Python, and PHP.

The book closes with a reference section that covers all of the tools and APIs we address in the book.*

On MySQL and mSQL

We have attempted to provide balanced and full coverage of both MySQL and mSQL in this book. A single book on both engines makes sense since they are so similar. While they do not have common code, the similarities are quite intentional. In order to be consistent, we have chosen always to use the expression "MySQL and mSQL" or "MySQL or mSQL" wherever something is true of both database engines. MySQL comes first only because we arbitrarily decided to make the most popular of the two appear first. Where MySQL or mSQL appear alone in a sentence without the other, the sentence is specifically addressing an issue associated with that database engine. Except for chapters dedicated solely to one engine or the other, you can assume that MySQL or mSQL appearing alone in a sentence means that the sentence is true only of the database being mentioned.

Conventions Used in This Book

The following conventions are used in this book:

Constant width
> Used for anything that might appear in a program, including keywords, function names, SQL commands, and variable names. This font is also used for code examples, output displayed by commands, and system configuration files.

Constant width bold
> Used for user input.

Constant width italic
> Indicates an element (e.g., a filename or variable) that you supply.

Italic
> Used for directory names, filenames, program names, Unix commands, and URLs. This font is also used to introduce new terms and for emphasis.

---

* Chapter 22, *JDBC Reference*, is a revised version of an appendix from O'Reilly's *Database Programming with JDBC and Java* by George Reese.

The owl symbol is used to indicate a tip, suggestion, or general note.

 The turkey symbol is used to indicate a warning.

Comments and Questions

Please address comments and questions concerning this book to the publisher:

O'Reilly & Associates
101 Morris Street
Sebastopol, CA 95472
800-998-9938 (in the U.S. or Canada)
707-829-0515 (international or local)
707-829-0104 (FAX)

You can also send us messages electronically. To be put on our mailing list or to request a catalog, send email to:

info@oreilly.com

To ask technical questions or comment on the book, send email to:

bookquestions@oreilly.com

Before submitting a bug report concerning MySQL, please check the online manual (and particularly the list of problems and common errors) at:

http://www.mysql.com/Manual_chapter/manual_toc.html

You can search the MySQL mailing list at:

http://www.mysql.com/doc.html

and the MySQL web site at:

http://www.mysql.com/search.html

Acknowledgments

The authors would first like to thank their editor Andy Oram for both his skill at making our work look more professional and for the less obvious and likely less enjoyable task of putting us back on focus when our minds would wander.

We also owe a huge debt of gratitude to those who provided us with a critical look at the book. Anyone familiar with MySQL knows the name Michael Widenius, the head of the MySQL project. He and another member of the MySQL team, Paul DuBois, sent in many valuable comments. Brian Jepson, one of the authors of the *Official Guide to Mini SQL* (John Wiley & Sons, Inc.), kindly offered us valuable input on our mSQL coverage. Finally, Glenn MacGregor and Michael Schecter provided useful comments on the book overall.

From Randy Yarger

I would like to thank my fiancée, Stacie Sheldon, for the support and love that has kept me sane. I would also like to thank Andy Oram for encouraging a relatively unknown author. Finally, but definitely not lastly, I would like to thank the ones that made it possible for me to be here, my mother, my father, and my creator.

From George Reese

I would specifically like to thank Monique Girgis for using her professional proofreading abilities on each one of my chapters. Leigh Caldwell also provided some critical eleventh-hour feedback on the last version of the MySQL chapters. Finally, I have to mention my cats, Misty, Gypsy, and Tia.

From Tim King

I wish to acknowledge Professor John Carlis for getting me interested in database technology and data modeling in the first place; Mark Kale for teaching me more about it than I ever learned in college; the lovely Ann Soter for her moral support and patience; and my mother and father for encouraging my interest in computers before it was cool to be a geek!

I

Getting Started with MySQL and mSQL

The first section of this book starts off by introducing you to relational database concepts and design. With the proper background in place, we will dive into the details of getting started with MySQL and mSQL. Perhaps you are already committed to one of these excellent database engines and are expecting this book to help you work with that database. In that case, you can focus on your database of choice and ignore areas devoted to the other. If, on the other hand, you have yet to make a choice, this section should cover enough of the basics to help you make the right choice for your situation. By the end of this section, you should have your database installed and configured, and you should be prepared to take on the subject of database programming, which is found in Part II, *Database Programming*.

1

Introduction to Relational Databases

Large corporate computing shops have been using complex and expensive database products for years. These full-featured, heavily optimized software systems are the only way for a big organization to manage its volumes of corporate information.

Home computer users haven't traditionally needed database products at all. They house their data—addresses, to-do lists, etc.—on their systems in small files or in specialized, off-the-shelf spreadsheet and phone book applications.

A new category of computer users who falls in between these two extremes has come into play. These persons maintain moderate-sized information sets required for small organizations, such as new businesses or nonprofit organizations. Alternatively, such users may not be just small, but instead may be a geographically isolated part of a larger company. Or the new kind of users might simply be individuals interested in maintaining complex, but personal data, such as a list of songs, from favorite bands, that can be served up on a personal web page. If you are the kind of person who wants a database, who is willing to do some work to set one up, but who does not want to spend six figures on a product and a fleet of programmers to maintain it, this book is for you.

This book introduces you to the world of small-scale database development through two popular database products, MySQL and mSQL. We start by introducing you to relational databases and application design in the relational world. If you have experience with relational databases and database design, you can skip on to Chapter 4, *MySQL*, or Chapter 5, *mSQL*, where we dive into the details of getting up and running with MySQL and mSQL. If you do skip on, you should note that we do provide a brief introduction and comparison of the two engines at the end of this chapter. The rest of the book—the vast majority of it—covers the use of MySQL and mSQL to build and support the type of applications important to users like you.

What Is a Database?

A *database* is, simply put, a collection of data. An example of a nonelectronic database is the public library. The library stores books, periodicals, and other documents. When you need to locate some data at the library, you search through the card catalog or the periodicals index, or maybe you even ask the librarian. Another similar example is the unsorted pile of papers you might find on your desk. When you need to find something, you rifle through the stack until you find the scrap of paper you are looking for. This database works (or maybe it doesn't) because the size of the database is incredibly small. A stack of papers certainly would not work with a larger set of data, such as the collections in the library. In the library, without the card catalog, periodicals index, and librarian, the library would still be a database; it would just be an unusable database. A database therefore generally requires some sort of organization to be of value. Your pile of papers would be much more reliable if you had some sort of filing system (then maybe you would not have lost that phone number!). So, restating our definition, we will define a database as an *organized* collection of data.

The library and the stack of papers have many similarities. They are both databases of documents. It makes no sense, however, to combine them because your papers are only interesting to you and the library contains documents of general interest. Both databases have a specific purpose and they are organized according to that purpose. We will therefore amend our definition a bit further: a database is a collection of data that is *organized* and stored according to some *purpose.*

Traditional paper-based databases have many disadvantages. They require a tremendous amount of physical space. Libraries occupy entire buildings and searching a library is relatively slow. Anyone who has spent time in a library knows that it can consume a nontrivial amount of time to find the information you seek. Libraries are also tedious to maintain and an inordinate amount of time is spent keeping the catalogs and shelves consistent. Electronic storage of a database helps to address these issues.

MySQL and mSQL are not databases. They are actually computer software that enable a user to create, maintain, and manage electronic databases. This category of software is known as a Database Management System (DBMS). A DBMS acts as a broker between the physical database and the users of that database.

When you first began managing electronic information, you almost certainly used a flat file. The file system file is the electronic version of the pile of papers on your desk. You likely came to the conclusion that this sort of ad hoc electronic database didn't meet your needs any more. A DBMS is the logical next step for your database needs, and MySQL and mSQL are the first stepping stones into the world of relational database management systems.

What Is a Relational Database?

According to our definition, a database is an organized collection of data. A relational database organizes data into tables. It is probably easier to illustrate the concept of a table than try to explain it. Table 1-1 is an example of a table that might appear in a book database.

Table 1-1. A Table of Books

ISBN	Title	Author
0-446-67424-9	L.A. Confidential	James Ellroy
0-201-54239-X	An Introduction to Database Systems	C.J. Date
0-87685-086-7	Post Office	Charles Bukowski
0-941423-38-7	The Man with the Golden Arm	Nelson Algren

Table 1-2 and Table 1-3 demonstrate two tables that might appear in an NBA database.

Table 1-2. A Table of NBA Teams

Team #	Name	Coach
1	Golden State Warriors	P.J. Carlesimo
2	Minnesota Timberwolves	Flip Saunders
3	L.A. Lakers	Kurt Rambis
4	Indiana Pacers	Larry Bird

Table 1-3. A Table of NBA Players

Name	Position	Team #
Rik Smits	Center	4
Kevin Garnett	Forward	2
Kobe Bryant	Guard	3
Reggie Miller	Guard	4
Stephon Marbury	Guard	2
Shaquille O'Neal	Center	3

We'll get into the specifics about tables later on, but you should note a few things about these examples. Each table has a name, several columns, and rows containing data for each of the columns. A relational database represents all of your data in tables just like this and provides you with retrieval operations that generate new tables from existing ones. As a result, the user sees the entire database in the form of tables.

A DBMS for a relational system is often called a Relational Database Management System (RDBMS). MySQL and mSQL are both examples of an RDBMS.

Where does SQL fit into all of this? We need some way to interact with the database. We need to define tables and retrieve, add, update, or delete data. SQL (Structured Query Language) is a computer language used to express database operations for data organized in a relational form (e.g., in tables). SQL is the industry standard language that most database programmers speak, and it is used by most RDBMS packages. As their names indicate, MySQL and mSQL are both SQL database engines. Due to their simplicity, however, they only support a subset of the current SQL standard, SQL2. We will discuss exactly how MySQL and mSQL support for SQL differs from the standard in later chapters.

Applications and Databases

According to our definition of a database, a database is an organized collection of data that serves some purpose. Just having a DBMS is not sufficient to give your database purpose. How you use your data defines its purpose. Imagine a library where nobody ever reads the books. There would not be much point in storing and organizing all of those books if they were never used. Now, imagine a library where you could not change or add to the collection. The utility of the library as a database would decrease over time since obsolete books could never be replaced and new books could never be added. In short, a library exists so that people may read the books and find the information they seek.

Databases exist so that people can interact with them. In the case of electronic databases, the interaction occurs not directly with the database, but instead indirectly through software applications. Before the emergence of the World Wide Web, databases typically were used by large corporations to support various business functions: accounting and financials, shipping and inventory control, manufacturing planning, human resources, and so on. The web and more complex home computing tasks have helped move the need for database applications outside the realm of the large corporation.

Databases and the Web

The area in which databases have experienced the most explosive growth—an area where MySQL and mSQL excel—is in web application development. As the demand for more complex and robust web applications grows, so does the need for databases. A database backend can support many critical functions on the web. Virtually any web content can be driven by a database.

Consider the example of a catalog retailer who would like to publish on the web and accept orders online. If the catalog were published as HTML files, someone would have to hand edit the catalog each time a new item was added or a price changed. If the catalog information were instead stored in a relational database, it would be possible to publish real time catalog updates simply by changing the product or price data in the database. It would also become possible to integrate the online catalog with existing electronic order processing systems. Using a database to drive such a web site thus has obvious advantages for both the retailer and the customer.

Here's how a web page typically interacts with a database. The database is on your web server or another machine that your server can talk to (a good DBMS makes this kind of distributed responsibility easy). You put a form on one web page that the user fills in with a query or data to submit. When the form's query is sent to your server, it runs a program that you write that extracts the data submitted by the user. These programs most often come in the form of CGI scripts and Java servlets, but can also occur by embedding programming right inside the HTML page. We will look at all of these methods in this book.

Now your program knows what the user is asking for or wishes to add to the database. The program issues an SQL query or update, and the database magically takes care of the rest. Any results obtained from the database can be formatted by your program into a new HTML page to send back to the user.

MySQL and mSQL

MySQL and mSQL are very similar, cheap, lightweight, and fast databases. This book covers both databases due to their overwhelming similarity. They are, however, different in very important ways and we will be sure to cover those differences as well. Both systems support C, Perl, Java (via Java DataBase Connectivity API [JDBC]), and Python programming. With the tools MySQL and mSQL provide these languages, it is possible to create full-blown client/server applications and database-integrated web sites and not spend a fortune. This is great news for the small web publisher or for anyone developing small-scale client/server applications who cannot afford to purchase one of the commercially available products.

The inexpensive—in some cases, free—nature of MySQL and mSQL does not come cost free. Neither DBMS supports the full range of SQL. These engines lack some features that may be required by more complex applications. For some applications you also have to work a little harder on the client side to meet needs that you get for free from expensive database engines. We will, however, teach you how to build portable MySQL and mSQL applications so that you have the option to try out more heavy-weight database engines when your needs demand them—you won't have to make a ton of changes to migrate to a big-time database. In order to understand what these two engines have to offer, it is best to take a brief look at their histories.

The History of mSQL

Before 1994, you were out of luck if you wanted a SQL-based RDBMS without paying large sums of money. The dominant commercial SQL solutions were Oracle, Sybase, and Informix. These database engines were designed to handle tremendous amounts of data with very complex relationships. They were powerful and full of features—and very resource intensive and expensive. In those days, you could not buy a $2000 200 MHz Pentium server. The resources required by these database engines cost tens of thousands of dollars.

Large corporations and major universities had no problem spending millions of dollars per year on these large DBMS/server combinations. As a small organization or individual user, however, you had to settle for weak desktop database programs. A few cheap client/server database engines did exist at that time, but none of them used SQL as their query language. The most notable of these database engines was Postgres, which was a DBMS descended from the same roots as the commercial Ingres RDBMS. Postgres, unfortunately, came with similar resource requirements as its commercial counterparts without the advantage of SQL as a query language. At the time, postgres used a variant of the QUEL language called PostQUEL.

David Hughes

As part of his Ph.D. thesis at Bond University in Australia, David Hughes (a.k.a. Bambi) was developing a system of monitoring and managing a variety of systems from one or more locations. This project was called the Minerva Network Management System. A key piece of Minerva was a DBMS for storing information about the machines on the network. As a university student without direct access to a server running one of the major commercial relational database engines, Hughes looked to Postgres as the obvious solution to his database needs.

Hughes' colleagues initially suggested that SQL should be the standard query language for Minerva. After all, SQL was—and still is—the most overwhelmingly accepted standard for a query language. By standardizing on SQL, Minerva could serve the needs of people all over the world just as long as they had some type of SQL DBMS installed. In other words, SQL exposed Minerva to a much wider audience that PostQUEL, which was limited to Postgres. As it turns out, today even Postgres speaks SQL.

The tug-of-war between the SQL standard and access to a SQL database engine left Hughes in a bind. If he based Minerva's query language on SQL, he would have no database engine. Because buying a multithousand dollar RDBMS was not an option, Hughes took a creative approach to the problem. He decided the solution was to create an application that could translate SQL into PostQUEL on the fly. This program would intercept all SQL statements sent from Minerva, convert them to PostQUEL, and then send the PostQUEL on to Postgres. Hughes created this product and named it miniSQL, or mSQL.

From PostQUEL translator to RDBMS

For a while, this configuration worked well for Hughes' needs. The Minerva system did not care what DBMS was in use so long as it understood SQL. As far as Minerva knew, Postgres did understand SQL because mSQL was there in the middle to handle PostQUEL translation. Unfortunately, as Minerva grew bigger, it also grew significantly slower. It eventually became clear that Postgres—or any other huge RDBMS—was not capable of supporting the small feature set demanded by Minerva in the limited resources available to Minerva. For example, Minerva required multiple simultaneous database connections. In order to support this, Postgres required multiple instances* of the database server to be running at the same time. In addition, several potential contributors to the Minerva project could not get involved because Postgres did not support their systems and they, too, did not have the option of purchasing an expensive SQL-based DBMS.

In the face of these problems, Hughes reevaluated his decision to use Postgres. As large and complex as it was, it was likely too complex for Minerva's needs. Most of Minerva's queries were simple INSERT, DELETE, and SELECT statements. All of the other stuff that cost Postgres in terms of performance simply was not required by Minerva.

Hughes already had mSQL doing SQL translation. He only needed to add data storage and retrieval capabilities to it and he had a database server that met his needs. This evolution led to the mSQL to that exists today.

The History of MySQL

It would be a mistake to characterize MySQL as a simple reaction to mSQL's failures. Its inventor, Michael Widenius (a.k.a. Monty) at the Swedish company TcX, has been working with databases since 1979. Until recently, Widenius was the only developer at TcX. In 1979, he developed an in-house database tool called

---

* Each process running the same program is called an instance of that program, because it occupies memory just as an instance of a variable takes up a program's memeory.

UNIREG for managing databases. Since 1979, `UNIREG` has been rewritten in several different languages and extended to handle big databases.

In 1994, TcX began developing web-based applications and used `UNIREG` to support this effort. Unfortunately, `UNIREG` created too much overhead to be successful in dynamically generating web pages. TcX began looking at SQL and mSQL. At that time, however, mSQL was still in its 1.x releases. As we mentioned, mSQL 1.x did not support any indices. mSQL's performance was therefore poor in comparison to UNIREG.

Widenius contacted David Hughes—the author of mSQL—to see if Hughes would be interested in connecting mSQL to UNIREG's B+ ISAM handler. Hughes was already well on his way to mSQL 2, however, and already had his indexing infrastructure in place. TcX decided to create a database server that was more compatible with its requirements.

TcX was smart enough not to try to reinvent the wheel. It built upon UNIREG and capitalized on the growing number of third party mSQL utilities by writing an API into its system that was, at least initially, practically identical to the mSQL API. As a result, an mSQL user who wanted to move to the TcX more feature-rich database server would only have to make trivial changes to any existing code. The code supporting this new database, however, was completely original.

By May 1995, TcX had a database that met its internal needs—MySQL 1.0. A business partner, David Axmark at Detron HB, began pressing TcX to release this server on the Internet. The goal of an Internet release would be to use a business model pioneered by Aladdin Peter Deutsch. The result was a very flexible copyright that makes MySQL "more free" than mSQL.

As for the name MySQL, Widenius says, "It is not perfectly clear where the name MySQL derives from. TcX's base directory and a large amount of their libraries and tools have had the prefix 'my' for well over 10 years. However, my daughter (some years younger) is also named My. So which of the two gave its name to MySQL is still a mystery."

Since the initial Internet release of MySQL, it has been ported to a host of Unix operating systems, Win32, and OS/2. TCX estimates that MySQL runs on about 500,000 severs.

Major changes in Version 3.22, the current recommended version, are:

- Better security
- Faster connections, faster parsing of SQL queries, and a better query optimizer
- Support for more operating systems
- `INSERT DELAYED`

- GRANT and REVOKE commands

- CREATE INDEX and DROP INDEX

- HIGH_PRIORITY and LOW_PRIORITY lock levels for SELECT, INSERT, UPDATE, and DELETE statements

- A new FLUSH command operating on TABLES, HOSTS, LOGS, and PRIVILEGES

- A new KILL command in SQL that works like *kill* under Unix or *msqladmin*

- A HAVING clause supporting expressions

- Compressed client/server protocol

- Saving default program options in my.cnf files

Major changes in Version 3.23, a development version, are:

- Tables directly portable between different operating systems and CPUs

- Temporary tables and HEAP tables, which are stored only in RAM

- Support for big files (63 bit) on operating systems that support them

- True floating point fields

- Comments on tables

- Sample ANALYSE ( ) procedure

- User-defined functions

- Much faster SELECT DISTINCT handling

- COUNT (DISTINCT)

Future enhancements planned for 3.23 include support for nesting one SELECT statement inside another and support for replicating databases, which permits load distribution among multiple servers and recovery in case of hardware failure.

MySQL is a very rapidly evolving database platform because of the army of volunteer coders who are helping to add to its strong base. You should therefore not be too surprised to find something that was true when we wrote this chapter is no longer true!

MySQL or mSQL?

We certainly have not yet provided you with enough information from which to make a decision. To get a full appreciation for the differences between the two engines as they exist today, you need to read on and understand the nuances as we present them in this book. On the surface, MySQL appears to be the obvious choice. mSQL fell behind after a time and is currently slower. David Hughes is not complacent. He is working on Version 2.1 of mSQL which should address many of its current shortcomings. At the same time, however, MySQL is moving ahead at the speed of light.

The case for mSQL may depend on the tools you are using. Because mSQL has been around longer, you may find more luck locating a tool that supports your specific needs. For example, only mSQL had a JDBC 2.0 compliant JDBC driver for Java database access at the time of this book's publication. Certainly this situation will have changed by the time you read this book. Nevertheless, you need to consider issues such as that when you decide which database to use.

No matter which database you use, you will be a winner. Both database engines are faster than any other choice you will make. Both database engines are perfect for mid-range database needs. For an objective comparison of these two databases with each other or any other database, we recommend you visit *http://www. mysql.com/crash-me-choose.htmy*. It is on the MySQL home page, but its criteria are openly verifiable and it is very well done.

2

Database Design

Once you install your DBMS software on your computer, it can be very tempting to just jump right into creating a database without much thought or planning. As with any software development, this kind of ad hoc approach works with only the simplest of problems. If you expect your database to support any kind of complexity, some planning and design will definitely save you time in the long run. You will need to take a look at what details are important to good database design.

Database Design

Suppose you have a large collection of compact discs and you want to create a database to track them. The first step is to determine what the data that you are going to store is about. One good way to start is to think about why you want to store the data in the first place. In our case, we most likely want to be able to look up CDs by artist, title, and song. Since we want to look up those items, we know they must be included in the database. In addition, it is often useful to simply list items that should be tracked. One possible list might include: CD title, record label, band name, song title. As a starting point, we will store the data in the table shown in Table 2-1.

Table 2-1. A CD Database Made Up of a Single Table

Band Name	CD Title	Record Label	Songs
Stevie Wonder	Talking Book	Motown	You Are the Sunshine of My Life, Maybe Your Baby, Superstition, . . .
Miles Davis Quintet	Miles Smiles	Columbia	Orbits, Circle, . . .
Wayne Shorter	Speak No Evil	Blue Note	Witch Hunt, Fee-Fi-Fo-Fum

Table 2-1. A CD Database Made Up of a Single Table (continued)

Band Name	CD Title	Record Label	Songs
Herbie Hancock	Headhunters	Columbia	Chameleon, Watermelon Man, . . .
Herbie Hancock	Maiden Voyage	Blue Note	Maiden Voyage

(For brevity's sake, we have left out most of the songs.) At first glance, this table seems like it will meet our needs since we are storing all of the data we need. Upon closer inspection, however, we find several problems. Take the example of Herbie Hancock. "Band Name" is repeated twice: once for each CD. This repetition is a problem for several reasons. First, when entering data in the database, we end up typing the same name over and over. Second, and more important, if any of the data changes, we have to update it in multiple places. For example, what if "Herbie" were misspelled? We would have to update the data in each of the two rows. The same problem would occur if the name Herbie Hancock changes in the future (à la Jefferson Airplane or John Cougar). As we add more Herbie Hancock CDs to our collection, we add to the amount of effort required to maintain data consistency.

Another problem with the single CD table lies in the way it stores songs. We are storing them in the CD table as a list of songs in a single column. We will run into all sorts of problems if we want to use this data meaningfully. Imagine having to enter and maintain that list. And what if we want to store the length of the songs as well? What if we want to perform a search by song title? It quickly becomes clear that storing the songs in this fashion is undesirable.

This is where database design comes into play. One of the main purposes of database design is to eliminate redundancy from the database. To accomplish this task, we use a technique called *normalization*. Before we start with normalization, let's start with some fundamental relational database concepts. A data model is a diagram that illustrates your database design. It is made up of three main elements: entities, attributes, and relationships. For now, let's focus on entities and attributes; we will take a look at relationships later.

Database Entities

An *entity* is a thing or object of importance about which data must be captured. All "things" are not entities, only those things about which you need to capture information. Information about an entity is captured in the form of attributes and/ or relationships. If something is a candidate for being an entity and it has no attributes or relationships, it is not really an entity. Database entities appear in a data model as a box with a title. The title is the name of the entity.

Entity Attributes

An *attribute* describes information about an entity that must be captured. Each entity has zero or more attributes that describe it, and each attribute describes exactly one entity. Each entity instance (row in the table) has exactly one value, possibly NULL, for each of its attributes. An attribute value can be numeric, a character string, date, time, or some other basic data value. In the first step of database design, logical data modeling, we do not worry about how the attributes will be stored.

 NULL provides the basis for the problem of dealing with missing information. It is specifically used for the case in which you lack a certain piece of information. As an example, consider the situation where a CD does not list the song lengths of each of its tracks. Each song has a length, but you cannot tell from the case what that length is. You do not want to store the length as zero, since that would be incorrect. Instead, you store the length as NULL. If you are thinking you could store it as zero and use zero to mean "unknown", you are falling into one of the same traps that led to one of the Y2K problems. Not only did old systems store years as two digits, but they often gave a special meaning to 9-9-99.

Our example database refers to a number of things: the CD, the CD title, the band name, the songs, and the record label. Which of these are entities and which are attributes?

Data Model

Notice that we capture several pieces of data (CD title, band name, etc.) about each CD, and we absolutely cannot describe a CD without those items. CD is therefore one of those things we want to capture data about and is likely an entity. To start a data model, we will diagram it as an entity. Figure 2-1 shows our sole entity in a data model.

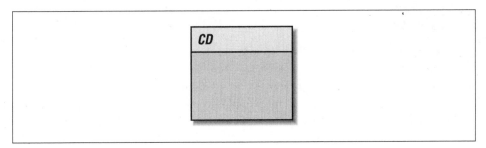

Figure 2-1. The CD entity in a data model

By common entity naming conventions, an entity name must be singular. We therefore call the table where we store CDs "CD" and not "CDs." We use this convention because each entity names an instance. For example, the "San Francisco 49ers" is an instance of "Football Team," not "Football Teams."

At first glance, it appears that the rest of the database describes a CD. This would indicate that they are attributes of CD. Figure 2-2 adds them to the CD entity in Figure 2-1. In a data model, attributes appear as names listed in their entity's box.

Figure 2-2. The CD entity with its attributes

This diagram is simple, but we are not done yet. In fact, we have only just begun. Earlier, we discussed how the purpose of data modeling is to eliminate redundancy using a technique called normalization. We have a nice diagram for our database, but we have not gotten rid of the redundancy as we set out to do. It is now time to normalize our database.

Normalization

E.F. Codd, then a researcher for IBM, first presented the concept of database normalization in several important papers written in the 1970s. The aim of normalization remains the same today: to eradicate certain undesirable characteristics from a database design. Specifically, the goal is to remove certain kinds of data redundancy and therefore avoid update anomalies. Update anomalies are difficulties with the insert, update, and delete operations on a database due to the data structure. Normalization additionally aids in the production of a design that is a high-quality representation of the real world; thus normalization increases the clarity of the data model.

As an example, say we misspelled "Herbie Hancock" in our database and we want to update it. We would have to visit each CD by Herbie Hancock and fix the artist's name. If the updates are controlled by an application which enables us to edit only one record at a time, we end up having to edit many rows. It would be much more desirable to have the name "Herbie Hancock" stored only once so we have to maintain it in just one place.

First Normal Form (1NF)

The general concept of normalization is broken up into several "normal forms." An entity is said to be in the first normal form when all attributes are single-valued. To apply the first normal form to an entity, we have to verify that each attribute in the entity has a single value for each instance of the entity. If any attribute has repeating values, it is not in 1NF.

A quick look back at our database reveals that we have repeating values in the Songs attribute, so the CD is clearly not in 1NF. To remedy this problem, an entity with repeating values indicates that we have missed at least one other entity. One way to discover other entities is to look at each attribute and ask the question "What thing does this describe?"

What does Song describe? It lists the songs on the CD. So Song is another "thing" that we capture data about and is probably an entity. We will add it to our diagram and give it a Song Name attribute. To complete the Song entity, we need to ask if there is more about a Song that we would like to capture. We identified earlier song length as something we might want to capture. Figure 2-3 shows the new data model.

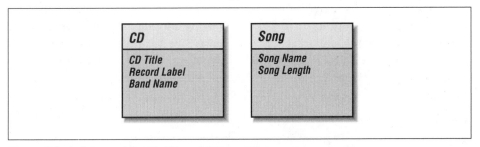

Figure 2-3. A data model with CD and Song entities

Now that the Song Name and Song Length are attributes in a Song entity, we have a data model with two entities in 1NF. None of their attributes contain multiple values. Unfortunately, we have not shown any way of relating a CD to a Song.

The Unique Identifier

Before discussing relationships, we need to impose one more rule on entities. Each entity must have a unique identifier—we'll call it the ID. An *ID* is an attribute of an entity that meets the following rules:

- It is unique across all instances of the entity.

- It has a non-NULL value for each instance of the entity, for the entire lifetime of the instance.

- It has a value that never changes for the entire lifetime of the instance.

The ID is very important because it gives us a way to know which instance of an entity we are dealing with. Identifier selection is critical because it is also used to model relationships. If, after you've selected an ID for an entity, you find that it doesn't meet one of the above rules, this could affect your entire data model.

Novice data modelers often make the mistake of choosing attributes that should not be identifiers and making them identifiers. If, for example, you have a `Person` entity, it might be tempting to use the `Name` attribute as the identifier because all people have a name and that name never changes. But what if a person marries? What if the person decides to legally change his name? What if you misspelled the name when you first entered it? If any of these events causes a name change, the third rule of identifiers is violated. Worse, is a name really ever unique? Unless you can guarantee with 100% certainty that the `Name` is unique, you will be violating the first rule. Finally, you do know that all `Person` instances have non-`NULL` names. But are you certain that you will always know the name of a `Person` when you first enter information about them in the database? Depending on your application processes, you may not know the name of a `Person` when a record is first created. The lesson to be learned is that there are many problems with taking a nonidentifying attribute and making it one.

The solution to the identifier problem is to invent an identifying attribute that has no other meaning except to serve as an identifying attribute. Because this attribute is invented and completely unrelated to the entity, we have full control over it and guarantee that it meets the rules of unique identifiers. Figure 2-4 adds invented ID attributes to each of our entities. A unique identifier is diagrammed as an underlined attribute.

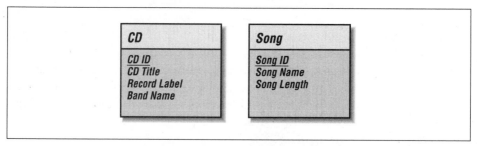

Figure 2-4. The CD and Song entities with their unique identifiers

Relationships

The identifiers in our entities enable us to model their relationships. A relationship describes a binary association between two entities. A relationship may also exist between an entity and itself. Such a relationship is called a *recursive relationship.*

Each entity within a relationship describes and is described by the other. Each side of the relationship has two components: a name and a degree.

Each side of the relationship has a name that describes the relationship. Take two hypothetical entities, an `Employee` and a `Department`. One possible relationship between the two is that an `Employee` is "assigned to" a `Department`. That `Department` is "responsible for" an `Employee`. The `Employee` side of the relationship is thus named "assigned to" and the `Department` side "responsible for."

Degree, also referred to as cardinality, states how many instances of the describing entity must describe one instance of the described entity. Degree is expressed using two different values: "one and only one" (1) and "one or many" (M). An employee is assigned to one department at a time, so `Employee` has a one and only one relationship with `Department`. In the other direction, a department is responsible for many employees. We therefore say `Department` has a "one or many" relationship with `Employee`. As a result a `Department` could have exactly one `Employee`.

It is sometimes helpful to express a relationship verbally. One way of doing this is to plug the various components of a direction of the relationship into this formula:

entity1 has [one and only one | one or many] *entity2*

Using this formula, `Employee` and `Department` would be expressed like so:

Each `Employee` must be assigned to one and only one `Department`.
Each `Department` may be responsible for one or many `Employees`.

We can use this formula to describe the entities in our data model. A CD contains one or many `Songs` and a `Song` is contained on one and only one CD. In our data model, this relationship can be shown by drawing a line between the two entities. Degree is expressed with a straight line for "one and only one" relationships or "crows feet" for "one or many" relationships. Figure 2-5 illustrates these conventions.

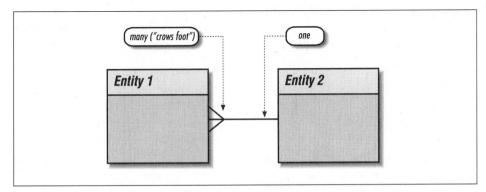

Figure 2-5. Anatomy of a relationship

How does this apply to the relationship between Song and CD? In reality, a Song can be contained on many CDs, but we ignore this for the purposes of this example. Figure 2-6 shows the data model with the relationships in place.

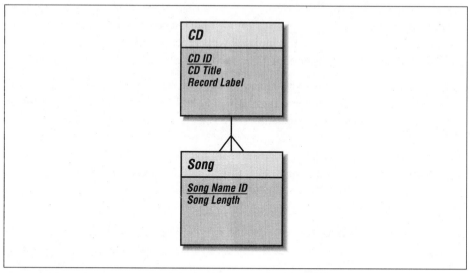

Figure 2-6. CD-Song relationship

With these relationships firmly in place, we can go back to the normalization process and improve upon the design. So far, we have normalized repeating song values into a new entity and modeled the relationship between it and the CD entity.

Second Normal Form (2NF)

An entity is said to be in the second normal form if it is already in 1NF and all nonidentifying attributes are dependent on the entity's entire unique identifier. If any attribute is not dependent entirely on the entity's unique identifier, that attribute has been misplaced and must be removed. Normalize these attributes either by finding the entity where it belongs or by creating an additional entity where the attribute should be placed.

In our example, "Herbie Hancock" is the Band Name for two different CDs. This fact illustrates that Band Name is not entirely dependent on CD ID. This duplication is a problem because if, for example, we had misspelled "Herbie Hancock," we would have to update the value in multiple places. We thus have a sign that Band Name should be part of a new entity with some relationship to CD. As before, we resolve this problem by asking the question: "What does a band name describe"? It describes a band, or more generally, an artist. Artist is yet another thing we are capturing data about and is therefore probably an entity. We will add it to our diagram with `Band Name` as an attribute. Since all artists may not be bands, we will rename the attribute `Artist Name`. Figure 2-7 shows the new state of the model.

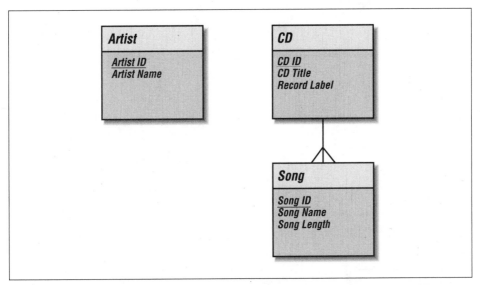

Figure 2-7. The data model with the new Artist entity

Of course, the relationships for the new Artist table are missing. We know that each `Artist` has one or many `CD`s. Each `CD` could have one or many `Artist`s. We model this in Figure 2-8.

We originally had the `Band Name` attribute in the `CD` entity. It thus seemed natural to make `Artist` directly related to `CD`. But is this really correct? On closer inspection, it would seem that there should be a direct relationship between an `Artist` and a `Song`. Each `Artist` has one or more `Song`s. Each `Song` is performed by one and only one `Artist`. The true relationship appears in Figure 2-9.

Not only does this make more sense than a relationship between `Artist` and `CD`, but it also addresses the issue of compilation `CD`s.

Kinds of Relationships

When modeling the relationship between entities, it is important to determine both directions of the relationship. After both sides of the relationship have been determined, we end up with three main kinds of relationships. If both sides of the relationship have a degree of one and only one, the relationship is called a "one-to-one" or "1-to-1" relationship. As we will find out later, one-to-one relationships are rare. We do not have one in our data model.

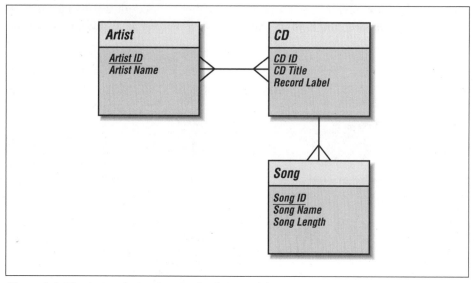

Figure 2-8. The Artist relationships in the data model

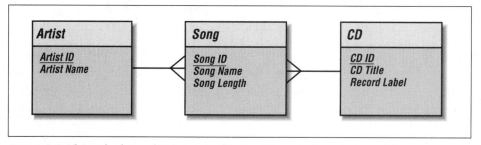

Figure 2-9. The real relationship between Artist and the rest of our data model

If one of the sides as a degree of "one or many" and the other side has a degree of "one and only one," the relationship is a "one-to-many" or "1-to-M" relationship. All of the relationships in our current data model are one-to-many relationships. This is to be expected since one-to-many relationships are the most common.

The final kind of relationships is where both sides of the relationship are "one or many" relationships. These kind of relationships are called "many-to-many" or "M-to-M" relationships. In an earlier version of our data model, the `Artist`-`CD` relationship was a many-to-many relationship.

Refining Relationships

As we noted earlier, one-to-one relationships are quite rare. In fact, if you encounter one during your data modeling, you should take a closer look at your design.

A one-to-one relationship may imply that two entities are really the same entity. If they do turn out to be the same entity, they should be folded into a single entity.

Many-to-many relationships are more common than one-to-one relationships. In these relationships, there is often some data we want to capture about the relationship. For example, take a look at the earlier version of our data model in Figure 2-8 that had the many-to-many relationship between Artist and CD. What data might we want to capture about that relationship? An Artist has a relationship with a CD because an Artist has one or more Songs on that CD. The data model in Figure 2-9 is actually another representation of this many-to-many relationship.

All many-to-many relationships should be resolved using the following technique:

1. Create a new entity (sometimes referred to as a *junction entity*). Name it appropriately. If you cannot think of an appropriate name for the junction entity, name it by combining the names of the two related entities (e.g., ArtistCD). In our data model, Song is a junction entity for the Artist-CD relationship.

2. Relate the new entity to the two original entities. Each of the original entities should have a one-to-many relationship with the junction entity.

3. If the new entity does not have an obvious unique identifier, inherit the identifying attributes from the original entities into the junction entity and make them together the unique identifier for the new entity.

In almost all cases, you will find additional attributes that belong in the new junction entity. If not, the many-to-many relationship still needs to be resolved, otherwise you will have a problem translating your data model into a physical schema.

More 2NF

Our data model is still not in 2NF. The value of the Record Label attribute has only one value for each CD, but we see the same Record Label in multiple CDs. This situation is similar to the one we saw with Band Name. As with Band Name, this duplication indicates that Record Label should be part of its own entity. Each Record Label releases one or many CDs. Each CD is released by one and only one Record Label. Figure 2-10 models this relationship.

Third Normal Form (3NF)

An entity is said to be in the third normal form if it is already in 2NF and no nonidentifying attributes are dependent on any other nonidentifying attributes. Attributes that are dependent on other nonidentifying attributes are normalized by moving both the dependent attribute and the attribute on which it is dependent into a new entity.

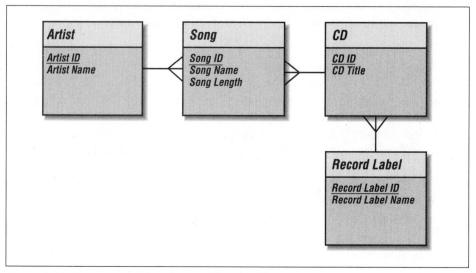

Figure 2-10. Our data model in the second normal form

If we wanted to track Record Label address information, we would have a problem for 3NF. The Record Label entity with address data would have State
Name and State Abbreviation attributes. Though we really do not need this
information to track CD data, we will add it to our data model for the sake of our
example. Figure 2-11 shows address data in the Record Label entity.

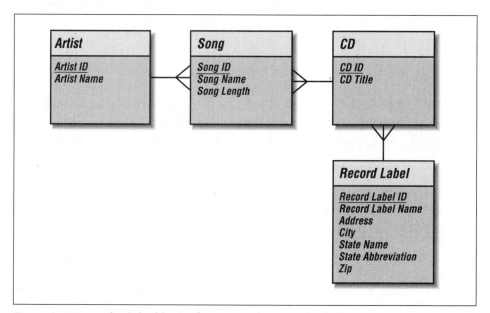

Figure 2-11. Record Label address information in our CD database

The values of State Name and State Abbreviation would conform to 1NF because they have only one value per record in the Record Label entity. The problem here is that State Name and State Abbreviation are dependent on each other. In other words, if we change the State Abbreviation for a particular Record Label—from MN to CA—we also have to change the State Name—from Minnesota to California. We would normalize this by creating a State entity with State Name and State Abbreviation attributes. Figure 2-12 shows how to relate this new entity to the Record Label entity.

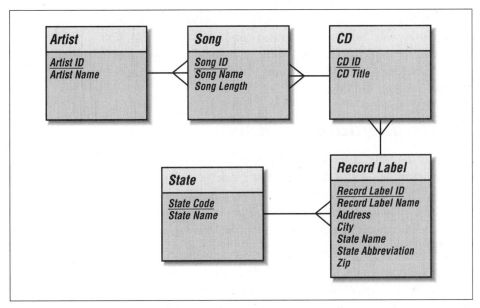

Figure 2-12. Our data model in the third normal form

Now that we are in 3NF, we can say that our data model is normalized. There are other normal forms which have some value from a database design standpoint, but these are beyond the scope of this book. For most design purposes, the third normal form is sufficient to guarantee a proper design.

A Logical Data Modeling Methodology

We now have a completed logical data model. Let's review the process we went through to get here.

1. Identify and model the entities.

2. Identify and model the relationships between the entities.

3. Identify and model the attributes.

4. Identify unique identifiers for each entity.

5. Normalize.

In practice, the process is rarely so linear. As shown in the example, it is often tempting and appropriate to jump around between entities, relationships, attributes, and unique identifiers. It is not as important that you follow a strict process as it is that you discover and capture all of the information necessary to correctly model the system.

The data model we created in this chapter is quite simple. We covered an approach to creating such a model which is in-line with the type and complexity of databases you are likely to encounter in developing MySQL or mSQL databases. We did not cover a whole host of design techniques and concepts that are not so important to small-scale database design, but these can be found in any text dedicated to database design.

Physical Database Design

What was the point in creating the logical data model? You want to create a database to store data about CDs. The data model is only an intermediate step along the way. Ultimately, you would like to end up with a MySQL or mSQL database where you can store data. How do you get there? Physical database design translates your logical data model into a set of SQL statements that define your MySQL or mSQL database.

Since MySQL and mSQL are relational database systems, it is relatively easy to translate from a logical data model, such as the one we described earlier, into a physical MySQL or mSQL database. Here are the rules for translation:

1. Entities become tables in the physical database.

2. Attributes become columns in the physical database. You have to choose an appropriate datatype for each of the columns.

3. Unique identifiers become columns that are not allowed to have NULLs. These are called *primary keys* in the physical database. You may also choose to create a unique index on the identifiers to enforce uniqueness. For your purposes, mSQL does not have a concept of a primary key. It simply has unique indices. This issue does not apply to MySQL.

4. Relationships are modeled as *foreign keys*. We will cover this later.

If we apply these rules to our data model—minus the Record Label address information—we will end up with the physical database described in Table 2-2.

Table 2-2. Physical Table Definitions for the CD Database

Table	Column	Datatype	Notes
CD	CDId	INT	primary key
	CDTitle	TEXT(50)	
Artist	ArtistId	INT	primary key
	ArtistName	TEXT(50)	
Song	SongId	INT	primary key
	SongName	TEXT(50)	
RecordLabel	RecordLabelId	INT	primary key
	RecordLabelName	TEXT(50)	primary key

The first thing you may notice is that all of the spaces are gone from the entity names in our physical schema. This is because these names need to translate into SQL calls to create these tables. Table names should thus conform to SQL naming rules. Another thing to notice is that we made all primary keys of type INT. Because these attributes are complete inventions on our part, they can be of any indexible datatype.* The fact that they are of type INT here is almost purely arbitrary. It is *almost* arbitrary because it is actually faster to search on numeric fields in many database engines and hence numeric fields make good primary keys. However, we could have chosen CHAR as the type for the primary key fields and everything would work just fine. The bottom line is that this choice should be driven by your criteria for choosing identifiers.

The rest of the columns are set to be of type TEXT with a length of 50. This definition works for both MySQL and mSQL. For MySQL, however, VARCHAR would be a better choice but not important to this example. Picking the right datatype for columns is very important, but we will not dwell on it here since we have not yet covered the datatypes for MySQL and mSQL.

We now have a starting point for a physical schema. We haven't yet translated the relationships into the physical data model. As we discussed earlier, once you have refined your data model, you should have mostly 1-to-1 and 1-to-M relationships—the M-to-M relationships were resolved via junction tables. We model relationships by adding a foreign key to one of the tables involved in the relationship. A foreign key is the unique identifier or primary key of the table on the other side of the relationship.

---

* Later in this book, we will cover the datatypes supported by MySQL and mSQL. Each database engine has different rules about which datatypes can be indexible. Neither database, for example, allows indices to be created on whole TEXT fields. It would therefore be inappropriate to have a primary key column be of type TEXT.

The most common relationship is the 1-to-M relationship. This relationship is mapped by placing the primary key on the "one" side of the relationship into the table on the "many" side. In our example, this rule means that we need to do the following:

- Place a `RecordLabelId` column in the CD table.

- Place a `CDId` column in the `Song` table.

- Place an `ArtistId` column in the `Song` table.

Table 2-3 shows the new schema.

Table 2-3. The Physical Data Model for the CD Database

Table	Column	Datatype	Notes
CD	CdId	INT	primary key
	CDTitle	TEXT(50)	
	RecordLabelId	INT	foreign key
Artist	ArtistId	INT	primary key
	ArtistName	TEXT(50)	
Song	SongId	INT	primary key
	SongName	TEXT(50)	
	CdId	INT	foreign key
	ArtistId	INT	foreign key
RecordLabel	RecordLabelId	INT	primary key
	RecordLabelName	TEXT(50)	

We do not have any 1-to-1 relationships in this data model. If we did have such a relationship, it should be mapped by picking one of the tables and giving it a foreign key column that matches the primary key from the other table. In theory, it does not matter which table you choose, but practical considerations may dictate which column makes the most sense as a foreign key.

We now have a complete physical database schema ready to go. The last remaining task is to translate that schema into SQL. For each table in the schema, you write one **CREATE TABLE** statement. Typically, you will choose to create unique indices on the primary keys to enforce uniqueness.

We are, in a sense, jumping ahead at this point. You may not be familiar with SQL yet, and it is not the purpose of this chapter to introduce the MySQL and mSQL variants of SQL. Nevertheless, here are two sample scripts to create the CD database. The first script, Example 2-1 is for MySQL. Example 2-2 is for mSQL.

Example 2-1. An Example Script for Creating the CD Database in MySQL

```
CREATE TABLE CD (CD_ID INT NOT NULL,
          RECORD_LABEL_I INT,
      CD_TITLE TEXT,
      PRIMARY KEY (CD_ID))
CREATE TABLE Artist (ARTIST_ID INT NOT NULL,
      ARTIST_NAME  TEXT,
          PRIMARY KEY (ARTIST_ID))
CREATE TABLE Song (SONG_ID INT NOT NULL,
            CD_ID INT,
            SONG_NAME TEXT,
            PRIMARY KEY (SONG_ID))
CREATE TABLE RecorLabel (RECORD_LABEL_ID INT NOT NULL,
          RECORD_LABEL_NAME TEXT,
          PRIMARY KEY(RECORD_LABEL_ID))
```

Example 2-2. An Example Script for Creating the CD Database in mSQL

```
CREATE TABLE CD (CD_ID           INT NOT NULL,
            RECORD_LABEL_ID  INT,
            CD_TITLE         TEXT(50))
CREATE UNIQUE INDEX CD_IDX ON CD (CD_ID)
CREATE TABLE Artist (ARTIST_ID    INT NO NULL,
              ARTIST_NAME  TEXT(50))
CREATE UNIQUE INDEX Artist_IDX ON Artist (ARTIST_ID)
CREATE TABLE Song (SONG_ID         INT NOT NULL,
            CD_ID           INT,
            SONG_NAME       TEXT(50))
CREATE UNIQUE INDEX Song_IDX ON Song (SONG_ID)
CREATE TABLE RecordLabel (RECORD_LABEL_ID   INT NOT NULL,
              RECORD_LABEL_NAME TEXT(50))
CREATE UNIQUE INDEX RecordLabel_IDX
            ON RecordLabel(RECORD_LABEL_ID)
```

Data models are meant to be database independent. You can therefore take the techniques and the data model we have generated in this chapter and apply them not only to MySQL and mSQL, but to Oracle, Sybase, Ingres, or any other relational database engine. In the following chapters, we will discuss the details of how you can merge your new database design knowledge into MySQL and mSQL.

3

Installation

Like most services, the MySQL and mSQL databases run as background processes (also called daemons on Unix systems). This chapter gives an overview on how to unpack and build them.

MySQL

Before you begin installing MySQL, you must answer a couple of questions.

1. Are you going to install MySQL as root or as another user?

   MySQL does not require root access to run, but installing it as root will enable you to make one copy available to everyone on your system. If you do not have root access, you will have to install it in your home directory. However, even if you install MySQL as root, it is a very good idea to run it as a different user. In this way, all data in the database can be protected from all other users by setting the permissions on the data files to only be readable by the special MySQL user. In addition, if the security of the database becomes compromised, the attacker only has access to the special MySQL user account which has no privileges beyond the database.

2. Are you going to install MySQL from source or from binary?

   There are many precompiled binary packages of MySQL available. Using this method can save time, but limits the amount of customization you can do on your installation. To install from source you need a C compiler and other development tools. If you have these, the benefits gained from installing from source usually outweigh the minor hassles.

These two questions are not mutually exclusive. If you install from a binary package you have to install as root. Binary installations will have certain path information hard coded into the binary, forcing you to install as the person who created your pre-built binary. MySQL does supply command line options to override these paths, but usually installing from source is less of a hassle.

The first step in installing MySQL, either from source or binary, is to obtain the distribution. Table 3-1 lists sites that contain copies of the MySQL source code and binaries.

Table 3-1. Sites that Contain Copies of MySQL Source Code and Binaries

Asia		
Korea	KREONet	*http://linux.kreonet.re.kr/mysql/*
Japan	Soft Agency	*http://www.softagency.co.jp/MySQL/*
	Nagoya Syouka University	*http://mirror.nucba.ac.jp/mirror/mysql/*
	Nagoya Syouka University	*ftp://mirror.nucba.ac.jp/mirror/mysql/*
	HappySize	*http://www.happysize.co.jp/mysql/*
	HappySize	*ftp://ftp.happysize.co.jp/pub/mysql/*
Singapore	HJC	*http://mysql.hjc.edu.sg/*
	HJC	*ftp://ftp.hjc.edu.sg/mysql/*
Taiwan	NCTU	*http://mysql.taconet.com.tw/*
	TTN	*http://mysql.ttn.net*
Australia		
Australia	AARNet/Queensland	*http://mirror.aarnet.edu.au/mysql/*
	AARNet/Queensland	*ftp://mirror.aarnet.edu.au/pub/mysql/*
	Blue Planet/Melbourne	*http://mysql.bluep.com*
	Blue Planet/Melbourne	*ftp://mysql.bluep.com/pub/mirror1/ mysql/*
	Tas	*http://ftp.tas.gov.au/mysql/*
	Tas	*ftp://ftp.tas.gov.au/pub/mysql/*
Africa		
South Africa	The Internet Solution/ Johannesburg	*ftp://ftp.is.co.za/linux/mysql/*
Europe		
Austria	University of Technology/ Vienna	*http://gd.tuwien.ac.at/db/mysql/*
	University of Technology/ Vienna	*ftp://gd.tuwien.ac.at/db/mysql/*

Table 3-1. Sites that Contain Copies of MySQL Source Code and Binaries (continued)

Bulgaria	Naturella	*ftp://ftp.ntrl.net/pub/mirror/mysql/*
Denmark	Ake	*http://mysql.ake.dk*
	SunSITE	*http://sunsite.auc.dk/mysql/*
	SunSITE	*ftp://sunsite.auc.dk/pub/databases/ mysql/*
Estonia	Tradenet	*http://mysql.tradenet.ee*
Finland	EUnet	*http://mysql.eunet.fi*
France	Minet	*http://www.minet.net/devel/mysql/*
Germany	Bonn University, Bonn	*http://www.wipol.uni-bonn.de/MySQL/*
	Bonn University, Bonn	*ftp://ftp.wipol.uni-bonn.de/pub/mirror/ MySQL/*
	Wolfenbuettel	*http://www.fh-wolfenbuettel.de/ftp/pub/ database/mysql/*
	Wolfenbuettel	*ftp://ftp.fh-wolfenbuettel.de/pub/ database/mysql/*
	Staufen	*http://mysql.staufen.de*
Greece	NTUA, Athens	*http://www.ntua.gr/mysql/*
	NTUA, Athens	*ftp://ftp.ntua.gr/pub/databases/mysql/*
Hungary	Xenia	*http://xenia.sote.hu/ftp/mirrors/ www.mysql.com*
	Xenia	*ftp://xenia.sote.hu/pub/mirrors/ www.mysql.com*
Israel	Netvision	*http://mysql.netvision.net.il*
Italy	Teta Srl	*http://www.teta.it/mysql/*
Poland	Sunsite	*http://sunsite.icm.edu.pl/mysql/*
	Sunsite	*ftp://sunsite.icm.edu.pl/pub/unix/mysql/*
Portugal	lerianet	*http://mysql.leirianet.pt*
	lerianet	*ftp://ftp.leirianet.pt/pub/mysql/*
Russia	DirectNet	*http://mysql.directnet.ru*
	IZHCOM	*http://mysql.udm.net*
	IZHCOM	*http://mysql.udm.net*
Romania	Bucharest	*http://www.lbi.ro/MySQL/*
	Bucharest	*ftp://ftp.lbi.ro/mirrors/ftp.tcx.se*
	Timisoara	*http://www.dnttm.ro/mysql/*
	Timisoara	*ftp://ftp.dnttm.ro/pub/mysql /*
Sweden	Sunet	*http://ftp.sunet.se/pub/unix/databases/ relational/mysql/*
	Sunet	*ftp://ftp.sunet.se/pub/unix/databases/ relational/mysql/*
	TCX	*http://www.tcx.se*

Table 3-1. Sites that Contain Copies of MySQL Source Code and Binaries (continued)

	TCX	*ftp://www.tcx.se*
	TCX	*http://www.mysql.com (Primary Site)*
	TCX	*ftp://ftp.mysql.com (Primary Site)*
UK	Omnipotent/UK	*http://mysql.omnipotent.net*
	Omnipotent/UK	*ftp://mysql.omnipotent.net*
	PliG/UK	*http://ftp.plig.org/pub/mysql/*
	PliG/UK	*ftp://ftp.plig.org/pub/mysql/*
Ukraine	PACO	*http://mysql.paco.net.ua*
	PACO	*ftp://mysql.paco.net.ua*
North America		
Canada	Tryc	*http://web.tryc.on.ca/mysql/*
USA	Circle Net/North Carolina	*http://www.mysql.net*
	DIGEX	*ftp://ftp.digex.net/pub/database/mysql/index.html/*
	Gina net/Florida	*http://www.gina.net/mysql/*
	Hurricane Electric/San Jose	*http://mysql.he.net*
	Netcasting/West Coast	*ftp://ftp.netcasting.net/pub/mysql/*
	Phoenix	*http://phoenix.acs.ttu.edu/mysql/*
	pingzero/Los Angeles	*http://mysql.pingzero.net*
South America		
Chile	Amerikanclaris	*http://www.labs.amerikanclaris.cl/mysql/*
	vision	*http://mysql.vision.cl*

Once you have connected to the FTP site, change to the *Downloads* directory. This directory will list several versions of MySQL like this:

```
MySQL-3.21
MySQL-3.22
MySQL-3.23
```

The highest version number is an unstable release where new features are being added and tested. Individual subversions of this stage will always be labeled 'alpha', 'beta', or 'gamma'. The previous version is the current stable version. This version has been thoroughly tested and is believed to be bug free. Earlier versions are also available for archive purposes.

If the development version is still in 'alpha' stage, you should definitely stick with the stable version unless you like living on the edge. Likewise, if the development version is in 'beta' stage, it's probably a good idea to use the stable version unless the new version has features that you really need, or if the system you are running it on is not absolutely critical. On the other hand, if the development version is at 'gamma', you should feel confident in using it, unless there is a known problem affecting your system.

You can see exactly what stage a particular version of MySQL is at by changing to the directory for that version. For example, the directory *MySQL-3.22* may look something like this:

```
mysql-3.22.19-beta-sgi-irix6,4-mip.tgz
mysql-3.22.21a-beta-ibm-aix4.2.1.0-rs6000.tgz
mysql-3.22.31-pc-linux-gnu-i586.tgz
mysql-3.22.33-sun-solaris2.6-sparc.tgz
mysql-3.22.33.tar.gz
```

The files with specific machine and operating system names are binary versions for that system. Files without a specific machine, such as the last file listed are the source code. If there is no stage label ('alpha', 'beta', 'gamma') attached to a file, it is a stable version. This is a case for the last two files in the list: One is a binary version for Sun Solaris 2.6 on Sparc hardware and the other is the source code. The other, older, versions exist because the development team does not always have the time and resources to compile every subversion of MySQL on every operating system and hardware configuration in existence. In fact, most of the pre-compiled versions are submitted by regular users who have had success compiling the latest version on their system.

With this information in mind, you should now choose the version of MySQL you wish to use and download the source distribution if you are going to compile MySQL, or the correct binary distribution for you machine, if it exists. If a binary distribution does not exist for your exact configuration, first check to see if one exists for a slightly different version of your system. For instance, *mysql-3.22.32a-ibm-aix4.2.1.0-powerpc.tgz* may also run for Version 4.1.4 of AIX on the same type of hardware. If you cannot find a working version this way, see if versions for your configuration exist for older versions of MySQL. If not, you will have to compile from source. If this is the case for you and you successfully compile and run MySQL, you should consider submitting a copy of your compiled binaries to the MySQL team for inclusion in the archive.

Installing from Source

Once you have downloaded the MySQL source distribution, unpack the archive using the following:

```
gunzip -c mysql-x.xx.xx.tar.gz | tar xvf -
```

Where `mysql-x.xx.xx.tar.gz` is the name of the file you downloaded. This will create a directory named `mysql-x.xx.xx` within the current directory. Change to this directory.

Run the `configure` script in the current directory. Invoke the script as `./configure` so that you do not accidentally run a program with the same name elsewhere on your system. Many installations will configure fine without any options, but for those that do not, `configure` provides a wide array. Running with the `--help` switch will list them all, but the following are the most common:

--without-server

> This will compile all of the included MySQL clients, but not the server.

--prefix

> This is used to set the installation directory to something other than the default (*/usr/local/*).

–with-low-memory

> This option tells the compiler to not use certain optimizations that use a great deal of memory during the compilation process. Using this option will fix most lack of memory errors encountered during installation.

--localstatedir

> This is used to set the directory containing the database data files to something other than the default (*/usr/local/var*).

--with-charset

> This will choose a different character set (default is 'latin1'). At the time of this writing, available character sets are `big5`, `danish`, `cp1251`, `cp1257`, `croat`, `czech`, `dec8`, `dos`, `euc_kr`, `german1`, `hebrew`, `hp8`, `hungarian`, `koi8_ru`, `koi8_ukr`, `latin1`, `latin2`, `swe7`, `usa7`, `win1251`, `win1251u`, `kr`, `ujis`, `sjis`, `tis620`.

After the `configure` script has completed, run **make** in the current directory. This will compile everything.

Once everything is finished compiling, **make install** will install everything into its proper place.

If this is the first time you are installing MySQL on this machine, or if all of the MySQL database files have been deleted since the last install, run the following to create the database structure and the administrative tables:

```
./scripts/mysql_install_db
```

This will also start the server daemon. To make sure it is running, change to the installation directory (/usr/local/ by default) and run the following:

```
./bin/mysqladmin version
```

The output should look something like this:

```
mysqladmin  Ver 7.11 Distrib 3.22.23b, for linux on i586
TCX Datakonsult AB, by Monty
```

```
Server version          3.22.23b-debug
Protocol version        10
Connection              Localhost via UNIX socket
UNIX socket             /tmp/mysql.sock
Uptime:                 6 sec

Threads: 1  Questions: 1  Slow queries: 0  Opens: 6  Flush tables: 1  Open
tables: 2  Memory in use: 1093K  Max memory used: 1093K
```

To summarize, a sequence of installation steps looks like this:

```
gzip -c mysql-x.xx.xx.tar.gz | tar xvf -
cd mysql-x.xx.xx
./configure
make
make install
./scripts/mysql_install_db
./bin/mysqladmin version
```

Installing a Binary Distribution

Once you have downloaded the binary distribution you must pick a directory to contain the MySQL files. The most common location is */usr/local/mysql,* but where you put your distribution largely depends on the needs of your users and the access rights you have to the machine.

Change to the directory just above the one you wish to house the MySQL distribution. For example, if you wish to use */usr/local/mysql,* change to */usr/local* now. Run the following to unpack the distribution:

```
gunzip -c /tmp/mysql-x.xx.xx-mymachine.tgz | tar xvf -
```

Here */tmp* is the directory where you downloaded MySQL and *mysql-x.xx.xx-mymachine.tgz* is the name of the file you downloaded.

This should create a directory called *mysql-x.xx.xx* within the current directory. If you want the files to be in a directory called just *mysql,* create a link:

```
ln -s mysql-x.xx.xx mysql
```

Next, check to see if the binary package contains the access grant tables. Change to the directory *mysql/mysql* from the current directory. If this directory does not exist or is empty, you must create the tables yourself. Change back one directory to the main *mysql* installation directory and run the following:

```
scripts/mysql_install_db
```

The previous command has to be run only once. To actually start the MySQL daemon, enter:

```
bin/safe_mysqld --log &
```

To see if the daemon is running properly, run the following:

```
bin/mysqladmin version
```

The output should look something like this:

```
Mysqladmin Ver 6.3 Distrib 3.21.33, for sun-solaris2.6 on sparc
TCX Datakonsult AB, by Monty

Server version          3.21.17-alpha
Protocol version        10
Connection                Localhost via UNIX socket
TCP Port                  3333
UNIX socket             /tmp/mysql.sock
Uptime:                   13 sec

Running threads: 1  Questions: 20  Reloads: 2  Open Tables: 3
```

mSQL

The first step in installing mSQL is obtaining the source distribution. At the time of this writing, the newest versions of mSQL were only distributed through the Hughes Technology web page at *http://www.hughes.com.avl*. The author of mSQL has chosen not to officially distribute binary copies of mSQL. If you are on a machine without a C compiler, you will either have to install one, or compile mSQL on another machine with the same hardware and operating system and copy over the results.

Once you have the mSQL source distribution, unpack it using the following:

```
gunzip -c msql-2.0.4.1.tar.gz | tar xvf -
```

This will create a directory with the name `msql-2.0.4.1` within the current directory. Change to the new directory.

Create the installation directory for your machine by running the following command:

```
make target
```

Now change to the *targets* directory. Within this directory there should be a new directory with the name of your operating system and hardware (e.g., Solaris-2.6-Sparc or Linux-2.0.33-i386). Change to this new directory.

Run the **setup** script in the current directory. Make sure you invoke it as `./setup` so that the shell doesn't run any program named *setup* in another directory instead. This script will configure the source code for compilation. After this script has competed, examine the *site.mm* file and change any parameters you wish in order to customize your local installation. In particular, you may wish to change the **INST_DIR** variable that determines the directory where mSQL will be installed.

After you are satisfied with the configuration, run the following to compile mSQL:

```
make all
```

After compilation, the following command will install mSQL in the directory you have chosen:

```
make install
```

To summarize, a sequence of installation steps looks like this:

```
gzip -c msql-x.x.x.tar.gz | tar xvf -
cd msql-x.x.x
make target
cd targets/myOS-mymachine
./setup
make all
make install
```

4

MySQL

MySQL may be one of the hottest grass-roots software projects since Linux. While mSQL certainly deserves credit for getting the ball rolling, MySQL has built upon that momentum. It is now nothing less than a serious competitor for the major database engines in the field of small-to-medium scale database development. In its beginnings, MySQL was simply a replacement for the aging mSQL 1 database engine. As we noted in Chapter 1, *Introduction to Relational Databases*, mSQL began showing signs of its age in the form of stability issues and an inability to meet the growing demands thrust upon it by its success. MySQL built upon the basic design goals of mSQL and now exceeds mSQL in its feature set while also managing to beat mSQL in performance.

Design

Working from the legacy of mSQL, TcX decided MySQL had to be at least as fast as mSQL in spite of its expanded feature base. At that time, mSQL defined database performance, so TcX's goal was no small task. MySQL's specific design goals are speed, robustness and ease of use. To get this sort of performance, TcX decided to make MySQL a multithreaded database engine. A multithreaded application performs many tasks at the same time just as if multiple instances of that application were running simultaneously.

By making MySQL multithreaded, TcX has given us many benefits. A separate thread handles each incoming connection with an extra thread always running in order to manage the connections. Clients therefore do not have to wait for queries from other clients to run. Any number of simultaneous queries can run. While any thread is writing to a table, all other threads requesting access to that table simply wait until the table is free. Your client can perform any allowed operation without any concern for other concurrent connections. The connection managing thread prevents two threads from writing to the same table at the same time.

This design is certainly more complex than mSQL's single-threaded design. The speed advantages of performing multiple simultaneous queries, however, far out-weighed the speed penalties of the increased complexity.

Another advantage to multithreaded processing is inherent to all multi-threaded applications. Even though the threads share the same process space, they execute individually. Because of this separation, multiprocessor machines can spread the load of each of the threads across the many CPUs. Figure 4-1 illustrates the multi-threaded nature of a MySQL database server.

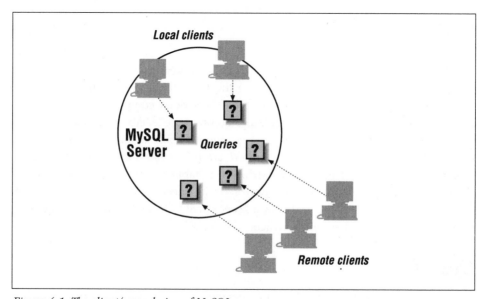

Figure 4-1. The client/sever design of MySQL

In addition to the performance gains introduced by multithreading, MySQL has a richer subset of SQL than mSQL. MySQL supports over a dozen datatypes and additionally supports SQL functions. Your application can access these functions through ANSI SQL statements.

MySQL actually extends ANSI SQL with a few features. These features include new functions (ENCRYPT, WEEKDAY, IF, and others), the ability to increment fields (AUTO_INCREMENT and LAST_INSERT_ID), and case sensitivity.

TcX did intentionally omit some SQL features found in the major database engines. Transactions and stored procedures are the two most notable omissions. Like David Hughes with mSQL, TcX decided that including these features would incur too much of a performance hit to be worth their addition. TcX is working on adding these features, however, in such a way that only users who really need these features are penalized by them.

Since 1996, TcX has been using MySQL in an environment with more than 40 databases containing 10,000 tables. Of these 10,000 tables, more than 500 have more than seven million records—about 100 GB of data.

Installing MySQL

The first step in using MySQL is installing it. MySQL runs on just about any Unix platform you can imagine as well as Windows 9x, Windows NT, and OS/2. The Windows 9x and Windows NT ports require the purchase of a license before you can use them. If you really want to take a test drive, an older shareware version is available.

MySQL comes in both binary and source code distributions. If you are looking to contribute to the MySQL project, want to add your own hacks, or simply cannot find a binary distribution for your platform, you should get the source code distribution. The vast majority of users, however, should get the binary distribution. You can find the latest binary and source distributions at *http://www.mysql.com*.

If you get the source distribution, you will have to compile MySQL in order to install it. Either way, you should refer to the instructions that come with your distribution as they will be the definitive resource on installing that distribution.

Running MySQL

Most people run their database servers all of the time. After all, it makes no sense to have a database if you cannot get to the data. TcX created MySQL with this in mind and thus MySQL runs as a daemon process under Unix or as a service under Windows NT. Windows 9x has only the rough analog of sticking a shortcut to the executable in the *StartUp* folder. One important issue to note under Windows 95 specifically is that Windows 95 leaks about 200 bytes of main memory for each thread creation. You therefore do not want to leave MySQL running under Windows 95 for extended periods of time. This problem does not apply to Windows 98 or Windows NT.

You run MySQL using the *safe_mysqld* script. Under Unix, this file is installed as */usr/local/bin/safe_mysqld* by default. This script is a Bourne script you can edit in order to change any of the default values. Any options that you supply to *safe_mysqld* will be passed on to the MySQL daemon itself.

MySQL is a forking daemon. As soon as you launch it, the program creates a copy of itself (forks itself) and runs as a background process. You thus do not need to do anything special to get MySQL to run in the background. If you use the wrapper *safe_mysqld* to start MySQL, then you do need to put it in the background:

```
/usr/local/mysql/bin/safe_mysqld &
```

The reason you need to run *safe_mysqld* in the background—and the reason you should run it instead of directly running *mysqld*—is that the *safe_mysqld* script starts *mysqld* and then continuously verifies that *mysqld* stays running. If MySQL dies unexpectedly, *safe_mysqld* will restart it.

Now that you know how to start MySQL, you need to get MySQL to start up and shut down with the computer on which it runs. Under Windows NT, of course, installing MySQL as a service is sufficient for the task. Under Windows 9x, you have to stick a shortcut to the MySQL startup script in the *StartUp* folder. As with just about everything else in the Unix world, getting MySQL to run at system startup and shut down at system shutdown is more complicated. Unix systems generally look for startup scripts somewhere under the */etc* directory—some under */etc/rc.d* or */etc/init.d*. You should check with your system administrator or system documentation for the exact details of where your startup/shutdown script should go. The MySQL distribution comes with a file in the *support_files* directory called *mysql.server*. This Unix shell script will serve as your startup/shutdown script.

Database Administration

You should now have a fresh MySQL installation up and running. The first thing you should do is change the root password for the server using the following command from inside the MySQL installation directory:

```
./bin/mysqladmin -u root password 'mynewpasswd'
```

With the MySQL server up and running securely, you can begin tackling some basic database administration issues so that MySQL can begin serving your needs.

The mysqladmin Utility

The *mysqladmin* is the primary tool for database administration under MySQL. Using this utility, you can create, destroy, and monitor your server and the databases it supports.

Database creation

Your database server is useless to you unless it actually has databases to serve. Using *mysqladmin*, you can create new databases:

```
mysqladmin -p create DATABASENAME
```

The *-p* option tells MySQL that you want to be prompted for the root password you specified earlier. If you enter the correct password, *mysqladmin* will create a new, blank database with the name you specify. Because a database under MySQL is a set of files in a specific directory, the *mysqladmin create* command creates a new directory to hold the files for the new database. For example, if you created a database called "mydata," the directory *mydata* will appear in the *data* directory of your MySQL installation.

 Because MySQL databases and tables are stored as file system files, you will encounter an unfortunate behavioral mismatch between Win32 implementations and Unix implementations. Specifically, all Win32 file systems are case-insensitive while Unix file systems are case-sensitive. The result is that database and table names are case-sensitive under Unix and case-insensitive under Win32.

Database destruction

During the process of developing a new database application, you will likely want to create several databases to support the development process. For example, it is common in database application development to have separate databases for development, testing, and production. When development is complete, it is time to get rid of the development and testing databases. The *mysqladmin* utility provides the "drop" option to let you delete a database:

```
mysqladmin -p drop DATABASENAME
```

As with the *mysqladmin create* command, *DATABASENAME* is the name of the database you wish to destroy. MySQL will not let you accidentally drop the database. After issuing this command, it will warn you that dropping a database is potentially a very bad thing to do and ask you to confirm the drop. You can examine the *data* directory after dropping the database to verify that the directory that once served as that database no longer exists.

Database renaming and copying

MySQL does not have a utility for renaming and copying databases. Because databases are simply files in a specific directory, you can, with care, use operating systems to copy or rename databases. Though using the file system commands will successfully copy or rename the database in question, they will not carry over the security configurations from the original table because MySQL keeps security information in a database table. In order to fully copy a database, you will have to also duplicate its security information in the MySQL system database. We will go into more detail on MySQL security later in the chapter.

Server status

MySQL provides a very rich array of commands in the mysqladmin utility for monitoring the MySQL server. Running the command *mysqladmin status* will provide a single line status display that looks like this:

```
Uptime: 395  Threads: 1  Questions: 14  Slow queries: 0
Opens: 10 Flush tables: 1  Open tables: 6
```

The values you see in the *mysqladmin status* output have the following meanings:

Uptime
> The number of seconds the server has been up and running.

Threads
> The number of threads that are currently interacting with the database. When examining the number of threads, you will always see at least one thread. The one thread is the one counting all the other threads. The server also has three other threads that are not visible to this command—one to handle signals, one to manage all of the other threads, and one to listen for incoming connections.

Questions
> The number of queries that have been sent to the database since it started.

Slow queries
> The number of queries that have taken longer than a configurable amount of time to execute. The configuration key is `long_query_time`. We will discuss configuration parameters later in the chapter.

Opens
> The number of tables that have been opened since the server started.

Flush tables
> The number of *flush, refresh,* and *reload* commands.

Open tables
> The number of tables currently open. Because MySQL is multithreaded, one table may be open more than once at any given time. For instance, any number of `SELECT` statements can be performed on the same table at the same time. Because of this trick, the value of "Open tables" can be larger than the number of tables in the system.

The *mysqladmin status* command also provides values for memory in use and maximum memory used if MySQL was compiled with the `--with-debug` option.

If you are looking for some more general, static information, then *mysqladmin version* is the command you are looking for. It provides the following output:

```
bin/mysqladmin  Ver 7.8 Distrib 3.22.17, for sun-solaris2.6 on sparc
TCX Datakonsult AB, by Monty
```

```
Server version          3.22.17
Protocol version        10
Connection              Localhost via Unix socket
Unix socket             /tmp/mysql.sock
Uptime:                 23 min 58 sec

Threads: 1  Questions: 15  Slow queries: 0  Opens: 10  Flush tables: 1  Open
tables: 6
```

The last line of information is, of course, identical to the information you saw from *mysqladmin status*. The rest of the display is entirely new.

Server version

The version of MySQL being run.

Protocol version

The version of the MySQL communications protocol that the server supports. If you are having problems with a tool that uses the MySQL communications protocol, you might want to check the value it expects against your MySQL protocol version from this display.

Connection

The method by which you are connected to the server. In the example above, the client is communicating with MySQL through a Unix socket. If you are looking at a remote MySQL server, this entry will hold the name of the machine from which you are connecting.

Unix socket

The file name of the socket you are using to communicate with the server. If you are communicating with MySQL via TCP/IP, this entry will disappear in favor of a **TCP port** entry that holds the port number of the MySQL server.

Uptime

The total time the server has been running.

Two other commands, *mysqladmin variables* and *mysqladmin extended-status*, offer more information.

Because MySQL is multithreaded, monitoring process activity is not as simple as using the Unix *ps* command. Though many threads are running, only one process will appear in the process list. To help address this problem, MySQL provides the *mysqladmin processlist* to display all of the running threads in a nicely formatted table:

```
+----+------+-----------+------+-----------+------+-------+------+
| Id | User | Host      | db   | Command   | Time | State | Info |
+----+------+-----------+------+-----------+------+-------+------+
| 920| joe  | client.com|mydata| Sleep     | 0    |       |      |
| 939| root | localhost |      | Processes | 0    |       |      |
+----+------+-----------+------+-----------+------+-------+------+
```

This output tells you exactly what each thread is doing. The values in the display have the following meaning:

Id

The internal identification number of the thread. This value has no relation to any operating system process IDs. You can use this number with the *mysqladmin kill* command to terminate the thread.

User

The user connected to the server with this thread.

Host

The host from which the user is connected.

db

The database to which the user is connected.

Command

The type of command being executed by the thread. The command can be one of the following:

Sleep

The thread is waiting for user input. Most processes should be in this state.

Quit

The thread is in the process of terminating.

Init DB

The thread is preparing the selected database for interaction. A client may communicate with only one database at a time, but it can switch any time it likes.

Query

The thread is performing an actual query. While most interaction with the database is in the form of queries, these commands occur very quickly and thus rarely appear in this output.

Field list

The thread is generating a list of the fields in a table.

Create DB

The thread is creating a new database.

Drop DB

The thread is deleting a database.

Reload

The thread is reloading the MySQL access tables. When the reload is finished, all new threads will use the refreshed access tables.

Shutdown

> The thread is in the process of terminating all other threads and shutting down the server.

Statistics

> The thread is generating statistics.

Processes

> This thread is examining other threads. The thread executing this command will show up with this value.

Connect

> The thread is negotiating an incoming connection from a client.

Kill

> The thread is terminating another thread.

Refresh

> The thread is flushing all of the caches and resetting the log files.

The MySQL log file provides yet another way to get useful administrative information about the MySQL server. MySQL generates the main log if *mysqld* is launched with the *--log* option. This log appears in */usr/local/var/HOSTNAME.log* where HOSTNAME is the name of the machine on which MySQL is running. This log tracks connections to the server and the commands that clients send to it.

By passing the *--debug* option to *mysqld* (or *safe_mysqld*), you can have MySQL send additional information to the log file. The debug package that MySQL uses has dozens of options, most of which you will never use. The most common debug setting, however, is *-d:t:o,FILENAME* where FILENAME is the name of the debug log you wish to use. This option will log almost everything the server does, step-by-step.

MySQL supports one more human-readable log. When you start MySQL with the --log-update option, MySQL will create a file with the name *HOSTNAME.#* where HOSTNAME is the name of the server machine and # is a unique number. This log will hold all changes to database tables. The log appears as SQL so that the operations can be replicated in another database server.

Server shutdown

The following command will perform a clean shutdown of the MySQL database server:

```
mysqladmin -p shutdown
```

This command is the most orderly way to shut down the server. If you started MySQL with *safe_mysqld* and try using some other method for shutting down the server, *safe_mysqld* will just start up a new instance of the server. One can also shut down the server safely with the traditional Unix *kill* command. But avoid using the drastic *kill-9* command.

Command line options for mysqladmin

The *mysqladmin* utility is a very rich tool with a handful of command line options. Its general format is

```
mysqladmin OPTIONS COMMAND1 COMMAND2 ... COMMANDn
```

In other words, you can issue multiple commands at one time with the *mysqladmin* utility. Just for grins, you could do

```
mysqladmin -p create silly drop silly
```

This command will both create and drop the database "silly" in one shot. The following is a list of commands you can send to *mysqladmin*:

create DATABASENAME
> Creates a new database with the specified name

drop DATABASENAME
> Drops an existing database with the specified name

extended-status
> Provides an extended status message from the server

flush-hosts
> Flushes all cached hosts

flush-logs
> Flushes all logs

flush-tables
> Flushes all tables

flush-privileges
> Same as *reload*

kill ID1,ID2, . . . ,IDn
> Terminates the threads with the specified thread IDs

password NEWPASSWORD
> Changes the old password to the specified value

ping
> Verifies that *mysqld* is still running

processlist
> Shows a list of active threads

reload
> Reloads all grant tables

refresh

Flushes all tables and closes and opens all log files

shutdown

Shuts down the server

status

Gives a short status message from the server

variables

Prints available variables

version

Shows server version information

In addition to the commands it supports, it also supports the following options:

-# LOG

Output debug log. Often this is '*d:t:o,FILENAME*'.

-f

Do not ask for confirmation of a dropped table and continue to the next command even if this one fails.

-? or --help

Show help for the *mysqladmin* utility.

-C

Use compression in the client/server protocol.

-h HOST

Connect to the specified host.

-p [PASSWORD]

Use the specified password to validate the user. If this option is used without specifying a password, then the user will be prompted to enter the password.

-P PORT

Use the specified port number for a connection.

-i SECONDS

Execute the commands repeatedly with the specified sleep interval in between executions.

-s

Silently exit if a connection to the server cannot be established.

-S SOCKET

The file to use for the Unix socket.

-t TIMEOUT

The timeout for the connection.

-u USER

    The user for the login if not the current user.

-V

    Show version information and exit.

-w COUNT

    Wait and retry the specified number of times if the server is not currently up.

Backups

The importance of regular backups in successful operation cannot be stressed enough. Without a usable backup, a single power outage can destroy months or years of work. However, with a properly planned backup schedule, you can recover from almost any catastrophe in a very short time.

Chapter 5, *mSQL*, provides a detailed discussion of the role of the *msqldump* command in mSQL backups. MySQL supports nearly identical functionality in the form of the *mysqldump* command. We recommend that you have a look at that discussion to understand the use of *mysqldump* and full backups. In this section, we will focus on the next most important form up backup: the incremental backup.

While full data backups are technically all that are needed to recover from data loss, they can be difficult to work with at times. When you have a great deal of data, the files required to backup all of the data can take up a large amount of space. Therefore, it is common practice to only back up all data once a week or some similar data. Then, every day, a backup is performed of all data that has changed since the last full backup. This is referred to as an incremental backup.

With MySQL, it is possible to perform an incremental backup using a feature of the database server known as the "update log." If the *mysqld* database server is launched with the *--log-update* option, all changes to any database will be logged in a file as an SQL command. These changes will be logged in the order they happen. The result is a file that, when fed into the *mysql* monitor, will replay all actions that have been performed on the database. If the log has been kept from the beginning of the database, it will go through the entire life of the database and end up with the data in its current state.

More usefully, if the log is kept since a certain defined point, say the last full data backup, the log can then be used to catch up the backup to the current state. In this way, the functionality of an incremental backup is obtained. At a regular interval (such as every week) perform a full data backup. Then every day copy the update log either to tape, or to a backup area on hard disk. Keep a separate copy of the update log for every day back to the last full data backup. This provides the ability to recreate the database in case of disaster and also to recover any partial data lost since the last full data backup. Because the update log is plain ASCII, SQL commands they can be searched for specific data.

Whatever method you use to back up your data, make sure that you do it often and that your periodically check your backups to make sure that you can indeed use them to recover your system. Many database administrators have faithfully kept backups only to find out in their time of need that because of some error—human, software, or physical media—their backups were absolutely useless.

Security

In addition to making sure you can get at your data reliably, you also want to make sure others cannot get to it at all. MySQL uses its own database server to implement security. When you first install MySQL, the installation process creates a database called "mysql." This database contains five tables: `db`, `host`, `user`, `tables_priv`, and `columns_priv`. Newer versions of MySQL also create a database called `func`, but it is unrelated to security. MySQL uses these tables to decide who is allowed to do what. The `user` table contains security information that applies to the server as a whole. The `host` table gives entire machines rights to the server. Finally, the `db`, `tables_priv`, and `columns_priv` tables control access to individual databases, tables, and columns.

We will take a brief look at all of MySQL's security tables and then discuss the details of how they work together to make MySQL a secure database engine.

The user table

The `user` table shown in Table 4-1 has the following structure:

Table 4-1. The User Table

Field	Type	Null	Key	Default	Extra
Host	char(60)		PRI		
User	char(16)		PRI		
Password	char(16)				
Select_priv	enum('N','Y')			N	
Insert_riv	enum('N','Y')			N	
Update_priv	enum('N','Y')			N	
Delete_priv	enum('N','Y')			N	
Create_priv	enum('N','Y')			N	
Drop_priv	enum('N','Y')			N	
Reload_priv	enum('N','Y')			N	
Shutdown_priv	enum('N','Y')			N	

Table 4-1. The User Table (continued)

Field	Type	Null	Key	Default	Extra
Process_priv	enum('N','Y')			N	
File_priv	enum('N','Y')			N	
Grant_priv	enum('N','Y')			N	
References_priv	enum('N','Y')			N	
Index_priv	enum('N','Y')			N	
Alter_priv	enum('N','Y')			N	

In both the Host and User columns, you can use "%" wildcard values. A host name of "chem%lab," for example, includes "chembiolab," "chemtestlab," and so on. The special user name "nobody" acts like a single "%." It covers any user not explicitly named elsewhere. Here is what the different access rights mean:

Select_priv

> The ability to perform **SELECT** statements

Insert_priv

> The ability to perform **INSERT** statements

Update_priv

> The ability to perform **UPDATE** statements

Delete_priv

> The ability to perform **DELETE** statements

Create_priv

> The ability to perform **CREATE** statements or to create databases

Drop_priv

> The ability to perform **DROP** statements or to drop databases

Reload_priv

> The ability to reload access information via *mysqladmin reload*

Shutdown_priv

> The ability to shutdown the server via *mysqladmin shutdown*

Process_priv

> The ability to manage server processes

File_priv

> The ability to read and write files using commands like **SELECT INTO OUTFILE** and **LOAD DATA INFILE**

Grant_priv

> The ability to grant your privileges to others

Index_priv

The ability to create or drop indices

Alter_priv

The ability to perform the `ALTER TABLE` statement

MySQL provides a special function to keep passwords safe from prying eyes. The `password()` function encrypts a password. The following statements show the `password()` function in action in the course of adding users to the system.

```
INSERT INTO user (Host, User, Password, Select_priv,
                  Insert_priv, Update_priv, Delete_priv)
VALUES ('%', 'bob', password('mypass'), 'Y', 'Y', 'Y','Y')
INSERT INTO user (Host, User, Password, Select_priv)
VALUES ('athens.imaginary.com', 'jane', '', 'Y')
INSERT INTO user(Host, User, Password)
VALUES ('%', 'nobody', '')
INSERT INTO user (Host, User, Password, Select_priv,
                  Insert_priv, Update_priv, Delete_priv)
VALUES ('athens.imaginary.com', 'nobody',
        password('thispass'), 'Y', 'Y', 'Y', 'Y')
```

MySQL user names are mostly unrelated to operating system user names. By default, the MySQL client tools use your operating system user name in attempting a login. There is, however, no necessary connection between the two. By using the *-u* option with most of the MySQL client utilities, you can connect to MySQL using any user name you like. Similarly, your operating system user name will not appear in the MySQL `user` table unless someone specifically adds it and grants you permissions.

The first user we created, "bob," can come from any host and can `SELECT`, `INSERT`, `UPDATE`, and `DELETE` records. The second user, "jane," can connect from "athens.imaginary.com." has no password, and can only execute `SELECT` statements. The third user is "nobody" from any host. This user is able to do absolutely nothing. The final user is "nobody" from "athens.imaginary.com" and can `SELECT`, `INSERT`, `UPDATE`, and `DELETE` records like "bob."

So how does MySQL do matching? Perhaps you noticed above that a given name could actually match several records. For example, "nobody@athens.imaginary. com" matches "nobody@%" and "nobody@athens.imaginary.com." Before checking the `user` table, MySQL sorts the data in the following manner:

1. MySQL first matches hosts that do not contain wildcards followed by hosts with wildcards. Empty `Host` fields are treated like they contain "%."

2. When hosts are the same, users without wildcards are checked before users with wildcards. As with `Host`, an empty `User` field is treated as if it contains "%."

3. The first match encountered is the only match considered.

In the earlier example, the user would be verified against "nobody" from "athens. imaginary.com" because "athens.imaginary.com" is sorted before "%." Because hosts are sorted before users, the values of any host from which you are connecting will take precedence over any specific privileges you might have. For example, if the `user` table contains the following entries:

Host	User
%	jane
athens.imaginary.com	

If "jane" connects from "athens.imaginary.com," the privileges associated with "athens.imaginary.com" are the privileges that MySQL will use.

The db table

You may have noticed that the `user` table makes no mention of specific databases or tables. The `user` table rules over the entire server. Most servers, however, have multiple databases. Different databases generally serve different purposes, and thus different user groups. The `db` table sets permissions for individual databases. The `db` table shown in Table 4-2 has the following structure:

Table 4-2. The db Table

Field	Type	Null	Key	Default	Extra
Host	char(60)		PRI		
Db	char(32)		PRI		
User	char(16)		PRI		
Select_priv	enum('N','Y')			N	
Insert_riv	enum('N','Y')			N	
Update_priv	enum('N','Y')			N	
Delete_priv	enum('N','Y')			N	
Create_priv	enum('N','Y')			N	
Drop_priv	enum('N','Y')			N	
References_priv	enum('N','Y')			N	
Index_priv	enum('N','Y')			N	
Alter_priv	enum('N','Y')			N	

This table looks a lot like the **user** table. The major distinction is that instead of having a **Password** column, this table has a **Db** column. This table manages a user's privileges within a specific database. Because **user** table permissions span the entire server, any activity granted to a user by the **user** table overrides that user's entry in the **db** table. Thus, if a user has **INSERT** access in the **user** table, that user will have **INSERT** access for all databases no matter what the **db** table says.

The most effective use of the **user** table is to create entries for each user in the **user** table with no permissions. This scheme enables a user to connect to the server, but do nothing else. The exception would be anyone who should be a server administrator. Everyone else should gain their permissions from the **db** table. Every user does have to appear in the **user** table, or they will not be allowed to connect to the database.

The same rules for user and host matching on the **User** and **Host** columns from the **user** table applies to this table—with a bit of a twist. A blank **Host** field will prompt MySQL to look for an entry matching the user's host in the **host** table. If no such match is found, MySQL denies the operation. If an entry is found, MySQL calculates the permission as the intersection of those found in the **db** and **host** entries. In other words, both entries must have a 'Y' in them or access is denied.

The host table

The **host** table serves a special purpose. The **host** table shown in Table 4-3 has the following structure:

Table 4-3. The Host Table

Field	Type	Null	Key	Default	Extra
Host	char(60)		PRI		
Db	char(32)		PRI		
Select_priv	enum('N','Y')			N	
Insert_riv	enum('N','Y')			N	
Update_priv	enum('N','Y')			N	
Delete_priv	enum('N','Y')			N	
Create_priv	enum('N','Y')			N	
Drop_priv	enum('N','Y')			N	
Grant_priv	enum('N','Y')			N	
References_priv	enum('N','Y')			N	
Index_priv	enum('N','Y')			N	
Alter_priv	enum('N','Y')			N	

The host table gives you a way of creating basic permissions on a host-by-host basis. When MySQL attempts to verify an operation, it seeks a match on the user name and host in the db table. If it finds a match on the user name with an empty Host field, it will consult the host table and use the intersection of the two sets of privileges to determine the outcome. For example, you may have a set of servers that you consider less secure than the rest of your network. You can deny them any kind of write access. If "bob" comes in from one of those machines and his entry in the db table has a blank Host field, he will be denied write access even though his db table entry would otherwise allow it.

The tables_priv and columns_priv tables

These two tables are basically refinements of what the db table provides. Specifically, any operation is checked with the relevant db entry, followed by any relevant tables_priv entry, followed by any relevant columns_priv entry. If one of these is allowed, then the operation is allowed. With these two tables, you can narrow permissions down to the table and column levels. You can manipulate the contents of the tables through the **GRANT** and **REVOKE** commands in SQL.

The stages of access control

You have had a look at the players in MySQL security. Now we need to put the players together and demonstrate how they are applied to real situations. MySQL divides access control into two stages. The first stage is connection. You must be able to connect to the server before you can do anything else.

Connection involves two checks. First, MySQL checks to see that the user name and host under which you are connecting has a corresponding entry in the user table. Matching an entry for you is based on the rules for matching we discussed earlier. If MySQL fails to find a match, your connection request is denied. If it finds a match and that match has a nonblank **Password** field entry, you must specify and match that password. Failure to match the password results in the denial of your connection request.

Once connected, the MySQL server enters the request verification stage. At this point, any specific requests you make are matched against your privileges. MySQL may take these privileges from any of the user, db, host, tables_priv, or columns_priv tables. If there is a match with the user table and the user table has a positive permission, then the operation is immediately allowed. Otherwise, MySQL looks for matches in the following tables in the following order:

1. db

2. tables_priv

3. columns_priv

If the db table has a positive entry, the operation is allowed and no further checking occurs. If the entry is negative, then MySQL checks with all matching **tables_priv** entries. If, for example, the operation is a **SELECT** that joins two tables, then the user must have positive entries for both tables in that database in the **tables_priv** table. If one or more of the entries is negative or nonexistent, then MySQL will perform the same logic for all of the columns in the **columns_priv** table.

The mysqlaccess utility

You may find learning the MySQL security system confusing at first. To simplify matters a bit, MySQL comes with a utility called *mysqlaccess*. This command is a Perl script* that will take the host, username, and database combination and provide you with the exact access rights for that user and why. For example, using the command *mysqlaccess nobody isp.com mydata* might report the following output:

```
Access-rights
for USER 'nobody', from HOST 'isp.com', to DB 'mydata'
        +-----------------+---+ +-----------------+---+
        | Select_priv     | Y | | Drop_priv       | N |
        | Insert_priv     | Y | | Reload_priv     | N |
        | Update_priv     | Y | | Shutdown_priv   | N |
        | Delete_priv     | Y | | Process_priv    | N |
        | Create_priv     | N | | File_priv       | N |
        +-----------------+---+ +-----------------+---+
BEWARE:  Everybody can access your DB as user 'nobody'
      :  from host 'isp.com' WITHOUT supplying a password.
      :  Be very careful about it!!

The following rules are used:
 db   : 'isp.com','mydata','nobody','Y','Y','Y','Y','N',
'N','N','N','N','N'
 host : 'Not processed: host-field is not empty in db-
table.'
 user : '%','nobody','','N','N','N','N','N','N','N','N','N'
```

As you can see, even if you understand MySQL security fully, *mysqlaccess* can be a valuable tool in auditing your server's security.

Making changes

MySQL loads the access tables at server startup. The advantage of this approach over constant lookups is speed. The downside, however, is that changes you make to the MySQL access tables are not immediately visible. In order to make those changes visible, you need to issue the command *mysqladmin reload*. If you

---

* For some reason, MySQL has shipped some distributions with the *mysqlaccess* script pointing to a nonstandard location for Perl binaries. If you get the response "command not found" when trying to execute *mysqlaccess*, you are almost certainly experiencing that problem. You will need to change line 1 of the *mysqlaccess* script so that it points to the proper location of your Perl binary, generally */usr/local/bin/perl*.

change the tables through GRANT or REVOKE commands in SQL, you do not have to explicitly reload the tables.

MySQL Utilities

TcX distributes MySQL with a very rich cast of support utilities. Even with all it has provided, the set of third party tools available is even richer. In this section, we attempt to give a brief overview of these tools with a full description in Chapter 18, *PHP and Lite Reference.*

Command Line Tools

isamchk

> Performs checks on the underlying data files within the database. These files are called ISAM (Indexed Sequential Access Method) files. This utility can repair almost any kind of damage to an ISAM file. We discuss this in more detail later in the chapter.

isamlog

> Reads logs generated by the MySQL server that relate to ISAM files. You can use a complete set of these logs to rebuild a table or to replay table changes after a certain period of time.

mysql

> Creates a direct connection to the database server and lets you enter queries directly from a MySQL prompt. You will likely find that you use this more than any other tool.

mysqlaccess

> Modifies the MySQL access rights tables and displays them in an easy to read form. Using this utility is a good way for you to learn about the structure of the MySQL access tables.

mysqladmin

> Performs administrative functions. This utility can add or delete entire databases as well as shutdown the server itself.

mysqlbug

> Reports a problem with MySQL to TcX. The output of this program will also be sent to the MySQL mailing list where the legion of MySQL volunteers will examine the problem.

mysqldump

> Sends the complete contents of a table, including the table structure itself, to a file in the form of SQL statements that can recreate the table. You can use the

output of this utility to recreate the table in another database or on another server.

mysqlimport

Reads a file of data and inserts it into a database table. This is a delimited file where the delimiters can be any of the common forms, like comma-delimited or quoted.

mysqlshow

Displays the structure of the databases on the server and the tables that make up those databases.

Third Party Tools

No vendor or developer can support everything a product might need all on their own. Open source products such as Linux have been so wildly successful due not only to the work of Linux Torvalds on the Linux kernel, but also to the hundreds, if not thousands, of third party products available for Linux. MySQL, too, has benefited from the work of third party developers. While we would like to list every third party product available, that list changes daily. Here we have tried to put together a representation of what is available. For a current list, visit the MySQL home page at *http://www.mysql.com/Contrib.*

Database conversion utilities

access_to_mysql

Converts Microsoft Access databases to MySQL tables. You insert this into Access as a function that enables you to save your table format in a manner that is exportable to MySQL.

dbf2mysql

Translates dBASE (DBF) files into MySQL tables. Even though dBASE is no longer as popular, the DBF format has become ingrained as the most common cross-application database file format. Every major desktop database can read and write DBF files. This application is thus useful when exporting data to or importing data from commercial desktop databases.

Exportsql/Importsql

Converts Microsoft Access databases to MySQL and vice versa. These tools are Access functions that can be used to export Access tables in a format readable by MySQL. They can also convert SQL output from MySQL and mSQL into a form readable by Access.

CGI interfaces

PHP

Creates HTML pages using special tags recognized by the PHP parser. PHP includes interfaces into most major databases, including MySQL and mSQL. We cover PHP in greater detail in Chapter 12, *PHP and Other Support for Database-driven HTML.*

Mysql-webadmin

Performs web administration of MySQL databases. This tool enables users to view tables and modify their content using HTML forms.

Mysqladm

Performs web administration of MySQL databases. This CGI program displays tables over the web and supports the addition and modification of tables.

www-sql

Creates HTML pages from MySQL database tables. This program parses HTML files for special tags and uses that information to perform SQL statements against MySQL.

Client applications

Mysqlwinadmn

Provides the ability to perform MySQL administration from Windows. This tool enables you to perform the functions of *mysqladmin* from inside a GUI.

xmysql

Provides full access to MySQL database tables for an X Window System client. This tool supports bulk inserts and deletes.

xmysqladmin

Provides the ability to perform MySQL administration from the X Window System. This tool is a graphical user interface that enables you to create and drop databases and manage tables. You can also use this tool to make sure the server is running, reload access tables, and manage threads.

Programming interfaces

MyODBC

Implements the database-independent ODBC (Open Database Connectivity) API for MySQL on Windows.

Db.py

Provides MySQL access to Python scripts. This module supports the caching of retrieved data for better performance. We discuss Python programming against MySQL in Chapter 11, *Python,* and provide a detailed reference in Chapter 20, *Python Reference.*

Vdb-dflts

> Provides a MySQL implementation of the Vdb database library. Vdb is a database-independent C API that enables common client code to access several different backend database servers. Vdb clients can use this API to access MySQL databases.

Delphi-interface

> Exposes the MySQL API to Inrpise's Delphi. Using this API, any Delphi application can access a MySQL database.

dump2h

> Converts MySQL table structures into C header files. This program takes the normal output of *mysqldump* and generates a C header file that describes the table as a C `struct`.

mm.mysql.jdbc

> Implements the Java standard JDBC (Java Database Connectivity) API. Chapter 14, *Java and JDBC*, discusses Java programming against this API in detail, while Chapter 22, *JDBC Reference*, provides a full reference for JDBC 2.0.

twzJdbcForMysql

> Implements the Java JDBC API.

Mysqltcl

> Provides a Tcl interface to MySQL.

MySQLmodule

> Provides Python access into MySQL.

Mysql-c++

> Wraps the MySQL C API in an object-oriented manner for access from C++ applications.

MySQL++

> Provides object-oriented access to MySQL for C++ applications.

Pike-mysql

> Enables users of the Roxen web server to write web applications that access MySQL.

Sqlscreens

> Generates databases screens in Tcl/Tk from a MySQL database. This tool enables developers to build a custom GUI tied to MySQL tables.

Squile

> Enables scripts written in Guile to access MySQL tables.

Wintcl

> Supports the embedding of Tcl code in HTML files. Using this tool, you can easily build web applications that can access MySQL databases.

Miscellaneous

Emacs-sql-mode

Adapts the standard SQL mode for Emacs to support the nuances of MySQL's syntax. This mode provides indenting, syntax highlighting, and statement completion so that writing SQL is easier.

findres

Finds reserved words in MySQL tables. This program examines MySQL tables for instances of reserved SQL words that may upset other SQL database engines.

Hyalog

Stores outgoing faxes in a MySQL table. This program will watch for faxes sent from the HylaFax program and save a copy into a MySQL table.

mod_auth_mysql

Authenticates users of the Apache web server. Apache normally controls access through plain text files with user names and encrypted passwords. This Apache module enables you to manage access control inside a MySQL database.

mod_log_mysql

Logs web traffic from an Apache web server into a MySQL database.

mysqlpasswd

Supports the addition, deletion, or modification of user records stored in MySQL by the mod_auth_mysql Apache module.

Mysql_watchdog

Monitors MySQL to make sure that it is continuously operational and functioning within normal parameters.

Nsapi_auth_mysql

Authenticates users of the Netscape web server.

Pam_mysql

Provides a PAM (Pluggable Authentication Module) interface for MySQL. PAM provides user verification for a variety of services, including standard system login.

Wuftpd-mysql

Enables logging of FTP traffic with the popular WuFTP daemon to a MySQL database.

Performance Tuning

The difference between being a good DBA (Database Administrator) and being a top-notch DBA is the difference between knowing how to manage your database server and knowing how your database server lives and breathes. Solving performance problems is often a matter of understanding just how MySQL works under the covers so that you can optimize application performance to take advantage of those features.

MySQL presents three main potential bottlenecks for any connection. The first possibility is the network connection between the client and the server. Second is the processing time needed for activities like building keys. Finally, disk I/O can be a problem. MySQL provides variables that enable you to match MySQL's operations to your application environment. You can set each of these variables using the -O option to mysqld.* For example, you set `back_log` to 15 by adding the option *-O back_log=15* to the options for *mysqld*. The following is a list of useful variables.

back_log

> The number of TCP/IP connections that are queued at once. If you have many remote users connecting to your database simultaneously, you may need to increase this value. The trade-off for a high value is slightly increased memory and CPU usage.

key_buffer

> A buffer allocated to store recently used keys. If you have slow queries, increasing this value could help. The trade-off is an increase in memory usage.

max_connections

> The number of simultaneous connections allowed by the database server. If some users are being denied access during busy times, you may need to increase this value. The trade-off is a more heavily loaded server. In other words, CPU usage, memory usage, and disk I/O will increase.

table_cache

> A buffer used to hold frequently accessed table data. If you gave the memory to hold them, keeping your tables in memory greatly reduces disk I/O. The trade-off is a significant increase in memory usage.

The MySQL Data Structure

MySQL stores each table as a set of three files. For example, a medium-sized table called `mytable` may look like this:

```
-rw-rw----  1 root  root  1034155 Jun  3 17:08 mytable.ISD
-rw-rw----  1 root  root    50176 Jun  3 17:08 mytable.ISM
-rw-rw----  1 root  root     9114 Jun  3 14:24 mytable.frm
```

The ISD file contains the actual data. The ISM file contains information about the keys and other internal data that enables MySQL to find data in the ISD file quickly. The frm file contains the structure of the table itself.

---

* Remember that the options to *safe_mysqld* are passed on to *mysqld*.

The ISM file is most important to the performance of MySQL. It is so important, in fact, that an entire utility, *isamchk*, is devoted to it. Running *isamchk -d* will display information about a table:

```
# isamchk -d mytable

ISAM file:     mytable
Data records:       1973  Deleted blocks:            0
Recordlength:        343
Record format: Packed

table description:
Key Start Len Index   Type
1   2     50  unique  text packed stripped
```

The important field to notice here is the "Deleted blocks" field. If this value is too high, then the file is wasting a lot of space. Fortunately, you can recover this space. The following command will examine the table and recreate it, removing most errors and eliminating unnecessary space:

```
isamchk -r mytable
```

You can obtain additional speed enhancements by running *isamchk -a* on the table. This command analyzes the distribution of data in a table. You should run it after you insert or delete numerous records from the table.

Repairing damaged tables

Due to server crashes or other acts of nature, a table in your database may become corrupted. When this happens, *isamchk* provides several different levels of repair:

```
isamchk mytable
```

 If you alter a table using isamchk while the database server is running, you may have to run *mysqladmin reload* to make the server see the updated table.

This command will repair most common problems with tables. Adding the *-i* and *-v* options will provide extra output about what is wrong. You can use more than one *-v* for extra information.

```
isamchk -rq mytable
```

This command will perform a quick check—and repair, if necessary—of only the ISM file. It will not check for corruption of the ISD file.

```
isamchk -e mytable
```

Using this option, you can perform a full check and repair of everything, eliminating any possible corruption. This sort of check will naturally take much longer than a regular check. The command will exit upon encountering the first severe error. If you want to continue reparations even after severe corruption is encountered, you can pass it the *-v* option. This option will guarantee the resulting table to be clean of corruption, but you may lose some data in the process.

Always back up your data before running any command that may alter the contents of a table. The *isamchk* utility is very good about repairing errors, but sometimes that means erasing corrupt data that is interfering with the rest of the table. If you have a backup, you can use it to recover any data that *isamchk* erased.

Removing and replacing keys

Keys can sometimes get in the way of database performance. If, for instance, you want to insert a large data set into a table, having MySQL index the keys after every insert can be very inefficient. In addition, if you have a table with corrupt keys, blindly repairing that table with *isamchk* could delete some of the data associated with the key.

In these situations, it can be helpful to temporarily remove the keys from a table and then replace them when the troublesome work is finished. The following command will remove the key information from a table:

```
isamchk -rq -k0
```

When you are ready to put them back in, issue this command to replace the keys:

```
isamchk -rq
```

Shut down the server before issuing *isamchk* with the *-r* option. If the server is running, *isamchk-r* could corrupt the table.

The *isamchk* command provides so many capabilities it can be hard to sift through them all. However, there are some basic guidelines to follow:

- While the database is young, run *isamchk -a* often. For most database applications, the bulk of data is inserted near the beginning of the life of the database. If you run *isamchk* with the analyze option every time the size of your database doubles you can make sure the data is always kept in the most efficient form.

- Run *isamchk -d* once or twice a year. If the number of deleted blocks used by your tables is a significant portion of your disk space run *isamchk -r* to rebuild your tables without the unneeded space. If you have an application that involves a great deal of deleting old data and inserting new data, run *isamchk -d* every couple of weeks and if the number of deleted blocks grows quickly, you may want to run *isamchk -r* routinely every month.

- Except for removing and replacing keys, which should always be done any-time more than a few dozen rows is being inserted at once, all other forms of *isamchk* should be run only reactively, whenever inconsistencies in the data-base appear.

Troubleshooting

Even in the best of products, problems occur. Fortunately, many problems you might run into have happened to others. The following is a collection of fre-quently encountered trouble spots dealing with MySQL administration:

Changes to the access tables are not working.
> Do not forget to issue the command *mysqladmin reload* after making changes to access tables.

MySQL is refusing connections at peak times.

1. You should first check how many connections the server allows. The command *mysqladmin variables* will show this value under `max_connections`. You can set this value higher by starting *mysqld* with the *-O max_connections=###* where ### is the limit you wish to set.

2. You can also check with the `back_log` value which determines the size of the queue that MySQL creates for incoming connections. The default value is 5. Versions of MySQL prior to 3.22.x could set this limit only as high as 64, but later versions can set it as high as 1024. Your operating system, however, may limit connections to 64.

3. Finally, this problem can also be caused by file descriptor limits. In this case, the symptoms are that no connections at all are being allowed when MySQL has a large number of threads running. Unix systems handle setting the num-ber of file descriptors in many different ways, so refer to your system docu-mentation on how to increase the limit.

MySQL claims to be unable to find a file that definitely exists, or it reports errors while reading it.
> Most of the time, this problem is a result of the file descriptor problem men-tioned above. If, however, you increase MySQL's table cache, it will not have to open the table files so many times and you may avoid this problem. By

default, the table cache value is 64. You can increase this value through the `table_cache` variable.

Threads start to pile up and they will not go away.

Certain systems, including Linux and some setups using NFS, have a problem with their file locking mechanism. This problem can result in a thread freezing. The *mysqladmin processlist* can help identify this problem. If the frozen threads report "System lock" under the "Command" field, use the *--skip-locking* option when starting *mysqld*.

5

mSQL

Database concepts and design are all extremely important, but you probably want to dive in and work with mSQL or MySQL. Chances are that you have chosen one database engine or the other to serve your needs. Perhaps, however, you are looking to this book to help you with that decision. In this chapter, we start diving into the details with mSQL. If you are already a committed MySQL user, you can skip over this chapter. If, on the other hand, you are a committed mSQL user or you want to learn about both database engines, this chapter is the place to start.

mSQL is the relational database management system (RDBMS) that initiated the era of cheap SQL database engines for small-to-medium sized database needs. Its small footprint, impressive speed, and short learning curve turned it into an excellent database choice for the growing population of start-up web developers who do not want to spend the time to become expert database programmers. The author of the mSQL database engine intentionally included all of these advantages when he set out to create a database product that could fill a gaping hole in database products.

Design

David Hughes had three specific design goals in mind for mSQL:

- mSQL had to be fast.
- mSQL had to have a small footprint.
- mSQL had to be able to handle multiple simultaneous connections.

Speed was the primary motivation behind mSQL. Because most commercial SQL servers try to implement the full SQL2 specification in addition to their own proprietary extensions, they pay for that support in terms of performance and footprint.

mSQL, however, sacrifices some of the more advanced features of the commercial database engines for speed. Minerva needed to be able to run many simple SQL queries quickly. mSQL does exactly that.

Speed and footprint go hand-in-hand. As Hughes discovered, if you start from the ground up and implement only the necessary functionality, you can design an SQL server that does not take up so many resources that it must be run on a machine by itself in order to be useful. As a result, mSQL has a large amount of the functionality of the major database engines using a fraction of the resources.

The speed and footprint improvements of mSQL would have been enough to make it a viable replacement for Postgres on the Minerva project. Hughes, however, also wanted to change the behavior that caused him to seek an alternative in the first place. Hughes specifically designed mSQL to handle multiple simultaneous connections within a single process. The result of these design goals is a small, fast, efficient SQL server capable of handling multiple connections, locally or over the network.

In order to implement this design, Hughes first needed to limit the functionality of the server. The mSQL dialect of SQL is a subset of the ANSI SQL2 standard that contains the most commonly used statements like CREATE, INSERT, SELECT, UPDATE, and DELETE.* Hughes left out resource intensive operations like transaction support. Because of the kind of applications mSQL supports, the functionality Hughes left out is generally not needed.

mSQL is a queuing, single-threaded server. Any number of clients may connect to mSQL at the same time—up to a defined limit. As each of these clients send queries to mSQL, the database engine sticks the queries into a synchronous queue and processes each query one at a time. The efficiency of this design is thus dependent on the ability of the server to handle each query quickly. If the queries are not processed in a timely manner, the queue will grow and eventually the server will crash from exceeding system limitations. Speed is therefore critical to the successful operation of mSQL. Figure 5-1 illustrates mSQL's queuing, single-threaded processing.

The single-threaded nature of mSQL eliminates the need for batch processing. Because queries are handled one at a time, SQL statements do not have the ability to overwrite each other. It would, of course, be nice if mSQL supported transactions, but they are not necessary for the proper operation of a database engine with mSQL's design goals.

On the client side, mSQL supports two kinds of connections. Remote clients connect to the server through a well-known TCP/IP port. By basing connectivity on

---

* We will cover the mSQL SQL dialect in Chapter 6, *SQL According to MySQL and mSQL.*

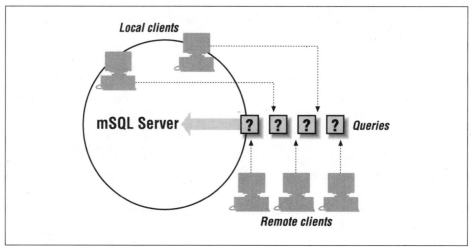

Figure 5-1. The client/server design of mSQL

TCP/IP, an mSQL database can be made available to any machine in the world via the Internet. Local connections can also make use of the TCP/IP port, but they can get better performance by using a standard Unix socket. Unix socket connections are about 20 percent faster than TCP/IP connections.

Bundled with mSQL is a suite of programs that enables complete access to the database system. The mSQL monitor, *msql*, enables a user to submit queries directly to the server. While this tool is useful during development, most users will want to interface with the database through some sort of application. In order to support application development, mSQL has a built-in C API that enables any C program to connect to a mSQL server through either a TCP/IP or Unix socket.

mSQL also provides a network protocol that enables other languages to connect to mSQL over a network without the need for using the C API. With these two types of interfaces, developers in a host of languages have put together libraries for connecting to mSQL in just about any language you can imagine. In this book, we cover the C, Perl, Java, and Python APIs.

mSQL Versions

When mSQL arrived on the scene, it made an immediate impact on the development community. For the first time, people had access to an affordable, SQL-based database engine. Among its more amazing aspects was that it not only compared with the major database engines in terms of performance, but that it was actually faster—sometimes over 100 times faster—in the areas for which it was designed.

Today, however, the computing environment does not stay still for long. With the advent of large-scale Internet collaboration, no project is beyond the reach of a dedicated base of programmers. By 1996, other cheap SQL implementations—one of which is MySQL—were appearing on the scene. mSQL was no longer alone.

Throughout the 1990s, Hughes has been developing and improving mSQL. The database engine, however, eventually reached the point where further development required some extensive rethinking of the entire project. Such a huge undertaking was bound to take a great deal of time as any new project has its share of new bugs and setbacks. During this time, it would also be necessary to maintain the existing product. mSQL 2 was thus born as the new rebuild of the mSQL engine while the existing product, mSQL 1, continued to be maintained.

mSQL 2 came along when the initial product was beginning to show its age. Stability problems and lack of important functionality, such as the support of important datatypes, were leading people to look for other solutions like MySQL. mSQL 2 provided fixes for a large range of bugs that plagued later releases of mSQL 1 and added a host of new features while remaining true to its original design goals. The subset of ANSI SQL supported by mSQL grew and a number of new datatypes were added. The indexing feature was reworked to provide much more powerful table indexing.

The major changes between mSQL 1 and 2 are:

Increased stability and performance
> The initial release of mSQL 2 fixed all of the known stability problems of mSQL 1. Memory leaks were eliminated and the code was extensively profiled to remove bugs. In addition, overall performance increased in spite of the new features.

Improved indexing support
> The first version of mSQL implemented a very weak indexing scheme. Each table could have exactly one index made up of exactly one column—the primary key. Indexing has been completely rewritten for mSQL 2 to support more complex and common indexing needs. You can now have multiple indices per table, and an index can be made up of more than one column. Indexing now also supports both B-Tree and AVL style index files.

More datatypes
> mSQL 2 has added many new datatypes, bringing it close to a complete implementation of the ANSI SQL2 specification. Along with MONEY, DATE, and TIME types, mSQL 2 now supports a TEXT datatype. In the initial mSQL release, all fields were fixed length so that all text fields—type CHAR—had their lengths predefined. In order to support common attributes, such as email addresses or book titles, you had to define a large CHAR field that largely wasted space for a

majority of addresses or titles. For example, for an email address field, you would have to define a `CHAR(35)` field. Even if your email address was "xxx@imaginary.com," mSQL used a full 35 characters for the entry. Furthermore, if you encountered an email address that was longer than 35 characters, you were out of luck. The new `TEXT` datatype takes care of both problems by enabling you to define an average length for the field. Anything over that length will be stored in an overflow buffer. Anything less will not cause extra characters to be stored. Unfortunately, `TEXT` fields are still lacking in that they cannot serve as indices and cannot be used in `LIKE` clauses.

Enhanced tools and API support

The standard tools provided with mSQL have been enhanced to support all of the new mSQL features. Hughes has added new functionality to the tools, such as the table copy and rename feature in *msqladmin*. The World Wide Web interactivity application W3-mSQL has been given a major overhaul with many enhancements. The scripting language has been reworked into Lite, a language with features that directly support web/database interactivity.

If you are new to mSQL, you almost certainly will be working with mSQL 2. If you are dealing with a legacy system, however, you should be very conscious of the distinctions between the two versions—especially if you intend to upgrade to mSQL 2.

Installing mSQL

Your first step in working with mSQL is naturally to download the product and install it. How you go about that depends on what platform you intend to use. mSQL was born as a Unix application and that is the platform Hughes supports. If you run some variant of Unix, mSQL is almost certain to work for you. Even if it does not, mSQL comes in source code form, meaning that an experienced C coder can fix any compatibility issues for oddball Unix systems. The Unix distribution is found at *http://www.hughes.com.au.*

If you are using Windows or OS/2, you are not left out in the cold. Both Win32 and OS/2 ports are being actively maintained. The mSQL PC home page at *http://blnet.com/msqlpc/* is the place to look for the most recent Win32 and OS/2 ports. While these ports are relatively current, they are always going to be a bit behind the latest and greatest from Hughes. At the time of this book's printing, the current Unix version was 2.0.7 while the current Win32 version is 2.0.4.1 and the current OS/2 version is 2.06. Mac users are mostly out of luck. Only the client tools for mSQL have been ported to the Mac.

The act of actually installing mSQL depends on your platform. Unix users will have to compile their distribution, while Win32 and OS/2 users are presented with the precompiled binaries. Because installation procedures can change from release to release, we will not go into the details of an mSQL install here. You should instead consult the documentation that comes with your release since it is certain to be up to date with the exact procedures for your release.

Running mSQL

mSQL is really the only database engine that is "install and go." In other words, you can install mSQL and start the server right up and be in business. The mSQL server process is called *msql2d* (for mSQL 1 servers, it is called *msqld*). This executable and all of the utilities that come with an mSQL distribution can be found in the *bin* directory. You can start up an mSQL instance simply by issuing the *msql2d* command with no command line options.

This default implementation will get you only so far. In most cases, you will want to edit a file in the mSQL distribution directory called *msql.conf*. This configuration file enables mSQL 2 users (it does not exist under mSQL 1) to specify a few common options. Configuring this file is generally necessary only when you are using some precompiled mSQL distribution.

The mSQL daemon process does not fork. This means that running it from the command line will leave the process running in your terminal unless you explicitly press CTRL-C to kill the process or put the process in the background. Under Unix, you can start the mSQL server from the command line in the background using the following command:

```
msqld2 &
```

The following script works to start up an mSQL server process at system start-up and to shut it down cleanly on system shutdown:

```
#!/bin/sh

if [ $1 = "start" ]; then
   if [ -x /usr/local/Hughes/bin/msql2d ]; then
       su msql -c '/usr/local/Hughes/bin/msql2d &'
   fi
else
   if [ $1 = "stop" ]; then
     if [ -x /usr/local/Hughes/bin/msqladmin ]; then
         su msql -c '/usr/local/Hughes/bin/msqladmin shutdown'
     fi
   fi
fi
```

This example script assumes that you want to run mSQL on Unix under the user ID "msql." You should naturally replace it with whatever user ID you wish to run mSQL under and replace */usr/local/Hughes* with the directory where you installed mSQL.

While the Win32 does not yet run as an NT service, you can run mSQL from the *StartUp* folder simply by sticking a shortcut to the *msql2d.exe* file into the *StartUp* folder. (We will cover the *msqladmin* command later in the chapter.)

While mSQL is a very stable product, every once and a while things just happen and the server dies. In particular, earlier versions of mSQL did have stability issues that caused the server to crash unexpectedly. For those occasions, you want to have something running that will check on the status of the database server.

The following Unix script will perform a thorough check to see that the *msql2d* daemon is still running. If the daemon is inactive, it is restarted and a message is sent to the administrator of the machine.

```sh
#!/bin/sh

# Retrieve the process ID of the database daemon
# This is for a default mSQL 2 installation, for mSQL 1
# the line should be:
# PID='cat /usr/local/Minerva/msqld.pid'
PID='cat /usr/local/Hughes/msql2d.pid'

# This checks to see if the server process is running.
# Use this line for BSD systems (Linux)
ALIVE='ps aux | grep $PID | grep -v grep | awk '{print $2}''
# Uncomment this line for SYSV systems (Solaris)
#ALIVE='ps -ef | grep $PID | grep -v grep | awk '{print $2}''

if [ $ALIVE ]
then
    REALLY_ALIVE='msqladmin version'
    DATE='date'

    # If the first word of the result is 'ERROR', or if
    # there was no output at all, the msqladmin
    # program was not able to connect to the database server
    if ! echo $REALLY_ALIVE | grep "^ERROR"
    then
        exit
    fi
    if [ ! $REALLY_ALIVE ]
    then exit; fi
else
    # This should be /usr/local/Minerva/bin/msqld &
    # for mSQL 1 installations
    /usr/local/Hughes/bin/msql2d &
mail -s "mSQL daemon restarted" root@yourmachine.com <<EOM
The mSQL daemon died unexpectedly and was restarted
on $DATE.
```

```
Sincerely,
The mSQL Watchdog
EOM


fi
```

Once started, mSQL is ready to communicate with the outside world in two differ-ent ways. Communication with the Internet happens through a TCP/IP port. mSQL listens to port 1112 by default. mSQL 2 listens to port 1114. You can, however, change which port the server listens to either at compile time (mSQL 1) or in the configuration file (mSQL 2).

Internal communication happens through Unix sockets. Unix sockets appear as regular files in the file system of a Unix server. You can distinguish them from reg-ular files because they are followed by the character when using the '-F' flag for the *ls* command. mSQL 1 uses the file */dev/msql* while mSQL 2 uses the file */usr/local/Hughes/msql2.sock*.

Running Multiple Daemons

You may find it useful at times to run more than one database server at a time. Performance is the most common cause for you to want to do this. Because of mSQL's single-threaded nature, it handles all requests serially. If one of your data-bases—or even one of your tables—is responsible for a large percentage of your database hits, applications which hit other databases or tables may end up spend-ing a lot of time waiting on queries that hit that database or table.

You will not encounter this problem with a multithreaded server like MySQL, but you can get around it in mSQL by running multiple mSQL processes. This solu-tion is limited in that only one daemon may have access to a particular database. Without this limitation, two daemons could overwrite each other's changes. You can accomplish this by giving each running *msql2d* instance its own base direc-tory under which its data is stored. You can do this in mSQL 2 via command line options and the configuration file. Under mSQL 1, you actually have to compile and install mSQL multiple times into multiple installation directories.

To set up the second directory for mSQL 2, use the following:

```
mkdir -p /usr/local/second_database/msqldb/.tmp
cp /usr/local/Hughes/msql.conf /usr/local/Hughes/msql.acl \
/usr/local/second_database
chown -R msql /usr/local/second_database
```

Some Unix systems use the *mkdirs* command instead of *mkdir -p* while some may not have that option at all. If the option does not exist, you will have to create each directory separately. Also, you need to substitute the user ID under which you run *msql2d* if it is different from "msql." Finally, the steps are identical if you are working under Windows or OS/2—only the command names and the path separator change.

Once the directories are created and the files copied, you need to edit *msql.conf* in the new directory to change `Inst_Dir` to point to */usr/local/second_database* and `TCP_Port` to some value that does not conflict with any other TCP service on the server. You can leave the `Unix_Port` option unchanged since the new socket will go in the new directory.

To launch the new daemon, run the old *msql2d* command with the following option:

```
msql2d -f /usr/local/second_database/msql.conf
```

If you are working with mSQL 1, life is a little more complicated. You specifically have to compile and install mSQL once for each server instance you wish to run. All of your utilities will work with any instance of your server.

The mSQL Configuration File

We have touched on the mSQL configuration file in places, but we have not really gone into any detail on it. Under mSQL 1, everything except security was defined at compile time. mSQL 2 provides a configuration file that enables you to configure the runtime behavior of your mSQL server. A mSQL configuration file might look like this:

```
[general]

Inst_Dir = c:\usr\local\Hughes
mSQL_User = msql
Admin_User = root
Pid_File = %I\msql2d.pid
TCP_Port = 1114
Unix_Port = %I\msql2.sock

[system]

Msync_Timer = 30
Host_Lookup = True
Read_Only = False
Remote_Access = True
Local_Access = True
```

```
[w3-msql]

Auth_Host = NULL
Footer = True
Force_Private = False
```

Like a Windows INI file, the mSQL configuration script is divided into sections, each with its own set of key/value pairs. At this point, the only parts of the mSQL configuration file of interest to us are in the *general* section.

Inst_Dir

> The mSQL installation directory. More specifically, this directory is where mSQL looks for your ACL file, the mSQL PID file, and the *msqldb* directory where the server's database directories are housed. Using this configuration key, you can support multiple mSQL servers with a single set of mSQL binaries.

mSQL_User

> The user ID under which the mSQL process is running.

Admin_User

> The user ID allowed to execute administrative commands such as the *msqladmin* command discussed in the next section of this chapter.

TCP_Port

> The TCP/IP port to which this server will be listening. Under Unix, you can only choose a port number less than 1024 if the mSQL server is running as the root user.

Unix_Port

> The name of the Unix socket file. In this file, we used the %I% variable to stand for the value of `Inst_Dir`.

Database Administration

Now that your server is running 24 hours a day, 7 days a week, your next task is to get it to serve your database needs. mSQL provides a set of utilities that support easy server administration.

The msqladmin Utility

The *msqladmin* utility is your primary database administration tool. It supports creating, deleting, copying, renaming, and examining your mSQL databases. If you look back to our discussion of what a database is in Chapter 1, *Introduction to Relational Databases*, you will remember that mSQL itself is not a database. Your databases are the collection of files under each directory in the *msqldb* directory.

mSQL is the database engine. One engine can serve many databases simultaneously. The msqladmin utility lets you administer the databases under a particular server.

Database creation

The first thing you want to do with your new mSQL installation is create a database that serves some purpose for you. The syntax of creating a database is:

```
msqladmin create DATABASENAME
```

In this syntax, *DATABASENAME* is the name of the new database you wish to create. This command will create a new, blank database with the name you specify. As we mentioned earlier, a database in mSQL is simply a directory under the *msqldb* directory in the mSQL installation. mSQL places all the data associated with your new database in files underneath this directory. For example, if you create a database called "mydata" using a default mSQL installation, the directory */usr/local/ Hughes/msqldb/mydata* will appear.

Database destruction

During the process of developing a new database application, you will likely want to create several databases to support the development process. For example, it is common in database application development to have separate databases for development, testing, and production. When development is complete, it is time to get rid of the development and testing databases. The *msqladmin* utility provides the "drop" option to let you delete a database:

```
msqladmin drop DATABASENAME
```

As with the *msqladmin create* command, *DATABASENAME* is the name of the database you wish to destroy. mSQL will not let you accidentally drop the database. After issuing this command, it will warn you that dropping a database is potentially a very bad thing to do and ask you to confirm the drop. You can examine the *msqldb* directory after dropping the database to verify that the directory that once served as that database no longer exists.

Database renaming and copying

A convenient new feature of mSQL 2 is the ability to copy and rename databases. Under mSQL 1, you could drop to the file system and do a manual rename or copy of the database directory using the renaming and copying tools of your operating system. If you go that route, however, you also have to remember to restart the mSQL server and make sure you have not messed up any permissions. With mSQL 2, however, a rename is as simple as:

```
msqladmin move OLDNAME NEWNAME
```

For example, if you had created a database with the misspelled name "midata" and you wanted to rename it to the proper spelling, you would issue the command:

```
msqladmin move midata mydata
```

Copying is just as simple:

```
msqladmin copy mydata mynewdata
```

Server status

If you have been playing with MySQL, you will notice that the monitoring of server status is one area in which mSQL is decidedly lacking. The msqladmin utility is your interface into monitoring your servers. The *msqladmin stats* command under mSQL 2 will produce the following output:

```
Server Statistics
-----------------

Mini SQL Version 2.0.4.1 - Forge Alpha Build #9
Copyright (c) 1993-94 David J. Hughes
Copyright (c) 1995-98 Hughes Technologies Pty Ltd.
All rights reserved.

Config file      : c:\usr\local\hughes\msql.conf
Max connections  : 61
Cur connections  : 1
Running as user  : UID 500

Connection table :
   Sock  Username    Hostname    Database    Connect   Idle   Queries
  +-----+----------+----------+ +----------+--------+------+--------+
  |   5 | randy    | Unix sock| No DB     | 0H  0M |    0 |     1 |
  |  13 | bob      | client.com| mydata    | 0H  5M |    2 |     4 |
  +-----+----------+------ ----+----------+--------+------+--------+
```

This output likely needs a little explanation:

Max connections
> The maximum number of simultaneous connections that the server can handle.

Cur connections
> The current number of connections to the database server.

Sock
> The Internet socket number used by mSQL to identify each connection.

Username
> The username of the person connected to the server.

Hostname
> The hostname of the machine connected to the server. "Unix sock" is shown if the client is connecting from the local host via a Unix socket.

Database

The name of the database to which the user is currently connected. "No DB" means that the client has not chosen a database.

Connect

The total time the client has been connected to the server in hours and minutes.

Idle

The amount of time in minutes since the client's last query.

Queries

The total number of queries the client has sent using this connection.

In addition to the *msqladmin stats* command, you can monitor other, more static, server information via the *msqladmin version* command. Your output might look something like this:

```
Version Details :-

        msqladmin version        2.0.4.1 - Forge Alpha Build #9
        mSQL server version      2.0.4.1 - Forge Alpha Build #9
        mSQL protocol version    23
        mSQL connection          127.0.0.1 via TCP/IP
        Target platform          CYGWIN32_NT-4.0-i586

Configuration Details :-

        Default config file      c:\usr\local\hughes/msql.conf
        TCP socket               1114
        Unix socket              c:\usr\local\Hughes\msql2.sock
        mSQL user                msql
        Admin user               root
        Install directory        c:\usr\local\Hughes
        PID file location        c:\usr\local\Hughes\msql2d.pid
        Memory Sync Timer        30
        Hostname Lookup          False
```

Each of the values in the output of *msqladmin version* can be set via the mSQL 2 configuration file.

If mSQL has been compiled with debugging enabled, mSQL will place information about the running server process into the debug file chosen at compile time. mSQL provides no other logging facilities.

Server shutdown

You saw an example of how to shutdown mSQL earlier in the chapter in the example Unix startup/shutdown script. The command is:

```
msqladmin shutdown
```

This command will perform a clean shutdown of the mSQL server.

Reloading server changes

If you make any changes to the mSQL ACL, you will need to tell the server to reload those changes. The command to do this is:

```
msqladmin reload
```

We will cover the mSQL ACL later in the chapter.

Command line options for msqladmin

In all of the examples we have given so far, *msqladmin* has been used to manage the mSQL server on the local host with the default configuration file. You can use this tool to manage servers on other machines or that use different configuration files. The full syntax for the *msqladmin* utility is:

```
msqladmin [-h host] [-f conf] [-q] COMMAND
```

The options have the following meanings:

-h   The host of the server you wish to manage.

-f   The configuration file for the server you wish to manage. You will only likely ever use this option if you are running multiple mSQL instances as described earlier in the chapter.

-q   Run in quiet mode. The *msqladmin* utility will not ask you for verification of commands. This option is useful if you are running the utility from a script.

Backups

Good backups are a vital part of any administration scheme. Database corruption can happen and, if severe enough, can cripple all applications that depend on the database. As the saying goes, data is only as good as the most recent backup.

There are a couple of backup methods available when using mSQL. Like most of mSQL, they do not provide all of the bells and whistles but they do get the job done. The *msqldump* command is the most commonly used method for backing up mSQL databases. This command produces a full standard SQL dump of an entire database. You must issue a separate msqldump command for each database on the system. For example:

```
msqldump database1 > /usr/backups/database1.sql.daily
msqldump database2 > /usr/backups/database2.sql.daily
msqldump database3 > /usr/backups/database3.sql.daily
```

This example creates a dump of three different databases into the same directory.

You use the file extension *daily* to indicate that the backup files are replaced every day. How often you backup your data will depend on the importance of the data and the amount and type of backup storage you have available. Because only full dumps are available from mSQL, the size of the backups can grow large on systems that contain a great deal of data. If you have enough space, a good backup plan is to keep separate daily backups for each day of the week—or for two weeks or even a month. At the end of the cycle, the tapes are reused as needed—or the files are overwritten if backing up to hard disk. This way there is always one week of data available. If backing up to hard disk, you can possibly condense the individual daily backups into a single daily backup that is overwritten each day. In this case, you should also keep a separate weekly backup in order to recover accidentally deleted data that cannot be found on the most recent backup. Because of the lack of redundancy, this plan should only be used if you have a limited amount of backup space available.

The other method of backing up mSQL databases involves taking advantage of the simple nature of the mSQL data files. Unlike some database packages, mSQL keeps its data in regular files stored in the native operating system's file system. Thus is it possibly to act on these files as if they were any other type of file. Therefore a complete backup of an mSQL system can be obtained by shutting down the mSQL server and then creating a tar archive of the mSQL data directory. You must shut down the server first or the archive data files could be incomplete or corrupt.

Restoring data from mSQL data backups is as simple as creating the backups. Dumps created with *msqldump* are in standard SQL that can be fed to the *msql* monitor. These dumps contain the instructions to create the tables as well as the data, so you should either remove the existing table, if it exists, or remove the `CREATE TABLE` statement from the backup file. If you are restoring only specific rows of data, you can simply copy them out of the backup file and feed them into the *msql* monitor.

When restoring data from a tar archive of the mSQL data directory, it is only possible to do a full restore to the backed up state. You cannot restore only parts of the data, and any data that has been added to the database since the backup will be lost. To perform this restore, simply shutdown the mSQL server then enter the backup file into the mSQL data directory. When you restart the server, it will be in exactly the state it was in when the backup was performed—except that any new databases added will still be there, untouched.

Which method you choose to use depends on your needs. Creating a binary archive is simple and complete and allows for a very fast recovery time. However, it is not possible to do a partial recovery and any data you have added since the backup will be lost. The SQL dump method on the other hand can be slow, but it allows for partial recovery, albeit with a little work. In addition, the SQL dump method can be performed at any time, while a binary archive required the server to be shut down, which can be a deciding factor in a busy installation.

One final concern to consider is portability. Unlike a binary backup, a SQL dump consists entirely of plain ASCII SQL commands. With little modification—mainly weeding out any of the mSQL specific SQL—a mSQL SQL dump can be imported into any standards compliant SQL server. This is a very handy way to transport your data if you ever need to switch SQL servers.

Security

Depending on your point of view, the mSQL security scheme is either one of its advantages or one of its disadvantages. On the one hand, mSQL's security is easier to manage than any other server-based relational database engine available. It accomplishes this ease of maintenance through simplicity. Unfortunately, this simplicity is insufficient for even moderately complex database applications.

mSQL manages security through a file called *msql.acl* stored in the mSQL installation directory. The .acl extension refers to "Access Control List," a very flexible form of authorization that has been in use on several operating systems and applications for some time. The format of the msql.acl file looks like this:

```
database=mydata
read=*
write=*
host=*
access=local,remote

database=mynewdata
read=*
wriite=admin,root
host=*
access=local
```

Each database has a stanza of options. The *read* and *write* lines indicate which users you want to give read (**SELECT**) or write (**INSERT,UPDATE,DELETE**) access to the database. The *host* line specifies which hosts can connect remotely to the database. If the *access* line contains "local," local Unix socket connections are allowed. Similarly, if the *access* line contains "remote," remote TCP connections are allowed.

The ACL file allows a "*" wildcard entry in the *read*, *write*, and *host* fields. You could therefore have the following ACL:

```
database=mynewdata
read=*
write=msql*
host=*.client.com,*isp.com
access=local,remote
```

Under this ACL, anyone from any host at client.com or anyone from any host at any domain ending in isp.com—for example, wisp.com and lisp.com—can connect to the database. These users can read from the database, but only user names beginning with "msql" can modify the database.

By default, everything is excluded. Thus, if you leave out a *write* entry, nobody can modify the database. Specific users and hosts may be excluded by prefixing their entries with a "-". Consider the following:

```
database=moredata
read=-bob,*
write=jane
host=-junk.isp.com,*.isp.com
access=local,remote
```

This ACL enables all machines from the isp.com domain to connect, except for junk.isp.com. In addition, everyone except "bob" can read from the database. Only "jane" can write to the database. Because rejection is mSQL's default, having specific rejection entries like "bob," is meaningless unless the line also contains a wildcard entry.

mSQL acts on the first match it encounters. If, for example, the wildcard in the *read* entry came before "-bob," the wildcard would have matched "bob" and "bob" would have read access.

The *msqladmin reload* command, as noted earlier in the chapter, reloads an ACL after you have made any changes. If you fail to issue the *msqladmin reload* command, your changes will not be seen until the server shuts down and starts back up.

mSQL Utilities

We have already covered one of the utilities that ships with mSQL, msqladmin. mSQL provides seven basic utilities for basic interaction with mSQL. In addition to those basic utilities, mSQL supports a lightweight scripting utility called Lite and a web interface called W3-mSQL. Third party developers support numerous tools beyond those that come with mSQL. We will now take a detailed look at the basic mSQL utilities beyond *msqladmin* and then skim over the list of third party tools. We will address Lite and W3-mSQL later in the book.

Command Line Tools

Each mSQL command line tool comes with detailed help to explain its syntax. In general, however, the syntax mirrors that of the *msqladmin* command. Specifically, a *-h* option enables you to specify a host and a *-f* options enables you to name a specific configuration file.

msql

> This tool is a command line interface into mSQL that enables you to interactively execute SQL against a specific database. In addition to the common options described above, you specify which database you wish to work against. Of all the commands that come with mSQL, this is likely the one you will use the most.

msqldump

> This command outputs the complete contents of a table or a whole database, including the table structure itself, as a series of SQL statements. The output of this utility can be used to backup a database and recreate it on another machine.

msqlimport

> This command reads a formatted file of data and inserts the data into the specified database table. The format of the file can come in any number of forms, including comma-delimited and quoted.

relshow

> This tool displays the structure of the database and tables within them. It is useful, for example, if you want to know what tables exist in a database or what columns exist within a specific table.

msqlexport

> This tool sends the contents of a table to the standard output in the form of a delimited text file. Many other database and applications like Microsoft Excel can read this file and import its data.

Third Party Support

As with any popular Internet product, the third party products that support mSQL are numerous. These products range from conversion utilities to programming interfaces. No matter how you use mSQL, you are certain to make use of at least one of the third party products outlined here. This list cannot, of course, be comprehensive as the availability of third party tools changes daily. You should check with the Hughes and mSQL PC web sites listed earlier in this chapter for the most up-to-date lists of third party tools.

Database conversion utilities

dbf2msql

> Translates DBF files into mSQL tables. DBF files are the format of the dBASE database that once was the leading desktop database. Even though dBASE is no longer as popular, the DBF format has become ingrained as the most common cross-application database file format. Every major desktop database can

read and write DBF files. This application is thus useful when exporting data to or importing data from commercial desktop databases.

mSQLpp

Converts Ingres Embedded SQL (ESQL) to SQL readable by mSQL. ESQL is embedded directly into C source files to provide easy access to databases in C programs. This program will translate a C source file with ESQL to a C source file using the standard mSQL API. It is intended to work as a preprocessor, so it is usually possible to use ESQL files—filtered through the program—with mSQL without any modification.

CGI interfaces

PHP

Creates HTML pages using special tags recognized by the PHP parser. PHP includes interfaces to most major databases, including MySQL and mSQL. PHP is covered in more detail in Chapter 12, *PHP and Other Support for Database-driven HTML.*

dbadmin

Provides a CGI interface to mSQL. This program is a CGI program that enables you to access any mSQL database table as if it were in an HTML form. You can modify table data and even perform operations on the database itself.

Jate

A complete CGI interface to mSQL. Jate comes with many features, all of which are accessible via HTML forms. You can view and modify tables and customize the output. Jate imports flat file data through HTML text fields. It also optimizes some data and searches before sending them to the database server.

mSQLCGI

Serves as another CGI interface to mSQL tables. This CGI program enables you to view and modify mSQL database tables over the web using HTML forms. This particular interface requires you to run a supplied program on each table you wish to use before you can access it over the web.

Client applications

dbview

Shows the structure of a mSQL database. This utility is similar to *relshow*, but it has a few added features. Most notably, *dbview* displays the number of records within each table.

XfSQL

Provides full access to mSQL table data as an Xforms client for the X Window System. Using this tool, you can insert, delete, and view table data under the X Windows System.

XmSQL

Provides full access to mSQL table data as a library-independent client for the X Window System. It will thus compile on any X Window system.

mSQLsql

Displays formatted tables. You can use this tool to view a mSQL table in a variety of ways, including customizable borders and delimiters for ASCII formatted tables. You can also produce HTML tables based on user-definable options.

mSQLwin-relshow

Provides a Windows-based GUI representation of the *relshow* tool.

Programming interfaces

ConNExS

Provides an interface between mSQL and the NExS spreadsheet application. NExS is a popular spreadsheet that can interactively link with an external data source. ConNExS enables mSQL database tables to serve as data sources for an NExS spreadsheet. Any changes to the spreadsheet will appear in the underlying mSQL table.

mSQLBase

Exposes the SQLBase API as a C wrapper to mSQL programs. The SQLBase API is a third party database connectivity API that supports several major SQL servers. This program translates the mSQL API into the SQLBase API so that SQLBase clients can work with mSQL.

mSQLCLI

Encapsulates the mSQL C API so that ODBC clients on OS/2 can run against mSQL. ODBC (Open Database Connectivity) is a popular database-independent API supported by most databases for access from OS/2 and Windows. This wrapper implements the common ODBC features that mSQL supports, but only for the OS/2 operating system. It includes the minimum allowed ODBC functionality.

msqldll

Packages the mSQL C API in the form of a Windows Data Linked Library (DLL). Using this DLL, you can write Windows applications using VisualBasic or any other Windows programming tool that works against DLLs.

MsqlJava

Wraps the mSQL TCP/IP network protocol into a Java API that resembles the mSQL C API. It provides a quick start to writing Java applications for developers who already know the mSQL C API but may not be familiar with the Java standard JDBC API. MsqlJava only works under JDK 1.0.

mSQL-JDBC

Implements the Java standard Java Database Connectivity (JDBC) API on top of the mSQL TCP/IP network protocol. This package supports the maximum level of JDBC functionality possible for mSQL in both JDK 1.1 and JDK 1.2 (Java 2) environments, including the JDBC 2.0 standard. Chapter 14, *Java and JDBC*, discusses, Java programming against this API in detail, while Chapter 22, *JDBC Reference*, provides a full reference for JDBC 2.0.

MsqlODBC

Implements the ODBC API for mSQL 1 on Windows. David Hughes is currently working on a mSQL 2 implementation.

mSQLPerl

Enables Perl scripts to access mSQL databases. Chapter 10, *Perl*, discusses Perl programming for MySQL and mSQL in detail, and Chapter 21, *Perl Reference*, provides a full reference for mSQLPerl.

mSQLPython

Enables Python scripts to access mSQL databases. Chapter 11, *Python*, discusses Python programming for MySQL and mSQL in detail, and Chapter 20, *Python Reference*, provides a full reference for mSQLPython.

mSQLRexx

Supports mSQL access from REXX, a scripting language most commonly found on the OS/2 operating system.

mSQLTCL

Enables any program in Tcl to access mSQL databases. This support encompasses many Tcl extensions, including Tcl/Tk and Expect.

mSQLVdb

Provides mSQL database access via the Vdb database library. Vdb is a database-independent C API that enables common client code to access several different backend database servers. Vdb clients can use this API to access mSQL databases.

zmsql

Provides object-oriented mSQL database access to C++ programs.

Miscellaneous

mod_auth_msql

Authenticates users of the Apache web server. Apache normally controls access through plain text files with user names and encrypted passwords. This Apache module enables you to manage access control inside a mSQL database.

mSQLEmacs

Expands the basic SQL-mode support in Emacs to handle special indenting and color highlighting for the mSQL variant of SQL.

msqlexpire

Deletes old data from mSQL tables. To use this program, a table must have a column that contains the age of the data. This program will examine the table for data that is older than desired and remove that data. You can configure msqlexpire to optionally send email notifications after each deletion.

mSQLSSL

Patches mSQL to support secure SSL-based network communications. In order to take advantage of this product, you need to compile mSQL with it. Once in place, your network communications are totally secure from prying eyes.

Sqs

Generates unique ID numbers for database tables. Using this program as a permanent daemon on a server, any number of clients can connect to the daemon and create, read, or delete sequences.

6

SQL According to MySQL and mSQL

The Structured Query Language (SQL) is the language used to read and write to MySQL and mSQL databases. Using SQL, you can search for data, enter new data, modify data, or delete data. SQL is simply the most fundamental tool you will need for your interactions with MySQL and mSQL. Even if you are using some application or graphical user interface to access the database, somewhere under the covers that application is generating SQL.

SQL is a sort of "natural" language. In other words, an SQL statement should read—at least on the surface—like a sentence of English text. This approach has both benefits and drawbacks, but the end result is a language very unlike traditional programming languages such as C, Java, or Perl.

In this chapter, we take a look at the SQL language as supported in MySQL and mSQL. For the most part, MySQL's dialect is a superset of mSQL's. We will carefully note the instances where the two dialects diverge. For the most part, however, this chapter applies to both database engines.

SQL Basics

SQL* is "structured" in the sense that it follows a very specific set of rules. A computer program can easily parse a formulated SQL query. In fact, the O'Reilly book *lex & yacc* by John Levine, Tony Mason, and Doug Brown implements a SQL grammar to demonstrate the process of writing a program to interpret language! A

---

* Pronounced either "sequel" or "ess-que-ell." Certain people get very religious about the pronunciation of SQL. Ignore them. It is important to note, however, that the "SQL" in mSQL and MySQL is properly pronounced "ess-que-ell."

query is a fully-specified command sent to the database server, which then performs the requested action. Below is an example of an SQL query:

```
SELECT name FROM people WHERE name LIKE 'Stac%'
```

As you can see, this statement reads almost like a form of broken English: "Select names from a list of people where the names are like Stac." SQL uses very few of the formatting and special characters that are typically associated with computer languages. Consider, for example, "$++;($*++/$|);$&$^,,;$!" in Perl versus "SELECT value FROM table" in SQL.

The SQL Story

IBM invented SQL in the 1970s shortly after Dr. E. F. Codd first invented the concept of a relational database. From the beginning, SQL was an easy to learn, yet powerful language. It resembles a natural language such as English, so that it might be less daunting to a nontechnical person. In the 1970s, even more than today, this advantage was an important one.

There were no casual hackers in the early 1970s. No one grew up learning BASIC or building web pages in HTML. The people programming computers were people who knew everything about how a computer worked. SQL was aimed at the army of nontechnical accountants and business and administrative staff that would benefit from being able to access the power of a relational database.

SQL was so popular with its target audience, in fact, that in the 1980s the Oracle corporation launched the world's first publicly available commercial SQL system. Oracle SQL was a huge hit and spawned an entire industry built around SQL. Sybase, Informix, Microsoft, and several other companies have since come forward with their implementations of a SQL-based Relational Database Management System (RDBMS).

At the time Oracle and its first competitors hit the scene, SQL was still brand new and there was no standard. It was not until 1989 that the ANSI standards body issued the first public SQL standard. These days it is referred to as SQL89. This new standard, unfortunately, did not go far enough into defining the technical structure of the language. Thus, even though the various commercial SQL languages were drawing closer together, differences in syntax still made it nontrivial to switch among implementations. It was not until 1992 that the ANSI SQL standard came into its own.

The 1992 standard is called both SQL92 and SQL2. The SQL2 standard expanded the language to accommodate as many of the proprietary extensions added by the commercial implementations as was possible. Most cross-DBMS tools have standardized on SQL2 as the way in which they talk to relational databases. Due to the extensive nature of the SQL2 standard, however, relational databases that implement the full standard are very complex and very resource intensive.

 SQL2 is not the last word on the SQL standard. With the growing popularity of object-oriented database management systems (OODBMS) and object-relational database management systems (ORDBMS), there has been increasing pressure to capture support for object-oriented database access in the SQL standard. SQL3 is the answer to this problem. It is not yet official, but it is currently very well defined and looks to become official sometime in 1999.

When MySQL and mSQL came along, they took a new approach to the business of database server development. Instead of manufacturing another giant RDBMS and risk having nothing more to offer than the big guys, they created small, fast implementations of the most commonly used SQL functionality.

The Design of SQL

As we mentioned earlier, SQL resembles a human language more than a computer language. SQL accomplishes this resemblance by having a simple, defined imperative structure. Much like an English sentence, individual SQL commands, called "queries," can be broken down into language parts. Consider the following examples:

```
CREATE    TABLE            people (name CHAR(10))
verb      object           adjective phrase

INSERT    INTO people      VALUES ('me')
verb      indirect object  direct object

SELECT    name             FROM people        WHERE name LIKE '%e'
verb      direct object    indirect object    adj. phrase
```

Most implementations of SQL, including MySQL and mSQL, are case-insensitive. Specifically, it does not matter how you type SQL keywords as long as the spelling is correct. The CREATE example from above could just as well appeared:

```
cREatE TAblE people (name cHaR(10))
```

The case-insensitivity only extends to SQL keywords.[*] In MySQL and mSQL, names of databases, tables, and columns are case-sensitive. This case-sensitivity is not necessarily true for all database engines. Thus, if you are writing an application that should work against all databases, you should act as if names are case-sensitive.

---

[*] For the sake of readability, we capitalize all SQL keywords in this book. We recommend this convention as a good "best practice" technique.

This first element of an SQL query is always a verb. The verb expresses the action you wish the database engine to take. While the rest of the statement varies from verb to verb, they all follow the same general format: you name the object upon which you are acting and then describe the data you are using for the action. For example, the query **CREATE TABLE people (CHAR(10))** uses the verb **CREATE**, followed by the object **TABLE**. The rest of the query describes the table to be created.

An SQL query originates with a client—the application that provides the façade through which a user interacts with the database. The client constructs a query based on user actions and sends the query to the SQL server. The server then must process the query and perform whatever action was specified. Once the server has done its job, it returns some value or set of values to the client.

Because the primary focus of SQL is to communicate actions to the database server, it does not have the flexibility of a general-purpose language. Most of the functionality of SQL concerns input to and output from the database: adding, changing, deleting, and reading data. SQL provides other functionality, but always with an eye towards how it can be used to manipulate the data within the database.

Creating and Dropping Tables

With MySQL or mSQL successfully installed, you should now be ready to create your first table. The *table*, a structured container of data, is the basic concept in a relational database. Before you can begin adding data to a table, you must define the table's structure. Consider the following layout:

```
+----------------------------------+
|                people            |
+-------------+--------------------+
| name        | char(10) not null  |
| address     | text(100)          |
| id          | int                |
+-------------+--------------------+
```

Not only does the table contain the names of the columns, but it also contains the types of each field as well as any additional information the fields may have. A field's datatype specified what kind of data the field can hold. SQL datatypes are similar to datatypes in other programming languages. The full SQL standard allows for a large range of datatypes. MySQL implements most of them, while mSQL contains only a few of the most useful types.

The general syntax for table creation is:

```
CREATE TABLE table_name (column_name1 type [modifiers]
                    [, column_name2 type [modifiers]]
    )
```

What constitutes a valid identifier—a name for a table or column—varies from DBMS to DBMS. mSQL provides close to the bare minimum support for names. It accepts any sequence of International Standards Organization (ISO) 8859-1 (Latin 1) letters, numbers, or '_' up to 20 characters as a valid identifier. An identifier must begin with a letter. Good database design only encounters problems with the ISO 8859-1 restriction. In other words, for good portable SQL, you do not want to have names that start with anything other than a valid letter. MySQL lets you go further. It allows up to 64 characters in an identifier, supports the character '$' in identifiers, and lets identifiers start with a valid number. More important, however, MySQL considers any valid letter for your local character set to be a valid letter for identifiers.

A *column* is the individual unit of data within a table. A table may have any number of columns, but large tables may be inefficient. This is where good database design, discussed in Chapter 2, *Database Design*, becomes an important skill. By creating properly normalized tables, you can "join" tables to perform a single search from data housed in more than one table. We discuss the mechanics of a join later in the chapter.

Like most things in life, destruction is much easier than creation. The command to drop a table from the database is:

```
DROP TABLE table_name
```

This command will completely remove all traces of that table from the database. MySQL will remove all data within the destroyed table from existence. If you have no backups of the table, you absolutely cannot recover from this action. The moral of this story is to always keep backups and be very careful about dropping tables. You will thank yourself for it some day.

With MySQL, you can specify more than one table to delete by separating the table names with commas. For example, DROP TABLE *people, animals, plants* would delete the three named tables. You can also use the IF EXISTS modifier under MySQL to avoid an error should the table not exist when you try to drop it. This modifier is useful for huge scripts designed to create a database and all its tables. Before the create, you do a DROP TABLE *table_name* IF EXISTS.

SQL Datatypes

In a table, each column has a type. As we mentioned earlier, a SQL datatype is similar to a datatype in traditional programming languages. While many languages define a bare-minimum set of types necessary for completeness, SQL goes out of its way to provide types such as **MONEY** and **DATE** that will be useful to every day users. You could store a **MONEY** type in a more basic numeric type, but having a type specifically dedicated to the nuances of money processing helps add to SQL's ease of use—one of SQL's primary goals.

Chapter 15, *SQL Reference*, provides a full reference of SQL types supported by MySQL or mSQL. Table 6-1 is an abbreviated listing of the most common types supported in both languages.

Table 6-1. The Most Often Used Datatypes Common to Both MySQL and mSQL

Datatype	Description
INT	An integer value. MySQL allows an **INT** to be either signed or unsigned, while mSQL provides a distinct type, **UINT**, for unsigned integers.
REAL	A floating point value. This type offers a greater range and precision than the **INT** type, but it does not have the exactness of an **INT**.
CHAR(length)	A fixed-length character value. No **CHAR** fields can hold strings greater in length than the specified value. Fields of lesser length are padded with spaces. This type is likely the most commonly used type in any SQL implementation.
TEXT(length)	A variable length character value. In mSQL, the given length is used as a suggestion as to how long the strings being stored will be. You may store larger values, but at a performance cost. Under MySQL, **TEXT** is just one of many variable-length datatypes.
DATE	A standard date value. While the format for storing a date differs between MySQL and mSQL, both database engines are capable of using the **DATE** type to store arbitrary dates for the past, present, and future. Both database engines are Y2K compliant in their date storage.
TIME	A standard time value. This type stores the time of day independent of a particular date. When used together with a date, a specific date and time can be stored. MySQL additionally supplies a **DATETIME** type that will store date and time together in one field.

 MySQL supports the **UNSIGNED** attribute for all numeric types. This modifier forces the column to accept only positive (unsigned) numbers. Unsigned fields have an upper limit that is double that of their signed counterparts. An unsigned **TINYINT**—MySQL's single byte numeric type—has a range of 0 to 255 instead of the -127 to 127 range of its signed counterpart.

Both database engines provide more types than those mentioned above. MySQL, in particular, is very rich in the number of datatypes it supports. In day-to-day programming, however, you will find yourself using mostly the types mentioned earlier. With mSQL, choosing a datatype is pretty much as simple as picking the type that most closely resembles the data you want to store. The size of the data you wish to store, however, plays a much larger role in designing MySQL tables.

Numeric Types

Before you create a table, you should have a good idea of what kind of data you wish to store in the table. Beyond obvious decisions about whether your data is character-based or numeric, you should know the approximate size of the data to be stored. If it is a numeric field, what is its maximum possible value? What is its minimum possible value? Could that change in the future? If the minimum is always positive, you should consider an unsigned type. You should always choose the smallest numeric type that can support your largest conceivable value. If, for example, we had a field that represented the population of a state, we would use an unsigned INT field. No state can have a negative population. Furthermore, in order for an unsigned INT field not to be able to hold a number representing a state's population, that state's population would have to be roughly the population of the entire Earth.

Character Types

Managing character types is a little more complicated. Not only do you have to worry about the minimum and maximum string lengths, but you also have to worry about the average size, the amount of variation likely, and the need for indexing. For our current purposes, an *index* is a field or combination of fields on which you plan to search—basically, the fields in your WHERE clause. Indexing is, however, much more complicated than this simplistic description, and we will cover indexing later in the chapter. The important fact to note here is that indexing one character fields works best when the field is fixed length. In fact, mSQL does not even provide an indexible variable-length character field! If there is little—or, preferably, no—variation in the length of your character-based fields, then a CHAR type is likely the right answer. An example of a good candidate for a CHAR field is a country code. The ISO provides a comprehensive list of standard two-character representations of country codes (US for the U.S.A., FR for France, etc.).* Since these codes are always exactly two characters, a CHAR(2) is always the right answer for this field.

A value does not need to be invariant in its length to be a candidate for a CHAR field. It should, however, have very little variance. Phone numbers, for example,

---

* Don't be lulled into believing states/provinces work this way. If you want to write an application that works in an international environment and stores state/province codes, make sure to make it a CHAR(3) since Australia uses three-character state codes. Also note that there is a 3-character ISO country-code standard.

can be stored safely in a CHAR(13) field even though phone number length varies from nation to nation. The variance simply is not that great, so there is no value to making a phone number field variable in length. The important thing to keep in mind with a CHAR field is that no matter how big the actual string being stored is, the field always takes up exactly the number of characters specified as the field's size—no more, no less. Any difference between the length of the text being stored and the length of the field is made up by padding the value with spaces. While the few potential extra characters being wasted on a subset of the phone number data is not anything to worry about, you do not want to be wasting much more. Variable-length text fields meet this need.

A good, common example of a field that demands a variable-length datatype is a web URL. Most web addresses can fit into a relatively small amount of space— *http://www.ora.com*, *http://www.hughes.com.au*, *http://www.mysql.com*—and consequentially do not represent a problem. Occasionally, however, you will run into web addresses like:

> *http://www.winespectator.com/Wine/Spectator/*
> *_notes | 55272939268343232214804313549Xv11=&Xr5=&Xv1=&type-region-*
> *search-code=&Xa14=flora+springs&Xv4=.*

If you construct a CHAR field large enough to hold that URL, you will be wasting a significant amount of space for most every other URL being stored. Variable-length fields let you define a field length that can store the odd, long-length value while not wasting all that space for the common, short-length values. MySQL and mSQL each take separate approaches to this problem.

Variable-length character fields in MySQL

If you are using only mSQL, you can skip this section. The advantage of variable-length text fields under MySQL is that such fields use precisely the minimum storage space required to store an individual field. A VARCHAR(255) column that holds the string "hello world," for example, only takes up twelve bytes (one byte for each character plus an extra byte to store the length).

In opposition to the ANSI standard, VARCHAR in MySQL fields are not padded. Any extra spaces are removed from a value before it is stored.

You cannot store strings whose lengths are greater than the field length you have specified. With a VARCHAR(4) field, you can store at most a string with 4 characters. If you attempt to store the string "happy birthday," MySQL will truncate the string to "happ." The downside of the MySQL approach to variable-length text fields over the mSQL approach is that there is no way to store the odd string that exceeds your designated field size. Table 6-2 shows the storage space required to store the 144 character Wine Spectator URL shown above along with an average-sized 30 character URL.

Table 6-2. The Storage Space Required by the Different MySQL Character Types

Datatype	Storage for a 144 Character String	Storage for a 30 Character String	Maximum String Size
CHAR(150)	150	150	255
VARCHAR(150)	145	31	255
TINYTEXT(150)	145	31	255
TEXT(150)	146	32	65535
MEDIUMTEXT(150)	147	33	16777215
LONGTEXT(150)	148	34	4294967295

If, after years of uptime with your database, you find that the world has changed and a field that once comfortably existed as a VARCHAR(25) now must be able to hold strings as long as 30 characters, you are not out of luck. MySQL provides a command called ALTER TABLE that enables you to redefine a field type without losing any data.

```
ALTER TABLE mytable MODIFY mycolumn LONGTEXT
```

Variable-length character fields in mSQL

You can skip this section if you are only interested in MySQL. Variable-length character fields in mSQL enable you to define a field's length to be the size of the average character string length it will hold. While every value you insert into this field will still take up at least the amount you specify, it can hold more. The database does this by creating an overflow table to hold the extra data. The downside of this approach comes in the form of performance and the inability to index variable-length fields.

Let's take a moment to examine the impact of different design choices with mSQL. In order to store all of the above URLs in a CHAR field, we would need to have a CHAR(144) column. Under this scenario, the four URLs in question would take up 576 bytes (144x3), even though you are only actually storing 216 bytes of data. The other 360 bytes is simply wasted space. If you multiple that times thousands or millions of rows, you can easily see how this becomes a serious problem. Using a variable-length TEXT(30) field, however, only 234 bytes (30x3+144) are required to store the 216 bytes of data. Only 18 bytes are wasted. That is a 41% savings!

Binary Datatypes

mSQL has no support for binary data. MySQL, on the other hand, provides a set of binary datatypes that closely mirror their character counterparts. The MySQL binary types are CHAR BINARY, VARCHAR BINARY, TINYBLOB, BLOB, MEDIUMBLOB, and LONGBLOB. The practical distinction between character types and their binary counterparts is the concept of encoding. *Binary data* is basically just a chunk of data that MySQL makes no effort to interpret. *Character data*, on the other hand, is assumed to represent textual data from human alphabets. It thus is encoded and sorted based on rules appropriate to the character set in question. Specifically, MySQL sorts binary in a case-insensitive, ASCII order.

Enumerations and Sets

MySQL provides two other special kinds of types with no mSQL analog. The ENUM type allows you specify at table creation a list of possible values that can be inserted into that field. For example, if you had a column named fruit into which you wanted to allow only "apple," "orange," "kiwi," or "banana," you would assign this column the type ENUM:

```
CREATE TABLE meal(meal_id INT NOT NULL PRIMARY KEY,
                  fruit ENUM('apple', 'orange', 'kiwi',
                             'banana'))
```

When you insert a value into that column, it must be one of the specified fruits. Because MySQL knows ahead of time what valid values are for the column, it can abstract them to some underlying numeric type. In other words, instead of storing "apple" in the column as a string, it stores it as a single byte number. You just use "apple" when you call the table or when you view results from the table.

The MySQL SET type works in the same way, except it lets you store multiple values in a field at the same time.

Other Kinds of Data

Every piece of data you will ever encounter can be stored using numeric or character types. Technically, you could even store numbers as character types. Just because you can do so, however, does not mean that you should do so. Consider, for example, storing money in the database. You could store that as an INT or a REAL. While a REAL might seem more intuitive—money requires decimal places, after all—an INT actually makes more sense. With floating point values like REAL fields, it is often impossible to capture a number with a specific decimal value. If, for example, you insert the number 0.43 to represent $0.43, MySQL and mSQL may store that as 0.42999998. This small difference can be problematic when applied to a large number of mathematical operations. By storing the number as an INT and inserting the decimal into the right place, you can be certain that the value represents exactly what you intend it to represent.

Isn't all of that a major pain? Wouldn't it be nice if MySQL and mSQL provided some sort of datatype specifically suited to money values? MySQL and, to a lesser degree, mSQL both provide special datatypes to handle special kinds of data. MONEY is an example of one of these kinds of data. DATE is another. For a full description of all datatypes, see Chapter 17, *MySQL and mSQL Programs and Utilities.*

Indices

While MySQL and mSQL both have greater performance than any of the larger database servers, some problems still call for careful database design. For instance, if we had a table with millions of rows of data, a search for a specific row would take a long time. As we discussed in Chapter 2, most database engines enable you to help it in these searches through a tool called an index.

Indices help the database store data in a way that makes for quicker searches. Unfortunately, you sacrifice disk space and modification speed for the benefit of quicker searches. The most efficient use of indices is to create an index for columns on which you tend to search the most. MySQL and mSQL support a common syntax for index creation:

```
CREATE INDEX index_name ON tablename (column1,
                                      column2,
                                      ...,
                                      columnN)
```

MySQL also lets you create an index at the same time you create a table using the following syntax:

```
CREATE TABLE materials (id        INT       NOT NULL,
                        name      CHAR(50) NOT NULL,
                        resistance INT,
                        melting_pt REAL,
                        INDEX index1 (id, name),
                        UNIQUE INDEX index2 (name))
```

The previous example creates two indices for the table. The first index—named index1—consists of both the id and name fields. The second index includes only the name field and specifies that values for the name field must always be unique. If you try to insert a field with a name held by a row already in the database, the insert will fail. All fields declared in a unique index must be declared as being NOT NULL.

Even though we created an index for name by itself, we did not create an index for just id. If we did want such an index, we would not need to create it—it is already there. When an index contains more than one column (for example: name, rank, and serial_number), MySQL reads the columns in order from left to right. Because of the structure of the index MySQL uses, any subset of the columns from left to right are automatically created as indices within the "main" index. For example, name by itself and name and rank together are both "free" indices created when you create the index name, rank, serial_number. An index of rank by itself or name and serial_number together, however, is not created unless you explicitly create it yourself.

MySQL also supports the ANSI SQL semantics of a special index called a primary key. In MySQL, a primary key is a unique key with the name PRIMARY. By calling a column a primary key at creation, you are naming it as a unique index that will support table joins. The following example creates a cities table with a primary key of id.

```
CREATE TABLE cities (id      INT  NOT NULL PRIMARY KEY,
                     name    VARCHAR(100),
                     pop     MEDIUMINT,
                     founded DATE)
```

Before you create a table, you should determine which fields, if any, should be keys. As we mentioned above, any fields which will be supporting joins are good candidates for primary keys. See Chapter 2 for a detailed discussion on how to design your tables with good primary keys.

Sequences and Auto-Incrementing

The best kind of primary key is one that has absolutely no meaning in the database except to act as a primary key. The best way to achieve this is to make a numeric primary key that increments every time you insert a new row. Looking at the cities table shown earlier, the first city you insert would have an id of 1, the second 2, the third 3, and so on. In order to successfully manage this sequencing of a primary key, you need some way to guarantee that a number can be read and incremented by one and only one client at a time. Under transactional databases, you could create a table called sequence that has a number representing the next id. When you need to insert a new row, you would read that table and insert a new number one more than the one you read. You must be assured that no one else will read from that table before you insert a new value, however, in order for that scheme to work. Otherwise, two clients could read the same value and attempt to use it as a primary key value in the same table.

Neither MySQL nor mSQL support transactions, so the previously identified mechanism cannot be used for generating unique ID numbers. The MySQL command LOCK TABLE is cumbersome for this task. However, both engines support their own variant of a concept called a sequence, which enables you to generate unique ID numbers without worrying about those transactional issues.

MySQL Sequences

When you create a table in MySQL, you can specify at most one column as being AUTO_INCREMENT. When you do this, you can automatically have this column insert the highest current value for that column + 1 when you insert a row and specify NULL or 0 for that row's value. The AUTO_INCREMENT row must be indexed. The following command creates the cities table with the id field being AUTO_INCREMENT:

```
CREATE TABLE cities (id       INT  NOT NULL PRIMARY KEY AUTO_INCREMENT,
                     name      VARCHAR(100),
                     pop       MEDIUMINT,
                     founded DATE)
```

The first time you insert a row, the id field for your first row will be 1 so long as you use NULL or 0 for that field in the INSERT statement. For example, this command takes advantage of the AUTO_INCREMENT feature:

```
INSERT INTO cities (id, name, pop)
VALUES (NULL, 'Houston', 3000000)
```

If no other values are in that table when you issue this command, MySQL will set this field to 1, not NULL (remember, it cannot be NULL). If other values are present in the table, the value inserted will be one greater than the largest current value for id.

Another way to implement sequences is by referring to the value returned by the LAST_INSERT_ID function:

```
UPDATE table SET id=LAST_INSERT_ID (id+1);
```

mSQL Sequences

Each mSQL table can have at most one sequence associated with it. The following syntax creates a sequence on a table:

```
CREATE SEQUENCE ON table_name [VALUE start STEP incr]
```

The start value is the number to start with. The incr value is the amount to increment on each access. By default, a sequence starts with 1 and increments 1 at a time. For example:

```
CREATE SEQUENCE ON mytable VALUE 100 STEP 5
```

This command creates a sequence on the mytable table whose first value will be 100 and will increase by 5 each time some accesses the sequence. The second value under this scheme would therefore be 105.

In order to access a sequence, you need to select a special column called _seq from the table:

```
SELECT _seq FROM table_name
```

This will both return to you the next value in the sequence and increment it.

Managing Data

The first thing you do with a newly created table is add data to it. With the data in place, you may want to make changes and eventually remove it.

Inserts

Adding data to a table is one of the more straightforward concepts in SQL. You have already seen several examples of it in this book. Both MySQL and mSQL support the standard SQL **INSERT** syntax:

```
INSERT INTO table_name (column1, column2, ..., columnN)
VALUES (value1, value2, ..., valueN)
```

When inserting data into numeric fields, you can insert the value as is; for all other fields, you must wrap them in single quotes. For example, to insert a row of data into a table of addresses, you might issue the following command:

```
INSERT INTO addresses (name, address, city, state, phone, age)
VALUES('Irving Forbush', '123 Mockingbird Lane', 'Corbin', 'KY',
       '(800) 555-1234', 26)
```

In addition, the escape character—'\' by default—enables you to escape single quotes and other literal instances of the escape character:

```
# Insert info for the directory Stacie's Directory which
# is in c:\Personal\Stacie
INSERT INTO files (description, location)
VALUES ('Stacie\'s Directory', 'C:\\Personal\\Stacie')
```

MySQL allows you to leave out the column names as long as you specify a value for every single column in the table in the exact same order they were specified in the table's **CREATE** call. If you want to use the default values for a column, however, you must specify the names of the columns for which you intend to insert nondefault data. If you do not have a default value set up for a column and that column is **NOT NULL**, you must include that column in the **INSERT** statement with a non-**NULL** value. If the earlier files table had contained a column called **size**, then the default value would be used. Under mSQL, the default value is always **NULL**. MySQL allows you to specify a custom default value in the table's **CREATE**.

Newer versions of MySQL support a nonstandard **INSERT** call for inserting multiple rows at once:

```
INSERT INTO foods VALUES (NULL, 'Oranges', 133, 0, 2, 39),
                         (NULL, 'Bananas', 122, 0, 4, 29),
                         (NULL, 'Liver', 232, 3, 15, 10)
```

While these nonstandard syntaxes supported by MySQL are useful for quick system administration tasks, you should not use them when writing database applications unless you really need the speed benefit they offer. As a general rule, you should stick as close to the ANSI SQL2 standard as MySQL and mSQL will let you. By doing so, you are making certain that you can move to some other database at some point in the future. Being flexible is especially critical for people with mid-range database needs because such users generally hope one day to become people with high-end database needs.

MySQL supports the SQL2 syntax for inserting the values of a **SELECT** call into a table:

```
INSERT INTO foods (name, fat)
SELECT food_name, fat_grams FROM recipes
```

You should note that the number of columns in the **INSERT** matches the number of columns in the **SELECT**. In addition, the datatypes for the **INSERT** columns must match the datatypes for the corresponding **SELECT** columns. Finally, the **SELECT** clause in an **INSERT** statement cannot contain an **ORDER BY** modifier and cannot be selected from the same table where the **INSERT** is occurring.

Updates

The insertion of new rows into a database is just the start of database use. Unless your database is read-only, you will probably also need to make periodic changes to the data. The standard SQL modification statement looks like this:

```
UPDATE table_name
SET column1=value1, column2=value2, ..., columnN=valueN
[WHERE clause]
```

Under mSQL, the value you assign to a column must be a literal of the column's datatype. MySQL, in contrast, enables you to calculate the assigned value. You can even calculate the value based on a value in another column:

```
UPDATE years
SET end_year = begin_year+5
```

This command sets the value in the **end_year** column equal to the value in the **begin_year** column plus 5 for each row in that table.

The WHERE Clause

You probably noted something earlier called the **WHERE** clause. In SQL, a **WHERE** clause enables you to pick out specific rows in a table by specifying a value that must be matched by the column in question. For example:

```
UPDATE bands
SET lead_singer = 'Ian Anderson'
WHERE band_name = 'Jethro Tull'
```

This **UPDATE** specifies that you should only change the **lead_singer** column for the row where **band_name** is identical to "Jethro Tull." If the column in question is not a unique index, that **WHERE** clause may match multiple rows. Many SQL commands employ **WHERE** clauses to help pick out the rows on which you wish to operate. Because the columns in the **WHERE** clause are columns on which you are searching, you should generally have indices created around whatever combinations you commonly use.

Deletes

Deleting data is a very straightforward operation. You simply specify the table from which you want to delete followed by a **WHERE** clause that identifies the rows you want to delete:

```
DELETE FROM table_name [WHERE clause]
```

As with other commands that accept a **WHERE** clause, the **WHERE** clause is optional. In the event you leave out the **WHERE** clause, you will delete all of the records in the table! Of all destructive commands in SQL, this is the easiest one to issue mistakenly.

Queries

The last common SQL command used is the one that enables you to view the data in the database: **SELECT**. This action is by far the most common action performed in SQL. While data entry and modifications do happen on occasion, most databases spend the vast majority of their lives serving up data for reading. The general form of the **SELECT** statement is as follows:

```
SELECT column1, column2, ..., columnN
FROM table1, table2, ..., tableN
[WHERE clause]
```

This syntax is certainly the most common way in which you will retrieve data from any SQL database. Of course, there are variations for performing complex and powerful queries, especially under MySQL. We cover the full range of the **SELECT** syntax in Chapter 15.

The first part of a **SELECT** statement enumerates the columns you wish to retrieve. You may specify a "*" to say that you want to select all columns. The **FROM** clause specifies which tables those columns come from. The **WHERE** clause identifies the specific rows to be used and enables you to specify how to join two tables.

Joins

Joins put the "relational" in relational databases. Specifically, a join enables you to match a row from one table up with a row in another table. The basic form of a join is what you may hear sometimes described as an *inner join*. Joining tables is a matter of specifying equality in columns from two tables:

```
SELECT book.title, author.name
FROM author, book
WHERE book.author = author.id
```

Consider a database where the **book** table looks like Table 6-3.

Table 6-3. A book Table

ID	Title	Author	Pages
1	The Green Mile	4	894
2	Guards, Guards!	2	302
3	Imzadi	3	354
4	Gold	1	405
5	Howling Mad	3	294

And the **author** table looks like Table 6-4.

Table 6-4. An author Table

ID	Name	Citizen
1	Isaac Asimov	US
2	Terry Pratchet	UK
3	Peter David	US
4	Stephen King	US
5	Neil Gaiman	UK

An inner join creates a table by combining the fields of both tables for rows that satisfy the query in both tables. In our example, the query specifies that the **author** field of the **book** table must be identical to the **id** field of the **author** table. The query's result would thus look like Table 6-5.

Table 6-5. Query Results Based on an Inner Join

Book Title	Author Name
The Green Mile	Stephen King
Guards, Guards!	Terry Pratchet
Imzadi	Peter David
Gold	Isaac Asimov
Howling Mad	Peter David

Neil Gaiman is nowhere to be found in these results. He is left out because there is no value for his `author.id` value found in the `book.author` table. An inner join only contains those rows that exactly match the query. We will discuss the concept of an outer join later in the chapter for situations where we would be interested in the fact that we have an author in the database who does not have a book in the database.

Aliasing

When you use column names that are fully qualified with their table and column name, the names can grow to be quite unwieldy. In addition, when referencing SQL functions, which will be discussed later in the chapter, you will likely find it cumbersome to refer to the same function more than once within a statement. The aliased name, usually shorter and more descriptive, can be used anywhere in the same SQL statement in place of the longer name. For example:

```
# A column alias
SELECT long_field_names_are_annoying AS myfield
FROM table_name
WHERE myfield = 'Joe'
# A table alias under MySQL
SELECT people.names, tests.score
FROM tests, really_long_people_table_name AS people
# A table alias under mSQL
SELECT people.names, tests.score
FROM tests, really_long_people_table_name=people
```

While mSQL fully supports table aliasing, it does not support column aliasing.

Grouping and Ordering

The results you get back from a select are, by default, indeterminate in the order they will appear. Fortunately, SQL provides some tools for imposing order on this seemingly random list. The first tool—available in both MySQL and mSQL—is ordering. You can tell a database that it should order any results you see by a certain column. For example, if you specify that a query should order the results by `last_name`, then the results will appear alphabetized according to the `last_name` value. Ordering comes in the form of the ORDER BY clause:

```
SELECT last_name, first_name, age
FROM people
ORDER BY last_name, first_name
```

In this situation, we are ordering by two columns. You can order by any number of columns, but the columns must be named in the **SELECT** clause. If we had failed to select the `last_name` above, we could not have ordered by the `last_name` field.

Grouping is an ANSI SQL tool that MySQL implements but mSQL does not. Because mSQL does not have any concept of aggregate functions, grouping simply does not make sense in mSQL. As its name implies, grouping lets you group rows with a similar value into a single row in order to operate on them together. You usually do this to perform aggregate functions on the results. We will go into functions a little later in the chapter.

Consider the following:

```
mysql> SELECT name, rank, salary FROM people\g
+--------------+----------+--------+
| name         | rank     | salary |
+--------------+----------+--------+
| Jack Smith   | Private  |  23000 |
| Jane Walker  | General  | 125000 |
| June Sanders | Private  |  22000 |
| John Barker  | Sargeant |  45000 |
| Jim Castle   | Sargeant |  38000 |
+--------------+----------+--------+
5 rows in set (0.01 sec)
```

If you group the results by rank, the output changes:

```
mysql> SELECT rank FROM people GROUP BY rank\g
+----------+
| rank     |
+----------+
| General  |
| Private  |
| Sargeant |
+----------+
3 rows in set (0.01 sec)
```

Now that you have the output grouped, you can finally find out the average salary for each rank. Again, we will discuss more on the functions you see in this example later in the chapter.

```
mysql> SELECT rank, AVG(salary) FROM people GROUP BY rank\g
+----------+-------------+
| rank     | AVG(salary) |
+----------+-------------+
| General  | 125000.0000 |
| Private  |  22500.0000 |
| Sargeant |  41500.0000 |
+----------+-------------+
3 rows in set (0.04 sec)
```

The power of ordering and grouping combined with the utility of SQL functions enables you to do a great deal of data manipulation even before you retrieve the data from the server. You should take great care not to rely too heavily on this power. While it may seem like an efficiency gain to place as much processing load as possible onto the database server, it is not really the case. Your client application is dedicated to the needs of a particular client, while the server is being shared by many clients. Because of the greater amount of work a server already has to do, it is almost always more efficient to place as little load as possible on the database server. MySQL and mSQL may be two of the fastest databases around, but you do not want to waste that speed on processing that a client application is better equipped to manage.

If you know that a lot of clients will be asking for the same summary information often (for instance, data on a particular rank in our previous example), just create a new table containing that information and keep it up to date as the original tables change. This is similar to caching and is a common database programming technique.

Extended Functionality

Both MySQL and mSQL have a few quirky extensions that do not really have counterparts in the other database engine. Most of MySQL's extensions are generally in line with the ANSI SQL standard. mSQL's extensions are simply related to special variables you can access while working with an mSQL database.

MySQL Features

MySQL goes well beyond mSQL's support for SQL by supporting functions and a limited concept of outer joins. Functions in SQL are similar to functions in other programming languages like C and Perl. The function takes zero or more arguments and returns some value. For example, the function SQRT(16) returns 4. Within a MySQL SELECT statement, functions may be used in either of two places:

As a value to be retrieved
> This form involves a function in the place of a column in the list of columns to be retrieved. The return value of the function, evaluated for each selected row, is part of the returned result set as if it were a column in the database. For example:

```
# Select the name of each event as well as the date of the event
# formatted in a human-readable form for all events more
# recent than the given time. The FROM_UnixTIME() function
# transforms a standard Unix time value into a human
# readable form.
SELECT name, FROM_UnixTIME(date)
FROM events
WHERE time > 90534323

# Select the title of a paper, the full text of the paper,
# and the length (in bytes) of the full text for all
# papers authored by Stacie Sheldon.
```

```
# The LENGTH() function returns the character length of
# a given string.
SELECT title, text, LENGTH(text)
FROM papers
WHERE author = 'Stacie Sheldon'
```

As part of a WHERE clause

This form involves a function in the place of a constant when evaluating a WHERE clause. The value of the function is used for comparison for each row of the table. For example:

```
# Randomly select the name of an entry from a pool of 35
# entries. The RAND() function generates a random number
# between 0 and 1 (multiplied by 34 to make it between 0
# and 34 and incremented by 1 to make it between 1 and
# 35). The ROUND() function returns the given number
# rounded to the nearest integer, resulting in a whole
# number between 1 and 35, which should match one of
# the ID numbers in the table.
SELECT name
FROM entries
WHERE id = ROUND( (RAND()*34) + 1 )


# You may use functions in both the value list and the
# WHERE clause. This example selects the name and date
# of each event less than a day old. The UNIX_TIMESTAMP()
# function, with no arguments, returns the current time
# in Unix format.
SELECT name, FROM_UnixTIME(date)
FROM events
WHERE time > (Unix_TIMESTAMP() - (60 * 60 * 24) )


# You may also use the value of a table field within
# a function. This example returns the name of anyone
# who used their name as their password. The ENCRYPT()
# function returns a Unix password-style encryption
# of the given string using the supplied 2-character salt.
# The LEFT() function returns the left-most n characters
# of the given string.
SELECT name
FROM people
WHERE password = ENCRYPT(name, LEFT(name, 2))
```

Finally, MySQL supports a more powerful joining than the simple inner joins we have used so far. Specifically, MySQL supports something called a *left outer join* (also known as simply *outer join*). This type of join is similar to an inner join, except that it includes data in the first column named that does not match any in the second column. If you remember our author and book tables from earlier in the chapter, you will remember that our join would not list any authors who did not have a book in our database. It is common that you may want to show entries from one table that have no corresponding data in the table to which you are joining. That is where an outer join comes into play:

```
SELECT book.title, author.name
FROM author
LEFT JOIN book ON book.author = author.id
```

Note that a outer join uses the keyword ON instead of WHERE. The results of our query would look like this:

```
+----------------+----------------+
| book.title     | author.name    |
+----------------+----------------+
| The Green Mile | Stephen King   |
| Guards, Guards!| Terry Pratchett|
| Imzadi         | Peter David    |
| Gold           | Isaac Asimov   |
| Howling Mad    | Peter David    |
| NULL           | Neil Gaiman    |
+----------------+----------------+
```

MySQL takes this concept one step further through the use of a natural outer join. A natural outer join will combine the rows from two tables where the two tables have identical column names with identical types and the values in those columns are identical:

```
SELECT my_prod.name
FROM my_prod
NATURAL LEFT JOIN their_prod
```

mSQL Features

mSQL has five "system variables" that you can include in any query. We have already covered one of those values, _seq. The others are:

_rowid

> A unique identifier corresponding to a row of data being returned. You can use it with subsequent UPDATE or DELETE statements to improve efficiency. This approach, however, is definitely not recommended because multiple clients can mess each other up. Specifically, two clients can select the same row. The first one deletes it and then a third client inserts a new row. The new row can have the same _rowid value as the deleted row. If the second client then tries to update or delete using that _rowid, it will affect data it did not intend to affect.

_timestamp

> The time when the row in question was last modified. Under the current version of mSQL, this value is in the standard Unix time format. This behavior may change in future versions, so you should only use this value to compare with timestamps in other rows.

_sysdate

Returns the current time on the mSQL server. This time can be used to ensure that all times used in the database are synchronized even if the clients are on systems with varying times. This time is given in the standard Unix format and will be the same no matter which table you select it from.

_user

This value holds the name of the user for the current client connection. As with **_sysdate**, this value is not dependent on the table from which you choose to select it.

7

Other Mid-Range Database Engines

When mSQL first appeared on the scene, it was the only mid-range database engine supporting SQL. It did not hold that distinction very long. Of course, you already know about one other such database: MySQL. In the years since mSQL's introduction, however, a handful of mid-range database engines have been released. In this book, we have focused on MySQL and mSQL due to their over-whelming similarities and their unequalled popularity. It would, however, be an injustice to fail to mention the other databases out there.

People use databases for so many things that it is hard to capture all of the tools for all possible uses in one package. The major database vendors attempt that goal. They pay for it in terms of performance and you pay for it in terms of price. The low-end database engines, on the other hand, are so very specialized as to be of little use to the small business or nonprofit organization or anyone else with unusual needs. The mid-range database engines fill an important void between the two extremes.

At this point, we have only looked at two very similar views of meeting mid-range database requirements. These approaches are definitely not the only ones. There is no law, for example, that says just because you are not a big company that you do not need transaction support. Some users in the mid-range may also need trig-gers, subselects, stored procedures, object-oriented support, or any of a host of potential features—they just do not need them all. The different mid-range data-base engines thus serve import needs that may not be served by MySQL or mSQL.

What Is "Free"?

You may occasionally hear people refer to MySQL and mSQL as being "free." When you hear people compare MySQL and mSQL, they may even make the claim that MySQL is "more free" than mSQL. Common sense chokes on the expression "more free." The software world, however, has actually invented the idea of "degrees of freeness."

Until now, we have been consciously avoiding discussing MySQL and mSQL as "free" database engines due to "free" being such a loaded term in the software world. Both engines may actually cost you money for a license. It depends on who you are. Under the licenses in play at the time of this book's printing, a university does not have to pay a licensing fee for either database engine. A commercial user of mSQL, however, must pay for a license. When people claim MySQL is "more free" than mSQL, what they mean is that MySQL costs nothing for more people than mSQL does.

Another issue that affects the concept of "free" in the software world has little to do with price. It has to do with the ability to view and modify the source code without paying extra. Under this model, both MySQL and mSQL are totally free database engines. You can go to their download sites and get them in source form. If you are one of those users who has to pay to use MySQL or mSQL, you do not have to pay any more for the source.

The software world has come up with a new term designed to get around the overloaded concept of "free". It is called Open Source. In fact, the term "Open Source" is now a trademark meaning software whose source code is open regardless of the charges associated with using the software. Linux, Netscape, FreeBSD, Perl, Apache, all GNU products, as well as many products in this book like MySQL, mSQL, mm.mysql.jdbc, and mSQL-JDBC (just to name a few) are all Open Source products.

The other database engines we mention in this chapter are also Open Source products. Open source is very important to the mid-range world because the big guys tend to view that market as too small to merit their attention and the low-end developers see the mid-range as too complicated to merit theirs.

What MySQL and mSQL Lack

The word "lack" is chosen here in absence of a better term. As we noted earlier in the book, both MySQL and mSQL have consciously chosen to leave out features that will impact performance. In other words, for MySQL and mSQL, performance is the name of the game. Some mid-range users, however, may be willing to sacrifice a little performance for some other features. In order to understand what other mid-range databases offer, then, it helps to know the things that MySQL and mSQL have left out.

MySQL intends to eventually include some of these features with the ability to turn them off if you do not want them. At the time of printing, we are aware that Monty wants to implement a stored procedure mechanism and subselects and perhaps even transactions.

Transactions

Transactions enable you to group multiple SQL statements together as one unit of work. By grouping statements together, you can be certain that no one else will see a partially changed database. You also know that if one of the statements fail, the entire unit of work fails. One way of visualizing transactions is as the intersection of a busy road. A single-threaded queuing system, such as mSQL, is like having a four-way stop at the intersection. Each car takes its turn, one at a time. If two cars are in a caravan through the intersection, they risk being split up at the stop sign.

A multithreaded locking system, such as MySQL, is more like having a traffic officer instead of stop signs. The traffic can fly through the intersection in any order and at any speed and the officer intelligently makes sure there are no collisions. If two cars come through the intersection from opposite directions at the same time, the officer tells one of them to halt and wait for the other to get through the intersection.

Transactions resemble a stop-light system. Incoming traffic halts at a red light for a period while traffic traveling together in the other direction moves through the intersection.

A practical example might be a banking application where a transfer from savings to checking involves changing the balance in the savings and then changing the balance in the checking. This application might have these two SQL statements:

```
# Deduct $100 from the $110 in the savings account
UPDATE account
SET balance = 10.00
WHERE id = 1234
# Add $100 to the $55 in the checking account
UPDATE account
SET balance = 155.00
WHERE id = 5678
```

Between the two updates, another transaction could be issued by another client that checks the balance of the checking and savings accounts to see if there is enough money for a check. If that were to happen, the check would bounce.

Worse still, if the server crashed between the two updates, your client would have just lost $100 to the bit bucket.

By wrapping those two statements in a transaction, you are saying that they both must succeed or fail together. If the first one succeeds but the second one fails, you can issue something called a "rollback" that returns the database to its state before you began the transaction. Similarly, no one else can touch the files you are modifying until you are done with your work.* MySQL lets you partially emulate transactions by using LOCK TABLES. Locks should work adequately for preventing corruption, but they do not provide the ability to roll back operations. mSQL has no transaction support.

Triggers

Triggers are a feature closely related to transactions. To carry the traffic analogy one step further, imagine a police officer sitting on a hill overlooking the intersection. Should one of the cars do something illegal, the officer enters traffic and pursues the offending car.

A *trigger* is one or more SQL statements stored in the database that are executed whenever some predefined event occurs. Triggers are a method of automating monitoring tasks. Whenever a certain condition is met, the trigger can act upon data or simply report that the triggering event took place.

Stored Procedures

At their simplest, stored procedures are simply one or more SQL statements stored in the database under some simple name to encapsulate a certain behavior. In the example of the account transfer mentioned above, you could simply store those two SQL statements as a single stored procedure called "transfer." Your application passes the stored procedure the two account numbers and an amount and it executes those two SQL statements in a single transaction.

On a more complex level, stored procedures may add to the basic SQL syntax so that it looks more like a traditional programming language. Oracle's PL/SQL and Sybase/Microsoft's TransactSQL are two examples of such SQL extensions. You may often hear of people using these kinds of stored procedures to "put the business logic in the database."

---

* There are special nuances to this feature called "transaction isolation" values. Sometimes you may not care if people have read-only views of inconsistent data. By allowing them to do so, you speed up the database by not having them wait on transactions to complete.

Subselects

The standard SQL SELECT statement enables complete access to all of the data stored within a table—if you know what you are looking for. Unless you are willing to retrieve the entire contents of the table, the most basic form of SELECT requires you to input at least a portion of the data you wish to retrieve. For example, SELECT name FROM friends WHERE name LIKE 'B%' requires you to know at least one letter of the name you are looking for. More specifically, what if you wanted to know who was making more than the average salary? The query would look something like:

```
SELECT name FROM people WHERE salary > ???
```

Greater than what? You do not have any idea what the average salary is unless you select that! You need to take the value of SELECT AVG(salary) FROM people and plug it into the earlier query. A subselect enables you to do this:

```
SELECT name
FROM people
WHERE salary > (SELECT AVG(salary) FROM people)
```

Objects

Relational databases are not the end of the line for databases. You will also find plenty of object-relational and object-oriented databases. In the high-end market, the idea of a pure relational database is slowly disappearing. The new SQL3 standard will incorporate many of the changes in the high-end market for support of objects.

To a Relational Database Management (RDBMS), all data is stored in tables, which are simply a list of records, which in turn are collections of bits that represent text, numbers, or other kinds of data. In an Object-oriented Database Management System (OODBMS), the fundamental unit of data is an object. An object may not only contain the kinds of data found in relational systems, but it may contain other objects or multidimensional data like arrays or even executable functions—more commonly called methods in the object world.

PostgreSQL

The current incarnation of the Postgres Object-Relational Database Management System is known as PostgreSQL (a.k.a. Postgres 6). While Postgres has had SQL capabilities for only three years, the system itself is over a decade old. In the early 1980s, Dr. Michael Stonebreaker of the University of California at Berkeley designed a database system that pioneered many of the concepts found in today's relational database systems. This database engine was known as Ingres (later

University Ingres). Ingres was a free, university funded project that quickly gathered a following among other computer scientists around the world.

One company saw the business potential in this academic product and it eventually trademarked and commercialized Ingres as a product. The original, free version of Ingres was renamed University Ingres and its development continued independent of the commercial version.

After a period of time, Dr. Stonebreaker's research led him further away from the original design goals of Ingres. He decided that it was time to design a completely new database system that extended the ideas of Ingres and went beyond into new territory. The database system became known as Postgres for Post-Ingres.

Postgres, like Ingres, was a university funded project that has been free to the public. Also like Ingres, the commercial sector took notice of Postgres and the commercial product Illustra* was born. Free Postgres has continued on and ranks up their in popularity with MySQL and mSQL for mid-range database servers.

In 1995, two developments happened that shaped the future of Postgres. First, two of Dr. Stonebreaker's graduate students, Andrew Yu and Jolly Chen, designed an SQL interface into Postgres. Here, a few years after David Hughes first developed MiniSQL as a SQL front-end to Postgres, Postgres finally had a true SQL front-end. With SQL support came increased popularity. As with both mSQL and MySQL, an increase in popularity brought on an increase for demand in new features. The result was an object-relational database engine for the mid-range that supports transactions, triggers, and subselects. You can find out more about PostgreSQL at *http://www.postgresql.org*.

GNU SQL

The GNU project is the symbol of freedom to many in the computer industry. An official GNU product is guaranteed to be freely available with full permission to modify and change the source code. You can find GNU versions of most any utility found in the Unix environment—including the editor (Emacs), shell (bash), and operating system kernel (Hurd). Until recently, one glaring omissions has been a database management system.

The Institute for System Programming at the Russian Academy of Science is working hard to change that. A couple of years ago, they released the first public beta of GNU SQL, a completely functional SQL RDBMS under the GNU Public License (GPL). A the time of this book's printing, GNU SQL is at version 0.7beta.

---

* Illustra was bought out by Informix in 1995 and is now part of their Universal Server product.

When GNU SQL was conceived, the SQL2 specification had not been finalized. Because of this, the initial releases of GNU SQL would provide only SQL89 functionality, with SQL2 features being added as they went.

GNU SQL currently supports many advanced features such as transactions, subselects, and cursors. Because this product is beta, we do not recommend it for production use. As it matures, however, it is certainly going to be worth looking at. You can find out more information on GNU SQL at *http://www.ispras.ru/~kml/gss/index.html.*

Beagle

Beagle is a free SQL engine designed and implemented by Robert Klein. Like GNU SQL, Beagle is planned to be a fully SQL compliant server with all of the features, including the object-relational extensions pioneered by PostgreSQL. Also like GNU SQL, Beagle is very much a work in progress. At the time of this book's printing, it had reached a level of sophistication where it is reliable and usable as a test or development server. It should not yet be used in a production environment.

One of the most interesting aspects of Beagle is that the author maintained a history log from the very beginning of the project. By examining the log, you can get a peek at the development of an SQL server from a simple TCP client/server test application to the almost fully functional SQL server it is today. The Beagle home page is located at *http://www.beaglesql.org.*

Making Comparisons

Like many applications, MySQL has a test suite that verifies that a newly compiled system does indeed support all of the features it is supposed to support. MySQL called their test suite "crash-me" because one of the things it was designed to do is attempt to crash the database server.

Somewhere along the way, someone noticed that "crash-me" was a portable program. Not only could it work on different operating systems, but you could use it to test different database engines. Since that discovery, "crash-me" has evolved from a simple test suite to a comparison program. The tests encompass all of standard SQL as well as extensions offered by many servers. In addition, the program tests the reliability of the server under stress. A complete test run gives a thorough picture of the capabilities of that database engine.

You can use "crash-me" to compare two or more database engines online. The "crash-me" page is *http://www.mysql.com/crash-me-choose.htmy.*

II

Database Programming

The power of a database is realized in the tools that use it. In this section, we talk about how you build those tools using a variety of today's popular programming languages. From web-based programming to business application development, we will discuss the APIs and tools necessary for using MySQL and mSQL to their fullest potential. This second section starts with a couple of high-level chapters on database application architectures and CGI programming. The meat of the section, however, deals with programming for MySQL and mSQL in various programming languages.

8

Database Application Architectures

Before we explore the details of database application development in various languages, we should take a moment to take a broader look at the question of how you architect database applications. The focus of this chapter is conceptual; we are going to take a look at the client/server architecture behind database programming. The issues are important for programming with MySQL and mSQL, but they are not specific to these database engines. They are instead issues you can apply to programming in any database environment. Without these concepts, however, you may find that your database applications neither meet your current needs nor adapt to meet any changing needs. Our look at database programming covers such complex issues as understanding common two-tier development, object-to-relational mapping, and two-tier's more cutting-edge sibling, three-tier client/server.

The Client/Server Architecture

At its simplest, the client/server architecture is about dividing up application processing into two or more logically distinct pieces. We have spent the entire book so far discussing the database as if it exists in some sort of vacuum. It serves its purpose only when being used by other applications. The database, at its simplest, makes up one piece of the client/server architecture. The database is the 'server'; any application that uses that data is a 'client.' In many cases, the client and server reside on separate machines; in most cases, the client application is some sort of user-friendly interface to the database. Figure 8-1 provides a graphical representation of a simple client/server system.

You have probably seen this sort of architecture all over the Internet. In fact, we will be addressing the specific problem of client/server Internet applications throughout this book. The web, for example, is a giant client/server application in which the web browser is the client and the web server is the server. In this

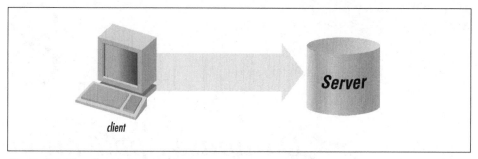

Figure 8-1. The client/server architecture

scenario, the server is not a relational database server, but instead a specialized file server. The essential quality of a server is that it serves data in some format to a client.

When you build a database application, you first need some way for the client to communicate with the database. Database vendors like to hide the underlying communication from developers in the form of language-specific APIs. When you write a database application, you write them with special libraries that translate your requests into TCP/IP packets that travel across the network to a database server.

The look of these database APIs varies both according to the language you are writing in and, in many cases, according to the database you are using. Because MySQL's APIs were designed to look a lot like mSQL's, however, all the APIs you will encounter in this book only have minor differences.

Data Processing

Part I, *Getting Started with MySQL and mSQL*, introduced the concepts of transaction management and result sets. A database application is nothing more than a tool for managing database transactions and processing result sets. For example, if you have an address book application, your processing of result sets is the grabbing of each row from the database and displaying it for the user. Your transaction management simply amounts to making sure that an update to the **address** and **person** tables are handled as a single unit.

As we have mentioned before, MySQL and mSQL have no support for transaction management. Any modification you make to the database is automatically committed when you send it. This limitation requires you to go to special lengths to make sure you do not end up with corrupt data from transactions that fail in the middle of two related accesses.

The other two important pieces to database application flow are connection and disconnection. It stands to reason that before you actually issue a query, you should first connect to the database. It is not uncommon, however, for people to forget the other piece of the puzzle—cleaning up after themselves. You should always free up any database resources you grab the minute you are done with them. In a long-running application like an Internet daemon process, a badly written system can eat up database resources until it locks up the system.

Part of cleaning up after yourself involves proper error handling. Better programming languages make it harder for you to fail to handle exceptional conditions (network failure, duplicate keys on insert, SQL syntax errors, etc.); but, regardless of your language of choice, you must make sure that you know what error conditions can arise from a given API call and act appropriately for each exceptional situation. The MySQL and mSQL C libraries provide a rowset-based look at your database. By rowset based, we mean that the C libraries enable you to deal directly with database data as it exists conceptually in the database. Chapter 13, *C and C++*, goes into the practical details of programming in this model using the MySQL and mSQL C APIs.

Accessing a relational database from an object-oriented environment exposes a special paradox: the relational world is entirely about the manipulation of data while the object world is about the encapsulation of data behind a set of behaviors. In an object-oriented application, the database serves as a tool for saving objects across application instances. Instead of seeing the query data as a rowset, an object-oriented application sees the data from a query as a collection of objects.

Object/Relational Modeling

The most basic question facing the object-oriented developer using a relational database is how to map relational data into objects. Your immediate thought might be to simply map object attributes to fields in a table. Unfortunately, this approach does not create the perfect mapping for several reasons.

- Objects do not store only simple data in their attributes. They may store collections or relationships with other objects.

- Most relational databases—MySQL and mSQL among them—have no way of modeling inheritance.

Think about that address book we talked about earlier. We probably have something like the **address** and **person** tables shown in Figure 8-2.

Rules of Thumb for Object/Relational Modeling

- Each persistent class has a corresponding database table.

- Object fields with primitive datatypes (integers, characters, strings, etc.) map to columns in the associated database table.

- Each row from a database table corresponds to an instance of its associated persistent class.

- Each many-to-many object relationship requires a join table just as database entities with many-to-many relationships require join tables.

- Inheritance is modeled through a one-to-one relationship between the two tables corresponding to the class and subclass.

The least apparent issue facing programmers is one of mindset. The basic task of object-oriented access to relational data is to grab that data and *immediately* instantiate objects. An application should only manipulate data through the objects. Most traditional programming methods, including most C, PowerBuilder, and VisualBasic development, require the developer to pull the data from the database and then process that data. The key distinction is that in object-oriented database programming, you are dealing with objects, not data.

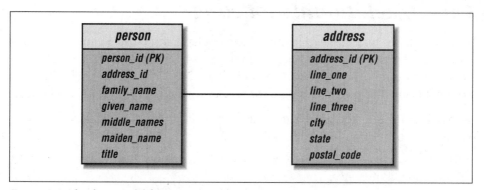

Figure 8-2. The data model for a simple address book application

Figure 8-3 shows the object model that maps to the data model from Figure 8-2. each row from the database turns into a program object. Your application therefore takes a result set and, for each row returned, instantiates a new `Address` or `Person` instance. The hardest thing to deal with here is the issue mentioned earlier: how do you capture the relationship between a person and her address in the database application? The `Person` object, of course, carries a reference to that person's `Address` object. But you cannot save the `Address` object within the `person` table of a relational database. As the data model suggests, you store object relationships through foreign keys. In this case, we carry the `address_id` in the `person` table.

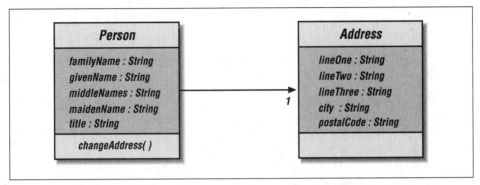

Figure 8-3. The object model supporting a simple address book application

With just a tiny amount of extra complexity to the object model, we can add a world of complexity to the challenge of mapping our objects to a data model. The extra bit of complexity could be to have `Person` inherit from `Entity` with a `Company` class also inheriting from `Entity`. How do we capture an `Entity` separate from a `Person` or a `Company`? The rule we outlined above is actually more of a guideline. In some instances, the base class may be purely abstract and subsequently have no data associated with it in the database. In that instance, you would not have an entity in the database for that class.

The Three-tier Architecture

We have so far discussed the most common architecture for web and simple business application processing, client/server. This architecture, however, has a hard time growing as your computing needs grow and change. It also does a poor job of taking advantage of the benefits of object-oriented programming. The first problem has been recently echoed throughout the industry in the discussion of thin clients. The desire for thin clients derives from the troublesome trend of throwing more and more processing onto the client. The poster children of this problem are PowerBuilder and VisualBasic, tools that pool data directly from a database into a GUI and then perform all operations on that data in the GUI.

Such a tight coupling of the user interface to the database engine results in applications that are difficult to modify and impossible to scale with growing user and data volume. If you have any experience with user interface design, you have experienced the fact that user interfaces are subject to changes based on user whims. The easiest way to isolate the impact of these changes would be to leave the job of the GUI to act only as a user interface. Such a user interface is a true thin client.

The impact on scalability comes from the other direction. Namely, when you need to modify an application to scale according to user demand or data volume, the modifications might come in the form of database changes including, but not limited to, distributing the database across multiple servers. By marrying your user interface to the database, you necessitate a change in that GUI in order to support scalability issues—issues that are purely server-related.

Thin clients are not today's only computing rage. Another trend is code reuse. Common code among applications tends to reside in data processing, commonly called business rules. With all of your business rules sitting in your user interface, you will find it difficult at best to attain any kind of code reuse. The answer to these problems lies in breaking an application into three pieces instead of two. This architecture is called the three-tier architecture.

When we speak of a user interface occurring on the client, we mean that as a logical distinction. A form of thin client, sometimes referred to as the "ultra-thin client." is what everyone commonly recognizes as a web page. A web page may be dynamically generated on a web server. In that case, the most client processing is occurring on the web server in the form of dynamic HTML page generation.

Contrast the two-tier architecture from Figure 8-1 with the three-tier architecture shown in Figure 8-4. With this design, we have added an intermediary layer between the user interface and database. This new layer, the application server, encapsulates the application processing logic—the business logic—that is common to the problem domain. The client becomes nothing more than a view of the middle-tier business objects and the database becomes nothing more than a storage mechanism for those objects. The most important advantage you gain is thus the separation of the user interface from the database. Suddenly, you do not have to build knowledge of the database into the GUI. Instead, all knowledge of how to deal with the database can sit in the middle tier.

The two main functions of the application server are to isolate database connectivity and provide a centralized repository for business logic. The user interface handles only display and input issues and the database engine handles only database issues. With data processing moved to a centralized location, multiple user interfaces can

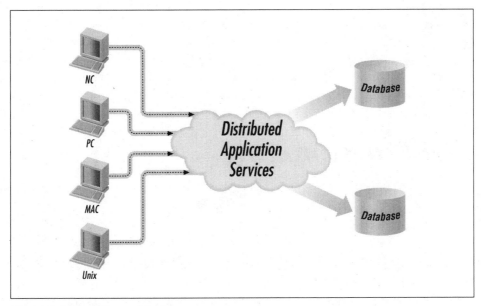

Figure 8-4. Three-tier architecture

use the exact same application server program—no more writing the data process-ing rules each time you build an application.

9

CGI Programming

Including a section on CGI within a book about databases may seem a bit like having a chapter on automotive repair in a cookbook: sure, you need a running car to go to the grocery, but isn't it a bit out of place? While it is true that the whole of CGI and web programming in general is vastly out of the scope of this book, a short primer is all that is needed to extend the capabilities of MySQL and mSQL to the high-visibility realm of the World Wide Web.

This chapter is primarily intended for those people who want to learn about databases but would not mind trying a little web programming. If your last name is Berners-Lee or Andressen you probably will not find anything here you do not already know. Even if you are not new to the world of CGI, it could be useful to keep a short reference handy while you ponder the mysteries of MySQL and mSQL.

What Is CGI?

As with most names that have acronyms, Common Gateway Interface (CGI) tells us very little about what it really means. What are we interfacing with? Where is this gateway? What's so common about it anyway? To answer these questions, we need to take a step back and look at the World Wide Web as a whole.

Tim Berners-Lee, a physicist at CERN, invented the web in 1990 (with planning going as far back as 1988). The idea was to give particle physicists the ability to exchange multimedia information—text, graphics, sounds—quickly and easily over the Internet. The World Wide Web had three major components: HTML, URLs, and HTTP. *HTML* is the formatting language used to display content on the web. *URLs* are the addresses used to retrieve the HTML (and other) content from a web server. Finally, *HTTP* is the language spoken by the web server, giving clients the ability to ask the server for documents.

While the ability to send content of all sorts over the Internet was revolutionary, another possibility was quickly realized. If it was possible to send any text through the web, why shouldn't it be possible to send text that does not come from a file, but rather is generated by a program? This opened up a whole realm of possibilities. As a simple example, a program that outputs the current time could be used, so that the reader sees the correct time every time he views the page. A few bright fellows at the National Center for Supercomputing Applications (NCSA) who were writing a web server saw the potential of this and CGI was soon born.

CGI is the set of rules by which programs on the server can send information via the web server to the client. The CGI specification was also accompanied by changes to HTML and HTTP to introduce a new feature known as forms.

Where CGI allows programs to send output to a client, forms extend that capability by allowing the client to send information to the CGI program. Now the user can not only view the current time, but he or she can also set the clock! Forms and CGI opened the door to true interactivity on the Internet. Popular applications of CGI include:

- Dynamic HTML. Entire sites of pages can be generated from a single CGI program.

- Search engines that retrieve documents that match keywords chosen by the user.

- Guestbooks and bulletin boards for users to add their own comments to a site.

- Order forms.

- Surveys.

- Information retrieval that serves up details from a database.

Over the next few chapters, we will discuss each of these CGI applications along with a couple of others. More specifically, all of these applications offer a perfect opportunity to combine CGI with a database. This topic is what interests us in this section.

HTML Forms

Before we examine the specifics of CGI, it is useful to review the most common method by which end users are presented with an interface to CGI programs: HTML forms. Forms are a part of the HTML markup language that enable fields of different types to be presented to the end user. Then data entered into the fields can be sent back to the web server. The fields can be lines or boxes of text or buttons which can be pushed or checked by the user. The following is an example of an HTML page that contains a form:

```
<HTML><HEAD><TITLE>My Forms Page</title></head>
<BODY>
<p>This is a page with a form.
<p><FORM ACTION="mycgi.cgi" METHOD=POST>
Enter your name: <INPUT NAME="firstname" SIZE=40><br>
<INPUT TYPE=SUBMIT VALUE="Submit Form">
</form>
</body></html>
```

This form creates a line 40 characters long into which the user can enter a first name. Underneath the input line is a button which, when clicked, will submit the form information to the server. The forms-related tags that are supported by HTML 3.2—currently the most widespread standard—are listed below. Incidentally, names of tags and attributes are case-insensitive. We adhere to the convention of using uppercase for opening tags and lowercase for closing tags, but that's just one way of doing it.

<FORM>

This tag indicates the beginning of a form. At the end of the form the closing </Form> is required. Within the <FORM> tag, three attributes are possible: ACTION gives the URL or relative path name of the CGI program to which the data will be sent; METHOD gives the HTTP method by which the form will be sent (this can be GET or POST, we will almost always use POST); ENCTYPE gives the method used to encode the data (this should only be used if you really know what you are doing).

<INPUT>

This is the most flexible way to allow users to enter data. There are actually nine different styles of <INPUT> tag. The style is given by the TYPE attribute. In the example above, two <INPUT> tags are used, one with TYPE=SUBMIT and one with the default type of TEXT. The nine types are as follows:

TEXT

A single line box in which the user may enter text.

PASSWORD

The same as TEXT except that the entered text is not displayed on the screen.

CHECKBOX

A checkbox which the user can check or uncheck.

RADIO

A radio button which must be paired with at least one other radio button. The user can choose only one.

SUBMIT

A button that submits the form to the web server when clicked.

RESET

A button that resets the form to its default values when clicked.

FILE

Like text, except that it expects the name of a file which it will upload to the server.

HIDDEN

An invisible field in which you can store data.

IMAGE

Like a submit button, except that you can specify an image to display on the button.

Besides TYPE, <INPUT> tags usually have a NAME attribute which associates the data entered in that field with a name; both the name and the data are passed to the server in key=value style. In the preceding example, the name of the text input field was firstname. A VALUE attribute can be used to give TEXT, PASSWORD, FILE and HIDDEN types a preset value. When used with SUBMIT or RESET it displays the text in the clickable box. RADIO and CHECKBOX types can be prechecked by using the CHECKED attribute (with no value).

The SIZE attribute is used to provide a line length for TEXT, PASSWORD, and FILE types. Likewise, MAXLENGTH can be used to provide a limit for the amount of text entered. The SRC attribute gives the URL of the image to use for the IMAGE type. Finally, the ALIGN attribute tells where to align the image for the IMAGE type; it can be TOP, MIDDLE, BOTTOM (the default), LEFT, or RIGHT.

<SELECT>

This tag provides a menu of choices from which the user can choose. The appearance can be either a drop-down menu from which the user can choose one item or a list from which the user can use one or more items. Each item appears in an <OPTION> tag. A closing </select> tag is required.

As with the <INPUT> tag, <SELECT> has a NAME attribute that gives a name to the entered data. A SIZE attribute is also available which determines how many options will be shown at once on the screen. If SIZE is missing, the list will be in a drop-down menu style. The MULTIPLE attribute, if present, indicates that more than one option can be chosen. The <OPTION> tag has two possible attributes. The VALUE attribute sets the value of the data to be returned. If no VALUE is present, the text after the <OPTION> tag to the end of the line will be used instead. If the SELECTED attribute is in an <OPTION> tag, that option will be preselected.

<TEXTAREA>

This last form-related tag enables users to enter blocks of text that will be sent
to the web server. A **<TEXTAREA>** tag presents the user with a blank box in
which they can enter any number of lines of text to be sent back to the web
server. A **</Textarea>** closing tag is required and any text between the
<TEXTAREA> and **</Textarea>** will be used as the default text for the box—
similar to the **VALUE** attribute for the **<INPUT>** tag. The three attributes for
<TEXTAREA> are all required. **NAME** gives a name to the data, just as with the
other form-related tags. **ROWS** and **COLS** specify the number of rows and columns to make the text box on the screen, although the user will be able to
enter data beyond those limits.

Example 9-1 showcases all of the different form elements.

Example 9-1. An HTML Form that Shows the Different Form Elements

```
<HTML><HEAD><TITLE>My Second Forms Page</title><BODY>
<p>This is a survey. Please enter the following information about yourself:

<!-- Now let's begin the form. We are using the 'POST' method and sending the
information to a CGI program called 'survey.cgi' -->
<FORM METHOD=POST ACTION="survey.cgi">

<p>Name: <INPUT SIZE=40 NAME='name'><br>
<!-- This is an <INPUT> tag of the (default) 'TEXT' style. It is 40 characters
long, and the data will have the name 'name' -->

Social Security Number: <INPUT TYPE=PASSWORD NAME='ssn' SIZE=20><br>
<!-- This is an <INPUT> tag of the 'PASSWORD' style, used here so that someone
looking over the user's shoulder won't see the SSN of the user. The data is saved
with the name 'ssn' and the field is 20 characters long on the screen. -->

Are you or have you ever been associated with the Communist party?
     <INPUT TYPE=CHECKBOX NAME='commie' VALUE='yes'><br>
<!-- This is an <INPUT> tag of the 'CHECKBOX' style, using the name 'commie' for
the data. If the form is submitted with the box checked, the value 'yes' will be
associated with the name 'commie' -->

Sex: <INPUT TYPE=RADIO NAME='sex' VALUE='male'> Male
     <INPUT TYPE=RADIO NAME='sex' VALUE='female'> Female
     <INPUT TYPE=RADIO NAME='sex' VALUE='neither' CHECKED> Neither<br>
<!-- These are three <INPUT> tags of the 'RADIO' style, using the name 'sex' for
the data. Only one of the three can be chosen, and since one of them is
prechecked, a value will be sent regardless of whether or not the user clicks on
any of them. The value sent to the server is in the 'VALUE' attribute and need
not have any relation to the text that comes after the tag. -->

<INPUT TYPE=HIDDEN NAME="form_number" VALUE="33a">
<!-- This is a little extra information that we would like to send to the CGI,
but which the user need not worry about, so we place it inside of an <INPUT> tag
of the 'HIDDEN' type -->
```

Example 9-1. An HTML Form that Shows the Different Form Elements (continued)

```
Please enter the path of your favorite game: <INPUT TYPE=FILE NAME='game'
SIZE=40><br>
<!-- If the user enters a valid path here, the file will be uploaded to the web
server with the name 'game', when the user submits the form. Most web browsers
will ask to confirm the transfer, however, so this example is not as insidious as
it looks. -->

What are your favorite color(s)?<br>
<SELECT NAME="color" MULTIPLE SIZE=5>
<OPTION>Red
<OPTION>Green
<OPTION>Yellow
<OPTION>Orange
<OPTION VALUE="Blue">A nice light sky azure
</select><br>
<!-- This is a <SELECT></select> pair with several <OPTION>s. The name given to
the data is 'color', and multiple selections are allowed with all 5 being
displayed on the screen at once. The last option uses a 'VALUE' attribute to
provide a shortened form of the text. -->

Describe the sociopolitical context of <I>War and Peace</I> in 50 words or less.
Be thorough.<br>
<TEXTAREA NAME='essay' COLS=70 ROWS=10></textarea><br>
<!-- This is a <TEXTAREA></textarea> pair which provides a space for the entry of
an essay. The data is given the name 'essay'. The text block is 70 characters
wide and 10 rows deep. The space between the <TEXTAREA> and </textarea> tags
could have been used to give an example essay. -->

<INPUT TYPE=SUBMIT VALUE="Enter Info"> <INPUT TYPE=RESET>
<!-- These are two <INPUT> tags of type 'SUBMIT' and 'RESET', respectively. The
'SUBMIT' button has the custom label 'Enter Info' while the 'RESET' button has
the default value (determined by the browser). Clicking the 'SUBMIT' button will
send the data to the web server. Clicking the 'RESET' button will restore the
form to its original state, erasing any of the user's data.  -->

</form></body></html>
```

The only input type not used in this example was the **IMAGE** style of the **<INPUT>**
tag. We could have used it on the page as an alternate way of submitting the form.
However, the **IMAGE** style is rarely compatible with text-based and hearing-
impaired accessible browsers so it may be wise to avoid it unless your site is
unavoidably tied to a heavily graphical style.

Now that the basics of HTML forms have been covered, the next step is to enter
the world of CGI itself.

The CGI Specification

So what are the exact "set of rules" that enable a CGI program in say, Batavia, Illinois to communicate with a web browser in Outer Mongolia? The official CGI specification along with lots of other nifty CGI information can be found on NCSA's web site at *http://hoohoo.ncsa.uiuc.edu/cgi/*. However, the reason this chapter exists is so that you don't have to make the long trek to your web browser and look it up yourself.

There are four methods by which CGI passes information between the CGI program and the web server—and hence to the web client:

- Environment variables
- Command line
- Standard input
- Standard output

Using these four methods, the server sends all of the information provided by the client to the CGI program. The CGI program then does its magic and sends the output back to the server where it is forwarded to the client.

> This information is written with the Apache HTTP server in mind. Apache is the most widely used web server and is available for virtually all platforms, including Windows 9x and Windows NT. However, this information should also apply to all HTTP servers that support CGI. Some of the more proprietary servers, such as those from Microsoft and Netscape, may have additional features or slightly different operation. As the face of the web is still changing at an incredible speed, standards are still in flux and there will undoubtedly be changes. However, CGI itself seems to have somewhat stabilized—at the expense of being overshadowed by other technologies, such as applets. Any CGI programs you write using this information will almost certainly be supported by most web servers for many years.

When a CGI program is invoked via a form, the most popular interface used, the browser passes the server a long string that begins with the path and name of the CGI program. Following that is various other data called path information, which is passed to the CGI program via the PATH_INFO environment variable (see Figure 9-1). After the path information comes a "?" symbol followed by form data that will be sent to the server using the HTTP GET method. This data will be available to the CGI program through the QUERY_STRING environment variable. Finally, any form data coming from the page itself through a POST form, the most common type, will be sent to the server using the HTTP POST method. This data will be passed to the CGI program through the standard input. A typical string passed from the browser to the server is shown in Figure 9-1. The program named *form-read*, in directory *cgi-bin*, is invoked by the server with the extra path information extra/information where the query data `choice=help` is included—most likely as part of the original URL. Finally the form data itself (the text "CGI programming" entered into a field labeled "keywords") is sent via an HTTP POST.

```
http://www.myserver.com/cgi-bin/formread/extra/information?choice=help
                                 program name   path info      query string
```

Figure 9-1. Parts of the string passed from browser to server

Environment Variables

When the server executes a CGI program, the first thing it does is give the program some information to work with in the form of environment variables. Seventeen variables are officially defined in the specification, while a great deal more unofficial ones that are used via the HTTP_ mechanism described later. Your CGI program can access these environment variables just as they would access the environment variables of the shell if the program was run from the command line. In a shell script, for instance, the environment variable FOO could be accessed as $FOO; in Perl it would be $ENV{'FOO'}; in C getenv("FOO"); etc. Listed in Table 9-1 are the variables that are always set—even if it is to a null value—by the server. In addition to these variables, information returned by the client in the header of the request is included as variables of the form HTTP_FOO, where FOO is the name of the header. For example, most web browsers include version information in a header labeled USER_AGENT. This can be accessed by your CGI program as the header HTTP_USER_AGENT. Table 9-1 lists the CCGI environment variables.

Table 9-1. The CGI Environment Variables

Environment Variable	Description
CONTENT_LENGTH	The length, in bytes, of the data provided by the POST or PUT method.
CONTENT_TYPE	The MIME type of any data attached via a POST or PUT method.
GATEWAY_INTERFACE	The version number of the CGI specification supported by the server.
PATH_INFO	Extra path information provided by the client. For example, in a request of the form *http://www.myserver.com/ test.cgi/this/is/a/path?field=green,* */this/is/a/path* will be the value of the PATH_INFO variable.

Table 9-1. The CGI Environment Variables (continued)

Environment Variable	Description
PATH_TRANSLATED	This is the same as PATH_INFO except any translation that is possible, such as expanding "~account" names, is done by the server.
QUERY_STRING	Any information following the "?" in the URL. This is also the information provided in a form if the REQUEST_METHOD is GET.
REMOTE_ADDR	The IP address of the client making the request.
REMOTE_HOST	The hostname, if available, of the client making the request.
REMOTE_IDENT	If the web server and the client both support identd-style identification, this will be the username of the account making the request.
REQUEST_METHOD	The method which the client used to make the request. For the run-of-the-mill CGI programs of the type we are going to make, this will usually be POST or GET.
SCRIPT_NAME	The path given by the client to run the script. This can be used for self-referencing URLs, and so that scripts that are linked in different places can react differently depending on their location.
SERVER_NAME	The hostname—or IP number, if the hostname is not available—of the machine on which the web server is running.
SERVER_PORT	The port number the web server is using.
SERVER_PROTOCOL	Protocol by which the client is communicating with the server. For our purposes, it will almost always be HTTP.
SERVER_SOFTWARE	Version information for the web server executing the CGI program.

The following is an example CGI script in Perl which prints out all of the environment variables set by the server—as well as any inherited variables, such as PATH, which are set by the shell that executed the server.

```perl
#!/usr/bin/perl -w

print <<HTML;
Content-type: text/html\n\n

<HTML><HEAD><TITLE></title></head><BODY>
<p>Environment Variables
<p>
HTML

foreach (keys %ENV) { print "$_: $ENV{$_}<br>\n"; }

print <<HTML;
</body></html>
HTML
```

Any of these variables can be used, even manipulated by your CGI program. However, none of the changes affect the web server which spawned your program.

Command Line

A little used feature of CGI allows arguments to be passed as command line parameters to a CGI program. The reason the feature is little used is because there are only a few practical applications, so we won't dwell on it here. Basically, if the QUERY_STRING environment variable does not contain an "=" symbol, the CGI program will be executed with the command line arguments as the QUERY_STRING. For instance, *http://www.myserver.com/cgi-bin/finger?root* will execute finger root on *www.myserver.com*.

Command line parameters are most commonly used in conjunction with the <ISINDEX> HTML tag. The <ISINDEX> tag is a miniform contained in a single tag. When a browser encounters an <ISINDEX> tag, it displays a text box in which the user can enter a query string. Upon submission—usually after the user presses the "Enter" key—the browser extracts a URL from the <ISINDEX> tag and calls it, passing the words of the query string as the command line.

For example, the finger CGI mentioned earlier could be written so that, if called with no arguments, it outputs an HTML page that contains an <ISINDEX> tag. The user would then enter an address into the field and the finger would be executed as described above.

Standard Input

As mentioned above, if a client sends information via a PUT or POST HTTP request, the length and MIME type of that information are put into the CONTENT_LENGTH and CONTENT_TYPE environment variables, respectively. The actual data is sent into the CGI program's standard input. No end-of-data marker is necessarily sent to the program, so it must examine the CONTENT_LENGTH variable and read only that number of bytes. This is the primary method of transferring form data from forms and we will use it almost exclusively in our examples.

Many libraries exist for almost all imaginable languages that perform the essential set-up tasks of a CGI program for you, including determining whether the incoming data was sent via the GET or POST method and either parsing the QUERY_STRING environment variable or reading the standard input, respectively. These libraries then place the data into easily accessible variables. A couple of the more common libraries are listed below. For the purely biased reason that we don't know every language out there, we will go into detail only for libraries that work with Perl and C. However, CGI can be very powerful in just about any language. An extensive list of CGI resources for various languages can be found on Yahoo at

*http://www.yahoo.com/Computers_and_Internet/Internet/World_Wide_Web/CGI__
Common_Gateway_Interface/.*

Accepting Input in Perl

Most of the rest of this section contains examples in Perl and C. This does not
mean that Perl and C are any better, or worse, than any others but simply that it
has been found very useful by many people in the area of CGI. In particular,
because of the popularity of Perl in this area, we still do the vast majority of our
CGI work in it. We would, however, also strongly recommend you take a look at
Python if you have not yet made a language decision for CGI programs.

Two major libraries provide CGI interfaces for Perl. The first is *cgi-lib.pl.** The *cgi-
lib.pl* utility is very common because for a while it was the only major library available. It is designed to work under Perl 4, but still works under Perl 5. The other
library, *CGI.pm*,† is more recent and in many ways supersedes *cgi-lib.pl. CGI.pm* is
written for Perl 5 and uses an entirely object-oriented scheme for dealing with CGI
data. The *CGI.pm* module parses the standard input and QUERY_STRING variable
and stores data in a CGI object. Your program needs only to create a new CGI
object and use simple methods like param() to retrieve the data in which you are
interested. Example 9-2 is a short example that shows how *CGI.pm* interprets data.
All of the Perl examples in this section will use *CGI.pm*.

Example 9-2. Parsing CGI Data in Perl

```
#!/usr/bin/perl -w

use CGI qw(:standard);   # Use the CGI.pm module. The qw(:standard) imports the
                         # namespace of the standard CGI functions to allow for
                         # clearer code. This can only be done if only one CGI
                         # object will be used throughout the script.

$mycgi = new CGI; # Create a CGI object, which will be our 'gateway' to the form
                  # data.

@fields = $mycgi->param; # This retrieves the names of the all of the form fields
                         # entered.


print header, start_html('CGI.pm test'); # The 'header' and 'start_html' methods
                         # are provided by CGI.pm as HTML shortcuts.
                         'header'
                         # prints out the required HTTP header, and
                         #'start_html' prints out the HTML header with the
                         #title given, along with the <BODY> tag.
```

---

* *http://www.bio.cam.ac.uk/cgi-lib/*

† *http://www-genome.wi.mit.edu/ftp/pub/software/WWW/cgi_docs.html*

Example 9-2. Parsing CGI Data in Perl (continued)

```
print "<p>Form information:<br>";


foreach (@fields) { print $_, ":", $mycgi->param($_), "<br>"; }
# For each of the fields, print out the field name along with the value (which
# is obtained through $mycgi->param('fieldname').

print end_html; # A shortcut provided to print the "</body></html>" ending tags.
```

Accepting Input in C

Since the primary MySQL and mSQL APIs are written in C, we will not completely abandon it for Perl, but instead provide a few C examples where appropriate. There are three widely used C libraries for CGI programming: *cgic* by Tom Boutell;[*] *cgihtml* by Eugene Kim;[†] and *libcgi* from EIT.[‡] We have found *cgic* to be the most complete and easiest to use. However, it lacks the ability to list all of the form variables if you do not know them beforehand. This ability can actually be added by means of a trivial patch, but that is beyond the scope of this chapter. Thus, to mimic the example Perl script used earlier we use the *cgihtml* library in Example 9-3.

Example 9-3. Parsing CGI Data in C

```
/* cgihtmltest.c - A generic CGI program to print out the keys and values
     of the submitted form data.
*/

#include <stdio.h>
#include "cgi-lib.h"  /* This contains all of the definitions for the CGI
                          functions */
#include "html-lib.h" /* This contains all of the definitions for the HTML
                          helper functions */

void print_all(llist l)
/* This functions prints out all of the data submitted by the form in the
same format as the above Perl example. Cgihtml also provides a built-in
function, print_entries(), which does the exact same thing using a set
HTML definition list format.
*/
{
  node* window;
/* The 'node' type is defined by the cgihtml library and refers to the
linked list which stores all of the form data. */
```

---

[*] *http://www.boutell.com/cgic/*

[†] *http://hcs.harvard.edu/~eekim/web/cgihtml/*

[‡] *http://wsk.eit.com/wsk/dist/doc/libcgi/libcgi.html*

Example 9-3. Parsing CGI Data in C (continued)

```
    window = l.head;
/* This sets a pointer at the beginning of the form data */

    while (window != NULL) {
/* Go through the linked list until you reach the last (the first empty) entry */

        printf("  %s:%s<br>\n",window->entry.name,
            replace_ltgt(window->entry.value));
/* Print out the data. Replace_ltgt() is a provided function which HTML encodes
the text so that it will show up correctly on the client browser. */

        window = window->next;
/* Go to the next entry in the list. */

    }
}


int main()
{
  llist entries; /* This is a pointer to the parsed data */
  int status; /* This is a status integer provided by the library */

  html_header();
/* This is an HTML-helper function which prints the HTML header */

  html_begin("cgihtml test");
/* This is an HTML-helper function which prints the beginning of the HTML
page with the specified title. */

  status = read_cgi_input(&entries);
/* This reads in and parses the form data */
  printf("<p>Form information:<br>");
  print_all(entries);
/* Call the print_all() function defined above. */
  html_end();
/* This is an HTML-helper function which prints the end of the HTML page. */
  list_clear(&entries);
/* This frees the memory used by the form data. */
  return 0;
}
```

Standard Output

Data sent by the CGI program to the standard output will be read by the web server and sent to the client. If the name of the script begins with *nph-*, the data is sent straight to the client without any interference from the web server. In this case, it is up to the CGI program to provide a valid HTTP header that will be understood by the client. Otherwise, let the web server create the HTTP header for you.

Even if you do not use an *nph-* script, you must still give the server one directive which tells it something about your output. Most commonly, this will be a `Content-Type` HTTP header, but it could also be a `Location` header. The headers should be followed by a blank line—that is, a bare linefeed or CR/LF combination.

The `Content-Type` header tells the server what type of data is being output by your CGI program. If the output is an HTML page, the line should be `Content-Type: text/html`. The `Location` header tells the server the name of another URL—or another path on the same server—to which to direct the client. It is of the form `Location: http://www.myserver.com/another/place/`.

After the HTTP headers and the blank line, you can send the body of your program's output, whether it be an HTML page, an image, plain text, or whatever. Among the CGI programs included with the Apache web server, the *nph-test-cgi* and *test-cgi* effectively show the difference between the nph and non-nph style headers, respectively.

In this section, we will be using libraries such as *CGI.pm* and *cgic* that provide functions for printing out the HTTP as well as the HTML headers. This will allow you to concentrate on generating the content itself. These helper functions are demonstrated in the examples earlier in this chapter.

Important Considerations for CGI Scripts

Now you have seen the basic operation of a CGI transaction: a client sends information, usually via form data, to the web server. The server then executes the CGI program, passing it the information. The CGI program then performs its magic and sends the output back to the server, where it is relayed to the client. From this point, you must make the leap from understanding how a CGI program works to understanding what makes them so popular.

While you've seen enough in this chapter to put together a rudimentary working CGI program, there are some critical topics you should learn before putting together real programs with MySQL or mSQL. First, you have to learn how to support multiple forms. You also need to study some security features that prevent malicious users from snooping or removing files on your site.

State Retention

Although it sounds like something done to hardened criminals, state retention is really a vitally important tool in providing advanced services to your users. The problem is this: HTTP is what is known as a 'stateless' protocol. That is, the client sends a request to the server, the server returns data to the client and both go their separate ways. The server keeps no special information about the client that would aid it in any future transactions. Likewise, there is no guarantee the client will remember anything about the transaction that it could use later. This puts an immediate and significant restriction on the usability of the World Wide Web.

Writing CGI scripts under this protocol is like not having the ability to remember past conversations. Every time you talked to someone, no matter how often you had talked to them before, you would have to reintroduce yourselves and find common ground all over again. Needless to say, this puts a hamper on productivity. Notice in Figure 9-2 that each time the request reaches the CGI program, it is a completely new instance of the program, with no connection to the previous one.

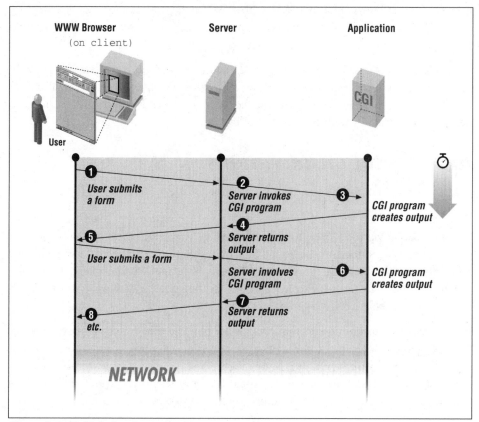

Figure 9-2. Multiple form requests

On the client side of things, the advent of Netscape Navigator introduced a kludge-like solution called HTTP cookies. This involved the creation of a new HTTP header that could be sent back and forth between the client and server, similar to the

`Content-Type` and `Location` headers. The client browser, upon receiving a cookie header, would save the information in the cookie as well as a domain—included in the cookie information—in which the cookie is valid. Then every time the browser accessed a URL within the given domain, the cookie header would be returned to the server for the use of any CGI program on that server.

The cookie method is used mainly to store user IDs. Information about a visitor can be stored in a file on the server machine. A unique ID for that user is then sent as a cookie to the user's browser. Now, whenever the user visits the site, the browser automatically sends the user's ID to the server. The server then passes the ID to the CGI program, which then opens the appropriate file and has access to all of the information about the user; all of this occurring transparently to the user.

Despite its usefulness, most large sites do not use cookies as the only method of state retention. There are a couple of reasons for this. First, not all browsers support cookies. Until very recently, the primary browser for the vision impaired—not to mention the fast-net connection impaired—Lynx, did not support cookies. It still does not "officially" support them, but some widely available offshoot versions now do. Secondly, and more importantly, cookies tie the user to a single machine. One of the great innovations of the web is that it is accessible from anywhere in the world. No matter where your web page was created and is stored you can show it off from any Internet-capable machine anywhere. However, if you try to access your cookie enhanced site from a machine other than your own, any personalization performed by the cookies will be lost.

Many sites still use cookies to provide users with personalized pages, but most augment the cookies with a traditional login/password style interface. If the site is accessed from a browser that does not provide a cookie, the page contains a form where a user enters a login name and password that was assigned at the time of his or her first visit. This form is usually small and discreet so as not to distract from the majority of users who have no interest in any kind of personalization, but are just passing through. When a user submits a login name and password via the form, a CGI then finds the correct information file for that user, just as if the name were sent as a cookie. Using this method, a person could log into a personalized web site from anywhere in the world.

Beyond the issue of user preferences and long-term information, a more subtle example of state retention can be provided by looking at popular search engines. When you perform a search through a search service such as AltaVista or Yahoo, you usually get back many more results than can be conveniently displayed. The way the search providers handle this is to show some small number of results—usually ten or twenty—combined with some sort of navigation tool that allows you to view the next set of results. While to a casual web surfer, this behavior has become commonplace and expected, the actual implementation is nontrivial and requires state retention.

When the user first makes a query to the search engine, the search engine gathers up all of the results, possibly stopping at some predefined limit. The trick is to then present these results to the user a few at a time, while remembering which user wanted the results and which set of results they wanted next. After stripping out the complexities of the search engine itself we are left with the problem of providing some sequence of information to a user, one page at a time. Consider Example 9-4 as an example CGI script that displays ten lines from a file and presents the user with the ability to view the next or previous ten lines depending on their position in the file.

Example 9-4. State Retention in a CGI Script

```perl
#!/usr/bin/perl -w

use CGI;

open(F,"/usr/dict/words") or die("Can't open! $!");
#This is the file that will be displayed. It can be any file.

$output = new CGI;

sub print_range { # This is the main function of the program.
        my $start = shift; # The starting line of the file.
        my $count = 0; # A placeholder.
        my $line = ""; # The current line of the file.
        print $output->header, $output->start_html('My Dictionary');
        # This starts the HTML with the title 'My Dictionary'.
        print "<pre>\n";
        while (($count < $start) and ($line = <F>)) { $count++; }
        # Skip all of the lines up to the starting line.
        while (($count < $start+10) and ($line = <F>) )
                { print $line; $count++; }
        # Then print the next ten lines.

        my $newnext = $start+10;
        my $newprev = $start-10;
        # Set up the starting lines for the 'Next' and 'Previous' URLs.

        print "</pre><p>";

        unless ($start == 0) { # Include a 'Previous' URL unless you're already
                                # at the beginning.
                print qq%<a href="read.cgi?start=$newprev">Previous</a>%;
        }

        unless (eof) { # Include a 'Next' URL unless you are at the end
                        # of the file.
                print qq% <a href="read.cgi?start=$newnext">Next</a>%;
        }
```

Example 9-4. State Retention in a CGI Script (continued)

```
        print <<HTML;
</body><html>
HTML
        exit(0);
}


# If there is no data provided, start at the beginning.
if (not $output->param) {
        &print_range(0);
}


# Else start at the line provided by the data.
&print_range($output->param('start'));
```

This example provides state retention using the simplest possible method. There's no problem keeping the data persistent, because we've stored it in a file on the server. All we need to know is where to start printing. So the script simply includes in the URL the starting point for the next or previous group of lines, all of the information needed to generate any subsequent pages.

However, once your needs grow beyond paging through a file, relying on the URL can become cumbersome. One way to lighten the burden is to use HTML forms and to include the state information in <INPUT> tags of type HIDDEN. This method can go far and is used by many sites today to link together related CGI programs or to stretch out the usefulness of one CGI program as in the dictionary example. Instead of referring to a specific item—such as the starting page—the data in the URL could refer to an automatically generated user ID number.

This is how AltaVista and the other search engines work. Your initial search generates a user ID number which is hidden in the subsequent URLs. This user ID number refers to one or more files on the server machine that contain the results of your query. Two more values are included in the URL: your current position in the results file, and the direction in wish you want to view next. These three values are all that are needed to provide the powerful navigation system used by the big search services.

There is still something missing, though. The file used in the example, */usr/dict/ words*, is a very big file. What if we got tired of reading it halfway through but wanted to come back to it later? Unless I peeked at the URL of the next link, we would have no way of getting back to where we left off. Even AltaVista does not provide this. If you restart your computer or use a different one, there is no way to get back to your old search without reentering the query. However, this long-term state retention is the basis of the personalized web sites we mentioned earlier and it is worth examining how this would work. Example 9-5 is a modified version of Example 9-4.

Example 9-5. Robust State Retention

```perl
#!/usr/bin/perl -w

use CGI;

umask 0;
open(F,"/usr/dict/words") or die("Can't open! $!");
chdir("users") or die("Can't chdir! $!");
# This is the directory where all of the user information will
# be stored.

$output = new CGI;

if (not $output->param) {
        print $output->header, $output->start_html('My Dictionary');
        print <<HTML;
        <FORM ACTION="read2.cgi" METHOD=POST>
        <p>Enter your username:
                <INPUT NAME="username" SIZE=30>
        <p>
        </form></body></html>
HTML
        exit(0);
}

$user = $output->param('username');

## If a file for the user does not exist, create one and set the
## Starting value to '0'.
if ( not -e "$user" ) {
        open (U, ">$user") or die("Can't open! $!");
        print U "0\n";
        close U;
        &print_range('0');

## Else, if the user does exist, and the URL didn't specify
## a starting value, read the users last value and start there.
} elsif ( not $output->param('start') ) {
        open(U,"$user") or die("Can't open user! $!");
        $start = <U>; close U;
        chomp $start;
        &print_range($start);

## Else, if the user does exist, and the URL did specify
## a starting value, write the starting value to the user's
## file and then start printing.
} else {
        open(U,">$user") or die("Can't open user to write! $!");
        print U $output->param('start'), "\n";
        close U;
        &print_range($output->param('start'));
}
```

Example 9-5. Robust State Retention (continued)

```
sub print_range {
        my $start = shift;
        my $count = 0;
        my $line = "";
        print $output->header, $output->start_html('My Dictionary');
        print "<pre>\n";
        while (($count < $start) and ($line = <F>)) { $count++; }
        while (($count < $start+10) and ($line = <F>) )
                { print $line; $count++; }
        my $newnext = $start+10;
        my $newprev = $start-10;
        print "</pre><p>";
        unless ($start == 0) {
                print
qq%<a href="read2.cgi?start=$newprev&username=$user">Previous</a>%;
        }
        unless (eof) {
                print
qq% <a href="read2.cgi?start=$newnext&username=$user">Next</a>%;
        # Note that the 'username' has been added to the URL.
        # Otherwise the CGI would forget which user it was dealing with.
        }
        print $output->end_html;
        exit(0);
}
```

Security

When it comes to running Internet servers, whether they are HTTP servers or otherwise, maintaining security is a primary concern. CGI, with its exchange of information between client and server, raises several important security related issues. The CGI protocol itself was designed to be reasonably secure. The information sent to the CGI program from the server is sent via the standard input or an environment variable, both secure methods. But once the CGI program has control of the data, there are no restrictions on what it can do. A poorly written CGI program can allow a malicious user to gain access to the server system. Consider the following CGI program:

```
#!/usr/bin/perl -w

use CGI;
my $output = new CGI;

my $username = $output->param('username');

print $output->header, $output->start_html('Finger Output'),
    "<pre>", `finger $username`, "</pre>", $output->end_html;
```

This program provides a functional CGI interface to the finger command. If the program is run as just *finger.cgi*, it will list all current users on the server system. If run as *finger.cgi?username=fred* it will finger the user "fred" on the server system. You could even run it as *finger.cgi?username=bob@foo.com* to finger a remote user. However, if a user ran it as *finger.cgi?username=fred;mail+hacker@bar.com</etc/passwd* unwanted things could happen. The backtick operator `` ` `` in Perl spawns a shell and executes a command returning the result. In this program `` `finger $username` `` is used as an easy way to run the finger command and retrieve its output. Most shells, however, allow the grouping of commands on a single line. Any Bourne-like shell does this via the ";" symbol, for example. So `` `finger fred;mail hacker@bar.com</etc/passwd` `` will run the *finger* command and then run *mail hacker@bar.com</etc/passwd*, possibly sending the entire password file of the server system to an unwanted user.

One solution to this is to parse the incoming form data, looking for possible malicious intent. You could scan for the ";" character and remove any characters after it, for instance. Another possibility is to make it impossible for such an attack to work, by using alternate methods. The above CGI program could be rewritten as follows:

```
#!/usr/local/bin/perl -w

use CGI;
my $output = new CGI;
my $username = $output->param('username');

$|++; # Disable buffering. This is to make sure that all the data makes it to
      # the client.

print $output->header, $output->start_html('Finger Output'), "<pre>\n";

$pid = open(C_OUT, "-|"); # This is a Perl idiom which spawns a child and opens a
                          # filehandle pipe between the parent and child.
if ($pid) { # This is the parent.
    print <C_OUT>; # Print the output from the child.
    print "</pre>", $output->end_html;
    exit(0); # End the program.
} elsif (defined $pid) { # This is the child.
    $|++; # Disable the buffering in the child as way.
    exec('/usr/bin/finger',$username) or die("exec() call failed.");
    # This executes the finger program with $username as the first and only
    # command line argument.
} else { die("fork() call failed."); } # Error checking.
```

As you can see, this is only a marginally more complex program. But if run as *finger.cgi?username=fred;mail+hacker@bar.com</etc/passwd*, the finger program is executed with the argument *fred;mail hacker@bar.com</etc/passwd* as if that were a single username.

As an added level of security, this script also executes finger explicitly as */usr/bin/finger*. In the unlikely event that the web server passed a strange PATH to your CGI program, running just finger could possibly execute something other than the desired program. Another security step you could take would be to examine the PATH environment variable and make sure it has reasonable values. Eliminating (the current working directory) from PATH is a good idea unless you know for sure where the current directory is and you have a special need to run a program there.

Another important security concern is that of user permissions. By default, a web server runs the CGI program as the same user that the server itself is running. Usually this is a pseudo-user, such as "nobody," with very few permissions. So the CGI program also has very few permissions. This is a generally good thing. This way, if a malicious remote user is able to remote access the server system via the CGI program, little damage can be done. The password-stealing example given earlier is one of the few things that could be done, but actual system damage can usually be contained.

However, running as a limited user also limits the ability of the CGI. If the CGI needs to read or write files, it can do so only in those places where it has permission. In the second persistent state example, for instance, a file is kept for each user. The CGI must have permission to read and write to the directory that contains these files, not to mention the files themselves. One way to do this would be to make the directory the same user as the server with read and write permissions for that user only. However, for a user such as "nobody," only root has that power. If you are a nonroot user you would have to contact your system administrator every time you wanted to change your CGI.

Another choice is to make the directory world readable and writable, essentially removing all protection from it. Since the outside world's only interface with these files is through your program, the danger here is not as great as it seems. However, if a loophole was found in your program, a remote user would have complete access to all of the files, including the ability to destroy them. In addition any legitimate users that are working on the server machine would also have the ability to alter the files. If you going to use this method, it must be on a server machine where all of the users are trusted. In addition, use the open directory only for files that are necessary to the CGI program. In other words, do not put any unnecessary files at risk.

Further Reading

If this is your first exposure to CGI programming, there are a many other places to go from here. Dozens of books have been written on the subject, and many of them assume no programming knowledge at all. *CGI Programming on the World Wide Web* from O'Reilly and Associates covers the material ranging from basic scripts in various languages to some really amazing tips and tricks. Free information is also in abundance on the World Wide Web. *CGI Made Really Easy* at *http://www.jmarshall.com/easy/cgi/* is a good starting place.

CGI and Databases

From the beginning of Internet time, databases have interacted with the development of the World Wide Web. In fact, many view the web as simply an enormous database of multimedia information.

Search engines are an everyday example of the benefits of databases. An engine does not go all over the web looking for keywords the moment you ask for them; instead the site's developers use other programs to create an enormous index that serves as a database from which the engine retrieves entries. Databases store information in a manner that allows quick, random-access retrieval.

Because databases are mutable, they lend even more power to the web: they turn it into a potential user interface for anything. System administration, for instance, could be performed remotely over a web interface instead of requiring the administrator to log into the affected system. Connecting databases to the web is the key to a new world of interactivity on the Internet.

 One reason for connecting databases to the web pops up repeatedly: much of the world's information is already in databases. Databases that existed before the creation of the web are referred to as legacy databases (as opposed to nonweb connected databases that were created recently, which are referred to as a bad idea). Many corporations (and even individuals) are now faced with the task of making these legacy databases available over the web. Unless your legacy database is in MySQL or mSQL, this topic is beyond the scope of this book.

As mentioned earlier, only your imagination limits the uses of database-web connectivity. Thousands of unique, useful databases currently exist that are available over the web for some reason or another. The types of database that are behind the scenes of these applications vary widely. Some of them use CGI programs to interface with a database server such as MySQL or mSQL. These are the types that we are most interested in. Others use commercial applications to interact with popular desktop databases, such as Microsoft Access and Claris FileMaker Pro. Still others simply deal with plain text files, which are the simplest databases of all.

Using these three types of databases, useful web sites of all sizes and levels of sophistication can be developed. One of our focuses over the next few chapters will be to apply the power of MySQL and mSQL to the web through CGI programming.

10

Perl

The Perl programming language has gone from a tool primarily used by Unix systems administrators to the most widely used development platform for the World Wide Web. Perl was not designed for the web, but its ease of use and powerful text handling abilities have made it a natural for CGI programming. Similarly, when mSQL first entered the scene, its extremely small footprint and execution time were very attractive to web developers who needed to serve thousands of transactions a day. MySQL, with its enhanced speed and capabilities provided an even greater incentive for web developers. Therefore, it was only natural that a Perl interface to both MySQL and mSQL was developed that allowed the best of both worlds.

 At the time of this writing there are two interfaces between MySQL and mSQL and Perl. The original consists of *Mysql.pm* and *Msql.pm*, custom interfaces that work only with MySQL and mSQL, respectively. The other, newer, interface is a plug-in for the Database Independent (DBI) set of modules. DBI is an attempt to provide a common Perl API for all database accesses and enable greater behind-the-scenes portability. The DBI interface has become the most robust and standard, and the makers of MySQL recommend that all work be done using DBI as development of the *Mysql.pm* and *Msql.pm* modules has ceased. However, many legacy systems still use these modules, so both will be covered here.

DBI

The recommended method for accessing MySQL and mSQL databases from Perl is the DBD/DBI interface. DBD/DBI stands for DataBase Dependent/DataBase

Independent. The name arises from the two-layer implementation of the interface. At the bottom is the database dependent layer. Here, modules exist for each type of database accessible from Perl. On top of these database dependent modules lies a database independent layer. This is the interface that you use to access the database. The advantage of this scheme is that the programmer only has to learn one API, the database independent layer. Every time a new database comes along, someone needs only to write a DBD module for it and it will be accessible to all DBD/DBI programmers.

As with all Perl modules, you must use DBI to get access:

```
#!/usr/bin/perl -w

use strict;
use CGI qw(:standard);
use DBI;
```

 When running any MySQL/mSQL Perl programs, you should always include the *-w* command line argument. With this present, DBI will redirect all MySQL and mSQL specific error messages to STDERR so that you can see any database errors without checking for them explicitly in your program.

All interactions between Perl and MySQL and mSQL are conducted through what is known as a database handle. The *database handle* is an object—represented as a scalar reference in Perl—that implements all of the methods used to communicate with the database. You may have as many database handles open at once as you wish. You are limited only by your system resources. The connect() method uses a connection format of DBI:servertype:database:hostname:port (hostname and port and optional), with additional arguments of username and password to create a handle:

```
my $dbh = DBI->connect('DBI:mysql:mydata', undef, undef);
my $dbh = DBI->connect('DBI:mSQL:mydata:myserver', undef, undef);
my $dbh = DBI->connect('DBI:mysql:mydata','me','mypass');
```

The *servertype* attribute is the name of the DBD database-specific module, which in our case will be either "mysql" or "mSQL" (note capitalization). The first version creates a connection to the MySQL server on the local machine via a Unix-style socket. This is the most efficient way to communicate with the database and should be used if you are connecting to a local server. If the hostname is supplied it will connect to the server on that host using the standard port unless the port is supplied as well. If you do not provide a username and password when connecting to a MySQL server, the user executing the program must have sufficient privileges within the MySQL database. The username and password should always be left undefined for mSQL databases.

Perl 5 has two different calling conventions for modules. With the object-oriented syntax, the arrow symbol "->" is used to reference a method in a particular class (as in DBI->connect). Another method is the indirect syntax, in which the method name is followed by the class name, then the arguments. The last connect method above would be written as connect DBI 'DBI:mysql:mydata', 'me', 'mypass'. Early versions of the *Msql.pm* used the indirect syntax exclusively and also enforced a specific method of capitalization inspired by the mSQL C API. Therefore, a lot of older *MsqlPerl* code will have lines in it like SelectDB $dbh 'test' where a simple $dbh->selectdb('test') would do. If you haven't guessed, we are partial to the object-oriented syntax, if only because the arrow makes the relationship between class and method clear.

Once you have connected to the MySQL or mSQL server, the database handle—$dbh in all of the examples in this section—is the gateway to the database server. For instance, to prepare an SQL query:

```
$dbh->prepare($query);
```

When using mSQL you may select only one database at a time for a particular database handle. The mSQL server imposes this limit. However, you may change the current database at any time by calling connect again. With MySQL, you may include other databases in your query by explicitly naming them. In addition, with both MySQL and mSQL, if you need to access more than one database concurrently, you can create multiple database handles and use them side by side.

Chapter 21, *Perl Reference*, describes the full range of methods and variables supplied by DBI as well as *Mysql.pm* and *Msql.pm*.

As an example of the use of DBI consider the following simple programs. In Example 10-1, *datashow.cgi* accepts a hostname as a parameter—"localhost" is assumed if no parameter is present. The program then displays all of the databases available on that host.

Example 10-1. The CGI datashow.cgi Shows All of the Databases on a MySQL or mSQL Server

```
#!/usr/bin/perl -w

use strict;
```

Example 10-1. The CGI datashow.cgi Shows All of the Databases on a MySQL
or mSQL Server (continued)

```perl
use CGI qw(:standard);
use CGI::Carp;
    # Use the DBI module
use DBI;
CGI::use_named_parameters(1);

my ($server, $sock, $host);

my $output = new CGI;
$server = param('server') or $server = '';

# Prepare the MySQL DBD driver
my $driver = DBI->install_driver('mysql');

    my @databases = $driver->func($server, '_ListDBs');

# If @databases is undefined we assume
# that means that the host does not have
# a running MySQL server. However, there could be other reasons
# for the failure. You can find a complete error message by
# checking $DBI::errmsg.
if (not @databases) {
        print header, start_html('title'=>"Information on $server",
        'BGCOLOR'=>'white');
        print <<END_OF_HTML;
<H1>$server</h1>
$server does not appear to have a running mSQL server.
</body></html>
END_OF_HTML
        exit(0);
}

        print header, start_html('title'=>"Information on $host",
                                'BGCOLOR'=>'white');
        print <<END_OF_HTML;
<H1>$host</h1>
<p>
$host\'s connection is on socket $sock.
<p>
Databases:<br>
<UL>
END_OF_HTML
foreach (@databases) {
        print "<LI>$_\n";
}
print <<END_OF_HTML;
</ul>
</body></html>
HTML
exit(0)
```

In Example 10-2, *tableshow.cgi* accepts the name of a database server (default is
"localhost") and the name of a database on that server. The program then shows
all of the available tables on that server.

Example 10-2. The CGI tableshow.cgi Shows All of the Tables Within a Database

```perl
#!/usr/bin/perl -w

use strict;
use CGI qw(:standard);
use CGI::Carp;
    # Use the Msql.pm module
use DBI;
CGI::use_named_parameters(1);

my ($db);
my $output = new CGI;
$db = param('db') or die("Database not supplied!");

# Connect to the requested server.
my $dbh = DBI->connect("DBI:mysql:$db:$server", undef, undef);

# If $dbh does not exist, the attempt to connect to the
# database server failed. The server may not be running,
# or the given database may not exist.
if (not $dbh) {
        print header, start_html('title'=>"Information on $host => $db",
            'BGCOLOR'=>'white');

        print <<END_OF_HTML;
<H1>$host</h1>
<H2>$db</h2>
The connection attempt failed for the following reason:<BR>
$DBI::errstr
</body></html>
END_OF_HTML
        exit(0);
}


print header, start_html('title'=>"Information on $host => $db",
        'BGCOLOR'=>'white');
print <<END_OF_HTML;
<H1>$host</h1>
<H2>$db</h2>
<p>
Tables:<br>
<UL>
END_OF_HTML
# $dbh->listtable returns an array of the tables that are available
# in the current database.
my @tables = $dbh->func( '_ListTables' );
foreach (@tables) {
        print "<LI>$_\n";
}
```

Example 10-2. The CGI tableshow.cgi Shows All of the Tables Within a Database (continued)

```
print <<END_OF_HTML;
</ul>
</body></html>
END_OF_HTML
        exit(0);
```

And, finally, Example 10-3 shows all of the information about a specific table.

Example 10-3. The CGI tabledump.cgi Shows Information About a Specific Table

```perl
#!/usr/bin/perl -w

use strict;
use CGI qw(:standard);
use CGI::Carp;
    # Use the DBI module
use DBI;
CGI::use_named_parameters(1);

my ($db,$table);
my $output = new CGI;
$server = param('server') or $server = '';
$db = param('db') or die("Database not supplied!");

# Connect to the requested server.
my $dbh = DBI->connect("DBI:mysql:$db:$server", undef, undef);

# We now prepare a query for the server asking for all of the data in
# the table.
my $table_data = $dbh->prepare("select * from $table");
# Now send the query to the server.
$table_data->execute;

# If the return value is undefined, the table must not exist. (Or it could
# be empty; we don't check for that.)
if (not $table_data) {
        print header, start_html('title'=>
        "Information on $host => $db => $table", 'BGCOLOR'=>'white');

        print <<END_OF_HTML;
<H1>$host</h1>
<H2>$db</h2>
The table '$table' does not exist in $db on $host.
</body></html>
END_OF_HTML
        exit(0);
}

# At this point, we know we have data to display. First we show the
# layout of the table.
print header, start_html('title'=>"Information on $host => $db => $table",
        'BGCOLOR'=>'white');
print <<END_OF_HTML;
```

Example 10-3. The CGI tabledump.cgi Shows Information About a Specific Table (continued)

```
<H1>$host</h1>
<H2>$db</h2>
<H3>$table</h3>
<p>
<TABLE BORDER>
<CAPTION>Fields</caption>
<TR>
 <TH>Field<TH>Type<TH>Size<TH>NOT NULL
</tr>
<UL>
END_OF_HTML

# $table_data->name returns a referece to an array
# of the fields of the database.
my @fields = @{$table_data->NAME};
# $table_data->type return an array reference of the types of fields.
# The types returned here are in SQL standard notation, not MySQL specific.
my @types = @{$table_data->TYPE};
# $table_data->is_not_null returns a Boolean array ref indicating which fields
# have the 'NOT NULL' flag.
my @not_null = @{$table_data->is_not_null};
# $table_data->length return an array ref of the lengths of the fields. This is
# fixed for INT and REAL types, but variable (defined when the table was
# created) for CHAR.
my @length = @{$table_data->length};

# All of the above arrays were returned in the same order, so that $fields[0],
# $types[0], $not_null[0] and $length[0] all refer to the same field.

foreach $field (0..$#fields) {
        print "<TR>\n";
print "<TD>$fields[$field]<TD>$types[$field]<TD>";
        print $length[$field] if $types[$field] eq 'SQL_CHAR';
        print "<TD>";
        print 'Y' if ($not_null[$field]);
        print "</tr>\n";
}


print <<END_OF_HTML;
</table>
<p>
<B>Data</b><br>
<OL>
END_OF_HTML

# Now we step through the data, row by row, using DBI::fetchrow_array().
# We save the data in an array that has the same order as the informational
# arrays (@fields, @types, etc.) we created earlier.
while(my(@data)=$table_data->fetchrow_array) {
        print "<LI>\n<UL>";
        for (0..$#data) {
                print "<LI>$fields[$_] => $data[$_]</li>\n";
```

Example 10-3. The CGI tabledump.cgi Shows Information About a Specific Table (continued)

```
        }
        print "</ul></li>";
}

print <<END_OF_HTML;
</ol>
</body></html>
        END_OF_HTML
```

An Example DBI Application

DBI allows for the full range of SQL queries supported by MySQL and mSQL. As an example, consider a database used by a school to keep track of student records, class schedules, test scores, and so on. The database would contain several tables, one for class information, one for student information, one containing a list of tests, and a table for each test. MySQL and mSQL's ability to access data across tables—such as the table-joining feature—enables all of these tables to be used together as a coherent whole to form a teacher's aide application.

To begin with we are interested in creating tests for the various subjects. To do this we need a table that contains names and ID numbers for the tests. We also need a separate table for each test. This table will contain the scores for all of the students as well as a perfect score for comparison. The **test** table has the following structure:

```
CREATE TABLE test (
    id INT NOT NULL AUTO_INCREMENT,
    name CHAR(100),
    subject INT,
    num INT
)
```

The individual tests have table structures like this:

```
CREATE TABLE t7 (
    id INT NOT NULL,
    q1 INT,
    q2 INT,
    q3 INT,
    q4 INT,
    total INT
)
```

The table name is **t** followed by the test ID number from the **test** table. The user determines the number of questions when he or she creates the table. The total field is the sum of all of the questions.

The program that accesses and manipulates the test information is *test.cgi*. This program, which follows, allows only for adding new tests. Viewing tests and changing tests is not implemented but is left as an exercise. Using the other scripts in this chapter as a reference, completing this script should be only a moderate challenge. As it stands, this script effectively demonstrates the capabilities of DBI:[*]

```perl
#!/usr/bin/perl -w

use strict;
require my_end;

use CGI qw(:standard);
my $output = new CGI;
use_named_parameters(1);

# Use the DBI module.
use DBI;
# DBI::connect() uses the format 'DBI:driver:database', in our case we are
# using the MySQL driver and accessing the 'teach' database.
my $dbh = DBI->connect('DBI:mysql:teach');
```

The add action itself is broken up into three separate functions. The first function, add, prints out the template form for the user to create a new test.

```perl
sub add {
    $subject = param('subject') if (param('subjects'));
    $subject = "" if $subject eq 'all';

    print header, start_html('title'=>'Create a New Test',
        'BGCOLOR'=>'white');
    print <<END_OF_HTML;
<H1>Create a New Test</h1>
<FORM ACTION="test.cgi" METHOD=POST>
<INPUT TYPE=HIDDEN NAME="action" VALUE="add2">
Subject:
END_OF_HTML
    my @ids = ();
    my %subjects = ();
    my $out2 = $dbh->prepare("select id,name from subject order by name");
    $out2->execute;
    # DBI::fetchrow_array() is exactly analogous to Msql::fetchrow()
    while(my($id,$subject)=$out2->fetchrow_array) {
        push(@ids,$id);
        $subjects{"$id"} = $subject;
    }
    print popup_menu('name'=>'subjects',
        'values'=>[@ids],
        'default'=>$subject,
        'labels'=>\%subjects);
    print <<END_OF_HTML;
<br>
```

---

[*] This example is a MySQL example. Of course, the API is identical for mSQL. The only "glitch" is with sequence generation. Remember that where MySQL automatically generates the next ID for the test table because of the AUTO_INCREMENT keyword, mSQL expects you to create a sequence on the test table and SELECT the _seq value before doing your insert.

```
Number of Questions: <INPUT NAME="num" SIZE=5><br>
A name other identifier (such as a date) for the test:
 <INPUT NAME="name" SIZE=20>
<p>
<INPUT TYPE=SUBMIT VALUE=" Next Page ">
 <INPUT TYPE=RESET>
</form></body></html>
END_OF_HTML
}
```

This function displays a form allowing the user to choose a subject for the test along with the number of questions and a name. In order to print out a list of available subjects, the table of subjects is queried. When using a **SELECT** query with DBI, the query must first be prepared and then executed. The DBI::prepare function is useful with certain database servers which allow you to perform operations on prepared queries before executing them. With MySQL and mSQL however, it simply stores the query until the DBI::execute function is called.

The output of this function is sent to the **add2** function as shown in the following:

```
sub add2 {
    my $subject = param('subjects');
    my $num = param('num');
    $name = param('name') if param('name');

    my $out = $dbh->prepare("select name from subject where id=$subject");
    $out->execute;
    my ($subname) = $out->fetchrow_array;

    print header, start_html('title'=>"Creating test for $subname",
        'BGCOLOR'=>'white');
    print <<END_OF_HTML;
<H1>Creating test for $subname</h1>
<h2>$name</h2>
<p>
<FORM ACTION="test.cgi" METHOD=POST>
<INPUT TYPE=HIDDEN NAME="action" VALUE="add3">
<INPUT TYPE=HIDDEN NAME="subjects" VALUE="$subject">
<INPUT TYPE=HIDDEN NAME="num" VALUE="$num">
<INPUT TYPE=HIDDEN NAME="name" VALUE="$name">
Enter the point value for each of the questions. The points need not
add up to 100.
<p>
END_OF_HTML
    for (1..$num) {
        print qq%$_: <INPUT NAME="q$_" SIZE=3> %;
        if (not $_ % 5) { print "<br>\n"; }
    }
    print <<END_OF_HTML;
<p>
Enter the text of the test:<br>
<TEXTAREA NAME="test" ROWS=20 COLS=60>
</textarea>
```

```
<p>
<INPUT TYPE=SUBMIT VALUE="Enter Test">
 <INPUT TYPE=RESET>
</form></body></html>
END_OF_HTML
  }
```

In this function, a form for the test is dynamically generated based on the parameters entered in the last form. The user can enter the point value for each question on the test and the full text of the test as well. The output of this function is then sent to the final function, **add3**, as shown in the following:

```
sub add3 {
    my $subject = param('subjects');
    my $num = param('num');

    $name = param('name') if param('name');

    my $qname;
    ($qname = $name) =~ s/'/\\'/g;
    my $q1 = "insert into test (id, name, subject, num) values (
        '', '$qname', $subject, $num)";



    my $in = $dbh->prepare($q1);
    $in->execute;

    # Retrieve the ID value MySQL created for us
    my $id = $in->insertid;

    my $query = "create table t$id (
        id INT NOT NULL,
        ";

    my $def = "insert into t$id values ( 0, ";

    my $total = 0;
    my @qs = grep(/^q\d+$/,param);
    foreach (@qs) {
        $query .= $_ . " INT,\n";
        my $value = 0;
        $value = param($_) if param($_);
        $def .= "$value, ";
        $total += $value;
    }
    $query .= "total INT\n)";
    $def .= "$total)";

    my $in2 = $dbh->prepare($query);
    $in2->execute;
    my $in3 = $dbh->prepare($def);
    $in3->execute;
```

```
            # Note that we store the tests in separate files. This is
            # useful when dealing with mSQL because of its lack of BLOBs.
            # (The TEXT type provided with mSQL 2 would work, but
            # inefficently.)
            # Since we are using MySQL, we could just as well
            # stick the entire test into a BLOB.
            open(TEST,">teach/tests/$id") or die("A: $id $!");
            print TEST param('test'), "\n";
            close TEST;

            print header, start_html('title'=>'Test Created',
                'BGCOLOR'=>'white');
            print <<END_OF_HTML;
<H1>Test Created</h1>
<p>
The test has been created.
<p>
<A HREF=".">Go</a> to the Teacher's Aide home page.<br>
<A HREF="test.cgi">Go</a> to the Test main page.<br>
<A HREF="test.cgi?action=add">Add</a> another test.
</body></html>
END_OF_HTML
            }
```

Here we enter the information about the test into the database. In doing so we take a step beyond the usual data insertion that we have seen so far. The information about the test is so complex that each test is best kept in a table of its own. Therefore, instead of adding data to an existing table, we have to create a whole new table for each test. First we create an ID for the new test using MySQL auto increment feature and enter the name and ID of the test into a table called **test**. This table is simply an index of tests so that the ID number of any test can be quickly obtained. Then we simultaneously create two new queries. The first is a **CREATE TABLE** query which defines our new test. The second is an **INSERT** query that populates our table with the maximum score for each question. These queries are then sent to the database server, completing the process (after sending a success page to the user). Later, after the students have taken the test, each student will get an entry in the test table. Then entries can then be compared to the maximum values to determine the student's score.

Msql.pm

The *Msql.pm* module is the original Perl interface to mSQL. While it has been replaced by the DBI modules, there are still many sites that depend on this old interface. To illustrate the use of *Msql.pm*, we will continue the teacher's aide example.

Since we need classes in which to give the tests, let's examine the table of subjects. The table structure looks like this:

```
CREATE TABLE subject (
   id INT NOT NULL,
   name CHAR(500),
   teacher CHAR(100)
)

CREATE UNIQUE  INDEX idx1 ON subject (
        id,
        name,
        teacher
)

CREATE SEQUENCE ON subject
```

The `id` number is a unique identifier for the class, while the name and teacher fields are the name of the course and the name of the teacher respectively. There is also an index of all three of the fields that speeds up queries. Finally, we define a sequence for the table. The ID numbers are generated by this sequence.

The CGI program to access and manipulate this data must to several things.

- Search for a subject in the database.

- Show the subject that is the result of a search.

- Add a new subject to the database.

- Change the values of a subject in the database.

With the power of Perl and mSQL, we can easily consolidate all of these functions into one file, *subject.cgi*. We can do this by separating each operation into its own function. The main portion of the program will be a switchboard of sorts that directs incoming requests to the proper function. We will describe the actions themselves later.

```
# Each of the different parts of the script is selected via the
# 'action'
# parameter. If no 'action' is supplied, the default() function is
# called.
# Otherwise the appropriate function is called.
&default if not param('action');
# This trick comes from Camel 2 and approximates the 'switch'
# feature of C.
foreach[AO4] (param('action')) {
    /view/ and do { &view; last; };
    /add$/ and do { &add; last; };
    /add2/ and do { &add2; last; };
    /add3/ and do { &add3; last; };
    /add4/ and do { &add4; last; };
    /schange$/ and do { &schange; last; };
    /schange2/ and do { &schange2; last; };
```

```
/lchange$/ and do { &lchange; last; };
/lchange2/ and do { &lchange2; last; };
/lchange3/ and do { &lchange3; last; };
/delete/ and do { &delete; last; };
&default;
}
```

 The "add," "schange," and "lchange" entries must have an anchoring "$" in the regular expression so that they do not match the other functions similar to them. Without the "$", "add" would also match add2, add3 and add4. An alternative method would be to place "add," "schange," and "lchange" after the other functions. That way they would only be called if none of the others matched. However, this method could cause trouble if other entries are added later. A third method would be to completely disambiguate all of the entries using /^view$/, /^add$/, etc. This involves slightly more typing but removes all possibility of error.

Now all we have to do is fill in the details by implementing each function.

The `default` function prints out the initial form seen by the user. This is the form that allows the user to choose which action to perform. This function is called if the CGI program is accessed without any parameters, as with *http://www.myserver. com/teach/subject.cgi,* or if the ACTION parameter does not match any of the existing functions. An alternative method would be to create a function that prints out an error if the ACTION parameter is unknown.

```
sub default {
    print header, start_html('title'=>'Subjects','BGCOLOR'=>'white');
    print <<END_OF_HTML;
<h1>Subjects</h1>
<p>Select an action and a subject (if applicable).
<FORM ACTION="subject.cgi" METHOD=POST>
<p><SELECT NAME="action">
<OPTION VALUE="view">View a Subject
<OPTION value="add">Add a Subject
<OPTION value="schange">Modify a Subject
<OPTION value="lchange" SELECTED>Modify a Class List
<OPTION value="delete">Delete a Subject
</select>
END_OF_HTML
    # See 'sub print_subjects' below.
    &print_subjects;
    print <<END_OF_HTML;
<p>
<INPUT TYPE=SUBMIT VALUE=" Perform Action ">
<INPUT TYPE=RESET>
</form></body></html>
HTML

}
```

There are five main actions: "view," "add," "schange" (change the information about a subject), "lchange" (change the class list for a subject), and "delete". For illustration, we will examine the "add" action in detail here. The "add" action is broken up into four separate functions because interaction with the user is required up to four times. Hidden variables are used to pass information from form to form until the class is finally created.

The first add function generates the form used to enter the initial information about the class, including its name, the teacher's name, and the number of students in the class.

```perl
sub add {
   my (%fields);
   foreach ('name','size','teacher') {
      if (param($_)) { $fields{$_} = param($_); }
      else { $fields{$_} = ""; }
   }

   print header, start_html('title'=>'Add a Subject','BGCOLOR'=>'white');
   print <<END_OF_HTML;
<H1>Add a Subject</h1>
<form METHOD=POST ACTION="subject.cgi">
<p>
Subject Name: <input size=40 name="name" value="$fields{'name'}"><br>
Teacher's Name: <input size=40 name="teacher" value="$fields{'teacher'}"><br>
Number of Students in Class: <input size=5 name="size"
value="$fields{'size'}">
<p>
<INPUT TYPE=HIDDEN NAME="action" VALUE="add2">
<INPUT TYPE=SUBMIT VALUE=" Next Page ">
<INPUT TYPE=RESET>
</form>
<p>
<A HREF="subject.cgi">Go</a> back to the main Subject page.<br>
<A HREF=".">Go</a> to the Teacher's Aide Home Page.
</body></html>
END_OF_HTML

}
```

The function checks to see if any of the fields have preassigned values. This adds extra versatility to the function in that it can now be used as a template for classes with default values—perhaps generated by another CGI program somewhere.

The values from the first part of the add process are passed back to CGI program into the **add2** function. The first thing that **add2** does is check whether the class already exists. If it does, an error message is sent to the user and he or she can change the name of the class.

If the class does not already exist, the function checks how many students were entered for the class. If none were entered, the class is created without any students. The students can be added later. If the number of students was specified, the class is created and a form is displayed where the user can enter the information about each student.

```perl
sub add2 {
    ...
    my $name = param('name');
    # We need one copy of the name that is encoded for the URL.
    my $enc_name = &cgi_encode($name);
    # We also need a copy of the name that is quoted safely for insertion
    # into the database. Msql provides the Msql::quote() function for that
    # purpose.
    my $query_name = $dbh->quote($name);

    # We now build a query to see if the subject entered already exists.
    my $query =
        "select id, name, teacher from subject where name=$query_name";

    # If the user supplied a teacher's name, we check for that teacher
    # specifically, since there can be two courses with the same name but
    # different teachers.
    if (param('teacher')) {
        $teacher = param('teacher');
        $enc_teacher = &cgi_encode($teacher);
        my $query_teacher = $dbh->quote($teacher);
        $query .= " and teacher=$query_teacher";
    }

    # Now we send the query to the mSQL server.
    my $out = $dbh->query($query);
    # We check $out->numrows to see if any rows were returned. If
    # there were any, and the user didn't supply an 'override'
    # parameter, then we exit with a message that the class already
    # exists, and giving the user a change to enter the class anyway
    # (by resubmitting the form with the 'override' parameter set.
    if ($out->numrows and not param('override')) {
        # Print 'Class already exists' page.
        ...
    } else {
        # Now we enter the information into the database.
        # First, we need to select the next number from the
        # table's sequence.
        $out = $dbh->query("select _seq from subject");
        my ($id) = $out->fetchrow;

        # Then we insert the information into the database, using
        # the sequence number we just obtained as the ID.
        $query = "INSERT INTO subject (id, name, teacher)
            VALUES ($id, '$name', '$teacher')";
        $dbh->query($query);
```

```
            # If the user did not specify a class size, we exit with
            # a message letting the user know that he or she can add
            # students later.
            if (not param('size')) {
                # Print success page.
                ...
            } else {
                # Now we print a form, allowing the user to enter the
                # names of each of the students in the class.
                print header, start_html('title'=>'Create Class List',
                    'BGCOLOR'=>'white');
                print <<END_OF_HTML;
<H1>Create Class List</h1>
<P>
<B>$name</b> has been added to the database. You can
now enter the names of the students in the class.
You may add or drop students later from the
<a href="subject.cgi">main
Subject page</a>.
<p>
<FORM METHOD=POST ACTION="subject.cgi">
<INPUT TYPE=HIDDEN NAME="action" VALUE="add3">
<INPUT TYPE=HIDDEN NAME="id" VALUE="$id">
<TABLE BORDER=0>
<TR><TH><TH>First Name<TH>Middle Name/Initial
<TH>Last Name<TH>Jr.,Sr.,III,etc
</tr>
END_OF_HTML
                for $i (1..$size) {
                    print <<END_OF_HTML;
<TR><TD>$i<TD><INPUT SIZE=15 NAME="first$i"><TD><INPUT SIZE=15
NAME="middle$i">
                    <TD><INPUT SIZE=15 NAME="last$i"><TD><INPUT SIZE=5
NAME="ext$i"></tr>
END_OF_HTML

                }
                print <<END_OF_HTML;
</table>
<INPUT TYPE=SUBMIT VALUE=" Submit Class List ">
<INPUT TYPE=RESET>
</form></body></html>
END_OF_HTML

            }
        }
}
```

Note that the function used three copies of the name parameter. To use a variable as part of a URL, all special characters must be URL-escaped. A function called **cgi_encode** is provided with the code for this example which performs this operation. Secondly, to insert a string into the mSQL database, certain characters must be escaped. The MsqlPerl interface provides the function quote—accessible through any database handle—to do this. Finally, an unescaped version of the variable is used when displaying output to the user.

When adding the class to the database, mSQL's sequence feature comes in handy. Remember that a sequence was defined on the class table. The values of this sequence are used as the unique identifiers for each class. In this way two classes can have the same name (or same teacher, etc.) and still be distinct. This also comes in handy when modifying the class later. As long as the unique ID is passed from form to form, any other information about the class can safely be changed.

Finally, notice that the student entry form displayed by this function is dynamically generated. The number of students entered for the class is used to print out a form with exactly the right number of entries. Always remember that the CGI program has complete control over the generated HTML. Any part, including the forms, can be programmatically created.

If the user did not enter any students for the class, we are now finished. The user can use the change feature to add students later. However, if students were requested, the information about those students is passed onto the stage in the **add3** function, as shown in the following:

```
sub add3 {
    if (not param('id')) { &end("An ID number is required"); }
    my $id = param('id');

    my @list = &find_last_student;
    my ($ref_students,$ref_notstudents) =
&find_matching_students(@list);

    @students = @$ref_students if $ref_students;
    @notstudents = @$ref_notstudents if $ref_notstudents;

    if (@notstudents) {
        # Print form telling the user that there are nonexisting
        # students in the list. The user can then automatically create
        # the students or go back and fix any typos.
        ...
    } else {
        &update_students($id,@students);
        # Print success page.
        ...
    }
}
```

The bulk of this function's work is performed by other functions. This is because other parts of the CGI program have similar needs so it is efficient to factor the common code into shared functions. The first such function is `find_last_student`, which examined the form data and returns a list of the form numbers—the form numbers are not related to the ID numbers in the database—of each student entered by the user. This is necessary because, as mentioned earlier, the previous form is dynamically generated and there is no way to immediately know how many students are included.

```perl
sub find_last_student {
    my @params = param;
    my @list = ();
    foreach (@params) {
        next if not param($_); # Skip any 'empty' fields
        if (/^(first|middle|last|ext)(\d+)/) {
            my $num = $2;
            if (not grep(/^$num$/,@list)) { push(@list,$num); }
        }
    }
    @list = sort { $a <=> $b} @list;
    return @list;
}
```

Note that the function returns all of the numbers, not just the last number—which would presumably be the number of students entered. Even though the previous form printed out the number of entries the user requested, there is no guarantee that the user filled all of them out. He or she may have missed or skipped a row, which would not be included with the form data. Therefore, it is necessary to find out each number that was entered. The output of this function is then sent to the next "helper" function: `find_matching_students`, as shown in the following:

```perl
sub find_matching_students {
    my @list = @_;
    my ($i,@students,@notstudents);
    @students = ();
    @notstudents = ();
    if (@list) {
        foreach $i (@list) {
            my @query = ();
            # Build a query that looks for a specific student.
            my $query = "select id, subjects from student where ";
            foreach ('first','middle','last','ext') {
                if (param("$_$i")) {
                    my $temp = param("$_$i");
                    # Single quotes are the field delimiters for mSQL (and MySQL),
                    # so they must be preceded with the escape character "\",
                    # which is escaped itself so that it is interpreted literally.
                    $temp =~ s/'/\\'/g;
                    push(@query,"$_ = '$temp'");
                }
            }
            $query .= join(" and ",@query);

            # Send the query to the database.
            my $out = $dbh->query($query);
            # If the database doesn't return anything, add the
```

```
                     # student to the @notstudents array.
                     if (not $out->numrows) {
                         push(@notstudents,[ param("first$i"),
                         param("middle$i"),
                         param("last$i"), param("ext$i") ]);
                         # Otherwise add the student to the @students array.
                     } else {
                         my ($id,$subjects) = $out->fetchrow;
                         push(@students,[$id,$subjects]);
                     }
                 }
             }
         return(\@students,\@notstudents);
     }
```

This function goes through each of the given student names and checks the database to see if they already exist. If they do exist their information is stored in an array called **@students**, otherwise they are put in **@notstudents**. The information about each student is kept in an anonymous array, creating a student object of sorts. Finally the function returns references to both of the arrays. It cannot return the data as regular arrays because there would be no way to tell where one array ended and the other began.

The final helper function is **update_students**, which adds the class to each existing student's list of classes.

```
     sub update_students {
         my $id = shift;
         my @students = @_;
         foreach (@students) {
             my($sid,$subjects)=@$_;
             if (not $subjects) { $subjects = ":$id:"; }
             elsif ($subjects !~ /:$id:/) { $subjects .= "$id:"; }
             my $query = "update student set subjects='$subjects'
                 where id=$id";
             $dbh->query($query);
         }
     }
```

This function queries the **student** table, which is entirely separate from the **subject** table. Within a single CGI program, you can interact with any number of different tables within a database. You can even switch between databases, but you can only have one database selected at a time. This function retrieves the subject list for each given student and adds the new subject to their list if it is not there already.

At this point all contingencies are taken care of except for the case where the subject has students that do not already exist in the **student** table. For this case, the list of new students are sent to the **add4** function as shown in the following:

```
sub add4 {
        # Get list of @students and @notstudents
        &update_students($id,@students) if @students;
        &insert_students($id,@notstudents) if @notstudents;

        # Print success page.
}
```

This function separates the list of students into existing and nonexisting students using the same method as **add3**. It then updates the existing students using **update_students** shown earlier. Nonexisting students, shown in the following, are sent to the new helper function **insert_students**:

```
sub insert_students {
    foreach $i (@list) {
        # This selects the next number in the sequence defined on the
        # table. We then use this number as the ID of the student.
        my $out = $dbh->query('select _seq from student');
        my($sid) = $out->fetchrow;

        # We have to quote all of the text strings for inclusion
        # in the database.
        my ($first, $middle, $last, $ext) = (
            $dbh->quote(param("first$i")),
            $dbh->quote(param("middle$i")),
            $dbh->quote(param("last$i")),
            $dbh->quote(param("ext$i"))
        );
        my $query = "insert into student (id, first, middle, last,
            ext, subjects) VALUES ($sid, $first, $middle,
            $last, $ext, ':$id:')";
        $dbh->query($query);
    }
}
```

This function again accesses the **student** table rather than the **subject** table. An ID number for the new students is retrieved from the sequence defined on the **student** table, and then the student is inserted into the table using that ID.

MysqlPerl

Monty Widenius, the author of MySQL, also wrote the Perl interface to MySQL, *Mysql.pm*. This was based on the mSQL module, *Msql.pm*. Thus, the interfaces of the two modules are almost identical. In fact, we recently converted an entire site from mSQL to MySQL by running "perl -e 's/^Msql/Mysql/" *.cgi" in every directory containing a CGI. This covers 95% of the work involved. Of course, this does not give you any of the advantages of MySQL, but it is a quick and easy way to start down the road to MySQL. Mysql.pm is maintained as part of msql-mysql-modules by Jochen Wiedmann.

One of the largest differences between MySQL and mSQL is the way they handle sequences. In mSQL, a sequence is defined on a table with a command like CREATE SEQUENCE on *tablename*. The sequence value is then read as if it were a normal table value with the command SELECT _seq from *tablename*. MySQL adds the flag AUTO_INCREMENT to the primary key. Whenever a null value is inserted into this field, it is automatically incremented. Both MySQL and mSQL allow only one sequence per table. For a full discussion on sequences in MySQL and mSQL, see Chapter 6, *SQL According to MySQL and mSQL*.

As an example of some of the features of *Mysql.pm*, let's go back to the tests example. Now that we have *subject.cgi* taken care of, the next step is the table of student information. The structure of the students table is as follows:

```
CREATE TABLE student (
    id INT NOT NULL auto_increment,
    first VARCHAR(50),
    middle VARCHAR(50),
    last VARCHAR(50),
    ext VARCHAR(50),
    subjects VARCHAR(100),
    age INT,
    sex INT,
    address BLOB,
    city VARCHAR(50),
    state VARCHAR(5),
    zip VARCHAR(10),
    phone VARCHAR(10),
    PRIMARY KEY (id)
)
```

All of the information used by the *subject.cgi* program is in this table, as well as other information pertaining to the student. The program that handles this table, *student.cgi* must perform all of the functions that *subject.cgi* did for the subject table.

It is not possible to access a mSQL database with the *Mysql.pm* module, or MySQL with *Msql.pm*. The *student.cgi* program expects to find a MySQL version of the subjects table. Likewise, the *subject.cgi* program expects an mSQL version of the students table.

To illustrate the operation of *Mysql.pm*, we will examine in detail the portion of *student.cgi* that enables a user to change the information about a student. Just like the "add" action in the *Msql.pm* example was broken up into four separate functions, the "change" action here is separated into three individual functions.

The first function, change, prints out a form that allows the user to search for a student to change, as shown in the following:

```
sub change {
    print header, start_html('title'=>'Student Change Search',
        'BGCOLOR'=>'white');
    &print_form('search2','Search for a Student to Change',1);
    print <<END_OF_HTML;
<p>
<INPUT TYPE=HIDDEN NAME="subaction" VALUE="change2">
<INPUT TYPE=SUBMIT VALUE=" Search for Students ">
 <INPUT TYPE=SUBMIT NAME="all" VALUE=" View all Students ">
 <INPUT TYPE=RESET>
</form></body></html>
END_OF_HTML
}
```

The form used for searching for a student to "change" is so similar to the form used to searching for a student to "view" and the one to "add" a student that a single function, **print_form**, is used for all three purposes, as shown in the following:

```
sub print_form {
    my ($action,$message,$any) = @_;

    print <<END_OF_HTML;
<FORM METHOD=post ACTION="students.cgi">
<INPUT TYPE=HIDDEN NAME="action" VALUE="$action">
<H1>$message</h1>
END_OF_HTML
    if ($any) {
        print <<END_OF_HTML;
<p>Search for <SELECT NAME="bool">
<OPTION VALUE="or">any
<OPTION VALUE="and">all
</select> of your choices.
END_OF_HTML
    }
    print <<END_OF_HTML;
<p>
First: <INPUT NAME="first" SIZE=20>
 Middle: <INPUT NAME="middle" SIZE=10>
 Last: <INPUT NAME="last" SIZE=20>
 Jr./III/etc.: <INPUT NAME="ext" SIZE=5>
<br>
Address: <INPUT NAME="address" SIZE=40><br>
City: <INPUT NAME="city" SIZE=20>
 State: <INPUT NAME="state" SIZE=5>
 ZIP: <INPUT NAME="zip" SIZE=10><br>
Phone: <INPUT NAME="phone" SIZE=15><br>
```

```
Age: <INPUT NAME="age" SIZE=5> Sex: <SELECT NAME="sex">
END_OF_HTML
    if ($any) {
        print <<END_OF_HTML;
<OPTION VALUE="">Doesn't Matter
END_OF_HTML
    }
    print <<END_OF_HTML;
<OPTION VALUE="1">Male
<OPTION VALUE="2">Female
</select><br>
<p>
Enrolled in:<br>
END_OF_HTML
    &print_subjects("MULTIPLE SIZE=5");

}
```

By using three parameters, this function customizes a form template so that it can be used for several very different purposes. Notice that this helper function calls another helper function, `print_subjects`. This function queries the `subject` table as seen in the *Msql.pm* example and prints out a list of all of the available subjects.

```
sub print_subjects {
    my $modifier = "";
    $modifier = shift if @_;
    print qq%<SELECT NAME="subjects" $modifier>\n%;
    my $out = $dbh->query("select * from subject order by name");
    while(my(%keys)=$out->fetchhash) {
        print qq%<OPTION VALUE="$keys{'id'}">$keys{'name'}\n%;
    }
    print "</select>\n";
}
```

The search parameters entered in this first form are then sent to the `search2` function, which actually performs the search. This is actually the function written to search for a student to view. Since its function is exactly what we need, we can piggy-back off of it as long as we tell it that we want to go to the next change function, `change2`, after the search. That is why we have the hidden variable `subaction=change2` in the form. It tells `search2`, as shown in the following, where to send the user next:

```
sub search2 {
    my $out = $dbh->query(&make_search_query);
    my $hits = $out->numrows;
    my $subaction = "view";
    $subaction = param('subaction') if param('subaction');
    print header, start_html('title'=>'Student Search Result',
        'BGCOLOR'=>'white');
```

```
    if (not $hits) {
        print <<END_OF_HTML;
<H1>No students found</h1>
<p>
No students matched your criteria.
END_OF_HTML
    } else {
        print <<END_OF_HTML;
<H1>$hits students found</h1>
<p>
<UL>
END_OF_HTML
        while(my(%fields)=$out->fetchhash) {
            print qq%<LI>
<A HREF="students.cgi?action=$subaction&id=$fields{'id'}">$fields{'first'}
 $fields{'middle'} $fields{'last'}%;
            print ", $fields{'ext'}" if $fields{'ext'};
            print "\n</a>";
        }
    }
    print <<END_OF_HTML;
</ul>
<p>
<A HREF="students.cgi?action=search">Search</a> again.
</body></html>
END_OF_HTML
}
```

With help from the `make_search_query` function, this function first searches for students that match the search term. It then displays a list of the matches from which the user can select. The ID number of the selected entry is then sent to the `change2` function, as shown in the following:

```
sub change2 {
    my $out = $dbh->query("select * from student where id=$id");

    my($did,$first,$middle,$last,$ext,$subjects,$age,$sex,$address,
        $city,$state,$zip,$phone) = $out->fetchrow;

    my @subjects = split(/:/,$subjects);
    shift @subjects;
    my $name = "$first $middle $last";
    if ($ext) { $name .= ", $ext"; }

    print header, start_html('title'=>"$name",'BGCOLOR'=>'white');
    print <<END_OF_HTML;
<H1>$name</h1>
<p>
<FORM ACTION="students.cgi" METHOD=POST>
<INPUT TYPE=HIDDEN NAME="action" VALUE="change3">
<INPUT TYPE=HIDDEN NAME="id" VALUE="$id">
First: <INPUT NAME="first" VALUE="$first" SIZE=20>
Middle: <INPUT NAME="middle" VALUE="$middle" SIZE=10>
Last: <INPUT NAME="last" VALUE="$last" SIZE=20>
Jr./III/etc.: <INPUT NAME="ext" VALUE="$ext" SIZE=5>
```

```
<br>
Address: <INPUT NAME="address" VALUE="$address" SIZE=40><br>
City: <INPUT NAME="city" VALUE="$city" SIZE=20>
State: <INPUT NAME="state" VALUE="$state" SIZE=5>
ZIP: <INPUT NAME="zip" VALUE="$zip" SIZE=10><br>
Phone: <INPUT NAME="phone" VALUE="$phone" SIZE=15><br>
Age: <INPUT NAME="age" VALUE="$age" SIZE=5> Sex:
END_OF_HTML
        my %sexes = ( '1' => 'Male',
            '2' => 'Female'
        );
        print popup_menu('name'=>'sex',
            'values'=>['1','2'],
            'default'=>"$sex",
            'labels'=>\%sexes);
        print <<END_OF_HTML;
<p>
Enrolled in:<br>
END_OF_HTML
        my @ids = ();
        my %subjects = ();
        my $out2 = $dbh->query("select id,name from subject order by name");
        while(my($id,$subject)=$out2->fetchrow) {
            push(@ids,$id);
            $subjects{"$id"} = $subject;
        }
        print scrolling_list('name'=>'subjects',
            'values'=>[@ids],
            'default'=>[@subjects],
            'size'=>5,
            'multiple'=>'true',
            'labels'=>\%subjects);
        print <<END_OF_HTML;
<p>
<INPUT TYPE=SUBMIT VALUE=" Change Student ">
 <INPUT TYPE=SUBMIT NAME="delete" VALUE=" Delete Student ">
 <INPUT TYPE=RESET>
</form></body></html>
END_OF_HTML
}
```

The primary purpose of this function is to print out a form very similar to the one generated from **print_from**. However, the values of this form must have the values of the chosen student preinserted as default values. This way, the user can edit whichever fields of the student he or she wishes without changing the rest.

A couple of functions provided by the *CGI.pm* module come in very handy when printing form with default values. Most importantly, the function CGI::scrolling_ list prints out an HTML **<SELECT>** block with the parameters you provide. Among other parameters, the function takes the parameters values, default, and labels which are references to the values of each <OPTION> tag, the ones which should be preselected and the labels that user sees respectively.

The output of this function is a complete set of information, just as if it were coming from an add form. The difference is that the data is for a student which already exists in the database. The **change3** function accepts this data and updates the student, as shown in the following:

```perl
sub change3 {
    if (param('delete')) { &delete2($id); }
    else {
        my $query = "update student set ";
        my @query = ();
        foreach ('first', 'middle', 'last', 'ext', 'address', 'city',
            'state', 'zip', 'phone') {
            if (param($_)) { push(@query,"$_ = ".
                $dbh->quote(param($_)));
            }
        }
        push(@query,"age=".param('age')) if param('age');
        push(@query,"sex=".param('sex')) if param('sex');

        my $subjects = "':";
        $subjects .= join(":",param('subjects'));
        $subjects .= ":" unless $subjects eq "':";
        $subjects .= "'";
        push(@query,"subjects=$subjects");

        $query .= join(", ",@query) . " where id=$id";
        $dbh->query($query);

        print header, start_html('title'=>'Student Changed',
            'BGCOLOR'=>'white');
        # Print success form
        ...
    }
}
```

Note that if the user chose the "Delete" button on the change page, this function automatically passes the ball to the delete function. This is one major advantage of integrating several functions into one program. If no user interaction is required, you can skip from function to function without sending redirect messages to the user.

The rest of this function is fairly straightforward. The information about the student is gathered into an **UPDATE** query, which is sent to the MySQL server. A success page is then sent to the user.

11

Python

If you are not familiar with Python and you do a lot of Perl programming, you definitely want to take a look at it. Python is an object-oriented scripting language that combines the strengths of languages like Perl and Tcl with a clear syntax that lends itself to applications that are easy to maintain and extend. The O'Reilly & Associates, Inc. book *Learning Python* by Mark Lutz and David Asher provides an excellent introduction into Python programming. This chapter assumes a working understanding of the Python language, including the ability to add new modules into a Python installation.

The Python support for the MySQL and mSQL databases that we are exploring in this chapter comes in the form of two Python modules. At the time of this book's printing, the mSQL module was available at *http://www.python.org* and the MySQL module at *http://www.mysql.com*. While there are several other modules providing MySQL and mSQL access to Python applications, they—like these two—are mostly API variations on the MySQL and mSQL C APIs. You need to install one or both of these modules in order to access your database of choice and run the examples in this chapter.

Both APIs are virtually the same. We will, therefore, approach both modules together and note where they differ.

Basic Connectivity

The Python APIs are likely the simplest database APIs of any in this book. As with the other APIs, we need to start with database connectivity—making the connection. Because Python has an interactive interface, the simplest way to demonstrate a connection is by using the command line interpreter. The following two Python sessions demonstrate simple database connections to MySQL and mSQL, respectively. The first example shows MySQL connectivity:

```
[4:30pm] athens> python
Python 1.5.1 (#1, Jun 13 1998, 22:38:15)  [GCC 2.7.2] on sunos5
Copyright 1991-1995 Stichting Mathematisch Centrum, Amsterdam
>>> import MySQL;
>>> db = MySQL.connect('athens.imaginary.com');
>>> db.selectdb('db_test');
>>> result = db.do('select test_val from test where test_id = 1');
>>> print result;
[['This is a MySQL test.']]
>>>
```

The mSQL code that does the same thing looks nearly identical:

```
[4:30pm] athens> python
Python 1.5.1 (#1, Jun 13 1998, 22:38:15)  [GCC 2.7.2] on sunos5
Copyright 1991-1995 Stichting Mathematisch Centrum, Amsterdam
>>> import mSQL;
>>> db = mSQL.connect('athens.imaginary.com');
>>> db.selectdb('db_test');
>>> result = db.query('select test_val from test where test_id = 1');
>>> print result;
[('This is a mSQL test.',)]
>>>
```

In both cases, your first task is to import the appropriate Python module. You should not use the from mSQL import * syntax since this import will pollute the namespace of your application. Instead, you should get a database handle instance via the connect() method in each module and perform your database access through that database handle.

The connect() call for both APIs is similar, though not identical. In the previous MySQL session, we are connecting to a database that allows global access. Because no user name or password is required, the connect() call for the MySQL session looks similar to the call for the mSQL session. You can, however, specify user name and password arguments when required by your MySQL database. For example, db = MySQL.connect('athens.imaginary.com', 'myuid', 'password'); will connect you to the MySQL server at *athens. imaginary.com* as the user "myuid" using the password "password." Neither API even requires a host name if you are connecting to the local machine. In such situations, they are smart enough to use a Unix domain socket (on Unix systems) for quicker connectivity.

The C API connection process is a two step process that requires you first to connect to the server, and then select which database you want to use. The Python APIs follow the same steps. In fact, under both MySQL and mSQL, the APIs for selecting a database are practically identical: selectdb(). For most uses, you will only ever pass this method a single parameter—the database name. MySQL does support an optional second parameter that enables you to direct result set data storage to stay on the server until each row is requested. You would only want to use this version of the API when you are on a client where you know memory is limited or are retrieving unusually large result sets.

Queries

The two APIs differ slightly in the way you send statements to the database and how you deal with whatever you get back. The mSQL API is very simple with no support for cursor management. The MySQL API, on the other hand, supports the simple mSQL API along with a more complex set of APIs that more accurately mirror the C API and provide cursor support. In the Python world, cursor support is of dubious value since neither database allows in-place edits and the simpler API shown in the interactive sessions above allows you to navigate back and forth through a result set as easily as a cursor. We will, however, find a use for the cursor API later in the chapter because the same API that provides cursor support also gives us support for dynamic database access.

mSQL and the simple form of the MySQL API enable an application to query a database and get results in the form of a list. Unfortunately, the two APIs have two trivial, but annoying, differences in how you do this. First of all, the mSQL query method is called **query()** and the MySQL one is called **do()**. Each method accepts any SQL string as an argument. If the statement produces a result set, that result set is returned in the form of a list: a list of tuples for mSQL and a list of lists for MySQL.

For most uses, the difference in the return types is meaningless—tuples are immutable. The code will almost always appear the same. You should nevertheless be aware that MySQL rows are lists and mSQL rows are tuples in the event you encounter a situation where the difference is relevant. Example 11-1 is a simple Python program that accesses MySQL and mSQL databases and prints out the results.

Example 11-1. Query Processing in Python for mSQL and MySQL

```
#!/usr/local/bin/python

# Import the modules
import mSQL, MySQL;

# Initialize database and query values
database = 'db_test';
query = 'SELECT test_id, test_val FROM test';

# Connect to the servers
```

Example 11-1. Query Processing in Python for mSQL and MySQL (continued)

```
msql = mSQL.connect();
mysql = MySQL.connect();

# Select the test databases
msql.selectdb(database);
mysql.selectdb(database);

# Run the query
m_result = msql.query(query);
my_result = mysql.do(query);

# Process the results from mSQL
for row in m_result:
    # Here, row is a tuple
    print "mSQL- test_id: ",row[0]," | test_val: ",row[1];

# Process the results from MySQL
for row in my_result:
    # Here, row is a list
    print "MySQL- test_id: ",row[0]," | test_val: ",row[1];

# Close the connections (mSQL only)
msql.close();
```

For both the MySQL and mSQL databases, the application loops through each row from the result set and prints out its data. Under mSQL, the first element in the tuple represents the first column from the query and the second element the second column. Similarly, the first element in the MySQL list represents the first column from the query and the second element the second column.

Updates

Issuing an update, insert, or delete to the database uses the same API as queries—you just don't need any result set processing. In other words, call `query()` or `do()` and do nothing else. MySQL does have the added functionality of returning the AUTO_INCREMENT value of the table in question has an AUTO_INCREMENT field.

Dynamic Connectivity

The API we have discussed so far in the chapter is really all you need for the simple, but most common database access of every day select, insert, update, and delete calls. Some more complex applications, however, may require that you not know everything—or perhaps anything—about the database to which you are connecting and the statements you are sending to it. While both APIs support database-level meta-data—runtime information about the database to which you

are connected—only the MySQL API provides full support for dynamically generated SQL calls, including result set meta-data.

MySQL Statement Handlers

As we noted earlier, MySQL has two query processing tools. The simple form
returns a result set in the form of a list of lists. The more complex form returns a
statement handler.

A statement handler represents the results of a MySQL query handled via the
query() method (as opposed to using the do() method). Example 11-2 shows
how you can use the statement handler to generate runtime information about a
query or update.

Example 11-2. Dynamic Database Access Using a MySQL Statement Handler

```
[7:20pm] athens> python
Python 1.5.1 (#1, Jun 13 1998, 22:38:15)  [GCC 2.7.2] on sunos5
Copyright 1991-1995 Stichting Mathematisch Centrum, Amsterdam
>>> import MySQL;
>>> db = MySQL.connect();
>>> db.selectdb('db_test');
>>> result = db.query("INSERT INTO test(test_id,test_val) VALUES(4, 'Bing!')");
>>> print result.affectedrows();
1
>>> result = db.query("SELECT * FROM test");
>>> print result.numrows();
3
>>> print result.fields();
[['test_id', 'test', 'long', 11, 'notnull'], ['test_val', 'test', 'string',
100, '']]
>>> print result.fetchrows(-1);
[[1, 'This is a test.'], [2, 'This is a test.'], [4, 'Bing!']]
>>>
```

With the statement handler, you now have access to the number of rows affected
by an update, insert, or delete in addition to a set of data about result sets from
queries. In Example 11-2, we accessed the number of rows retrieved by a query
and detailed information about the columns represented in the result set.

Of the new methods introduced in Example 11-2, only fetchrows() is not self-
evident. This method fetches the next series of rows matching the number passed
to it. In other words, if you call result.fetchrows(2), a list of the next two
rows will be returned. This method will return a list of all rows—as in the example above—if you pass it a number less than 0. Combining this method with a call
to seek() enables you to move around a result set. The seek() method accepts
an integer parameter specifying which row you wish to work on where 0 represents the first row.

Database Meta-data

Though only the MySQL API supports dynamic result set management (at least at the time of publishing of this book), both APIs support database meta-data through a nearly identical set of methods. Database meta-data is basically information about a database connection. Example 11-3 shows a Python session that interrogates MySQL and mSQL connections about themselves.

Example 11-3. Data

```
[7:56pm] athens> python
Python 1.5.1 (#1, Jun 13 1998, 22:38:15)   [GCC 2.7.2] on sunos5
Copyright 1991-1995 Stichting Mathematisch Centrum, Amsterdam
>>> import mSQL, MySQL;
>>> msql = mSQL.connect();
>>> mysql = MySQL.connect();
>>> print msql.listdbs();
['db_test', 'db_web']
>>> print mysql.listdbs();
[['db_test'], ['mysql'], ['test']]
>>> msql.selectdb('db_test');
>>> mysql.selectdb('db_test');
>>> print msql.listtables();
['test', 'hosts']
>>> print mysql.listtables();
[['test']]
>>> print msql.serverinfo;
2.0.1
>>> print mysql.serverinfo();
3.21.17a-beta-log
>>> print mysql.clientinfo();
MySQL-Python-1.1
>>> print msql.hostname;
None
>>> print mysql.hostinfo();
Localhost via UNIX socket
>>> print mysql.stat();
Uptime: 4868410  Running threads: 1  Questions: 174  Reloads: 4  Open tables: 4
>>> print mysql.listprocesses();
None
>>>
```

In this example, we have a litany of method calls that provide extended information about database connections. In a couple of instances, mSQL provides this information via immutable attributes rather than methods. The MySQL API, on the other hand, provides a lot more information than does the mSQL one. See the reference section, Part III, *Reference*, for a full description of each of these methods and attributes.

12

PHP and Other Support for Database-driven HTML

Several easy-to-use program HTML extensions provide support for accessing MySQL and mSQL database servers within web pages. In this chapter, we will start with W3-mSQL—a mSQL-specific tool. We will then show how to take the more database-independent approach with PHP and two minor Perl extensions. The W3-mSQL scripting language, Lite, lets you embed entire programs into an HTML file. A CGI program executes the script and sends the result to the reader as a dynamically created HTML document.

Since W3-mSQL and the other extensions in this chapter use their own scripting languages and hide all evidence of CGI, knowledge of the previous chapters of this section is not necessary for this chapter. However, understanding how CGI works, as well as having some prior programming experience (Lite is similar to both C and Perl), can be useful when reading this chapter.

Alternatives for Dynamic Content on the Web

The World Wide Web's first encounter with what we now call Dynamic HTML was Server Side Includes (SSI). The idea behind SSI is that there are certain common values, such as the current date and time, that would be useful to include in an HTML page but impracticable because they change so often. SSI provided a method by which an HTML page could tell the server to insert a value into the HTML page before sending it to the end user. That way the value would always be current, but the creator of the page would not have to continuously update it. Within an HTML page, a typical SSI directive looks like this:

```
<!--#echo var="DATE_LOCAL" -->
```

The problem with SSI is that there is a very limited set of information that the server can easily provide. Once you get past date, time, and the ability to include other files there is not much else available without seriously bloating the web server itself.

It quickly became apparent that if the web server itself did not provide dynamic HTML, it could come from only two other sources. The client—that is, the web browser—could interpret the commands or some other program on the server machine could preprocess the commands, outputting plain HTML to the end users.

The first road is what led to JavaScript and other similar technologies. With JavaScript, as with SSI, commands are embedded within the HTML. Unlike SSI, the server does not touch JavaScript commands; instead, the web browser handles them. This method allows for much greater interaction with the user. For instance, using JavaScript you may specify that an action take place when the user moves the mouse over different parts of the screen. In this way, it becomes possible to create a feeling of immediacy and interactivity not otherwise possible. Following is an example of typical JavaScript code:

```
<SCRIPT>
<! onMouseOver("do the jig"); -->
</script>
```

The problem with client-side solutions, such as JavaScript, is that as soon as the client is finished downloading the page, the connection with the server is lost. Very often there are resources on the server machine, such as database servers, with which we would like to interact. However, with client-side scripting it is usually either impossible or impractical to communicate with the server or any other remote machine after the page has loaded. This type of functionality is best suited for a server side solution,.

With a server-side interpreter, an HTML document is examined before being sent to the end user. Some program, usually a CGI program, looks for and executes programming code embedded in the HTML. The advantage of this system is that you gain all of the power of a CGI program while hiding much of the complexity.

Consider a marine foundation that has a database containing information about sharks. This database has vital statistics of the various shark species, as well as filenames pointing to images of the creatures. Creating a web interface to this database is an ideal application of server-side interpreted HTML. All of the output pages containing information about a particular shark will be formatted similarly. In the few places where dynamic data from the database is required, commands can be inserted which will be executed before the user sees the page. You can even generate dynamic <IMG> tags that show the desired pictures. Later in the chapter we will look at how to implement this example using a variety of server-side interpreters.

W3-mSQL

W3-mSQL is actually a single CGI program called *w3-msql*. The program filters HTML pages that have embedded W3-mSQL commands and sends the resultant purified HTML to the client. W3-mSQL commands are written in a custom programming language called Lite. Lite is in many ways similar to Perl and C, but is specifically designed to interact with the mSQL database. A quick reference of Lite functions is included at the end of Chapter 18, *PHP and Lite Reference*. To accomplish this, the path of the W3-mSQL enhanced HTML file is added to the w3-msql URL, e.g. *http://www.me.com/cgi-bin/w3-msql/~me/mypage.html*.

Within the HTML file, anything within the `<!  >` tag is interpreted as Lite commands. For instance, the Lite equivalent of the "Hello world!" program would be:

```
<HTML><HEAD><TITLE>Hello world!</title></head>
<BODY>
<!
   echo("Hello world!");
>
</body></html>
```

Anything in the file that is not within `<!  >` tags is left as plain HTML.

mSQL installs the *w3-msql* program automatically, so all you should have to do is place it into your *cgi-bin* directory and you will be set to go.

W3-Auth

W3-Auth is a mechanism for providing security to W3-mSQL driven pages. It is included with W3-mSQL and is installed automatically along with mSQL. With W3-Auth you can create a hierarchy of users and groups that are allowed to use various W3-mSQL enhanced pages.

W3-Auth works on the idea of using three separate levels of security access: user, group, and area. A *user* is a single name that usually refers to a single person, much like usernames in Unix. A *group* is just a collection of users. An *area* is a section of your web site that you wish to protect.

This scheme is particularly useful for sites that use multiple virtual hosts on the same web server. For instance, let's say that your machine goes by the names *server1*, *server2*, and *server3*. A different group of people administers each of these different names. With W3-Auth you can set up usernames for each person, then set up groups for each site name. Finally, you can create three different areas encompassing the three sites. The members of each group would then be able to administer the permissions for their W3-mSQL enhanced page without being able to affect the other sites.

Installation

Both the W3-mSQL and W3-Auth programs are compiled and installed automatically with the mSQL distribution. After installation they can be found in *MSQL_ HOME/bin* where MSQL_HOME is the location of the mSQL files—*/usr/local/Hughes* by default. Both the *w3-msql* and *w3-auth* binaries should be copied to the *cgi-bin* directory or its equivalent of your web server.

Upon installation W3-Auth assumes that the *w3-msql* program and itself will be made available through the *cgi-bin* directory of your web site. If you wish to place these programs in another directory, you must manually modify the source code before installing mSQL. Using Perl, this may be done as follows. From the *src/w3-msql* directory of the mSQL distribution type *perl -pi -e 's/cgi-bin/yourcgidirectory/g' *.c.* Alternatively, the following shell script will do the job:

```
#!/bin/sh

# Run this from the src/w3-msql directory of your mSQL source distribution.

for file in 'ls *.c';
do
        sed -e "s/cgi-bin/$1/" $file > $file.tmp
        mv $file.tmp $file
done
```

Copy this script into your *src/w3-msql* directory and type the following:

```
./scriptname yourcgidirectory
```

Where *scriptname* is the name of the script and yourcgidirectory is the name of the directory that will hold the w3-msql and w3-auth binaries.

W3-Auth is currently incompatible with the distributed version of the Apache web server due to a minor security feature of Apache. Apache currently does not allow CGI programs to access authentication information. Without this ability, no CGI program (including W3-Auth) can display a standard username/password box to the user and retrieve the results. Because of the importance of Apache to the mSQL community, a patch was quickly released which allows W3-Auth to run with Apache. After applying this patch, you must recompile Apache. Note that applying this patch allows all CGI programs to retrieve username and password information from users browsing the site. Unless you do not trust the people with access to the CGI programs on your machine, this patch is relatively safe.

After you have installed mSQL, there is a script in the *misc* directory of your mSQL home called *setup_www*. Running this script creates the databases and tables needed to use W3-Auth on your machine. The script will create a username and password for a person with total control over W3-Auth. Once this script is finished, you can use W3-Auth itself to create and modify other permissions.

W3-mSQL Example

To illustrate the use of W3-mSQL and Lite, consider again the marine foundation. The foundation runs its own web site. On this web site is an interactive database containing information on the various species of sharks in the oceans. For our example, the user will first encounter a plain HTML page that contains a form. By choosing the values on the form, the user can search through the shark database to retrieve information about a specific species. The HTML form could look something like the following:

```
<HTML><HEAD><TITLE>SHARKS!</title></head>
<BODY BGCOLOR="white">
<h1>Search the shark database</h1>
<p>
<FORM METHOD=POST ACTION="/cgi-bin/w3-msql/~sharks/search_result.html">
Species: <SELECT NAME="species">
<OPTION>
<OPTION>Heterodontus Portusjackson
<OPTION>Galeocerdo Cuvier
<OPTION>Carcharodon Carcharias
<OPTION>Isurus Paucus
</select>
Age: <SELECT NAME="age">
<OPTION>
<OPTION>Young
<OPTION>Adult
<OPTION>Old
</select>
Location: <SELECT NAME="location">
<OPTION>
<OPTION>Atlantic
<OPTION>Pacific
<OPTION>Caribean
<select>
<p>
<INPUT TYPE="SUBMIT" VALUE=" SUBMIT "> <INPUT TYPE=RESET>
</form>
</body>
</html>
```

The mSQL containing the information about the sharks has the following structure:

```
+-----------------+----------+--------+----------+--------------+
|      Field      |   Type   | Length | Not Null | Unique Index |
+-----------------+----------+--------+----------+--------------+
| id              | int      | 100    | Y        | N/A          |
| species         | char     | 1000   | N        | N/A          |
| age             | int      | 2000   | N        | N/A          |
| location        | char     | 1000   | N        | N/A          |
+-----------------+----------+--------+----------+--------------+
```

The HTML file */~sharks/search_result.html* is a W3-mSQL enhanced file that retrieves the information about the requested species and displays an information file about that shark.

```
<HTML>
<HEAD><TITLE>Shark Search Result</title></head>
<BODY>
<H1>Here are the sharks that match your search...</h1>
<p>
<!
    $sock = msqlConnect();
    if ($sock < 0) {
        echo("Error : $ERRMSG\n");
        exit(1);
    }
    if (msqlSelectDB($sock,"sharks") < 0) {
        echo("Error : $ERRMSG\n");
        exit(1);
    }
    /* We now start to build the query. When finished, a typical query
     * will look something like this:
     * SELECT * FROM SHARK WHERE SPECIES='Isurus Paucus' AND AGE=2
     */
    $query = "select * from sharks ";

    if ($species || $age || $location) {
        $query += " where ";
    }

    if ($species) { $query += "species = '$species'"; }
    if ($age) {
        if ($species) { $query += " and "; }
        $query += "age = $age";
    }
    if ($location) {
        if ($species || $age) { $query += " and "; }
        $query += "location = '$location'";
    }
    if (msqlQuery($sock,$query) < 0) {
        echo("Error : $ERRMSG\n");
        exit(1);
    }
    $result = msqlStoreResult();
    $numresults = msqlNumRows($result);
>

<UL>

<!
    if (! $numresults ) {
        echo ("<H2>No results matched</h2>");
    else {
        $shark = msqlFetchRow($result);
        while (#$shark > 0) {
```

```
           $id = $shark[0];
           echo("<LI>");
           printf("<IMG SRC=\"graphics/shark%s.gif\" ALIGN=LEFT>", $shark[0]);
           echo("<B>Species:</b> $shark[1]<br>");
           if ($shark[2] == 1) { $age = "Young"; }
           else if ($shark[2] == 2) { $age = "Adult"; }
           else if {$shark[2] == 3) { $age = "Old"; }
           echo("<B>Age:</b> $age<br>");
           echo("<B>Location</b> $shark[3]<br>");
           $shark = msqlFetchRow($result);
       }
    }
>
</ul>
<A HREF="search.html">Search again</a>
</body></html>
```

Notice that the Lite code and the HTML can be arbitrarily intermixed. Anywhere that there is static HTML you can end the Lite code and enter just the HTML. This becomes particularly useful when you have a largely static page where some dynamic content is desired.

Also, notice that at one point in the page, a tag for an image of the current shark is generated using the ID number of the shark. This is a useful way to include information that is not conveniently stored in a database. Because of mSQL's inability to handle blobs, it is often useful to store pictures, other binary data, or even large amounts of text as plain files tagged with the unique ID of the database entry.

PHP

By its very nature, W3-mSQL is highly specialized for use with the mSQL database server. If you are using MySQL, or if your needs are not covered by W3-mSQL, there are other HTML preprocessors available that offer database support.

PHP, which stands for "PHP: Hypertext Preprocessor," is an application very similar to W3-mSQL in spirit. They are both CGI programs that interpret HTML before sending a final page to the browser. They both have their own built-in scripting language. Moreover, they both have tightly integrated database capabilities. However, PHP extends beyond the range of W3-mSQL by offering compatibility with several database servers, including both MySQL and mSQL.

PHP's scripting language is also more extensive, covering more possible applications than W3-mSQL. In short, you should use PHP unless you are definitely wedded to mSQL as a database server, in which case some of W3-mSQL's optimizations may suit you.

If you use PHP, the HTML example shown earlier which retrieve information from a shark database would now look as follows:

```
<HTML>
<HEAD><TITLE>Shark Search Result</title></head>
<BODY>
<H1>Here are the sharks that match your search...</h1>
<p>
<?
/* We now start to build the query. When finished, a typical query
 * will look something like this:
 * SELECT * FROM SHARK WHERE SPECIES='Isurus Paucus' AND AGE=2
 */

    $query = "select * from sharks where ";

    if ($species || $age || $location) {
        $query += " where ";
    }

    if ($species) { $query += "species = '$species'"; }
    if ($age) {
        if ($species) { $query += " and "; }
        $query += "age = $age";
    }
    if ($location) {
        if ($species || $age) { $query += " and "; }
        $query += "location = '$location'";
    }
    $result = msql("sharks",$query);
    if (result == -1) {
        echo("Error : $phperrmsg\n");
        exit(1);
    }
    $numresults = msql_numrows($result);
>

<UL>

<!
    if (! $numresults );
>
 <H2>No results matched</h2>
<!
    else {
        while ($i < $numresults) {
            $id[$i] = msql_result($result,$i,"id");
            $species[$i] = msql_result($result,$i,"species");
            $age[$i] = msql_result($result,$i,"age");
            $loc[$i] = msql_result($result,$i,"location");
            echo("<LI>");
            printf("<IMG SRC=\"graphics/shark%s.gif\" ALIGN=LEFT>", $id[$i]);
            echo("<B>Species:</b> $species[$i]<br>");
            if ($age[$i] == 1) { $age = "Young"; }
```

```
        else if ($age[$i] == 2) { $age = "Adult"; }
        else if {$age[$i] == 3) { $age = "Old"; }
        echo("<B>Age:</b> $age<br>");
        echo("<B>Location</b> $location[$i]<br>");
    }
}
>
</ul>
<A HREF="search.html">Search again</a>
</body></html>
```

Embedded Perl

Several Perl modules and related programs let you embed Perl code into an HTML document. A CGI program then executes this code before sending the final HTML file to the browser.

The most obvious advantage that these solutions have over W3-mSQL and PHP is that the scripting language used in the HTML file is regular Perl. Although they may be easy to learn and similar to C and Perl in style, Lite and the PHP scripting language are unique, proprietary languages that exist only for their one use. Perl, on the other hand, is virtually ubiquitous. It is a standardized programming language with years of bug elimination and extensive security features. There is a persuasive argument to using this sort of solution.

ePerl

The first application that allowed embedding Perl code within ASCII text, such as an HTML document, was ePerl. The ePerl program itself is written in C and is meant to be a general purpose Perl interpreter for ASCII documents. It works fine for HTML but does not have the HTML- or web-specific enhancements of some other packages.

EmbPerl

EmbPerl is a more recent creation than ePerl, which is more specifically focused on HTML and the web. There are additional "metacommands"—HTML style tags processed by EmbPerl—that allow flow control and other programming features within the HTML itself.

As an example of Perl code embedded within an HTML file, consider the shark database output form used earlier. We will use EmbPerl for our example, but since we are using a standard language (Perl) the code in the page would be nearly identical between the different Perl embedders.

```
<HTML>
<HEAD><TITLE>Shark Search Result</title></head>
<BODY>
<H1>Here are the sharks that match your search...</h1>
<p>
[-
    use Msql;
    use CGI qw(:standard);

    $dbh = Msql->connect;
    $dbh->selectdb("sharks");

    %age = ( '0' => 'Young',
             '1' => 'Adult',
             '2' => 'Old'
           );
    # We now start to build the query. When finished, a typical query
    # will look something like this:
    # SELECT * FROM SHARK WHERE SPECIES='Isurus Paucus' AND AGE=2

    $query = "select * from sharks where ";

    if ($species or $age or $location) {
        $query .= " where ";
        $query .= join(" and ", param);
    }

    $result = $dbh->query($query);
    if (result == -1) {
        echo("Error : " . Msql->errmsg . "\n");
        exit(1);
    }
    $numresults = $result->numrows;
-]

<UL>

[$if (! $numresults ) $]
 <H2>No results matched</h2>
[$else$]
    [$while (%shark = $Msql->fetchhash($result)) $]
       <LI>
       <IMG SRC="graphics/shark[+$shark{'id'}+].gif" ALIGN=LEFT>
       <B>Species:</b> [+$shark{'species'}+]<br>
       <B>Age:</b> [+$age{$shark{'age'}}+]<br>
       <B>Location</b> [+$shark{'location'}+]<br>
    [$endwhile$]
[$endif]
</ul>
<A HREF="search.html">Search again</a>
</body></html>
```

13

C and C++

In this book, we examine several different programming languages, Python, Java, Perl, and C. Of these languages, C/C++ is by far the most challenging. With the other languages, your primary concern is the formulation of SQL, the passing of that SQL to a function call, and the manipulation of the resulting data. C adds the very complex issue of memory management into the mix.

Both MySQL and mSQL provide C libraries that enable the creation of MySQL and mSQL database applications. In fact, MySQL derives its API very heavily from mSQL, meaning that experience programming against one API translates well to the next. As we explored in the first section, however, MySQL is much more feature-rich than mSQL. These extra features naturally result in a few differences between the two APIs. In this chapter, we will examine these differences while coming to understand the details of each API by building an object-oriented C++ API that can be conditionally compiled to run with either API.

The Two APIs

Whether you are using C or C++, the MySQL and mSQL C APIs are your gateway into the database. How you use them, however, can be very different depending on whether you are using C or the object-oriented features of C++. C database programming must be attacked in a linear fashion, where you step through your application process to understand where the database calls are made and where clean up needs to occur. Object-oriented C++, on the other hand, requires an OO interface into the API of your choice. The objects of that API can then take on some of the responsibility for database resource management.

Table 13-1 shows the function calls of each API side by side. We will go into the details of how these functions are used later in the chapter. Right now, you should just take a minute to see how the two APIs compare and note what is available to you. Naturally, the reference section lists each of these methods with detailed prototype information, return values, and descriptions.

Table 13-1. The C APIs for MySQL and mSQL

MySQL	mSQL
mysql_affected_rows( )	See msqlQuery()
mysql_close( )	msqlClose( )
mysql_connect( )	msqlConnect( )
myql_create_db( )	
mysql_data_seek( )	msqlDataSeek( )
mysql_drop_db( )	
mysql_eof( )	
mysql_error( )	
mysql_fetch_field( )	msqlFetchField( )
mysql_fetch_lengths( )	
mysql_fetch_row( )	msqlFetchRow( )
mysql_field_count( )	
mysql_field_seek( )	msqlFieldSeek( )
mysql_free_result( )	msqlFreeResult( )
mysql_get_client_info( )	
mysql_get_host_info( )	
mysql_get_proto_info( )	
mysql_get_server_info( )	
mysql_init( )	
mysql_insert_id( )	
mysql_list_dbs( )	msqlListDBs( )
mysql_list_fields( )	msqlListFields( )
	msqlListIndex( )
mysql_list_processes( )	
mysql_list_tables( )	msqlListTables( )
mysql_num_fields( )	msqlNumFields( )
mysql_num_rows( )	msqlNumRows( )
mysql_query( )	msqlQuery( )
mysql_real_query( )	
mysql_reload( )	
mysql_select_db( )	msqlSelectDB( )
mysql_shutdown( )	
mysql_stat( )	

Table 13-1. The C APIs for MySQL and mSQL (continued)

MySQL	mSQL
mysql_store_result( )	msqlStoreResult( )
mysql_use_result( )	

The MySQL API is much larger than the mSQL API in order to account for MySQL's extended feature set. In many cases, MySQL is actually only providing an API interface into database administration functions that are present in both database engines. By just reading the function names, you might have gathered that any database application you write might minimally look something like this:

1. Connect

2. Select DB

3. Query

4. Fetch row

5. Fetch field

6. Close

Example 13-1 shows a simple select statement that retrieves data from a MySQL database using the MySQL C API.

Example 13-1. A Simple Program that Selects All Data in a Test Database and Displays the Data

```
#include <sys/time.h>
#include <stdio.h>
#include <mysql.h>

int main(char **args) {
    MYSQL_RES *result;
    MYSQL_ROW row;
    MYSQL *connection, mysql;
    int state;

     /* connect to the mySQL database at athens.imaginary.com */
    mysql_init(&mysql);
    connection = mysql_real_connect(&mysql,
                                    "athens.imaginary.com",
                                    0, 0,
                                    "db_test", 0, 0);
    /* check for a connection error */
    if( connection == NULL ) {
        /* print the error message */
        printf(mysql_error(&mysql));
        return 1;
    }
    state = mysql_query(connection,
```

Example 13-1. A Simple Program that Selects All Data in a Test Database and Displays the Data (continued)

```
                          "SELECT test_id, test_val FROM test");
    if( state != 0 ) {
        printf(mysql_error(connection));
        return 1;
    }
    /* must call mysql_store_result() before we can issue any
     * other query calls
     */
    result = mysql_store_result(connection);
    printf("Rows: %d\n", mysql_num_rows(result));
    /* process each row in the result set */
    while( ( row = mysql_fetch_row(result)) != NULL ) {
        printf("id: %s, val: %s\n",
                (row[0] ? row[0] : "NULL"),
                (row[1] ? row[1] : "NULL"));
    }
    /* free the result set */
    mysql_free_result(result);
    /* close the connection */
    mysql_close(connection);
    printf("Done.\n");
}
```

Of the `#include` files, both *mysql.h* and *stdio.h* should be obvious to you. The *mysql.h* header contains the prototypes and variables required for MySQL, and *stdio.h* the prototype for `printf()`. The *sys/time.h* header, on the other hand, is not actually used by this application. It is instead required by the *mysql.h* header as the MySQL file uses definitions from *sys/time.h* without actually including it. To compile this program using the GNU C compiler, use the command line:

```
gcc -L/usr/local/mysql/lib -I/usr/local/mysql/include -o select select.c\
-lmysql -lnsl -lsocket
```

You should of course substitute the directory where you have MySQL installed for */usr/local/mysql* in the preceding code.

The `main()` function follows the steps we outlined earlier—it connects to the server, selects a database, issues a query, processes the result sets, and cleans up the resources it used. We will cover each of these steps in detail as the chapter progresses. For now, you should just take the time to read the code and get a feel for what it is doing. In addition, compare it to the same program written for mSQL shown in Example 13-2.[*]

---

[*] MySQL comes with a utility called msql2mysql which ostensibly converts any application written against the mSQL API to the MySQL API. It does provide a start at converting mSQL applications, but it leaves a bit of work to be done since MySQL requires extra arguments to some functions.

Example 13-2. The Simple Select Application for mSQL

```c
#include <sys/time.h>
#include <stdio.h>
#include <msql.h>

int main(char **args) {
    int connection, state;
    m_result *result;
    m_row row;

    /* connect to the mSQL database at athens.imaginary.com */
    state = msqlConnect("athens.imaginary.com");
    /* check for a connection error */
    if( state == -1 ) {
        /* print the error message stored in MsqlErrMsg */
        printf(msqlErrMsg);
        return 1;
    }
    else {
        /* the return balue from msqlConnect() is our connection handle */
        connection = state;
    }
    /* select which database to use on the server */
    state = msqlSelectDB(connection, "db_test");
    /* again, -1 means an error */
    if( state == -1 ) {
        printf(msqlErrMsg);
        /* close up our connection before exiting */
        msqlClose(connection);
        return 1;
    }
    state = msqlQuery(connection, "SELECT test_id, test_val FROM test");
    if( state == -1 ) {
        printf(msqlErrMsg);
        return 1;
    }
    else {
        printf("Rows: %d\n", state);
    }
    /* must call msqlStoreResult() before we can issue any
     * other Query() calls
     */
    result = msqlStoreResult();
    /* process each row in the result set */
    while( ( row = msqlFetchRow(result)) != NULL ) {
        printf("id: %s, val: %s\n",
                (row[0] ? row[0] : "NULL"),
                (row[1] ? row[1] : "NULL"));
    }
    /* free the result set */
    msqlFreeResult(result);
    /* close the connection */
    msqlClose(connection);
    printf("Done.\n");
}
```

The two programs are nearly identical. Other than name differences, there are only a few really dramatic distinguishing features. The most striking difference is the database connection. There are two main qualities of this difference:

- MySQL is a one-step connect process, where mSQL is a two step process.*

- MySQL looks for a user name and password. mSQL does not.

As we discussed earlier in the book, MySQL supports a complex level of user authentication with user name and password combinations. mSQL, on the other hand, has a simple authentication scheme based on the user ID of the process connecting to the database. The more robust MySQL scheme is much more desirable in a client/server environment, but it is also much harder to manage as an administrator. For application developers, the result is the need to pass a user name and password to the `mysql_real_connect()` call when using MySQL in addition to the basic server name used in mSQL.

The first argument of the connection API for MySQL is peculiar at first inspection. It is basically a way to track all calls not otherwise associated with a connection. For example, if you try to connect and the attempt fails, you need to get the error message associated with that failure. The MySQL `mysql_error()` function, however, requires a pointer to a valid MySQL connection. The null connection you allocate early on provides that connection. You must, however, have a valid reference to that value for the lifetime of your application—an issue of great importance in more structured environment than a straight "connect, query, close" application. The C++ examples later in the chapter will shed more light on this issue.

The other two major API distinctions lie in the way error handling is done and result set counting is done. The mSQL API creates a global variable that stores error messages. Because MySQL is multithreaded, such a global error variable would not function for its API. It, therefore, uses the `mysql_error()` function to retrieve error messages associated with the last error raised for the specified connection.

The connection API and error handling are two places where MySQL differs from mSQL in order to provide functionality not found in mSQL. Result set counting is done differently in mSQL in order to provide a better interface than MySQL

---

* MySQL does support a connection process that directly mirrors the mSQL connection process. If you want, you can use `mysql_connect()` followed by `mysql_select_db()` to make a connection along the mSQL model. Unless you are trying to quickly port an application from mSQL, however, `mysql_real_connect()` is really the proper way to make a connection.

provides. Specifically, when you send SQL to msqlQuery(), the number of affected rows is returned as the return value (or -1 if an error occurred). Counting affected rows for updates versus rows in a result set for queries thus uses the same paradigm. In MySQL, however, you have to use different paradigms for dealing with queries than with result sets. For queries, you pass the result set to mysql_num_rows() to get the number of rows in the result set. Updates, on the other hand, require you to call another API, mysql_affected_rows(). Where msqlQuery() provides the number of rows matched by the WHERE clause in an update, mysql_affected_rows() actually reports the number of changed rows. As a final note, mSQL does provide a msqlNumRows() method that provides the same interface for result set counting that MySQL provides. It does not provide a counterpart to mysql_affected_rows().

Object-oriented Database Access in C++

The C APIs work great for procedural C development. They do not, however, fit into the object-oriented world of C++ all that well. In order to demonstrate how these two APIs work in real code, we will spend the rest of the chapter using them to create a C++ API for object-oriented database development.

Because we are trying to illustrate MySQL and mSQL database access, we will focus on issues specific to MySQL and mSQL and not try to create the perfect general C++ API. In the MySQL and mSQL world, there are three basic concepts: the connection, the result set, and the rows in the result set. We will use these concepts as the core of the object model on which our library will be based. Figure 13-1 shows these objects in a UML diagram.*

The Database Connection

Database access in any environment starts with the connection. As you saw in the first two examples, MySQL and mSQL have two different ways of representing the same concept—a connection to the database. We will start our object-oriented library by abstracting on that concept and creating a Connection object. A Connection object should be able to establish a connection to the server, select the appropriate database, send queries, and return results. Example 13-3 is the header file that declares the interface for the Connection object.

---

* UML is the new Unified Modeling Language created by Grady Booch, Ivar Jacobson, and James Rumbaugh as a new standard for documenting the object-oriented design and analysis.

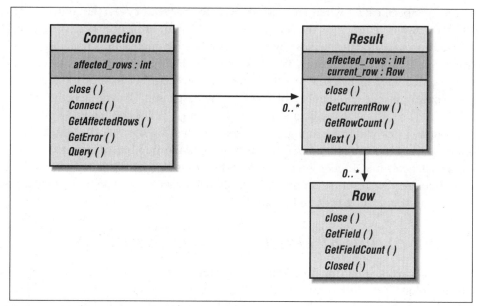

Figure 13-1. Object-oriented database access library

Example 13-3. The Connection Class Header

```
#ifndef l_connection_h
#define l_connection_h

#include <sys/time.h>

#if defined(HAS_MSQL)
#include <msql.h>
#elif defined(HAS_MYSQL)
#include <mysql.h>
#endif

#include "result.h"

class Connection {
private:
    int affected_rows;
#if defined(HAS_MSQL)
    int connection;
#elif defined(HAS_MYSQL)
    MYSQL mysql;
    MYSQL *connection;
#else
    #error No database defined.
#endif

public:
    Connection(char *, char *);
    Connection(char *, char *, char *, char *);
    ~Connection();
```

Example 13-3. The Connection Class Header (continued)

```
        void Close();
        void Connect(char *host, char *db, char *uid, char *pw);
        int GetAffectedRows();
        char *GetError();
        int IsConnected();
        Result *Query(char *);
};
```

```
#endif // 1_connection_h
```

The methods the `Connection` class will expose to the world are uniform no matter which database engine you use. Underneath the covers, however, the class will have private data members specific to the library you compile it against. For making a connection, the only distinct data members are those that represent a database connection. As we noted earlier, mSQL uses an `int` to represent a connection and MySQL uses a `MYSQL` pointer with an additional MYSQL value to handle establishing the connection.

Connecting to the database

Any applications we write against this API now need only to create a new `Connection` instance using one of the associated constructors in order to connect to the database. Similarly, an application can disconnect by deleting the `Connection` instance. It can even reuse a `Connection` instance by making direct calls to `Close()` and `Connect()`. Example 13-4 shows the implementation for the constructors and the `Connect()` method.

Example 13-4. Connecting to MySQL and mSQL Inside the Connection Class

```
#include "connection.h"

Connection::Connection(char *host, char *db) {
#if defined(HAS_MSQL)
    connection = -1;
#elif defined(HAS_MYSQL)
    connection = (MYSQL *)NULL;
#else
    #error No database linked.
#endif
    Connect(host, db, (char *)NULL, (char *)NULL);
}

Connection::Connection(char *host, char *db, char *uid, char *pw) {
#if defined(HAS_MSQL)
    connection = -1;
#elif defined(HAS_MYSQL)
    connection = (MYSQL *)NULL;
#else
    #error No database linked.
```

Example 13-4. Connecting to MySQL and mSQL Inside the Connection Class (continued)

```
#endif
    Connect(host, db, uid, pw);
}

void Connection::Connect(char *host, char *db, char *uid, char *pw) {
    int state;

    if( IsConnected() ) {
        throw "Connection has already been established.";
    }
#if defined(HAS_MSQL)
    connection = msqlConnect(host);
    state = msqlSelectDB(connection, db);
#elif defined (HAS_MYSQL)
    mysql_init(&mysql);
    connection = mysql_real_connect(&mysql, host,
                                    uid, pw,
                                    db, 0, 0);
#else
    #error No database linked.
#endif
    if( !IsConnected() ) {
        throw GetError();
    }
    if( state < 0 ) {
        throw GetError();
    }
}
```

The two constructors are clearly designed to support the different parameters required by MySQL and mSQL connections. The API, nevertheless, should allow for both constructors to work against either database. The API accomplishes this by ignoring the user ID and password when an application using a mSQL calls the 4-argument constructor. Similarly, null values are passed to MySQL for the user ID and password when the 2-argument constructor is called. The actual database connectivity occurs in the Connect() method.

The Connect() method encapsulates all steps required for a connection. For MySQL, it calls mysql_real_connect(). For mSQL, it instead calls msqlConnect() followed by msqlSelectDB(). If either step fails, Connect() throws an exception.

Disconnecting from the database

A Connection's other logic function is to disconnect from the database and free up the resources it has hidden from the application. This functionality occurs in the Close() method. Example 13-5 provides all of the functionality for disconnecting from MySQL and mSQL.

Example 13-5. Freeing up Database Resources

```
Connection::~Connection() {
    if( IsConnected() ) {
        Close();
    }
}

void Connection::Close() {
    if( !IsConnected() ) {
        return;
    }
#if defined(HAS_MSQL)
    msqlClose(connection);
    connection = -1;
#elif defined(HAS_MYSQL)
    mysql_close(connection);
    connection = (MYSQL *)NULL;
#else
    #error No database linked.
#endif
}
```

The `mysql_close()` and `msqlClose()` methods respectively free up the resources associated with connections to MySQL and mSQL.

Making Calls to the database

In between opening a connection and closing it, you generally want to send statements to the database. The `Connection` class accomplishes this via a `Query()` method that takes a SQL statement as an argument. If the statement was a query, it returns an instance of the `Result` class from the object model in Figure 13-1. If, on the other hand, the statement was an update, the method will return `NULL` and set the `affected_rows` value to the number of rows affected by the update. Example 13-6 shows how the `Connection` class handles queries against MySQL and mSQL databases.

Example 13-6. Querying the Database

```
Result *Connection::Query(char *sql) {
    T_RESULT *res;
    int state;

    // if not connectioned, there is nothing we can do
    if( !IsConnected() ) {
        throw "Not connected.";
    }
    // execute the query
#if defined(HAS_MSQL)
    state = msqlQuery(connection, sql);
#elif defined(HAS_MYSQL)
    state = mysql_query(connection, sql);
```

Example 13-6. Querying the Database (continued)

```
#else
    #error No database linked.
#endif
    // an error occurred
    if( state < 0 ) {
        throw GetError();
    }
    // grab the result, if there was any
#if defined(HAS_MSQL)
    res = msqlStoreResult();
#elif defined(HAS_MYSQL)
    res = mysql_store_result(connection);
#else
    #error No database linked.
#endif
    // if the result was null, it was an update or an error occurred
    // NOTE: mSQL does not throw errors on msqlStoreResult()
    if( res == (T_RESULT *)NULL ) {
        // just set affected_rows to the return value from msqlQuery()
#if defined(HAS_MSQL)
        affected_rows = state;
#elif defined(HAS_MYSQL)
        // field_count != 0 means an error occurred
        int field_count = mysql_num_fields(connection);

        if( field_count != 0 ) {
            throw GetError();
        }
        else {
            // store the affected_rows
            affected_rows = mysql_affected_rows(connection);
        }
#else
        #error No database linked.
#endif
        // return NULL for updates
        return (Result *)NULL;
    }
    // return a Result instance for queries
    return new Result(res);
}
```

The first part of a making-a-database call is calling either `mysql_query()` or `msqlQuery()` with the SQL to be executed. Both APIs return a nonzero on error. The next step is to call `mysql_store_result()` or `msqlStoreResult()` to check if results were generated and make those results usable by your application. At this point, the two database engines differ a bit on the processing details.

Under the mSQL API, `msqlStoreResult()` will not generate an error. This function is used by an application to move a newly generated result set into storage to be managed by the application instead of by the mSQL API. In other words, when you call msqlQuery(), it stores any results in a temporary area in memory managed by the API. Any subsequent call to msqlQuery() will wipe out that storage area. In order to store that result in an area of memory managed by your application, you need to call msqlStoreResult().

Because msqlStoreResult() does not generate an error, you need to worry about only two possibilities when you make an msqlStoreResult() call. If the call to the database was a query that generated a result set, msqlStoreResult() returns a pointer to an m_result structure to be managed by the application. For any other kind of call (an update, insert, delete, or create), msqlStoreResult() returns NULL. You can then find out how many rows were affected by a nonquery through the return value from the original msqlQuery() call.

Like the msqlStoreResult() call, mysql_store_result() is used to place the results generated by a query into storage managed by the application. Unlike the mSQL version, you need to wrapper mysql_store_result() with some exception handling. Specifically, a NULL return value from mysql_store_result() can mean either the call was a nonquery or an error occurred in storing the results. A call to mysql_num_fields() will tell you which is in fact the case. A field count not equal to zero means an error occurred. The number of affected rows, on the other hand, may be determined by a call to mysql_affected_rows().*

Other Connection behaviors

Throughout the Connection class are calls to two support methods, IsConnected() and GetError(). Testing for connection status is simple—you just check the value of the connection attribute. It should be non-NULL for MySQL and something other than -1 for mSQL. Error messages, on the other hand, require some explanation.

Retrieving error messages under mSQL is very simple and straightforward. You just use the value of the msqlErrMsg global variable. This value is exactly what our GetError() method returns for mSQL. MySQL, however, is a little more complicated. Being multithreaded, it needs to provide threadsafe access to any error messages. It manages to make error handling work in a multithreaded environment by hiding error messages behind the mysql_error() function. Example 13-7 shows MySQL and mSQL error handling in the GetError() method as well as connection testing in IsConnected().

---

* One particular situation behaves differently. MySQL is optimized for cases where you delete all records in a table. This optimization incorrectly causes some versions of MySQL to return 0 for a mysql_affected_rows() call.

Example 13-7. Reading Errors and Other Support Tasks of the Connection Class

```
int Connection::GetAffectedRows() {
    return affected_rows;
}

char *Connection::GetError() {
#if defined(HAS_MSQL)
    return msqlErrMsg;
#elif defined(HAS_MYSQL)
    if( IsConnected() ) {
        return mysql_error(connection);
    }
    else {
        return mysql_error(&mysql);
    }
#else
    #error No database linked.
#endif
}

int Connection::IsConnected() {
#if defined(HAS_MSQL)
    return !(connection < 0);
#elif defined(HAS_MYSQL)
    return !(!connection);
#else
    #error No database linked.
#endif
)
```

Error Handling Issues

While the error handling above is rather simple because we have encapsulated it into a simple API call in the Connection class, you should be aware of several potential pitfalls you can encounter. First, under mSQL, error handling is global to an application. For applications supporting multiple connections, the value of msqlErrMsg represents the last error from the most recent call to any mSQL API function. More to the point, even though mSQL itself is single threaded, you can write multithreaded applications against it—but you need to be very careful about how you manage access to error messages. Specifically, you will need to write your own threadsafe API on top of the mSQL C API that copies error messages and associates them with the proper connections.

Both database engines manage the storage of error messages inside their respective APIs. Because you have no control over that storage, you may run into another issue regarding the persistence of error messages. In our C++ API, we are handling the error messages right after they occur—before the application makes any other database calls. If we wanted to move on with other processing before dealing with an error message, we would need to copy the error message into storage managed by our application.

Result Sets

The `Result` class is an abstraction on the MySQL and mSQL result concepts. Specifically, should provide access to the data in a result set as well as the meta-data surrounding that result set. According to the object model from Figure 13-1, our `Result` class will support looping through the rows of a result set and getting the row count of a result set. Example 13-8 is the header file for the `Result` class.

Example 13-8. The Interface for a Result Class in result.h

```
#ifndef l_result_h
#define l_result_h

#include <sys/time.h>

#if defined(HAS_MSQL)
#include <msql.h>
#elif defined(HAS_MYSQL)
#include <mysql.h>
#endif

#include "row.h"

class Result {
private:
    int row_count;
    T_RESULT *result;
    Row *current_row;

public:
    Result(T_RESULT *);
    ~Result();

    void Close();
    Row *GetCurrentRow();
    int GetRowCount();
    int Next();
};

#endif // l_result_h
```

Navigating results

Our `Result` class enables a developer to work through a result set one row at a time. Upon getting a `Result` instance from a call to `Query()`, an application should call `Next()` and `GetCurrentRow()` in succession until `Next()` returns 0. Example 13-9 shows how this functionality looks for MySQL and mSQL.

Example 13-9. Result Set Navigation

```
int Result::Next() {
    T_ROW row;

    if( result == (T_RESULT *)NULL ) {
        throw "Result set closed.";
    }
#if defined(HAS_MSQL)
    row = msqlFetchRow(result);
#elif defined(HAS_MYSQL)
    row = mysql_fetch_row(result);
#else
    #error No database linked.
#endif
    if( !row ) {
        current_row = (Row *)NULL;
        return 0;
    }
    else {
        current_row = new Row(result, row);
        return 1;
    }
}

Row *Result::GetCurrentRow() {
    if( result == (T_RESULT *)NULL ) {
        throw "Result set closed.";
    }
    return current_row;
}
```

The *row.h* header file in Example 13-11 defines T_ROW and T_RESULT based on which database engine the application is being compiled for. The functionality for moving to the next row in both databases is identical and simple. You simple call `mysql_fetch_row()` or `msqlFetchRow()`. If the call returns NULL, there are no more rows left to process.

In an object-oriented environment, this is the only kind of navigation you should ever use. A database API in an OO world exists only to provide you access to the data—not as a tool for the manipulation of that data. Manipulation should be encapsulated in domain objects. Not all applications, however, are object-oriented applications. MySQL and mSQL each provides a function that allows you to move to specific rows in the database. These methods are `mysql_data_seek()` and `msqlDataSeek()` respectively.

Cleaning up and row count

Database applications need to clean up after themselves. In talking about the Connection class, we mentioned how the result sets associated with a query are moved into storage managed by the application. The Close() method in the

Result class frees the storage associated with that result. Example 13-10 shows how to clean up results and get a row count for a result set.

Example 13-10. Clean up and Row Count

```
void Result::Close() {
    if( result == (T_RESULT *)NULL ) {
        return;
    }
#if defined(HAS_MSQL)
    msqlFreeResult(result);
#elif defined(HAS_MYSQL)
    mysql_free_result(result);
#else
    #error No database linked.
#endif
    result = (T_RESULT *)NULL;
}

int Result::GetRowCount() {
    if( result == (T_RESULT *)NULL ) {
        throw "Result set closed.";
    }
    if( row_count > -1 ) {
        return row_count;
    }
    else {
#if defined(HAS_MSQL)
        row_count = msqlNumRows(result);
#elif defined(HAS_MYSQL)
        row_count = mysql_num_rows(result);
#else
        #error No database linked.
#endif
        return row_count;
    }
}
```

Rows

An individual row from a result set is represented in our object model by the Row class. The Row class enables an application to get at individual fields in a row. Example 13-11 shows the declaration of a Row class.

Example 13-11. The Row Class from row.h

```
#ifndef l_row_h
#define l_row_h

#include <sys/types.h>

#if defined(HAS_MSQL)
#include <msql.h>
```

Example 13-11. The Row Class from row.h (continued)

```
#define T_RESULT m_result
#define T_ROW     m_row
#elif defined(HAS_MYSQL)
#include <mysql.h>
#define T_RESULT MYSQL_RES
#define T_ROW     MYSQL_ROW
#endif

class Row {
private:
    T_RESULT *result;
    T_ROW fields;

public:
    Row(T_RESULT *, T_ROW);
    ~Row();

    char *GetField(int);
    int GetFieldCount();
    int IsClosed();
    void Close();
};

#endif // l_row_h
```

Both APIs have macros for datatypes representing a result set and a row within
that result set. In both APIs, a row is really nothing more than an array of strings
containing the data from that row. Access to that data is controlled by indexing on
that array based on the query order. For example, if your query was SELECT
user_id, password FROM users, then index 0 would contain the user ID and
index 1 the password. Our C++ API makes this indexing a little more user friendly.
GetField(1) will actually return the first field, or fields[0]. Example 13-12
contains the full source listing for the Row class.

Example 13-12. The Implementation of the Row Class

```
#include <malloc.h>

#include "row.h"

Row::Row(T_RESULT *res, T_ROW row) {
    fields = row;
    result = res;
}

Row::~Row() {
    if( !IsClosed() ) {
        Close();
    }
}
```

Example 13-12. The Implementation of the Row Class (continued)

```cpp
void Row::Close() {
    if( IsClosed() ) {
        throw "Row closed.";
    }
    fields = (T_ROW)NULL;
    result = (T_RESULT *)NULL;
}

int Row::GetFieldCount() {
    if( IsClosed() ) {
        throw "Row closed.";
    }
#if defined(HAS_MSQL)
    return msqlNumFields(result);
#elif defined(HAS_MYSQL)
    return mysql_num_fields(result);
#else
    #error No database linked.
#endif
}

// Caller should be prepared for a possible NULL
// return value from this method.
char *Row::GetField(int field) {
    if( IsClosed() ) {
        throw "Row closed.";
    }
    if( field < 1 || field > GetFieldCount() ) {
        throw "Field index out of bounds.";
    }
    return fields[field-1];
}

int Row::IsClosed() {
    return (fields == (T_ROW)NULL);
}
```

An example application using these C++ classes is packaged with the examples from this book.

14

Java and JDBC

In Chapter 13, *C and C++*, we introduced you to the C APIs for MySQL and mSQL. Unfortunately, each API only enables you to program for the database it supports. If you are looking to port an application between MySQL and mSQL, or even worse, if you are looking to make an application work on Oracle or Sybase or any other database engine, you must rewrite your database code to make use of that database engine's proprietary API. Java programmers, however, are mostly freed from database portability issues. They have a single API, the Java DataBase Connectivity API (JDBC), that provides them with a unified interface into all SQL databases.

Because JDBC is a single interface to all databases, you need only to learn it in order to be able to write applications that run on both MySQL and mSQL. In fact, as long as you write proper JDBC code, the Java applications you write will be able to run against any database engine. If you have access to a database other than MySQL or mSQL, you should give this claim a test by running this chapter's examples on that database.

In this chapter, we are assuming a basic understanding of the Java programming language and Java concepts. If you do not already have this background, we strongly recommend taking a look at *Exploring Java* (O'Reilly & Associates, Inc.). For more details on how to build the sort of three-tier database applications we discussed in Chapter 8, *Database Application Architectures*, take a look at *Database Programming with JDBC and Java* (O'Reilly & Associates, Inc.).

What Is JDBC?

Like all Java APIs, JDBC is a set of classes and interfaces that work together to support a specific set of functionality. In the case of JDBC, this functionality is naturally database access. The classes and interfaces that make up the JDBC API are thus abstractions from concepts common to database access for any kind of database. A `Connection`, for example, is a Java interface representing a database connection. Similarly, a `ResultSet` represents a result set of data returned from a SQL `SELECT` statement. Java puts the classes that form the JDBC API together in the `java.sql` package which Sun introduced in JDK 1.1.

The details of database access naturally differ from vendor to vendor. JDBC does not actually deal with those details. Most of the classes in the `java.sql` package are in fact interfaces—and thus no implementation details. Individual database vendors provide implementations of these interfaces in the form of something called a JDBC driver. As a database programmer, however, you need to know only a few details about the driver you are using—the rest you manage via the JDBC interfaces. The vendor specific information you need in order to use JDBC includes:

- The JDBC URL for the driver
- The name of the class that implements `java.sql.Driver`

 The new JDBC 2.0 specification adds an optional standard extension API for vendors to implement. If your JDBC vendor implements this standard extension, you do not even need to know the JDBC URL or `Driver` class implementation. It prescribes a `DataSource` class that you can look up by a configurable name in a JNDI*-supported directory.

Both of these items can be supplied at runtime, either on the command line or in a properties file. Your code never needs to mention these two implementation-dependent pieces. We will cover what the JDBC URL and `Driver` class do in a few paragraphs when we cover database connections. Figure 14-1 diagrams the interfaces of JDBC.

The Database Connection

Your first step is to connect to the database. One of the few implementation classes in the `java.sql.package` is the `DriverManager` class. It maintains a list of JDBC implementations and provides you with database connections based on JDBC URLs you provide it. A JDBC URL comes in the form of *jdbc:protocol:subprotocol*. It tells a `DriverManager` which database engine you wish to connect to and it provides the `DriverManager` with enough information to make a connection.

---

* JNDI is the Java Naming and Directory Interface API. It lets you store Java objects in a naming and directory service like an Lightweight Directory Access Protocol (LDAP) server and then look them up by name.

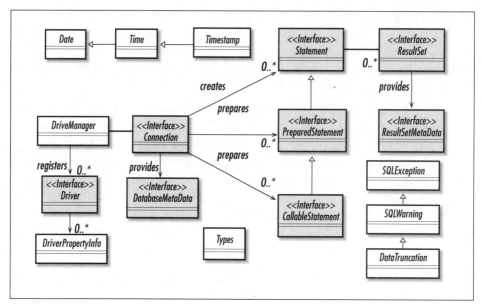

Figure 14-1. The classes and interfaces of the JDBC API

 JDBC uses the word "driver" in multiple contexts. In the lower-case sense, a JDBC driver is the collection of classes that together implement all of the JDBC interfaces and provide an application with access to at least one database. In the upper-case sense, the `Driver` is the class that implements `java.sql.Driver`. Finally, JDBC provides a `DriverManager` that can be used to keep track of all of the different `Driver` implementations.

The protocol part of the URL refers to a given JDBC driver. In the case of MySQL and mSQL, the protocol is *mysql* and *msql*, respectively. The subprotocol provides the implementation-specific connection data. Both MySQL and mSQL require a host name and database name in order to make a connection. Optionally, they may require a port if your database engine is not running as root. The full mSQL URL therefore looks like: *jdbc:msql://athens.imaginary.com:1114/test.* It says that the `DriverManager` should find the mSQL JDBC driver and connect to the database test at *athens.imaginary.com* on port 1114. All of this is done via a single call to the `DriverManager getConnection()` method. Example 14-1 shows how to make a connection to an mSQL database.

Example 14-1. A Code Snippet from the Examples that Come with the Imaginary JDBC Driver for mSQL Showing How to Make a Connection

```
import java.sql.*;

public class Connect {
    public static void main(String argv[]) {
        Connection con = null;

        try {
            // here is the JDBC URL for this database
            String url = "jdbc:msql://athens.imaginary.com:1114/db_test";
            // more on what the Statement and ResultSet classes do later
            Statement stmt;
            ResultSet rs;

            // either pass this as a property, i.e.
            // -Djdbc.drivers=com.imaginary.sql.msql.MsqlDriver
            // or load it here like we are doing in this example
            Class.forName("com.imaginary.sql.msql.MsqlDriver");
            // here is where the connection is made
            con = DriverManager.getConnection(url, "borg", "");
        }
        catch( SQLException e ) {
            e.printStackTrace();
        }
        finally {
            if( con != null ) {
                try { con.close(); }
                catch( Exception e ) { }
            }
        }
    }
}
```

The line `con = DriverManager.getConnection(url, "borg", "")` makes the database connection in this example. In this case, the JDBC URL and `Driver` implementation class names are actually hard coded into this application. The only reason this is acceptable is because this application is a demo for the mSQL-JDBC driver. For a serious application, you would want to load this information from a properties file, pass it as command line arguments, or pass it as system properties. The `Driver` implementation will automatically be loaded if you pass it as the system property *jdbc.drivers*—in other words, you do not have to call `Class.forName().newInstance(driver_name)` when you pass the driver name as the *jdbc.drivers* system property. The second and third arguments to `getConnection()` are the user ID and password to use for the connection. Because mSQL does not use passwords for user authentication, this example just uses an empty string. In MySQL, however, you will need to provide a password.*

---

* MySQL actually has several JDBC drivers. At least one of them allows you to specify the user ID and password as part of the URL.

Maintaining Portability Using Properties Files

Though our focus is on two specific databases, it is good Java programming practice to make your applications completely portable. To most people, portability
means that you do not write code that will run on only one platform. In the Java
world, however, the word "portable" is a much stronger term. It means no hardware resource dependencies, and that means no database dependencies.

We discussed how the JDBC URL and **Driver** name are implementation dependent, but we did not discuss how to avoid hard coding them. Because both are
simple strings, you can pass them on the command line as runtime arguments or
as parameters to applets. While that solution works, it is hardly elegant since it
requires command line users to remember long command lines. A similar solution
might be to prompt the user for this information; but again, you are requiring that
the user remember a JDBC URL and a Java class name each time they run an
application.

A more elegant solution than either of the above solutions would be to use a
properties file. Properties files are supported by the `java.util.ResourceBundle`
and its subclasses to enable an application to extract runtime specific information
from a text file. For a JDBC application, you can stick the URL and **Driver** name in
the properties file, leaving the details of the connectivity up to an application administrator. Example 14-2 shows a properties file that provides connection information.

Example 14-2. The SelectResource.properties File with Connection Details for a Connection

```
Driver=com.imaginary.sql.msql.MsqlDriver
URL=jdbc:msql://athens.imaginary.com:1114/db_test
```

Example 14-3 shows the portable **Select** class.

Example 14-3. Specific Information

```java
import java.sql.*;
import java.util.*;

public class Connect {
    public static void main(String argv[]) {
        Connection con = null;
        ResourceBundle bundle = ResourceBundle.getBundle("SelectResource");

        try {
            String url = bundle.getString("URL");
            Statement stmt;
            ResultSet rs;

            Class.forName(bundle.getString("Driver"));
            // here is where the connection is made
            con = DriverManager.getConnection(url, "borg", "");
        }
```

Example 14-3. Specific Information (continued)

```
        catch( SQLException e ) {
            e.printStackTrace();
        }
        finally {
            if( con != null ) {
                try { con.close(); }
                catch( Exception e ) { }
            }
        }
    }
}
```

We have gotten rid of anything specific to mSQL in the sample connection code. One important issue still faces portable JDBC developers—one that stings mSQL developers in particular. JDBC requires any driver to support SQL2 entry level. This is an ANSI standard for minimum SQL support. As long as you use SQL2 entry level SQL in your JDBC calls, your application will be 100% portable to other database engines. Unfortunately, while MySQL is SQL2 entry level, mSQL is not. Applications you write for mSQL will very likely port to other databases without issue, but applications written to use the full range of SQL92 entry level will not port back to mSQL without pain.

Simple Database Access

The Connect example did not do much. It simply showed you how to connect to a database. A database connection is useless unless you actually talk to the database. The simplest forms of database access are SELECT, INSERT, UPDATE, and DELETE statements. Under the JDBC API, you use your database Connection instance to create Statement instances. A Statement naturally represents any kind of SQL statement. Example 14-4 shows how to insert a row into a database using a Statement.

Example 14-4. Inserting a Row into mSQL Using a JDBC Statement Object

```
import java.sql.*;
import java.util.*;

public class Insert {
    // We are inserting into a table that has two columns: test_id (int)
    // and test_val (char(55))
    // args[0] is the test_id and args[1] the test_val
    public static void main(String argv[]) {
        Connection con = null;
        ResourceBundle bundle = ResourceBundle.getBundle("SelectResource");

        try {
            String url = bundle.getString("URL");
```

Example 14-4. Inserting a Row into mSQL Using a JDBC Statement Object (continued)

```
            Statement stmt;

            Class.forName(bundle.getString("Driver"));
            // here is where the connection is made
            con = DriverManager.getConnection(url, "borg", "");
            stmt = con.createStatement();
            stmt.executeUpdate("INSERT INTO test (test_id, test_val) " +
                               "VALUES(" + args[0] + ", '" + args[1] + "')");
        }
        catch( SQLException e ) {
            e.printStackTrace();
        }
        finally {
            if( con != null ) {
                try { con.close(); }
                catch( Exception e ) { }
            }
        }
    }
}
```

If this were a real application, we would of course verified that the user entered an INT for the test_id, that it was not a duplicate key, and that the test_val entry did not exceed 55 characters. This example nevertheless shows how simple performing an insert is. The createStatement() method does just what it says: it creates an empty SQL statement associated with the Connection in question. The executeUpdate() method then passes the specified SQL on to the database for execution. As its name implies, executeUpdate() expects SQL that will be modifying the database in some way. You can use it to insert new rows as shown earlier, or instead to delete rows, update rows, create new tables, or do any other sort of database modification.

Queries are a bit more complicated than updates because queries return information from the database in the form of a ResultSet. A ResultSet is an interface that represents zero or more rows matching a database query. A JDBC Statement has an executeQuery() method that works like the executeUpdate() method— except it returns a ResultSet from the database. Exactly one ResultSet is returned by executeQuery(), however, you should be aware that JDBC supports the retrieval of multiple result sets for databases that support multiple result sets. Neither MySQL or mSQL support multiple result sets. It is nevertheless important for you to be aware of this issue in case you are ever looking at someone else's code written against another database engine. Example 14-5 shows a simple query. Figure 14-2 shows the data model behind the test table.

Example 14-5. A Simple Query

```java
import java.sql.*;
import java.util.*;

public class Select {
    public static void main(String argv[]) {
        Connection con = null;
        ResourceBundle bundle =
                ResourceBundle.getBundle("SelectResource");

        try {
            String url = bundle.getString("URL");
            Statement stmt;
            ResultSet rs;

             Class.forName(bundle.getString("Driver"));
            // here is where the connection is made
            con = DriverManager.getConnection(url, "borg", "");
            stmt = con.createStatement();
            rs = stmt.executeQuery("SELECT * from test ORDER BY test_id");
            System.out.println("Got results:");
            while(rs.next()) {
                int a= rs.getInt("test_id");
                String str = rs.getString("test_val");

                System.out.print(" key= " + a);
                System.out.print(" str= " + str);
                System.out.print("\n");
            }
            stmt.close();
        }
        catch( SQLException e ) {
            e.printStackTrace();
        }
        finally {
            if( con != null ) {
                try { con.close(); }
                catch( Exception e ) { }
            }
        }
    }
}
```

The `Select` application executes the query and then loops through each row in the `ResultSet` using the `next()` method. Until the first call to `next()`, the `ResultSet` does not point to any row. Each call to `next()` points the `ResultSet` to the subsequent row. JDBC 2.0 introduces the concept of a scrollable result set. If your `ResultSet` instance is set to be scrollable, you can also make calls to `previous()` to navigate backwards through the results. You are done processing rows when `next()` returns `false`.

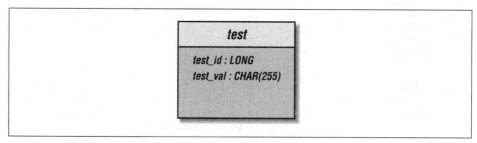

Figure 14-2. The test table from the sample database

Dealing with a row means getting the values for each of its columns. Whatever the value in the database, you can use the getter methods in the `ResultSet` to retrieve the column value as whatever Java datatype you like. In the `Select` application, the call to `getInt()` returned the `test_id` column as an `int` and the call to `getString()` returned the `test_val` column as a `String`. These getter methods accept either the column number—starting with column 1—or the column name. You should, however, avoid retrieving values using a column name at all costs since retrieving results by column name is many, many times slower than retrieving them by column number.

Error Handling and Clean Up

All JDBC method calls can throw `SQLException` or one of its subclasses if something happens during a database call. Your code should be set up to catch this exception, deal with it, and clean up any database resources that have been allocated. Each of the JDBC classes mentioned so far has a `close()` method associated with it. Practically speaking, however, you only really need to make sure you close things whose calling process might remain open for a while. In the examples we have seen so far, you only really need to close your database connections. Closing the database connection closes any statements and result sets associated with it automatically. If you intend to leave a connection open for any period of time, however, it is a good idea to go ahead and close the statements you create using that connection when you finish with them. In the JDBC examples you have seen, this clean up happens in a finally clause. You do this since you want to make sure to close the database connection no matter what happens.

Dynamic Database Access

So far we have dealt with applications where you know exactly what needs to be done at compile time. If this were the only kind of database support that JDBC provided, no one could ever write tools like the *mysql* and *msql* interactive command line tools that determine SQL calls at runtime and execute them. The JDBC

`Statement` class provides the `execute()` method for executing SQL that may be either a query or an update. Additionally, `ResultSet` instances provide runtime information about themselves in the form of an interface called `ResultSetMetaData` which you can access via the `getMetaData()` call in the `ResultSet`.

Meta Data

The term meta data sounds officious, but it is really nothing other than extra data about some object that would otherwise waste resources if it were actually kept in the object. For example, simple applications do not need the name of the columns associated with a `ResultSet`—the programmer probably knew that when the code was written. Embedding this extra information in the `ResultSet` class is thus not considered by JDBC's designers to be core to the functionality of a `ResultSet`. Data such as the column names, however, is very important to some database programmers—especially those writing dynamic database access. The JDBC designers provide access to this extra information—the meta data—via the `ResultSetMetaData` interface. This class specifically provides:

- The number of columns in a result set

- Whether **NULL** is a valid value for a column

- The label to use for a column header

- The name for a given column

- The source table for a given column

- The datatype of a given column

Another example class that comes with the mSQL-JDBC driver is the **Exec** application. It will accept any SQL you specify on a command line and execute it. Example 14-6 shows that source code.

Example 14-6. The Source to the Exec Application for Executing Dynamic SQL

```
import java.sql.*;

public class Exec {
    public static void main(String args[]) {
        Connection con = null;
        String sql = "";

        for(int i=0; i<args.length; i++) {
            sql = sql + args[i];
            if( i < args.length - 1 ) {
                sql = sql + " ";
            }
        }
        System.out.println("Executing: " + sql);
        try {
```

Example 14-6. The Source to the Exec Application for Executing Dynamic SQL (continued)

```
    Class.forName("com.imaginary.sql.msql.MsqlDriver").newInstance();
    String url = "jdbc:msql://athens.imaginary.com:1114/db_test";
    con = DriverManager.getConnection(url, "borg", "");
    Statement s = con.createStatement();

    if( s.execute(sql) ) {
        ResultSet r = s.getResultSet();
        ResultSetMetaData meta = r.getMetaData();
        int cols = meta.getColumnCount();
        int rownum = 0;

        while( r.next() ) {
            rownum++;
            System.out.println("Row: " + rownum);
            for(int i=0; i<cols; i++) {
                System.out.print(meta.getColumnLabel(i+1) + ": "
                                 + r.getObject(i+1) + ", ");
            }
            System.out.println("");
        }
    }
    else {
        System.out.println(s.getUpdateCount() + " rows affected.");
    }
    s.close();
    con.close();
}
catch( Exception e ) {
    e.printStackTrace();
}
finally {
    if( con != null ) {
        try { con.close(); }
        catch( SQLException e ) { }
    }
}
```

Each result set provides a `ResultSetMetaData` instance via the `getMetaData()` method. In the case of dynamic database access, we need to find out the how many columns are in a result set so that we are certain to retrieve each column as well as the names of each of the columns for display to the user. The meta data for our result set provides all of this information via the `getColumnCount()` and `getColumnLabel()` methods.

Processing Dynamic SQL

The concept introduced in Example 14-6 is the dynamic SQL call. Because we do not know whether we will be processing a query or an update, we need to pass the SQL call through the `execute()` method. This method returns `true` if the statement returned a result set or `false` if none was produced. In the example, if it returns `true`, the application gets the returned `ResultSet` through a call to `getResultSet()`. The application can then go on to do normal result set processing. If, on the other hand, the statement performed some sort of database modification, you can call `getUpdateCount()` to find out how many rows were modified by the statement.

A Guest Book Servlet

You have probably heard quite a bit of talk about Java applets. We discussed in Chapter 8, however, how doing database access in the client is a really bad idea. We have packaged with the examples in this book an example that contains a real application that uses the JDBC knowledge we have discussed in this chapter to create a server-side Java class known as a servlet. While servlets are not in themselves part of the three-tier solution we discussed in Chapter 8, this example should provide a useful example of how JDBC can be used. The servlet in question is a web page that lets people visiting your site enter comments about it. Others can then view these comments. For this example, all you need to know about servlets is that the `doPost()` method handles HTTP POST events and `doGet()` handles HTTP GET events.

There are two pieces to this servlet: the get and the post. In both pieces, a call is made to `printComments()` to show the comments in the guest book. In this method, we encounter something we have not yet seen in the previous simple examples, a call to `wasNull()` after each column value is retrieved. As its name implies, `wasNull()` returns `true` if the last value fetched was SQL NULL. For calls returning a Java object, the value will generally be NULL when a SQL NULL is read from the database. In these instances, `wasNull()` may appear somewhat redundant. For primitive datatypes, however, a valid value may be returned on a fetch. The `wasNull()` method gives you a way to see if that value was NULL in the database. For example, a NULL for an integer column will return 0 when you call `getInt()`. In order to know whether or not the column held 0 or NULL, you must call `wasNull()`.

III

Reference

This section provides reference materials for all of the APIs and tools we have covered in this book.

15

SQL Reference

MySQL SQL

ALTER/MODIFY

```
ALTER [IGNORE] TABLE table ADD [COLUMN] create_clause
ALTER [IGNORE] TABLE table ADD INDEX [name] (column, . . .)
ALTER [IGNORE] TABLE table ADD UNIQUE [name] (column, . . . .)
ALTER [IGNORE] TABLE table ALTER [COLUMN] column SET DEFAULT value
ALTER [IGNORE] TABLE table ALTER [COLUMN] column DROP DEFAULT
ALTER [IGNORE] TABLE table CHANGE [COLUMN] column create_clause
ALTER [IGNORE] TABLE table DROP [COLUMN] column
ALTER [IGNORE] TABLE table DROP FOREIGN KEY key
ALTER [IGNORE] TABLE table DROP INDEX key
ALTER [IGNORE] TABLE table DROP PRIMARY KEY
ALTER [IGNORE] TABLE table MODIFY [COLUMN] create_clause
ALTER [IGNORE] TABLE table RENAME [AS] new_name
```

The ALTER statement covers a wide range of actions that modify the structure of a table. This statement is used to add, change, or remove columns from an existing table as well as to remove indexes. Multiple ALTER statements may be combined into one using commas as in the following example:

```
ALTER TABLE mytable DROP myoldcolumn, ADD mynewcolumn INT
```

To perform modifications on the table, MySQL creates a copy of the table and changes it, meanwhile queuing all table altering queries. When the change is done, the old table is removed and the new table put it its place. At this point the queued queries are performed. As a safety precaution, if any of the queued queries create duplicate keys that should be unique, the ALTER statement is rolled back and cancelled. If the IGNORE keyword is present in the statement, duplicate unique keys are ignored and the ALTER statement proceeds as if normal. Be warned that using IGNORE on an active table with unique keys is inviting table corruption.

As mentioned earlier, there are several different, often orthogonal, actions performed by ALTER:

ADD [COLUMN] *create_clause*
> Inserts a new column into the table. The create_clause is of the same type as used by the CREATE statement (see later). The table must already exist and must not have a column with the same name as the new one. (The COLUMN keyword is optional and has no effect.)

ADD INDEX [*name*] (*column*, ...)
> Creates an index out of the given columns. Up to 15 columns may be combined in an index. Naming an index is optional. If no name is given, the index will be named after the first column listed (with a numerical suffix _2, _3, etc., for uniqueness if necessary).

ADD UNIQUE [*name*] (*column*, ...)
> Is identical to ADD INDEX except that the values of the indexed columns are guaranteed to be unique. That is, if a user attempts to add a value that already exists to a unique index, an error will be returned.

ALTER [COLUMN] *column* SET DEFAULT *value*
ALTER [COLUMN] *column* DROP DEFAULT
> Creates, modifies or deletes the default value of a column. When the SET DEFAULT phrase is used, the default value of the column is set to the new value (even if no default previously existed). When DROP DEFAULT is used, any existing default value is removed. If the default is dropped, any existing rows that were created with the default value are left untouched. (The COLUMN keyword is optional and has no effect.)

CHANGE [COLUMN] *new_column_name create_clause*
MODIFY [COLUMN] *create_clause*
> Alters the definition of a column. This statement is used to change a column from one type to a different type while affecting the data as little as possible. The create clause is a full clause as specified in the CREATE statement. This includes the name of the column. Because of this, you change the name of the column using this statement. (For example, ALTER TABLE mytable CHANGE name newname CHAR(30)). The MODIFY version is the same as CHANGE if the new column has the same name as the old. The COLUMN keyword is optional and has no effect. The following conversions are done automatically:
>
> — Integer to Floating Point, and vice versa (e.g., BIGINT to DOUBLE).
>
> — Smaller numerical value to larger numerical value (e.g., INTEGER to BIGINT).

— Larger numerical value to smaller numerical value (e.g., DOUBLE to FLOAT). If a value is beyond the limits of the new type, the highest (or greatest negative) possible value of the new type is used instead.

— Numerical to character (e.g., SMALLINT to CHAR(5)).

— Character to numerical (e.g., VARCHAR to MEDIUMINT). Either integer or floating point conversion is performed upon the text (whichever is appropriate for the new type).

— Smaller character to larger character (e.g., BLOB to LONGTEXT).

— Larger character to smaller character (e.g., TEXT to VARCHAR(255)). If a value is longer than the limits of the new type, the text is truncated to fit the new type.

— Even for conversions that are not mentioned here (e.g., TIMESTAMP to YEAR), MySQL will try its best to perform a reasonable conversion. Under no circumstance will MySQL give up and return an error when using this statement; a conversion of some sort will always be done. With this in mind you should (1) make a backup of the data before the conversion and (2) immediately check the new values to see if they are reasonable.

DROP [COLUMN] *column*

Deletes a column from a table. This statement will remove a column and all of its data from a table permanently. There is no way to recover data destroyed in this manner other than from backups. All references to this column in indices will be removed. Any indices where this was the sole column will be destroyed as well. (The COLUMN keyword is optional and has no effect.)

DROP INDEX *key*

Removes an index from a table. This statement will completely erase an index from a table. This statement will not delete or alter any of the table data itself, only the index data. Therefore, an index removed in this manner can be recreated using the ALTER TABLE ... ADD INDEX statement.

DROP PRIMARY KEY

Identical to DROP INDEX except that it looks for the special index known as the Primary Key. If no Primary Key is found in the table, the first unique key is deleted.

RENAME [AS] *new_table*

Changes the name of the table. This operation does not affect any of the data or indices within the table, only the table's name. If this statement is performed alone, without any other ALTER TABLE clauses, MySQL will not create a temporary table as with the other clauses, but simply perform a fast Unix-level rename of the table files.

The FOREIGN KEY operation is currently not implemented in MySQL. While the syntax is there, attempting an action on a FOREIGN KEY will do nothing.

To perform any of the ALTER TABLE actions, you must have SELECT, INSERT, DELETE, UPDATE, CREATE, and DROP privileges for the table in question.

Examples

```
# Add the field 'address2' to the table 'people' and make it of type
'VARCHAR'
# with a maximum length of 200.
ALTER TABLE people ADD COLUMN address2 VARCHAR(100)
# Add two new indexes to the 'hr' table, one regular index for the 'salary'
# field and one unique index for the 'id' field. Also, continue operation if
# duplicate values are found while creating the 'id_idx' index (very
dangerous!).
ALTER TABLE hr ADD INDEX salary_idx ( salary )
ALTER IGNORE TABLE hr ADD UNIQUE id_idx ( id )
# Change the default value of the 'price' field in the 'sprockets' table to
# $19.95.
ALTER TABLE sprockets ALTER price SET DEFAULT '$19.95'
# Remove the default value of the 'middle_name' field in the 'names' table.
ALTER TABLE names ALTER middle_name DROP DEFAULT
# Change the type of the field 'profits' from its previous value (which was
# perhaps INTEGER) to BIGINT.
ALTER TABLE finanaces CHANGE COLUMN profits profits BIGINT
# Remove the 'secret_stuff' field from the table 'not_private_anymore'
ALTER TABLE not_private_anymore DROP secret_stuff
# Delete the named index 'id_index' as well as the primary key from the
# table 'cars'.
ALTER TABLE cars DROP INDEX id_index, DROP PRIMARY KEY
# Rename the table 'rates_current' to 'rates_1997'
ALTER TABLE rates_current RENAME AS rates_1997
```

CREATE

```
CREATE DATABASE dbname
CREATE TABLE name ( field_name field_type, ... )
CREATE INDEX name ON table ( column, ... )
CREATE FUNCTION name RETURNS values SONAME library
```

Creates new database elements (or entirely new databases). This statement is used to create databases, tables, and user defined functions (UDFs).

The CREATE INDEX statement is provided for compatibility with other implementations of SQL. In older versions of SQL this statement does nothing. As of 3.22, this statement is equivalent to the ALTER TABLE ADD INDEX statement. To perform the CREATE INDEX statement, you must have INDEX privileges for the table in question.

The CREATE DATABASE statement creates an entirely new, empty database. This is equivalent to running the mysqladmin create utility. As with running mysqladmin, you must be the administrative user for MySQL (usually root or mysql) to perform this statement.

The CREATE FUNCTION statement allows MySQL statements to access precompiled executable functions. These functions can perform practically any operation, since they are designed and implemented by the user. The return value of the function can be STRING, for character data; REAL, for floating point numbers; or INTEGER for integer numbers. MySQL will translate the return value of the C function to the indicated type. The library file that contains the function must be a standard shared library that MySQL can dynamically link into the server.

The CREATE TABLE statement defines the structure of a table within the database. This statement is how all MySQL tables are created. This statement consists of the name of the new table followed by any number of field definitions. The syntax of a field definition is the name of the field followed by its type, followed by any modifiers (e.g., name char(30) not null). MySQL supports the following datatypes, as shown in Table 15-1.

Table 15-1. Datatypes

Type	Size (in bytes)	Comments
TINYINT(*length*) / INT1(*length*)	1	Integer with unsigned range of 0-255 and signed range of -128-127.
SMALLINT(*length*) / INT2(*length*)	2	Integer with unsigned range of 0-65535 and signed range of -32768-32767.
MEDIUMINT(*length*) / INT3(*length*) / MIDDLEINT(*length*)	3	Integer with unsigned range of 0-16777215 and signed range of -8388608-8388607.
INT(*length*) / INTEGER(*length*) / INT4(*length*)	4	Integer with unsigned range of 0-4294967295 and signed range of -2147483648-2147483647.
BIGINT(*length*) / INT8(*length*)	8	Integer with unsigned range of 0-18446744-7370955165 and signed range of -9223372036854775808-9223372036854775807.
FLOAT / FLOAT(4) / FLOAT(*length, decimal*) / FLOAT4(*length, decimal*)	4	Floating point number with maximum value +/-3.402823466E38 and minimum (non-zero) value +/-1.175494351E-38.
DOUBLEPRECISION (*length, decimal*) / DOUBLE(*length, decimal*) / REAL(*length, decimal*) / FLOAT8(*length, decimal*) / FLOAT(8)	8	Floating point number with maximum value +/-1.7976931348623157E308 and minimum (non-zero) value +/-2.2250738585072014E-308.

Table 15-1. Datatypes (continued)

Type	Size (in bytes)	Comments
DECIMAL(*length*, *decimal*)/ NUMERIC(*length*, *decimal*)	length	Floating point number with the range of the DOUBLE type that is stored as a CHAR field. DECIMAL and NUMERIC are always treated as CHAR fields that just happen to contain a numeric value.
TIMESTAMP(*length*)	4	A timestamp value that updates every time the row is modified. You may also assign a value to field manually. Assigning a NULL value sets the field to the current time. The (optional) length field determines the output formatting of the statement. A length of 14 (the default) produces a string of the form 'YYYYMMDDHHMMSS', 12 gives 'YYMMDDHHMMSS', eight produces 'YYYYMMDD' and six gives 'YYMMDD'.
DATE	3	A date value that stores the year, month and date. Values are always output with the format 'YYYY-MM-DD', but may be entered in any of the following formats: 'YY-MM-DD', 'YYYY-MM-DD', 'YYMMDD', or 'YYYYMMDDHHMSS' (the time portion is ignored).
TIME	3	A time value that stores the hour, minute and second. Values are always output with the format 'HH:MM:SS' but may be entered in any of the following formats: 'HH:MM:SS', 'HHMMSS', 'HHMM' (seconds are set to 0), or 'HH' (minutes and seconds are set to 0).
DATETIME	8	A value that stores both the date and the time. Values are both input and output as 'YYYY-MM-DD HH:MM:SS'.
YEAR	1	A value that stores the year. Values can be input in either the 'YYYY' or 'YY' format and will be output as two- or four-digit years depending on the input format. Two digit years are assumed to lie between 1970 and 2069, inclusive. This type currently only understands years within the range of 1901 to 2155.

Table 15-1. Datatypes (continued)

Type	Size (in bytes)	Comments
CHAR(*length*) / BINARY(*length*)	length	A fixed length text string. Any input that is shorter than the length is padded with spaces at the end. All trailing spaces, whether inserted by MySQL or not, are removed when outputting values. MySQL treats text as case-insensitive by default (see the BINARY modifier, below). The BINARY type is equivalent to CHAR with the BINARY modifier.
CHAR(*length*) VARYING/ VARCHAR(*length*) / VARBINARY(*length*)	length	A variable length text string (case-insensitive) with a predefined maximum length. The maximum length must be between 1 and 255 characters. Any trailing spaces are removed before storing data of this type. The VARBINARY type is equivalent to VARCHAR with the BINARY modifier.
TINYTEXT	length+1	A text field (case-insensitive) with a maximum length of 255 characters.
TINYBLOB	length+1	A binary field (case-sensitive) with a maximum length of 255 characters. Binary data is case-sensitive.
TEXT/LONG VARCHAR	length+2	A text field with a maximum length of 64KB of text.
BLOB/LONG VARBINARY	length+2	A binary field with a maximum length of 64KB of data.
MEDIUMTEXT	length+3	A text field with a maximum length of 16MB of text.
MEDIUMBLOB	length+3	A binary field with a maximum length of 16MB of data.
LONGTEXT	length+4	A text field with a maximum length of 4GB of text.
LONGBLOB	length+4	A binary field with a maximum length of 4GB of data.
ENUM	1,2	A field that can contain one of a number of predefined possible values (e.g., ENUM("apples," "oranges," "bananas"). Data may be either entered as one of the text options or as a number corresponding to the index of an option (the first option is number 1). A NULL value may always be entered for the field. A maximum of 65535 different options may be defined per enumeration. If there are less than 256 options, the field will take up only one byte of space (otherwise it will use two).

Table 15-1. Datatypes (continued)

Type	Size (in bytes)	Comments
SET	1-8	A field that can contain any number of a set of predefined possible values (e.g., SET("rock," "pop," "country," "western"). Data may be entered as a comma-separated list of values or as an integer that is the bit representation of the values (e.g., 12, which is 1100 in binary, would correspond to "country, western" in the example above). There is a maximum of 64 values in a single set.

In addition to the main types, several modifiers can also be used to qualify the type:

decimal

> This is the maximum number of decimals allowed in a floating point value. Any values entered that have more decimal places will be rounded off. For example, for the field **price FLOAT(5,2)** the value 4.34 would be displayed as 4.34, the value 234.27 would be displayed as 234.3 (to satisfy the maximum total length) and the value 3.331 would be displayed as 3.33 (to satisfy the maximum decimal length).

length

> For numerical values, this is the number of characters used to display the value to the user. This includes decimal points, signs, and exponent indicators. For example, the field **peanuts INT(4)** has a legal range of -999 to 9999. MySQL will store values outside the given range, however, as long as it is inside the maximum range of the type. If you store a value that is outside the defined range, MySQL will issue a warning, but everything will work normally.

> When used with the **TIMESTAMP** type, the length determines the format used for the timestamp.

> When used with a character type, the length determines the number of characters in the data. For fixed character types, the length is exactly the number of characters used to store the data. For variable characters types, the length is the length of the longest allowed string.

> The length attribute is optional for all types except for **DECIMAL/NUMERIC**, **CHAR** and **VARCHAR**.

Since the DECIMAL/NUMERIC type is stored as a character string, it is bound by the maximum length the same way a CHAR field would be. Therefore, inserting numbers outside of the range defined on the field will fail and generate an error just as if an overly long string were inserted into a CHAR field.

precision

This attribute is available in the FLOAT type to provide compatibility with the ODBC system. The value of this attribute can be 4 to define a normal float (same as FLOAT without a precision attribute) or 8 to define a double precision float (same as the DOUBLE field).

AUTO_INCREMENT

This attribute allows a numeric field to be automatically updated. This is useful for creating unique identification numbers for the rows in the table. Data can be inserted and read normally from an AUTO_INCREMENT field, but if a value of NULL or 0 is inserted, the existing value of the field is increased by one automatically. The current value of an AUTO_INCREMENT field can be obtained by using the LAST_INSERT_ID function (see SELECT, below).

BINARY

This attribute can be used with CHAR and VARCHAR types to indicate binary data in the text string. The only effect that BINARY has is to make any sorting of the values case-sensitive. By default, MySQL ignores case when sorting text.

DEFAULT *value*

This attribute assigns a default value to a field. If a row is inserted into the table without a value for this field, this value will be inserted. If a default is not defined, a null value is inserted unless the field is defined as NOT NULL in which case MySQL picks a value based on the type of the field.

NOT NULL

This attribute guarantees that every entry in the column will have some non-NULL value. Attempting to insert a NULL value into a field defined with NOT NULL will generate an error.

NULL

This attribute specifies that the field is allowed to contain NULL values. This is the default if neither this nor the NOT NULL modifier are specified. Fields that are contained within an index cannot contain the NULL modifier. (It will be ignored, without warning, if it does exist in such a field.)

PRIMARY KEY

This attribute automatically makes the field the primary key (see later) for the table. Only one primary key may exist for a table. Any field that is a primary key must also contain the NOT NULL modifier.

REFERENCES *table* [(*column*, . . .)] [MATCH FULL | MATCH PARTIAL] [ON DELETE *option*] [ON UPDATE *option*]

> This attribute currently has no effect. MySQL understands the full references syntax but does not implement its behavior. The modifier is included to make it easier to import SQL from different SQL sources. In addition, this functionality may be included in a future release of MySQL.

UNSIGNED

> This attribute can be used with integer types to define an unsigned integer. The maximum value of an unsigned integer is twice that of its signed counterpart, but it cannot store negative values. Without any modifiers, all types are considered to be signed.

ZEROFILL

> The attribute can be used with integer types to add zeros to the left of every number until the maximum length is reached. For example, the field `counter` `INT(5) ZEROFILL` would display the number 132 as 00132.

Indexes

MySQL supports the concept of an index of a table, as described in Chapter 2, *Database Design*. Indexes are created by means of special "types" that are included with the table definition:

KEY/INDEX [*name*] (*column*, [*column2*, . . .])

> Creates a regular index of all of the named columns (KEY and INDEX, in this context, are synonyms). Optionally the index may be given a name. If no name is provided, a name is assigned based on the first column given and a trailing number, if necessary, for uniqueness. If a key contains more than one column, leftmost subsets of those columns are also included in the index. Consider the following index definition.
>
> ```
> INDEX idx1 ( name, rank, serial );
> ```
>
> When this index is created, the following groups of columns will be indexed:
>
> — name, rank, serial
>
> — name, rank
>
> — name

PRIMARY KEY

> Creates the primary key of the table. A primary key is a special key that can be defined only once in a table. The primary key is a UNIQUE key with the name "PRIMARY." Despite it's privileged status, in function it is the same as every other unique key.

UNIQUE [*name*] (*column*, [*column2*, . . .])

Creates a special index where every value contained in the index (and there-fore in the fields indexed) must be unique. Attempting to insert a value that already exists into a unique index will generate an error. The following would create a unique index of the "nicknames" field:

```
UNIQUE (nicknames);
```

 In the current implementation of MySQL's indices, NULL values are not allowed in any fild that is part of an index.

When indexing character fields (CHAR, VARCHAR and their synonyms only), it is possible to index only a prefix of the entire field. For example, this following will create an index of the numeric field 'id' along with the first 20 characters of the character field 'address':

```
INDEX adds ( id, address(20) );
```

When performing any searches of the field 'address', only the first 20 characters will be used for comparison unless more than one match is found that contains the same first 20 characters, in which case a regular search of the data is per-formed. Therefore, it can be a big performance bonus to index only the number of characters in a text field that you know will make the value unique.

Fields contained in an index must be defined with the NOT NULL modifier (see earlier). When adding an index as a separate declaration, MySQL will generate an error if NOT NULL is missing. However, when defining the primary key by adding the PRIMARY KEY modifier to the field definition, the NOT NULL modifier is auto-matically added (without a warning) if it is not explicitly defined.

In addition to the above, MySQL supports the following special "types":

- FOREIGN KEY *(name (column, [column2, . . .])*

- CHECK

These keywords do not actually .perform any action. They exist so that SQL exported from other databases can be more easily read into MySQL. Also, some of this missing functionality may be added into a future version of MySQL.

You must have CREATE privileges on a database to use the CREATE TABLE statement.

Examples

```
# Create the new empty database 'employees'
CREATE DATABASE employees;
```

```
# Create a simple table
CREATE TABLE emp_data ( id INT, name CHAR(50) );
# Make the function make_coffee (which returns a string value and is stored
# in the myfuncs.so shared library) available to MySQL.
CREATE FUNCTION make_coffee RETURNS string SONAME "myfuncs.so";
```

DELETE

```
DELETE FROM table [WHERE clause]
```

Deletes rows from a table. When used without a **WHERE** clause, this will erase the entire table and recreate it as an empty table. With a clause, it will delete the rows that match the condition of the clause. This statement returns the number of rows deleted to the user.

As mentioned above, not including a **WHERE** clause will erase this entire table. This is done using an efficient method that is much faster than deleting each row individually. When using this method, MySQL returns 0 to the user because it has no way of knowing how many rows it deleted. In the current design, this method simply deletes all of the files associated with the table except for the file that contains the actual table definition. Therefore, this is a handy method of zeroing out tables with unrecoverably corrupt data files. You will lose the data, but the table structure will still be in place.

You must have **DELETE** privileges on a database to use the following statement:

Examples

```
# Erase all of the data (but not the table itself) for the table 'olddata'.
DELETE FROM olddata
# Erase all records in the 'sales' table where the 'year' field is '1995'.
DELETE FROM sales WHERE year=1995
```

DESCRIBE

DESC

```
DESCRIBE table [column]
DESC table [column]
```

Gives information about a table or column. While this statement works as advertised, its functionality is available (along with much more) in the **SHOW** statement. This statement is included solely for compatibility with Oracle SQL. The optional column name can contain SQL wildcards, in which case information will be displayed for all matching columns.

Example

```
# Describe the layout of the table 'messy'
DESCRIBE messy
# Show the information about any columns starting with 'my_' in the 'big'
table.
```

```
# Remember: '_' is a wildcard, too, so it must be escaped to be used
literally.
DESC big my\_%
```

DROP

```
DROP DATABASE name
DROP INDEX name
DROP TABLE [IF EXISTS] name[, name2, ...]
DROP FUNCTION name
```

Permanently remove a database, table, index, or function from the MySQL system.

DROP DATABASE

Will remove an entire database with all of its associated files. The number of files deleted will be returned to the user. Because three files represent most tables, the number returned is usually the number of tables times three. This is equivalent to running the *mysqladmin drop* utility. As with running *mysqladmin*, you must be the administrative user for MySQL (usually root or mysql) to perform this statement.

DROP INDEX

Statement provides for compatibility with other SQL implementations. In older versions of MySQL, this statement does nothing. As of 3.22, this statement is equivalent to ALTER TABLE . . . DROP INDEX. To perform the DROP INDEX statement, you must have SELECT, INSERT, DELETE, UPDATE, CREATE and DROP privileges for the table in question.

DROP TABLE

Will erase an entire table permanently. In the current implementation, MySQL simply deletes the files associated with the table. As of 3.22, you may specify IF EXISTS to make MySQL not return an error if you attempt to remove a table that does not exist. You must have DELETE privileges on the table to use this statement.

DROP FUNCTION

Will remove a user defined function from the running MySQL server process. This does not actually delete the library file containing the function. You may add the function again at any time using the CREATE FUNCTION statement. In the current implementation DROP FUNCTION simply removes the function from the function table within the Mysql database. This table keeps track of all active functions.

You must have DROP privileges on that table to execute this statement.

DROP is by far the most dangerous SQL statement. If you have drop privileges, you may permanently erase a table or even an entire database. This is done without warning or confirmation. The only way to undo a DROP is to restore the table or database from back-ups. The lessons to be learned here are: (1) always keep backups; (2) don't use DROP unless you are really sure; and (3) always keep backups.

Examples

```
# Completely remove the 'important_data' database from the face of the Earth.
DROP DATABASE important_data
# Delete the tables 'oh_no', 'help_me' and 'dont_do_it'
DROP TABLE oh_no, help_me, dont_do_it
# Remove the named index 'my_index'
DROP INDEX my_index
# Remove the function 'myfunc' from the running server. This can be added
again
# at anytime using the CREATE FUNCTION statement.
DROP FUNCTION myfunc
```

EXPLAIN

```
EXPLAIN SELECT statement
```

Displays verbose information about the order and structure of a **SELECT** statement. This can be used to see where keys are not being used efficiently.

Example

```
EXPLAIN SELECT customer.name, product.name FROM customer, product, purchases
WHERE purchases.customer=customer.id AND purchases.product=product.id
```

FLUSH

```
FLUSH option[, option...]
```

Flushes or resets various internal processes depending on the option(s) given. You must have `reload` privileges to execute this statement. The option can be any of the following:

HOSTS

Empties the cache table that stores hostname information for clients. This should be used if a client changes IP addresses, or if there are errors related to connecting to the host.

LOGS

Closes all of the standard log files and reopens them. This can be used if a log file has changed inode number. If no specific extension has been given to the update log, a new update log will be opened with the extension incremented by one.

PRIVILEGES

Reloads all of the internal MySQL permissions grant tables. This must be run for any changes to the tables to take effect.

STATUS

Resets the status variables that keep track of the current state of the server.

TABLES

Closes all currently opened tables and flushes any cached data to disk.

GRANT

```
GRANT privilege [ (column, ...) ] [, privilege [( column, ...) ] ...]
    ON {table} TO user [IDENTIFIED BY 'password']
        [, user [IDENTIFIED BY 'password'] ...] [WITH GRANT OPTION]
```

Previous to MySQL 3.22.11, the **GRANT** statement was recognized but did nothing. In current versions, **GRANT** is functional. This statement will enable access rights to a user (or users). Access can be granted per database, table or individual column. The table can be given as a table within the current database, '*' to affect all tables within the current database, '*.*' to affect all tables within all databases or 'database.*' to effect all tables within the given database.

The following privileges are currently supported:

ALL PRIVILEDGES/ALL

Effects all privileges

ALTER

Altering the structure of tables

CREATE

Creating new tables

DELETE

Deleting rows from tables

DROP

Deleting entire tables

FILE

Creating and removing entire databases as well as managing log files

INDEX

Creating and deleting indices from tables

INSERT

Inserting data into tables

PROCESS

Killing process threads

REFERENCES

Not implemented (yet)

RELOAD

Refreshing various internal tables (see the FLUSH statement)

SELECT

Reading data from tables

SHUTDOWN

Shutting down the database server

UPDATE

Altering rows within tables

USAGE

No privileges at all

The `user variable` is of the form *user@hostname*. Either the user or the host-name can contain SQL wildcards. If wildcards are used, either the whole name must be quoted, or just the part(s) with the wildcards (e.g., `joe@"%.com "` and *"joe@%. com"* are both valid). A user without a hostname is considered to be the same as *user@"%"*.

If you have a global `GRANT` privilege, you may specify an optional `INDENTIFIED BY` modifier. If the user in the statement does not exist, it will be created with the given password. Otherwise the existing user will have his or her password changed.

Giving the `GRANT` privilege to a user is done with the `WITH GRANT OPTION` modi-fier. If this is used, the user may grant any privilege they have onto another user.

INSERT

```
INSERT [DELAYED | LOW_PRIORITY ] [INTO] table [ (column, ...) ] VALUES ( values )
    [, ( values )... ]
INSERT [LOW_PRIORITY] [INTO] table [ (column, ...) ] SELECT ...
INSERT [LOW_PRIORITY] [INTO] table SET column=value, column=value,...
```

Inserts data into a table. The first form of this statement simply inserts the given values into the given columns. Columns in the table that are not given values are set to their default value or `NULL`. The second form takes the results of a `SELECT` query and inserts them into the table. The third form is simply an alternate ver-sion of the first form that more explicitly shows which columns correspond with which values. If the `DELAYED` modifier is present in the first form, all incoming `SELECT` statements will be given priority over the insert, which will wait until the other activity has finished before inserting the data. In a similar way, using the `LOW_PRIORITY` modifier with any form of `INSERT` will cause the insertion to be postponed until all other operations from the client have been finished.

When using a **SELECT** query with the **INSERT** statement, you cannot use the **ORDER BY** modifier with the **SELECT** statement. Also, you cannot insert into the same table you are selecting from.

Starting with MySQL 3.22.5 it is possible to insert more than one row into a table at a time. This is done by adding additional value lists to the statement separated by commas.

You must have **INSERT** privileges to use this statement.

Examples

```
# Insert a record into the 'people' table.
INSERT INTO people ( name, rank, serial_number ) VALUES ( 'Bob Smith',
    'Captain', 12345 );
# Copy all records from 'data' that are older than a certain date into
# 'old_data'. This would usually be followed by deleting the old data from
# 'data'.
INSERT INTO old_data ( id, date, field ) SELECT ( id, date, field) FROM data
    WHERE date < 87459300;
# Insert 3 new records into the 'people' table.
INSERT INTO people (name, rank, serial_number ) VALUES ( 'Tim O\'Reilly',
'General', 1), ('Andy Oram', 'Major', 4342), ('Randy Yarger', 'Private',
9943);
```

KILL

```
KILL thread_id
```

Terminates the specified thread. The thread ID numbers can be found using the **SHOW PROCESSES** statement. Killing threads owned by users other than yourself require process privilege.

Example

```
# Terminate thread 3
KILL 3
```

LOAD

```
LOAD DATA [LOCAL] INFILE file [REPLACE|IGNORE] INTO TABLE table [delimiters]
[(columns)]
```

Reads a text file that is in a readable format and inserts the data into a database table. This method of inserting data is much quicker than using multiple **INSERT** statements. Although the statement may be sent from all clients just like any other SQL statement, the file referred to in the statement is assumed to be located on the server. If the filename does not have a fully qualified path, MySQL looks under the directory for the current database for the file. As of MySQL 3.22, if the LOCAL modifier is present, the file will be read from the client's local filesystem.

With no delimiters specified, LOAD DATA INFILE will assume that the file is tab delimited with character fields, special characters escaped with the backslash (\), and lines terminated with a newline character.

In addition to the default behavior, you may specify your own delimiters using the following keywords:

FIELDS TERMINATED BY 'c'

Specifies the character used to delimit the fields. Standard C language escape codes can be used to designate special characters. This value may contain more than one character. For example, FIELDS TERMINATED BY ',' denotes a comma delimited file and FIELDS TERMINATED BY '\t' denotes tab delimited. The default value is tab delimited.

FIELDS ENCLOSED BY 'c'

Specifies the character used to enclose character strings. For example, FIELD ENCLOSED BY '"' would mean that a line containing "this, value", "this", "value" would be taken to have three fields: "this,value", "this", and "value". The default behavior is to assume that no quoting is used in the file.

FIELDS ESCAPED BY 'c'

Specifies the character used to indicate that the next character is not special, even though it would usually be a special character. For example, with FIELDS ESCAPED BY '^' a line consisting of First,Second^,Third,Fourth would be parsed as three fields: "First", "Second,Third" and "Fourth". The exceptions to this rule are the null characters. Assuming the FIELDS ESCAPED BY value is a backslash, \0 indicates an ASCII NULL (character number 0) and \N indicates a MySQL null value. The default value is the backslash character. Note that MySQL itself considers the backslash character to be special. Therefore to indicate backslash in that statement you must back-slash the backslash like this: FIELDS ESCAPED BY '\\'.

LINES TERMINATED BY 'c'

Specifies the character that indicates the start of a new record. This value can contain more than one character. For example, with LINES TERMINATED BY '.', a file consisting of a,b,c.d,e,f.g,h,k. would be parsed as three separate records, each containing three fields. The default is the newline character. This means that by default, MySQL assumes that each line is a separate record.

The keyword FIELDS should only be used for the entire statement. For example:

```
LOAD DATA INFILE data.txt FIELDS TERMINATED BY ',' ESCAPED BY '\\'.
```

By default, if a value read from the file is the same as an existing value in the table for a field that is part of a unique key, an error is given. If the REPLACE keyword is added to the statement, the value from the file will replace the one already in the table. Conversely, the `IGNORE` keyword will cause MySQL to ignore the new value and keep the old one.

The word `NULL` encountered in the data file is considered to indicate a null value unless the `FIELDS ENCLOSED BY` character encloses it.

Using the same character for more than one delimiter can confuse MySQL. For example, `FIELDS TERMINATED BY ',' ENCLOSED BY ','` would produce unpredictable behavior.

If a list of columns is provided, the data is inserted into those particular fields in the table. If no columns are provided, the number of fields in the data must match the number of fields in the table, and they must be in the same order as the fields are defined in the table.

You must have `SELECT` and `INSERT` privileges on the table to use this statement.

Example

```
# Load in the data contained in 'mydata.txt' into the table 'mydata'. Assume
# that the file is tab delimited with no quotes surrounding the fields.
LOAD DATA INFILE 'mydata.txt' INTO TABLE mydata
# Load in the data contained in 'newdata.txt' Look for two comma delimited
# fields and insert their values into the fields 'field1' and 'field2' in
# the 'newtable' table.
LOAD DATA INFILE 'newdata.txt' INTO TABLE newtable FIELDS TERMINATED BY ','
    ( field1, field2 )
```

LOCK

```
LOCK TABLES name [AS alias] READ|WRITE [, name2 [AS alias] READ|WRITE, ...]
```

Locks a table for the use of a specific thread. This command is generally used to emulate transactions as described in Chapter 7, *Other Mid-Range Database Engines*. If a thread creates a `READ` lock all other threads may read from the table but only the controlling thread can write to the table. If a thread creates a `WRITE` lock, no other thread may read from or write to the table.

Using locked and unlocked tables at the same time can cause the process thread to freeze. You must lock all of the tables you will be accessing during the time of the lock. Tables you access only before or after the lock do not need to be locked. The newest versions of MySQL generate an error if you attempt to access an unlocked table while you have other tables locked.

Example

```
# Lock tables 'table1' and 'table3' to prevent updates, and block all access
# to 'table2'. Also create the alias 't3' for 'table3' in the current thread.
LOCK TABLES table1 READ, table2 WRITE, table3 AS t3 READ
```

OPTIMIZE

```
OPTIMIZE TABLE name
```

Recreates a table eliminating any wasted space. This is done by creating the optimized table as a separate, temporary table and then moving over to replace the current table. While the procedure is happening, all table operations continue as normal (all writes are diverted to the temporary table).

Example

```
OPTIMIZE TABLE mytable
```

REPLACE

```
REPLACE INTO table [(column, ...)] VALUES (value, ...)
REPLACE INTO table [(column, ...)] SELECT select_clause
```

Inserts data to a table, replacing any old data that conflicts. This statement is identical to INSERT except that if a value conflicts with an existing unique key, the new value replaces the old one. The first form of this statement simply inserts the given values into the given columns. Columns in the table that are not given values are set to their default value or NULL. The second form takes the results of a SELECT query and inserts them into the table.

Examples

```
# Insert a record into the 'people' table.
REPLACE INTO people ( name, rank, serial_number ) VALUES ( 'Bob Smith',
    'Captain', 12345 )
# Copy all records from 'data' that are older than a certain date into
# 'old_data'. This would usually be followed by deleting the old data from
# 'data'.
REPLACE INTO old_data ( id, date, field ) SELECT ( id, date, field) FROM data
    WHERE date < 87459300
```

REVOKE

```
REVOKE privilege [(column, ...)] [, privilege [(column, ...) ...]
    ON table FROM user
```

Removes a privilege from a user. The values of privilege, table, and user are the same as for the GRANT statement. You must have the GRANT privilege to be able to execute this statement.

SELECT

```
SELECT [STRAIGHT_JOIN] [DISTINCT|ALL] value[, value2...]
[INTO OUTFILE 'filename' delimiters] FROM table[, table2...] [clause]
```

Retrieve data from a database. The SELECT statement is the primary method of reading data from database tables.

If you specify more than one table, MySQL will automatically join the tables so that you can compare values between the tables. In cases where MySQL does not perform the join in an efficient manner, you can specify STRAIGHT_JOIN to force MySQL to join the tables in the order you enter them in the query.

If the DISTINCT keyword is present, only one row of data will be output for every group of rows that is identical. The ALL keyword is the opposite of distinct and displays all returned data. The default behavior is ALL.

The returned values can be any one of the following:

Aliases

Any complex column name or function can be simplified by creating an alias for it. The value can be referred to by its alias anywhere else in the SELECT statement (e.g., SELECT DATE_FORMAT(date,"%W, %M %d %Y") as nice_ date FROM calendar).

Column names

These can be specified as column, table.column or database.table. column. The longer forms are necessary only to disambiguate columns with the same name, but can be used at any time (e.g., SELECT name FROM people; SELECT mydata.people.name FROM people).

Functions

MySQL supports a wide range of built-in functions (see later). In addition, user defined functions can be added at any time using the CREATE FUNCTION statement (e.g., SELECT COS(angle) FROM triangle).

By default, MySQL sends all output to the client that sent the query. It is possible however, to have the output redirected to a file. In this way you can dump the contents of a table (or selected parts of it) to a formatted file that can either be human readable, or formatted for easy parsing by another database system.

The INTO OUTFILE 'filename' delimiters modifier is the means in which output redirection is accomplished. With this the results of the SELECT query are put into filename. The format of the file is determined by the delimiters arguments, which are the same as the LOAD DATA INFILE statement with the following additions:

- The OPTIONALLY keyword may be added to the FIELDS ENCLOSED BY modifier. This will cause MySQL to thread enclosed data as strings and non-enclosed data as numeric.

- Removing all field delimiters (i.e., FIELDS TERMINATED BY '' ENCLOSED BY '') will cause a fixed-width format to be used. Data will be exported according to the display size of each field. Many spreadsheets and desktop databases can import fixed-width format files.

The default behavior with no delimiters is to export tab delimited data using back-slash (\) as the escape character and to write one record per line.

The list of tables to join may be specified in the following ways:

Table1, Table2, Table3, . . .
> This is the simplest form. The tables are joined in the manner that MySQL deems most efficient. This method can also be written as `Table1 JOIN Table2 JOIN Table3, ....`. The `CROSS` keyword can also be used, but it has no effect (e.g., `Table1 CROSS JOIN Table2`) Only rows that match the conditions for both columns are included in the joined table. For example, `SELECT * FROM people, homes WHERE people.id=homes.owner` would create a joined table containing the rows in the `people` table that have `id` fields that match the `owner` field in the `homes` table.

> Like values, table names can also be aliased (e.g., `SELECT` t1.name, t2.address `FROM` long_table_name t1, longer_table_name t2)

Table1 STRAIGHT_JOIN *Table2*
> This is identical to the earlier method, except that the left table is always read before the right table. This should be used if MySQL performs inefficient sorts by joining the tables in the wrong order.

Table1 LEFT [OUTER] JOIN *Table2* ON *clause*
> This checks the right table against the clause. For each row that does not match, a row of NULLs is used to join with the left table. Using the previous example `SELECT * FROM people, homes LEFT JOIN people, homes ON people.id=homes.owner`, the joined table would contain all of the rows that match in both tables, as well as any rows in the `people` table that do not have matching rows in the `homes` table, NULL values would be used for the `homes` fields in these rows. The OUTER keyword is optional and has no effect.

Table1 LEFT [OUTER] JOIN *Table2* USING *(column[, column2 . . .])*
> This joins the specified columns only if they exist in both tables (e.g., `SELECT * FROM old LEFT OUTER JOIN new USING (id)`)

Table1 NATURAL LEFT [OUTER] JOIN *Table2*
> This joins only the columns that exist in both tables. This would be the same as using the previous method and specifying all of the columns in both tables (e.g., `SELECT rich_people.salary, poor_people.salary FROM rich_people NATURAL LEFT JOIN poor_people`)

{ oj Table1 LEFT OUTER JOIN *Table2* ON *clause }*

This is identical to *Table1* LEFT JOIN *Table2* ON *clause* and is only included for ODBC compatibility. (The "oj" stands for "Outer Join".)

If no clause is provided, SELECT returns all of the data in the selected table(s).

The search clause can contain any of the following substatements:

WHERE *statement*

The WHERE statement construct is the most common way of searching for data in SQL. This statement is usually a comparison of some type but can also include any of the functions listed below, except for the aggregate functions. Named values, such as column names and aliases, and literal numbers and strings can be used in the statement. The following operators are supported:

( ) Parentheses are used to group operators in order to force precedence.

+ Adds two numerical values

- Subtracts two numerical values

* Multiplies two numerical values

/ Divides two numerical values

% Gives the modulo of two numerical values

| Performs a bitwise OR on two integer values

& Performs a bitwise AND on two integer values

<< Performs a bitwise left shift on an integer value

>> Performs a bitwise right shift on an integer value

NOT *or !*

Performs a logical NOT (returns 1 if the value is 0 and returns 0 otherwise).

OR *or* | |

Performs a logical OR (returns 1 if any of the arguments are not 0, otherwise returns 0)

AND *or &&*

Performs a logical AND (returns 0 if any of the arguments are 0, otherwise returns 1)

= Match rows if the two values are equal. MySQL automatically converts between types when comparing values.

<> *or !=*

Match rows if the two values are not equal.

<= Match rows if the left value is less than or equal to the right value.

< Match rows if the left value is less than the right value.

>= Match rows if the left value is greater than or equal to the right value.

> Match rows if the left value is greater than the right value.

value BETWEEN *value1* AND *value2*

Match rows if *value* is between *value1* and *value2*, or equal to one of them.

value IN (*value1*,*value2*,...)

Match rows if *value* is among the values listed.

value NOT IN (*value1*, *value2*,...)

Match rows if *value* is not among the values listed.

value1 LIKE *value2*

Compares *value1* to *value2* and matches the rows if they match. The right-hand value can contain the wildcard '%' which matches any number of characters (including 0) and '_' which matches exactly one character. The is probably the single most used comparison in SQL. The most common usage is to compare a field value with a literal containing a wildcard (e.g., SELECT name FROM people WHERE name LIKE 'B%').

value1 NOT LIKE *value2*

Compares *value1* to *value2* and matches the rows if they differ. This is identical to NOT (value1 LIKE value2).

value1 REGEXP/RLIKE *value2*

Compares *value1* to *value2* using the extended regular expression syntax and matches the rows if they match. The right hand value can contain full Unix regular expression wildcards and constructs (e.g., SELECT name FROM people WHERE name RLIKE '^B.*').

value1 NOT REGEXP *value2*

Compares *value1* to *value2* using the extended regular expression syntax and matches the rows if they differ. This is identical to NOT (value1 REXEXP value2).

The WHERE clause returns any of the expression values that are not 0 or NULL (that is, anything that is not logically false). Therefore, SELECT age FROM people WHERE age>10 will return only those ages that are greater than 10.

GROUP BY *column*[, *column2*,...]

This gathers all of the rows together that contain data from a certain column. This allows aggregate functions to be performed upon the columns (e.g., SELECT name,MAX(age) FROM people GROUP BY name).

HAVING *clause*

This is the same as a WHERE clause except that it is performed upon the data that has already been retrieved from the database. The HAVING statement is a good place to perform aggregate functions on relatively small sets of data that have been retrieved from large tables. This way, the function does not have to act upon the whole table, only the data that has already been selected (e.g., SELECT name,MAX(age) FROM people GROUP BY name HAVING MAX(age)>80).

ORDER BY *column* [*ASC*|*DESC*] [, *column2* [*ASC*|*DESC*],...]

Sorts the returned data using the given column(s). If DESC is present, the data is sorted in descending order, otherwise ascending order is used. Ascending order can also be explicitly stated with the ASC keyword (e.g., SELECT name, age FROM people ORDER BY age DESC).

LIMIT [*start,*] *rows*

Returns Only the specified number of rows. If the start value is supplied, that many rows are skipped before the data is returned. The first row is number 0 (e.g., SELECT url FROM links LIMIT 5,10 (returns URL's numbered 5 through 14).

PROCEDURE *name*

In mSQL and early versions of MySQL, this does not do anything. It was provided to make importing data from other SQL servers easier. Starting with MySQL 3.22, this substatement lets you specify a procedure that modifies the query result before returning it to the client.

SELECT supports the concept of functions. MySQL defines several built-in functions that can operate upon the data in the table, returning the computed value(s) to the user. With some functions, the value returned depends on whether the user wants to receive a numerical or string value. This is regarded as the "context" of the function. When selecting values to be displayed to the user, only text context is used, but when selecting data to be inserted into a field, or to be used as the argument of another function, the context depends upon what the receiver is expecting. For instance, selecting data to be inserted into a numerical field will place the function into a numerical context.

The following are all of the named functions built into MySQL:

ABS(*number*)

Returns the absolute value of *number* (e.g., ABS(-10) returns 10).

ACOS(*number*)

Returns the inverse cosine of *number* in radians (e.g., ACOS(0) returns 1. 570796).

ASCII(*char*)

Returns the ASCII value of the given character (e.g., ASCII('h') returns 104).

ASIN(*number*)

Returns the inverse sine of number in radians (e.g., ASIN(0) returns 0. 000000).

ATAN(*number*)

Returns the inverse tangent of number in radians (e.g., ATAN(1) returns 0. 785398.)

ATAN2(*X, Y*)

Returns the inverse tangent of the point (*X, Y*) (e.g., ATAN(-3,3) returns -0. 785398).

CHAR(*num1*[,*num2*,. . .])

Returns a string made from converting each of the numbers to the character corresponding to that ASCII value (e.g., CHAR(122) returns 'z').

CONCAT(*string1,string2*[,*string3*,. . .])

Returns the string formed by joining together all of the arguments (e.g., CONCAT('Hi',' ','Mom','!') returns "Hi Mom!").

CONV(*number, base1, base2*)

Returns the value of *number* converted from *base1* to *base2*. *Number* must be an integer value (either as a bare number or as a string). The bases can be any integer from 2 to 36 (e.g., CONV(8,10,2) returns 1000 (the number 8 in decimal converted to binary)).

BIN(*decimal*)

Returns the binary value of the given decimal number. This is equivalent to the function CONV(decimal,10,2) (e.g., BIN(8) returns 1000).

BIT_COUNT(*number*)

Returns the number of bits that are set to 1 in the binary representation of the number (e.g., BIT_COUNT(17) returns 2).

CEILING(*number*)

Returns the smallest integer larger than or equal to *number* (e.g., CEILING (5.67) returns 6).

COS(*radians*)

Returns the cosine of the given number, which is in radians (e.g., COS(0) returns 1.000000).

COT(*radians*)

Returns the cotangent of the given number, which must be in radians (e.g., COT(1) returns 0.642093).

CURDATE()/CURRENT_DATE()

Returns the current date. A number of the form YYYYMMDD is returned if this is used in a numerical context, otherwise a string of the form 'YYYY-MM-DD' is returned (e.g., CURDATE() could return "1998-08-24").

`CURTIME()`/`CURRENT_TIME()`

> Returns the current time. A number of the form HHMMSS is returned if this is used in a numerical context, otherwise a string of the form HH:MM:SS is returned (e.g., `CURRENT_TIME()` could return 13:02:43).

`DATABASE()`

> Returns the name of the current database (e.g., `DATABASE()` could return "mydata").

`DATE_ADD(date, INTERVAL amount type)`/`ADDDATE(date, INTERVAL amount type)`

> Returns a date formed by adding the given amount of time to the given date. The type of time to add can be one of the following: SECOND, MINUTE, HOUR, DAY, MONTH, YEAR, MINUTE_SECOND (as "minutes:seconds"), HOUR_MINUTE (as "hours:minutes"), DAY_HOUR (as "days hours"), YEAR_MONTH (as "years-months"), HOUR_SECOND (as "hours:minutes:seconds"), DAY_MINUTE (as "days hours:minutes") and DAY_SECOND (as "days hours:minutes:seconds"). Except for those types with forms specified above, the amount must be an integer value (e.g., `DATE_ADD("1998-08-24 13:00:00", INTERVAL 2 MONTH)` returns "1998-10-24 13:00:00").

`DATE_FORMAT(date, format)`

> Returns the date formatted as specified. The format string prints as given with the following values substituted:
>
> *%a* Short weekday name (Sun, Mon, etc.)
>
> *%b* Short month name (Jan, Feb, etc.)
>
> *%D* Day of the month with ordinal suffix (1st, 2nd, 3rd, etc.)
>
> *%d* Day of the month
>
> *%H* 24-hour hour (always two digits, e.g., 01)
>
> *%h/%I*
>
> > 12-hour hour (always two digits, e.g., 09)
>
> *%i* Minutes
>
> *%j* Day of the year
>
> *%k* 24-hour hour (one or two digits, e.g., 1)
>
> *%l* 12-hour hour (one or two digits, e.g., 9)
>
> *%M* Name of the month
>
> *%m*
>
> > Number of the month (January is 1).
>
> *%p* AM or PM

%r 12-hour total time (including AM/PM)

%S Seconds (always two digits, e.g., 04)

%s Seconds (one or two digits, e.g., 4)

%T 24-hour total time

%U

   Week of the year (new weeks begin on Sunday)

%W

   Name of the weekday

%w

   Number of weekday (0 is Sunday)

%Y Four digit year

%y Two digit year

%%

   A literal "%" character.

DATE_SUB(*date*, **INTERVAL** *amount type*)/**SUBDATE**(*date*, **INTERVAL** *amount type*)

   Returns a date formed by subtracting the given amount of time from the given date. The same interval types are used as with **DATE_ADD** (e.g., **SUBDATE**("1999-05-20 11:04:23", **INTERVAL** 2 **DAY**) returns "1999-05-18 11:04:23").

DAYNAME(*date*)

   Returns the name of the day of the week for the given date (e.g., **DAYNAME**('1998-08-22') returns "Saturday").

DAYOFMONTH(*date*)

   Returns the day of the month for the given date (e.g., **DAYOFMONTH**('1998-08-22') returns 22).

DAYOFWEEK(*date*)/**WEEKDAY**(*date*)

   Returns the number of the day of the week (1 is Sunday) for the given date (e.g., **DAY_OF_WEEK**('1998-08-22') returns 7).

DAYOFYEAR(*date*)

   Returns the day of the year for the given date (e.g., **DAYOFYEAR**('1983-02-15') returns 46).

DEGREES(*radians*)

   Returns the given argument converted from radians to degrees (e.g., **DEGREES**(2*PI()) returns 360.000000).

`ELT(number,string1,string2, . . .)`

Returns *string1* if *number* is 1, *string2* if *number* is 2, etc. A null value is returned if *number* does not correspond with a string (e.g., `ELT(3,` `"once","twice","thrice","fourth")` returns "thrice").

`ENCRYPT(string[, salt])`

Password-encrypts the given string. If a salt is provided, it is used to generate the password (e.g., `ENCRYPT('mypass','3a')` could return "3afi4004idgv").

`EXP(power)`

Returns the number *e* raised to the given power (e.g., `EXP(1)` returns 2. 718282).

`FIELD(string,string1,string2, . . .)`

Returns the position in the argument list (starting with *string1*) of the first string that is identical to *string*. Returns 0 if no other string matches *string* (e.g., `FIELD('abe','george','john','abe','bill')` returns).

`FIND_IN_SET(string,set)`

Returns the position of *string* within *set*. The *set* argument is a series of strings separated by commas (e.g., `FIND_IN_SET ('abe', 'george, john, abe, bill')` returns 3).

`FLOOR(number)`

Returns the largest integer smaller than or equal to *number* (e.g., `FLOOR (5.67)` returns 5).

`FORMAT(number, decimals)`

Neatly formats the given number, using the given number of decimals (e.g., `FORMAT(4432.99134,2)` returns "4,432.99").

`FROM_DAYS(days)`

Returns the date that is the given number of days (where day 1 is the Jan 1 of year 1) (e.g., `FROM_DAYS(728749)` returns "1995-04-02").

`FROM_UNIXTIME(seconds [, format])`

Returns the date (in GMT) corresponding to the given number of seconds since the epoch (January 1, 1970 GMT). If a format string (using the same format as DATE_FORMAT) is given, the returned time is formatted accordingly (e.g., `FROM_ UNIXTIME(903981584)` returns "1998-08-24 18:00:02").

`GET_LOCK(name,seconds)`

Creates a named user-defined lock that waits for the given number of seconds until timeout. This lock can be used for client-side application locking between programs that cooperatively use the same lock names. If the lock is successful, 1 is returned. If the lock times out while waiting, 0 is returned. All others errors return a NULL value. Only one named lock may be active at a time for a singe session. Running `GET_LOCK()` more than once will silently remove any previous locks (e.g., GET_LOCK("mylock",10) could return 1 within the following 10 seconds).

GREATEST(*num1, num2*[, *num3, . . .*])

Returns the numerically largest of all of the arguments (e.g., GREATEST(5,6,68,1,4) returns 68).

HEX(*decimal*)

Returns the hexadecimal value of the given decimal number. This is equivalent to the function CONV(decimal,10,16) (e.g., HEX(90) returns "3a").

HOUR(*time*)

Returns the hour of the given time (e.g., HOUR('15:33:30') returns 15).

IF(*test, value1, value2*)

If *test* is true, returns *value1*, otherwise returns *value2*. The *test* value is considered to be an integer, therefore floating point values must be used with comparison operations to generate an integer (e.g., IF(1>0,"true","false") returns true).

IFNULL(*value, value2*)

Returns *value* if it is not null, otherwise returns *value2* (e.g., IFNULL(NULL, "bar") returns "bar").

INSERT(*string,position,length,new*)

Returns the string created by replacing the substring of *string* starting at *position* and going *length* characters with *new* (e.g., INSERT('help',3,1,' can jum') returns "he can jump").

INSTR(*string,substring*)

Identical to LOCATE except that the arguments are reversed (e.g., INSTR('makebelieve','lie') returns 7).

ISNULL(*expression*)

Returns 1 if the expression evaluates to NULL, otherwise returns 0 (e.g., ISNULL(3) returns 0).

INTERVAL(*A,B,C,D, . . .*)

Returns 0 if *A* is the smallest value, 1 if *A* is between *B* and C, 2 if *A* is between *C* and *D,* etc. All of the values except for *A* must be in order (e.g., INTERVAL(5,2,4,6,8) returns 2 (because 5 is in the second interval, between 4 and 6).

LAST_INSERT_ID()

Returns the last value that was automatically generated for an AUTO_INCREMENT field (e.g., LAST_INSERT_ID() could return 4).

LCASE(*string*)/LOWER(*string*)

Returns *string* with all characters turned into lower case (e.g., LCASE('BoB') returns "bob").

LEAST(*num1, num2*[, *num3, . . .*])

>Returns the numerically smallest of all of the arguments (e.g., LEAST(5,6,68,1,4) returns 1).

LEFT(*string,length*)

>Returns *length* characters from the left end of *string* (e.g., LEFT("12345",3) returns "123").

LENGTH(*string*)/OCTET_LENGTH(*string*)/CHAR_LENGTH(*string*)/
CHARACTER_LENGTH(*string*)

>Returns the length of *string* (e.g., CHAR_LENGTH('Hi Mom!') returns 7). In character sets that use multibyte characters (such as Unicode, and several Asian character sets), one character may take up more than one byte. In these cases, MySQL's string functions should correctly count the number of characters, not bytes, in the string. However, in versions prior to 3.23, this did not work properly and the function returned the number of bytes.

LOCATE(*substring,string*[,*number*])/POSITION(*substring,string*)

>Returns the character position of the first occurrence of *substring* within *string*. If *substring* does not exist in *string*, 0 is returned. If a numerical third argument is supplied to LOCATE, the search for *substring* within *string* does not start until the given position within *string* (e.g., LOCATE('SQL','MySQL') returns 3).

LOG(*number*)

>Returns the natural logarithm of *number* (e.g., LOG(2) returns 0.693147).

LOG10(*number*)

>Returns the common logarithm of *number* (e.g., LOG10(1000) returns 3.000000).

LPAD(*string,length,padding*)

>Returns *string* with *padding* added to the left end until the new string is *length* characters long (e.g., LPAD(' Merry X-Mas',18,'Ho') returns "HoHoHo Merry X-Mas").

LTRIM(*string*)

>Returns *string* with all leading whitespace removed (e.g., LTRIM(' Oops') returns "Oops").

MID(*string,position,length*)/SUBSTRING(*string,position,length*)/
SUBSTRING(*string* FROM *position* FOR *length*)

>Returns the substring formed by taking *length* characters from *string*, starting at *position* (e.g., SUBSTRING('12345',2,3) returns "234").

MINUTE(*time*)

>Returns the minute of the given time (e.g., MINUTE('15:33:30') returns 33).

MOD(*num1, num2*)

Returns the modulo of *num1* divided by *num2*. This is the same as the % operator (e.g., MOD(11,3) returns 2).

MONTH(*date*)

Returns the number of the month (1 is January) for the given date (e.g., MONTH('1998-08-22') returns 8).

MONTHNAME(*date*)

Returns the name of the month for the given date (e.g., MONTHNAME('1998-08-22') returns "August").

NOW()/SYSDATE()/CURRENT_TIMESTAMP()

Returns the current date and time. A number of the form YYYYMMDDHHMMSS is returned if this is used in a numerical context, otherwise a string of the form 'YYYY-MM-DD HH:MM:SS' is returned (e.g., SYSDATE() could return "1998-08-24 12:55:32").

OCT(*decimal*)

Returns the octal value of the given decimal number. This is equivalent to the function CONV(decimal,10,8) (e.g., OCT(8) returns 10).

PASSWORD(*string*)

Returns a password-encrypted version of the given string (e.g., PASSWD('mypass') could return "3afi4004idgv").

PERIOD_ADD(*date,months*)

Returns the date formed by adding the given number of months to *date* (which must be of the form YYMM or YYYYMM) (e.g., PERIOD_ADD(9808,14) returns 199910).

PERIOD_DIFF(*date1, date2*)

Returns the number of months between the two dates (which must be of the form YYMM or YYYYMM) (e.g., PERIOD_DIFF(199901,8901) returns 120).

PI()

Returns the value of pi: 3.141593.

POW(*num1, num2*)/POWER(*num1, num2*)

Returns the value of *num1* raised to the *num2* power (e.g., POWER(3,2) returns 9.000000).

QUARTER(*date*)

Returns the number of the quarter of the given date (1 is January-March) (e.g., QUARTER('1998-08-22') returns 3).

RADIANS(*degrees*)

Returns the given argument converted from degrees to radians (e.g., RADIANS(-90) returns -1.570796).

RAND([*seed*])

> Returns a random decimal value between 0 and 1. If an argument is specified, it is used as the seed of the random number generator (e.g., RAND(3) could return 0.435434).

RELEASE_LOCK(*name*)

> Removes the named locked created with the GET_LOCK function. Returns 1 if the release is successful, 0 if it failed because the current thread did not own the lock and a NULL value if the lock did not exist (e.g., RELEASE_ LOCK("mylock")).

REPEAT(*string,number*)

> Returns a string consisting of the original *string* repeated *number* times. Returns an empty string if *number* is less than or equal to zero (e.g., REPEAT('ma',4) returns 'mamamama').

REPLACE(*string,old,new*)

> Returns a string that has all occurrences of the substring *old* replaced with *new* (e.g., REPLACE('*black jack*','*ack*','*oke*') returns "bloke joke").

REVERSE(*string*)

> Returns the character reverse of *string* (e.g., REVERSE('my bologna') returns "angolob ym").

RIGHT(*string,length*)/SUBSTRING(string FROM length)

> Returns *length* characters from the right end of *string* (e.g., SUBSTRING("12345" FROM 3) returns "345").

ROUND(*number*[,*decimal*])

> Returns *number*, rounded to the given number of decimals. If no *decimal* argument is supplied, *number* is rounded to an integer (e.g., ROUND(5.67,1) returns 5.7).

RPAD(*string,length,padding*)

> Returns *string* with padding added to the right end until the new string is *length* characters long (e.g., RPAD('Yo',5,'!') returns "Yo!!!").

RTRIM(*string*)

> Returns *string* with all trailing whitespace removed (e.g., RTRIM('Oops   ') returns "Oops").

SECOND(*time*)

> Returns the seconds of the given time (e.g., SECOND('15:33:30') returns 30).

SEC_TO_TIME(*seconds*)

> Returns the number of hours, minutes and seconds in the given number of seconds. A number of the form HHMMSS is returned if this is used in a numerical context, otherwise a string of the form HH:MM:SS is returned (e.g., SEC_TO_ TIME(3666) returns "01:01:06").

SIGN(*number*)

Returns -1 if *number* is negative, 0 if it's zero, or 1 if it's positive (e.g., SIGN(4) returns 1).

SIN(*radians*)

Returns the sine of the given number, which is in radians (e.g., SIN(2*PI()) returns 0.000000).

SOUNDEX(*string*)

Returns the Soundex code associated with string (e.g., SOUNDEX('Jello') returns "J400").

SPACE(*number*)

Returns a string that contains *number* spaces (e.g., SPACE(5) returns "   ").

SQRT(*number*)

Returns the square root of *number* (e.g., SQRT(16) returns 4.000000).

STRCMP(*string1, string2*)

Returns 0 if the strings are the same, -1 if *string1* would sort before than *string2*, or 1 if *string1* would sort after than *string2* (e.g., STRCMP('bob','bobbie') returns -1).

SUBSTRING_INDEX(*string,character,number*)

Returns the substring formed by counting *number* of *character* within *string* and then returning everything to the right if count is positive, or everything to the left if count is negative (e.g., SUBSTRING_INDEX('1,2,3,4,5',',',-3) returns "1,2,3").

SUBSTRING(*string,position*)

Returns all of *string* starting at *position* characters (e.g., SUBSTRING("123456",3) returns "3456").

TAN(*radians*)

Returns the tangent of the given number, which must be in radians (e.g., TAN(0) returns 0.000000).

TIME_FORMAT(*time, format*)

Returns the given time using a format string. The format string is of the same type as DATE_FORMAT, as shown earlier.

TIME_TO_SEC(*time*)

Returns the number of seconds in the *time* argument (e.g., TIME_TO_SEC('01:01:06') returns 3666).

TO_DAYS(*date*)

Returns the number of days (where day 1 is the Jan 1 of year 1) to the given date. The date may be a value of type DATE, DATETIME or TIMESTAMP, or a number of the form YYMMDD or YYYYMMDD (e.g., TO_DAYS(19950402) returns 728749).

`TRIM([[BOTH|LEADING|TRAILING]` `[remove]` `[FROM]` `string)`

> With no modifiers, returns *string* with all trailing and leading whitespace removed. You can specify whether to remove either the leading or the trailing whitespace, or both. You can also specify another character other than space to be removed (e.g., `TRIM(both '-' from '---look here---')` returns "look here").

`TRUNCATE(number, decimals)`

> Returns *number* truncated to the given number of decimals (e.g., `TRUNCATE(3.33333333,2)` returns 3.33).

`UCASE(string)/UPPER(string)`

> Returns *string* with all characters turned into uppercase (e.g., `UPPER ('Scooby')` returns "SCOOBY").

`UNIX_TIMESTAMP([date])`

> Returns the number of seconds from the epoch (January 1, 1970 GMT) to the given date (in GMT). If no date is given, the number of seconds to the current date is used (e.g., `UNIX_TIMESTAMP('1998-08-24 18:00:02')` returns 903981584).

`USER()/SYSTEM_USER()/SESSION_USER()`

> Returns the name of the current user (e.g., `SYSTEM_USER()` could return "ryarger").

`VERSION()`

> Returns the version of the MySQL server itself (e.g., `VERSION()` could return "3.22.5c-alpha").

`WEEK(date)`

> Returns the week of the year for the given date (e.g., `WEEK('1998-12-29')` returns 52).

`YEAR(date)`

> Returns the year of the given date (e.g., `YEAR('1998-12-29')` returns 1998).

The following functions are aggregate functions that perform upon a set of data. The usual method of using these is to perform some action on a complete set of returned rows. For example, `SELECT AVG(height) FROM kids` would return the average of all of the values of the `height` field in the `kids` table.

`AVG(expression)`

> Returns the average value of the values in *expression* (e.g., `SELECT AVG(score) FROM tests`).

`BIT_AND(expression)`

> Returns the bitwise AND aggregate of all of the values in *expression* (e.g., `SELECT BIT_AND(flags) FROM options`).

BIT_OR(*expression*)

> Returns the bitwise OR aggregate of all of the values in *expression* (e.g., SELECT BIT_OR(flags) FROM options).

COUNT(*expression*)

> Returns the number of times *expression* was not null. COUNT(*) will return the number of rows with some data in the entire table (e.g., SELECT COUNT(*) FROM folders).

MAX(*expression*)

> Returns the largest of the values in *expression* (e.g., SELECT MAX (elevation) FROM mountains).

MIN(*expression*)

> Returns the smallest of the values in *expression* (e.g., SELECT MIN(level) FROM toxic_waste).

STD(*expression*)/STDDEV(*expression*)

> Returns the standard deviation of the values in *expression* (e.g., SELECT STDDEV(points) FROM data).

SUM(*expression*)

> Returns the sum of the values in *expression* (e.g., SELECT SUM(calories) FROM daily_diet).

Examples

```
# Find all names in the 'people' table where the 'state' field is 'MI'.
SELECT name FROM people WHERE state='MI'
# Display all of the data in the 'mytable' table.
SELECT * FROM mytable
```

SET

```
SET OPTION SQL_OPTION=value
```

Defines an option for the current session. Values set by this statement are not in effect anywhere but the current connection, and they disappear at the end of the connection. The following options are current supported:

CHARACTER SET *charsetname* or DEFAULT

> Changes the character set used by MySQL. Currently the only other built-in character set is cp1251_koi8, which refers to the Russian alphabet. Specifying DEFAULT will return to the original character set.

LAST_INSERT_ID=*number*

> Determines the value returned from the LAST_INSERT_ID() function.

SQL_BIG_SELECTS=0 or 1

> Determines the behavior when a large SELECT query is encountered. If set to 1, MySQL will abort the query with an error if the query would probably take

too long to compute. MySQL decides that a query will take too long it will have to examine more rows than the value of the `max_join_size` server variable. The default value is 0, which allows all queries.

SQL_BIG_TABLES=0 or 1

Determines the behavior of temporary tables (usually generated when dealing with large data sets). If this value is 1, temporary tables are stored on disk, which is slower than primary memory but can prevent errors on systems with low memory. The default value is 0, which stores temporary tables in RAM.

SQL_LOG_OFF=0 or 1

When set to 1, turns off standard logging for the current session. This does not stop logging to the ISAM log or the update log. You must have PROCESS LIST privileges to use this option. The default is 0, which enables regular logging. Chapter 4, *MySQL*, describes the various MySQL logging schemes.

SQL_SELECT_LIMIT=*number*

The maximum number of records returned by a SELECT query. A LIMIT modifier in a SELECT statement overrides this value. The default behavior is to return all records.

SQL_UPDATE_LOG=0 or 1

When set to 0, turns off update logging for the current session. This does not affect standard logging or ISAM logging. You must have PROCESS LIST privileges to use this option. The default is 1, which enables regular logging.

TIMESTAMP=*value* or DEFAULT

Determines the time used for the session. This time is logged to the update log and will be used if data is restored from the log. Specifying DEFAULT will return to the system time.

Example

```
# Turn off logging for the current connection.
SET OPTION SQL_LOG_OFF=1
```

SHOW

```
SHOW DATABASES [LIKE clause]
SHOW KEYS FROM table [FROM database]
SHOW INDEX FROM table [FROM database]
SHOW TABLES [FROM database] [LIKE clause]
SHOW COLUMNS FROM table [FROM database] [LIKE clause]
SHOW FIELDS FROM table [FROM database] [LIKE clause]
SHOW STATUS
SHOW TABLE STATUS [FROM database] [LIKE clause]
SHOW VARIABLES [LIKE clause]
```

Displays various information about the MySQL system. This statement can be used to examine the status or structure of almost any part of MySQL.

Examples

```
# Show the available databases
SHOW DATABASES
# Display information on the indexes on table 'bigdata'
SHOW KEYS FROM bigdata
# Display information on the indexes on table 'bigdata' in the database
'mydata'
SHOW INDEX FROM bigdata FROM mydata
# Show the tables available from the database 'mydata' that begin with the
# letter 'z'
SHOW TABLES FROM mydata LIKE 'z%'
# Display information about the columns on the table 'skates'
SHOW COLUMNS FROM stakes
# Display information about the columns on the table 'people' that end with
# '_name'
SHOW FIELDS FROM people LIKE '%\_name'
# Show server status information.
SHOW STATUS
# Display server variables
SHOW VARIABLES
```

UNLOCK

```
UNLOCK TABLES
```

Unlocks all tables that were locked using the **LOCK** statement during the current connection.

Example

```
# Unlock all tables
UNLOCK TABLES
```

UPDATE

```
UPDATE table SET column=value, ... [WHERE clause]
```

Alters data within a table. This statement is used to change actual data within a table without altering the table itself. You may use the name of a column as a value when setting a new value. For example, **UPDATE health SET miles_ ran=miles_ran+5** would add five to the current value of the **miles_ran** column. The statement returns the number of rows changed.

You must have **UPDATE** privileges to use this statement.

Example

```
# Change the name 'John Deo' to 'John Doe' everywhere in the people table.
UPDATE people SET name='John Doe' WHERE name='John Deo'
```

USE

```
USE database
```

Selects the default database. The database given in this statement is used as the default database for subsequent queries. Other databases may still be explicitly specified using the `database.table.column` notation.

Example

```
# Make db1 the default database.
USE db1
```

mSQL SQL

CREATE

```
CREATE TABLE name field_name field_type, [field2  type2, ...]
CREATE SEQUENCE ON table [STEP value] [VALUE value]
CREATE INDEX name ON table ( column, ... )
```

Creates new database elements (or entirely new databases). This statement is used to create tables, indices, and sequences.

The **CREATE SEQUENCE** statement adds a sequence to a table. A sequence is simply a value associated with a table that the mSQL server keeps track of. Most commonly, a sequence is used to generate unique identification numbers for tables. The value of the sequence is incremented every time the sequence value is read. The **STEP** modifier determines how much the sequence value is increased each time. The **VALUE** modifier gives the initial value of the sequence.

The **CREATE INDEX** statement defines an index for the table. The mSQL system supports indexes that contain more than one field. You must provide a name for the index, although it need not be meaningful because it is rarely needed by the end user.

The **CREATE TABLE** statement defines the structure of a table within the database. This statement is how all mSQL tables are created. The syntax of the create definition is the name of a field followed by the type of the field, followed by any modifiers (e.g., `name char(30) not null`). The following datatypes are supported by mSQL:

CHAR(*length*)
    Fixed length character value. No values can be greater than the given length.

DATE
    Standard date type.

INT

Standard 4-byte integer. Range is -2147483646 to 2147483647.

MONEY

Monetary type suitable for accurately storing money values. This type allows for storing decimal values (like 19.99) without the imprecision of using a floating point type.

REAL

Standard 8-byte floating point value. Minimum nonzero values are +/- 4.94E-324 and maximum are +/- 1.79E+308.

TEXT(*length*)

Variable length character value. The given length is the maximum value for most of the data, but longer data can be entered.

TIME

Standard time type.

UINT

Standard 4-byte unsigned integer. Range is 0 to 4294967295.

In addition to the main types, several modifiers can also be used to qualify the type:

length

This value is the maximum length of a character type. For CHAR, this is the absolute maximum. For TEXT this is only an approximate maximum that should apply to most of the data. Longer data can be inserted into a TEXT field, but it will make the table slower.

NOT NULL

Specifies that the field cannot contain a null value. Attempting to insert a null value into such a field will result in an error.

Examples

```
# Create a simple table
CREATE TABLE emp_data ( id INT, name CHAR(50) )
# Add a sequence to the table 'checks' with the initial value '1000' and the
# default step of 1.
CREATE SEQUENCE ON checks VALUE 1000
# Create an index on the table 'music' that covers the fields 'artist',
# 'publisher', and 'title'.
CREATE INDEX idx1 ON music ( artist, publisher, title )
```

DELETE

```
DELETE FROM table [WHERE clause]
```

Deletes rows from a table. When used without a **WHERE** clause, this will erase the entire table and recreate it as an empty table. With a clause, it will delete the rows that match the condition of the clause.

Examples

```
# Erase all of the data (but not the table itself) for the table 'olddata'.
DELETE FROM olddata
# Erase all records in the 'sales' table where the 'year' field is '1995'.
DELETE FROM sales WHERE year=1995
```

DROP

```
DROP INDEX name
DROP TABLE name
DROP SEQUENCE FROM table
```

Permanently remove a table, index, or sequence from the mSQL system.

 DROP is by far the most dangerous SQL statement. If you have drop privileges, you may permanently erase a table or even an entire database. This is done without warning or confirmation. The only way to undo a DROP is to restore the table or database from backups. The lessons to be learned here are (1) always keep backups and (2) don't use DROP unless you are really sure.

Examples

```
# Delete the tables 'oh_no'
DROP TABLE oh_no
# Remove the named index 'my_index'
DROP INDEX my_index
# Erase the sequence defined on the table 'counter'. Another sequence can be
# recreated at any time using the 'CREATE SEQUENCE' statement.
DROP SEQUENCE FROM counter
```

INSERT

```
INSERT INTO table [ (column, ...) ] VALUES ( values )
```

Inserts data into a table. This statement inserts the given values into the given columns. Columns in the table that are not given values are set to **NULL**. If you leave out the list of columns, the number of value given must exactly match the number of columns in the table.

Examples

```
# Insert a record into the 'people' table.
INSERT INTO people ( name, rank, serial_number ) VALUES ( 'Bob Smith',
    'Captain', 12345 )
```

SELECT

```
SELECT [DISTINCT] columns FROM table [clause]
```

Retrieves data from a database. The SELECT statement is the primary method of reading data from database tables.

If you specify more than one table, mSQL will automatically join the tables so that you can compare values between the tables.

If the DISTINCT keyword is present, only one row of data will be output for every group of rows that is identical.

The column names can be specified as column or table.column. The longer form is necessary only to disambiguate columns with the same name, but can be used at any time (e.g., SELECT name FROM people; SELECT people.name FROM people).

The list of tables to join are specified as Table1, Table2, Table3, ... The tables are joined in the manner that mSQL deems most efficient. Table names can also be aliased (e.g., SELECT t1.name, t2.address FROM long_table_name=t1, longer_table_name=t2).

If no clause is provided, SELECT returns all of the data in the selected table(s).

The search clause can contain any of the following substatements:

WHERE statement

> The WHERE statement construct is the most common way of searching for data in SQL. The statement is a comparison of two or more values. Named values (such as column names and aliases) and literal numbers and strings can be used in the statement. The following operators are supported:

> AND

>> Performs a logical AND (returns 0 if any of the arguments are 0, otherwise returns 1)

> OR

>> Performs a logical OR (returns 1 if any of the arguments are not 0, otherwise returns 0)

> ( )

>> Parentheses are used to group operators in order to force precedence.

= Returns 1 if the two values are equal, otherwise returns 0. MySQL automatically converts between types when comparing values.

<> Returns 1 if the two values are not equal, otherwise returns 0.

<= Returns 1 if the left value is less than or equal to the right value, otherwise returns 0.

< Returns 1 if the left value is less than the right value, otherwise returns 0.

>= Returns 1 if the left value is greater than or equal to the right value, otherwise returns 0.

> Returns 1 if the left value is greater than the right value, otherwise returns 0.

ORDER BY *column* [DESC][, *column2* [DESC],...]

Sorts the returned data using the given column(s). If DESC is present, the data is sorted in descending order, otherwise ascending order is used (e.g., **SELECT** name, age FROM people ORDER BY age DESC).

value1 LIKE *value2*

Compares *value1* to *value2* and returns 1 if they match and 0 otherwise. The right-hand value can contain the wildcard "%" which matches any number of characters (including 0) and '_' which matches exactly one character. This is probably the single most used comparison in SQL. The most common usage is to compare a field value with a literal containing a wildcard (e.g., **SELECT** name FROM people WHERE name LIKE 'B%').

value1 RLIKE *value2*

Compares *value1* to *value2* using the extended regular expression syntax and returns 1 if they match and 0 otherwise. The right hand value can contain full Unix regular expression wildcards and constructs (e.g., **SELECT** name FROM people WHERE name RLIKE '^B.*').

value1 CLIKE *value2*

Compares *value1* to *value2* using a case insensitive version of the LIKE operator (e.g., **SELECT** name FROM people WHERE name CLIKE 'b%').

The WHERE clause returns any of the expression values that are not 0 or NULL. Therefore, **SELECT** age FROM people WHERE age>10 will return only those ages that are greater than 10.

Examples

```
# Find all names in the 'people' table where the 'state' field is 'MI'.
SELECT name FROM people WHERE state='MI'
# Display all of the data in the 'mytable' table.
SELECT * FROM mytable
```

UPDATE

```
UPDATE table SET column=value, ... [WHERE clause]
```

Alters data within a table. This statement is used to change actual data within a table without altering the table itself.

Example

```
# Change the name 'John Deo' to 'John Doe' everywhere in the people table.
UPDATE people SET name='John Doe' WHERE name='John Deo'
```

16

MySQL and mSQL System Variables

Several variables can be used to customize the operation of MySQL and mSQL. Many of these are environment variables that are inherited from the user's shell, while others are set via command line options and configuration files.

MySQL System Variables

Environment Variables

The following variables are specific to MySQL programs. They may be defined in the current shell or as part of a shell script. To set a variable for the MySQL daemon (*mysqld*), define the variable in the *safe_mysqld* script that is used to start the daemon or define the variables in the MySQL configuration file (described later in this chapter).

MY_BASEDIR

MY_BASEDIR_VERSION

> The root directory containing the subdirectories *'bin'*, *'var'* and *'libexec'* that contain the MySQL programs and data. A default value of this (usually compiled into MySQL as */usr/local*) is used if this variable does not exist. This option affects only the *mysqld* program.

MYSQL_DEBUG

> The debugging level for the program. This option can be used with any MySQL program. The debugging library used by MySQL has many options. A list of all of the available options can be found at *http://www.turbolift.com/ mysql/appendixC.html*. The most common set of options is `d:t:o,/tmp/ debugfile`.

MYSQL_HOST

The hostname used to connect to a remote MySQL database server. This option can be used with any of the MySQL client programs (*mysql, mysqlshow, mysqladmin,* etc.).

MYSQL_PWD

The password used to connect to the MySQL database server. This option can be used with any of the MySQL client programs.

 Be careful where you put your passwords. A common use for environment variables is to set them within scripts. Of course, setting this particular variable in a script would make your password visible to anyone who can run the script. Even setting the variable manually on the command line exposes it to the superuser and any else who has the ability to examine the system memory.

MYSQL_TCP_PORT

When used with a client program, this is the TCP port on a remote machine used to connect to the MySQL database server. When used with *mysqld*, this is the port used to listen for incoming connections.

MYSQL_UNIX_PORT

When used with a client program, this is the Unix socket file used to connect to the MySQL database server. When used with *mysqld*, this is the name of the Unix socket file created that allows local connections.

In addition, the MySQL programs use the following environment variables that are routinely set as part of the Unix environment.

EDITOR

VISUAL

The path of the default editor. The *mysql* program uses this program to edit SQL statements if a \e or **edit** command is encountered.

HOME

The home directory of the current user.

LOGIN

LOGNAME

USER

The username of the current user.

PATH

The list of directories used to find programs.

POSIXLY_CORRECT

> If this variable is defined, no special processing is done on command line options. Otherwise, command line options are reordered so that extended options can be used. This variable can be used with any MySQL program.

TMP

TMPDIR

> The directory in which temporary files are kept. If this variable is not defined '/tmp' is used.

TZ

> The time zone of the local machine.

UMASK

> The umask used when creating new files.

Command line variables

These options are supplied via the –O or –set-variable command line option that is available in most MySQL programs.

back_log

> The number of TCP connections that can be queued at once. The default value is 5. This option is available for *mysqld* only.

connect_timeout

> The number of seconds the *mysqld* server waits for a connect packet before responding with Bad handshake.

decode-bits

> The number of bits used for generating certain internal tables. This should be a number between 4 and 9 (between 4 and 6 on a 16-bit operating system). The default value is 9. This option is available only for *isamchk* and should be used only if you understand the details of the ISAM table structure.

delayed_insert_limit

> Causes the INSERT DELAYED handler to check whether there are any SELECT statements pending after inserting *delayed_insert_limit* rows. If so, the handler allows the statements to execute before continuing.

delayed_insert_timeout

> How long an INSERT DELAYED thread should wait for INSERT statements to finish before terminating.

delayed_queue_size

> How big a queue (in rows) should be allocated for handling INSERT DELAYED. If the queue becomes full, any client that does an INSERT DELAYED must wait until there is room in the queue again.

dritebuffer

> The size of the buffer used to store outgoing data. The default value is 260KB. This option is only available for *isamchk*.

flush_time

> If set, all tables are closed then every flush_time seconds to free resources and synchronize changes to disk.

join_buffer

> The size of a buffer used when performing table joins. Increasing this can speed up performance for queries that join tables. The default value is 130 KB. This option is available only for *mysqld*.

key_buffer_size

> The size of a buffer allocated to store recently accessed keys. Increasing this can speed up performance for queries that involve the repeated use of the same keys. This option is available for *isamchk* (where the default value is 0.5 MB) and *mysqld* (default value of 1 MB).

long_query_time

> If set, the slow_queries counter is incremented each time a query takes longer than *long_query_time* seconds.

max_allowed_packet

> The maximum size of the buffer used to store incoming data. Each client connection has a separate buffer. The default value is 64KB. This option is available only for *mysqld*.

max_connect_errors

> If set, the server blocks further connections from a remote host when the number of interrupted connections from that host exceeds *max_connect_errors*. You can unblock a host with the command FLUSH HOSTS.

max_connections

> The maximum number of simultaneous client connections. The default value is 90. This option can be used only with *mysqld*.

max_delayed_threads

> Start no more than this number of threads to handle INSERT DELAYED. If a client tries to use INSERT DATA to insert new data after this limit is reached, the request is handled as if the DELAYED attribute was not specified.

max_join_size

> The maximum size of a temporary table created by joining tables. The default value is 4 GB. This option can be used only with *mysqld*.

max_sort_length

> The maximum number of characters to examine when sorting a BLOB or VARCHAR field. The default value is 1KB.

max_tmp_tables

(To be implemented later for Version 3.23.) Maximum number of temporary tables a client can keep open at the same time.

net_buffer_length

The initial size of the buffer used to store incoming data. Each client connection has a separate buffer. The default value is 8KB. This option is available for *mysql, mysqld,* and *mysqldump.*

readbuffer

The size of the buffer used to store data being read from files. The default value is 260KB. This option is available only for *isamchk.*

record_buffer

The size of a buffer used to read data from the tables directly (that is, not using keys). Increasing this can speed up performance for queries that do not involve keys. The default value is 130KB. This option is available only for *mysqld.*

sortbuffer

The size of the buffer used when sorting table data. The default value is 1MB. This option is available only for *isamchk.*

sort_buffer

The size of the buffer used when performing sorts on retrieved data. Increasing this can speed up performance for queries that use ORDER BY or GROUP BY statements. The default value is 2MB. This option is available only for *mysqld.*

sort_key_blocks

The number of blocks of keys used when sorting keys. This default value is 16. This option is only available for *isamchk* and should be used only if you understand the details of the ISAM table structure.

table_cache

The maximum number of tables the database server can have open at once. The default value is 64. This option is only available for *mysqld.*

tmp_table_size

The maximum size of temporary tables used by the database server. The default value is 1MB. This option is only available for *mysqld.*

thread_stack

The size of the memory stack for each thread. The default value is 64KB. This option is only available for *mysqld.*

wait_timeout

The number of seconds the server waits for activity on a connection before closing it.

The MySQL Configuration File

As of MySQL 3.22, you may specify both server and client options within a text configuration file. There is one format for this file which takes on different meaning depending on the location of the file. If the configuration file is stored in */etc/ my.cnf*, the options apply to all MySQL servers and clients on the machine. If it located in the data directory of a MySQL server (e.g., */usr/local/mysql/data/my.cnf*) the options effect the operation of that MySQL server. Lastly, if the configuration file is named *.my.cnf* (note the initial period) and is located in the home directory of a user, it effects any clients run by that user.

The format of the file is similar to the one popularized by Windows initialization files. The file is broken up into stanzas, each with a group name enclosed in brackets. Underneath the group name is a list of options. Comments are indicated by a line beginning with # or ;. Each group name is the name of a MySQL client or server program you wish the option to affect. The special group name `client` affects all MySQL client programs (everything except *mysqld*).

The options given in this file can be any long form command line option to any MySQL command (excluding the double-dash "--" option indentifier). Following is a sample server-wide *my.cnf* file.

```
[client]
port=9999
socket=/dev/mysql

[mysqld]
port=9999
socket=/dev/mysql
set-variable = join_buffer=1M

[mysql]
host=dbhost
unbuffered
```

mSQL System Variables

Before mSQL 2, the only post-install configuration that could be performed was through a few global environment variables. However, mSQL 2.0 introduced a configuration file that allows for a much greater flexibility in setting mSQL's parameters. This section covers both the environment variables and the mSQL 2 specific configuration file.

Environment Variables

The following variables are specific to mSQL programs. They may be defined in the current shell or as part of a shell script.

MSQL_DEBUG

> The debugging level for the program. This is a number from 0 (no output) to 3 (maximum output).

MSQL_CONF_FILE

> The path to the mSQL configuration file as shown later.

In addition, the mSQL programs use the following environment variables that are routinely set as part of the Unix environment.

USER

> The username of the current user.

EDITOR
VISUAL

> The path of the default editor. The *msql* program uses this program to edit SQL statements if a \e command is encountered.

The mSQL Configuration File

The mSQL configuration file contains the values of several variables that effect the operation of the mSQL programs. By default, the location of the configuration file is */usr/local/Hughes/msql.conf*. This value can be changed by setting the MSQL_CONF_FILE environment variable. The configuration file begins with a section name in brackets followed by the variables for that section. Following is a sample `msql.conf` file:

```
[general]

Inst_Dir = /usr/local/Hughes
mSQL_User = msql
Admin_User = root
Pid_File = %I/msql2d.pid
TCP_Port = 1114
UNIX_Port = %I/msql2.sock

[system]

Msync_Timer = 30
Host_Lookup = True
Read_Only = False

[w3-msql]

Auth_Host = NULL
Footer = True
Force_Private = False
```

The **general** section affects the operation of all mSQL programs, the *msqld* database server uses the **system** section and the w3-msql section is for the W3-mSQL web/database interaction system. When mSQL reads the configuration files, it replaces the characters %I with the location of the mSQL installation on the server machine. The available variables for each section are listed below.

general

Admin_User

> The username of the account allowed to make changes to the mSQL database as a whole. The default value is `root`.

Inst_Dir

> The location of the mSQL installation. All occurrences of %I in the configuration file are replaced with this value. The default value is */usr/local/Hughes*.

mSQL_User

> The username of the account that runs the mSQL server daemon. The default value is `msql`.

Pid_File

> The location of the file containing the process ID of the running mSQL daemon. The default is `%I/msql2d.pid`.

TCP_Port

> The TCP port number used to connect to a mSQL server (in the case of the client programs) or to listen for incoming connections (in the case of *msql2d*). The default value is `1114`.

UNIX_Port

> The filename of the Unix socket used to connect to the local mSQL server (in the case of the client programs) or to allow local connections (in the case of *msql2d*). The default value is `%I/msql2.sock`.

system

Host_Lookup

> If set to 'True', all client connections must be from machines that have valid, verifiable hostnames.

Msync_timer

> The interval (in seconds) at which the data used by the server in RAM is synchronized with the data on disk.

Read_Only

> If set to 'True', no modifications are allowed on the database. Only `SELECT` queries are permitted.

w3-msql

Auth_Host

The hostname of the machine containing the database server with the W3-Auth tables. If set to NULL or omitted, the local server is used.

Footer

If set to 'True', the standard Hughes Technologies footer will be appended to every page.

Force_Private

If set to 'True', only pages that are protected by W3-Auth can be accessed through W3-mSQL. This prevents regular HTML files from being processed through W3-mSQL.

17

MySQL and mSQL Programs and Utilities

Both MySQL and mSQL come prepackaged with a wealth of programs and utilities to make interacting with the database server easier. Some of these programs are used by the end user to read and write from the database, while others are meant for the database administrator to maintain and repair the database as a whole.

MySQL Utilities

isamchk

```
isamchk [options] table [table...]
```

Performs operations on the database table files themselves (called ISAM files for Indexed Sequential Access Method). This utility is used to check and repair the files, as well as report information about them. You must provide the correct path to the ISAM file you wish to examine. The default location for the ISAM files is */usr/local/ var/databasename/tablename.ISM.*

Options

-?, --help
> Display usage information.

-# debuglevel, --debug=debuglevel
> Set the debugging level to **debuglevel**. The debugging library used by MySQL has many options. A list of all of the available options can be found at *http://www.turbolift.com/mysql/appendixC.html.* The most common set of options is **d:t:o,/tmp/debugfile.**

-a, --analyze
> Analyze the distribution of keys within a table and make adjustments if performance would be improved.

-d, --description
Display short description of a table.

-e, --extend-check
Perform additional checks on the integrity of a table. With this option, you can be absolutely sure that the table is not damaged.

-f, --force
Overwrite without warning files that already exist. Also automatically recover damaged tables without notice.

-i, --information
Display full statistics the table(s) being checked.

-k=number, --keys-used=number
Update only number of keys used. This option is used mainly to disable the keys (-k=0) to speed up other operations on the table such as a bulk load.

-l, --no-symlinks
Do not repair a table that is a symlink.

-q, --quick
Speed up repair by not examining the data file.

-r, --recover
Perform general repair on the table. Does not fix duplicate keys which are supposed to be unique.

-o, --safe-recover
Use an older, slower method of recovery that can repair some things that "–r" will miss.

-O, --set-variable
Set an option variable. See Chapter 16, *MySQL and mSQL System Variables*, for a full list of usable variables.

-s, --silent
Display only errors

-S, --sort-index
Sort the index block of the table.

-R=index, --sort-records=index
Sort the records of the table by index within the table.

-u, --unpack
Decompress a file packed with *pack_isam*.

-v, --verbose
Display extra information.

-V, --version

> Display version information.

-w, --wait

> If the table is locked, wait for it to be unlocked. Without this option, *ismchk* will exit if it encounters a locked table.

isamlog

```
isamlog [options] [logfile] [table]
```

Displays information about ISAM logs. An ISAM log is generated if the MySQL server is started with the **–log-isam** option. The information in the ISAM log can be used to recover damaged tables using the –r option. However, modifying the data files directly can be dangerous and you should always back up your data before doing so.

Options

-?, --help

> Display usage information

-# debuglevel

> Set debugging level. A list of all of the available options can be found at *http://www.turbolift.com/mysql/appendixC.html.*

-c number

> Examine only the last **number** commands.

-f number

> Maximum number of open files. When repairing large logs *isamlog* can have a number of tables open at once. If you consistently run out of file descriptors on your system, this option will limit the number of files *isamlog* uses. Instead of using more files, it will juggle data between the open files and memory, resulting in slower operation.

-F directory

> Directory containing the ISAM log file.

-i   Display additional information.

-o number

> Offset number commands before examining the log.

-p   Remove components from the path.

-r   Ignore errors while examining log. This option allows you to recover all of the information within a log file.

-R datafile recordnumber

Open an ISAM data file (a file ending with .ISM) and retrieve the data at recordnumber.

-u   Update the tables using the log information.

-v   Display extra information about the process.

-V   Display version information.

-w file

Write all records found using –R to a file.

mysql

```
mysql [options] [database]
```

The MySQL command line monitor. This program is the most basic way to communicate with the MySQL server. SQL commands can be typed directly on the command line and the results are displayed on the screen. If **database** is supplied, it is automatically selected as the current database.

The command line monitor works much like a bash shell, because it uses the same GNU readline function that bash uses. For example, you can complete a word by using the tab key, press Ctrl-a to jump to the start of the current line or Ctrl-e to jump to the end, press Ctrl-r to perform a reverse search, and use the up arrow to retrieve the previous command.

Statements can continue over multiple lines and are not acted upon until a command is given. When using full word commands (go, print, etc.) the command must be entered on a line by itself. Escape character commands (\g, \p, etc.) can be used at the end of any line. In addition, a semicolon can be used to end an SQL statement just like \g.

Commands

help, ?, \h

Display the list of commands.

clear, \c

Clear (ignore) the current statement.

edit, \e

Edit the current statement using the default editor.

exit.

Exit the program.

go, \g, ;

Send the current statement to the database server.

ego, \G

Send the current statement to the server and display the results vertically.

print, \p

Display the current statement.

quit, \q

Same as *exit.*

rehash, \#

Rebuild the index of completion terms.

status, \s

Display status information about the server and the current session.

use, \u

Select another database.

Options

-?, --help

Display usage information.

-# debuglevel. --debug=debuglevel

Set the debugging level. A list of all of the available options can be found at *http://www.turbolift.com/mysql/appendixC.html* -A, --no-auto-rehash.

Do not automatically rehash database information.

-B, --batch

Print results in 'batch' mode. This provides minimally formatted output which can easily be used in other database applications.

-e statement, --execute=statement

Execute the given statement and quit. Automatically implies –B.

-f, --force

Do not stop processing when an SQL error is encountered.

-h host, --host=host

Connect to the database server on the specified host.

-n, --unbuffered

Do not buffer output between queries.

-O variable=value, --set-variable variable=value

Set an option variable. See Chapter 16 for a full list of usable variables.

-p [password], --password[=password]

The password used to connect to the database server. If this option is used without a value, the password is asked from the command line.

-P port, --port=port

> The port number used to connect to the database server.

-q, --quick

> Display output as it comes from the server. If you suspend your terminal while using this option, the server could pause.

-r. --raw

> Display output without any conversion. Only useful in conjunction with –B.

-s, --silent

> Suppress some output.

-S file, --socket=file

> The Unix socket file used to connect to the database server.

-t, --table

> Display output in table format.

-T, --debug-info

> Display debugging information when the program exits.

-u username, --user=username

> Username used for connection with the database.

-v, --verbose

> Display extra output.

-V, --version

> Display version information

-w, --wait

> Wait and attempt connection later if unable to connect to the database server.

mysqlaccess

```
mysqlaccess [options] [host] user database
```

Displays and modifies access rights for the MySQL server. You may examine the rights of users for any database and in connection with any host. Unix shell wildcards '*' and '?' may be used to match multiple hosts, users and databases. All actions are performed on a copy of the actual grant tables until a `mysqlaccess` `--commit` command is sent.

Options

-?, --help

> Display usage information.

-b, --brief

> Display results as a brief single line table.

--commit
> Move changes from temporary table to the actual grant tables. You must run mysqladmin reload before the changes will take effect.

--copy
> Renew the temporary table from the actual grant tables.

-d database, --db=database
> The database to which to connect.

--debug=debuglevel
> Set the debugging level (0 through 3).

-h host, --host=host
> The host whose access rights are examined.

--howto
> Usage examples for the program.

-H host, --rhost=host
> Connect to a database server on a remote host.

--old-server
> Connect to a pre-3.21 MySQL server.

-p password, --password=password
> Check the password of the user being examined.

--plan
> Display suggestions for future releases.

--preview
> Show difference between temporary table and actual grant tables.

-P password, --spassword=password
> Administrative password used to access the grant tables.

--relnotes
> Display the release notes for the program.

--rollback
> Undo the changes made to the temporary table.

-t, --table
> Display results in full table format.

-u username, --user=username
> User to be examined.

-U username. --superuser=username
> Administrative username used to access the grant tables.

-v, --version
> Display version information.

mysqladmin

mysqladmin [*options*] command [*command...*]

Performs operations that affect the database server as a whole. This utility is used to shutdown the database server, add and delete entire databases, and other administrative functions.

Commands

create database
Create a new database.

drop database
Remove and destroy a database.

extended-status
Report a fuller status from the server than the *status* command.

flush-hosts
Send all buffered information to the clients.

flush-logs
Flush all buffered log data.

flush-privileges
Same as *reload*.

flush-status
Clear the status variables.

flush-tables
Commit all buffered table operations.

kill thread-id [thread-id...]
Kill one or more *mysqld* server threads.

password password
Set the administration password for the database server.

ping
Check if the MySQL server is alive.

processlist
Show the active *mysqld* server threads.

reload
Reload access information from the grant tables.

refresh
Perform all buffered table operations and reopen the log files.

shutdown
Shutdown the database server.

status

> Report the status of the server.

variables

> Display the system variables used by the server.

version

> Display the version number of the server.

Options

-?, --help

> Display usage information.

-# debuglevel, --debug=debuglevel

> Set the debugging level. See *isamchk* for more information.

-f, --force

> Drop tables without confirmation. Also, do not quit if an error is encountered.

-h host, --host=host

> Connect to the MySQL server on the given host.

-i seconds, --sleep=seconds

> Perform the commands repeatedly, sleeping the given number of seconds between each run.

-p [password], --password=[password]

> Password used to connect to database server. If this options is used without an argument, the password is asked from the command line.

-P port, --port=port

> Port numbed used to connect to a remove database server.

-s, --silent

> Do not give an error if unable to connect to the database server.

-S file, --socket=file

> The Unix socket used to connect to the local database server.

-u username, --user=username

> User used to connect to the database server.

-V, --version

> Display version information for the *mysqladmin* program.

mysqlbug

```
mysqlbug
```

Report a bug in a MySQL program or utility. This program collects information about your MySQL installation and sends a detailed problem report to the MySQL team.

mysqld

```
mysqld [options]
```

The MySQL server daemon. All other programs interact with the database through this server, so it should be left running at all times (except when down for maintenance). The daemon is usually started from a script called *safe_mysqld*. This script sets the appropriate environment variables and launches *mysqld* with the necessary arguments.

Options

-?, -I, --help

Display usage information.

-# debuglevel, --debug=debuglevel

Set the debugging level. See isamchk for more information.

-b directory, --basedir=directory

The base directory used to determine all other directories.

--big-tables

Allow large result sets by saving temporary results in a file.

--bind-address=ip-number

The IP address the server binds to.

-h directory, --datadir=directory

The directory containing the database data files.

-l [logfile], --log[=logfile]

Log various information, including connections and errors. If no argument is provided, `hostname.log` is used as the log file, where `hostname` is the name of the server machine.

--log-isam[=logfile]

Log changes to the data (ISAM) files. If no argument is provided, *isam.log* is used as the log file. The log generated by this option can be read and manipulated with the *isamlog* utility.

--log-update[=number]

Log database updates. The log file is named *hostname.num*, where `hostname` is the name of the server machine and `num` is the argument to the option or a unique number if no argument is given.

-L=language, --language=language

The language (English, French, etc.) for the server to use.

-n, --new

Enable new (and possibly unsafe) routines.

-o, --old-protocol
>   Use the 3.20.x protocol.

-O variable=value, --set-variable variable=value
>   Set an option variable. See Chapter 16 for a full list of usable variables.

--pid-file=file
>   The name of the file containing the process ID (PID) of the running server. The default value is `hostname.pid` where `hostname` is the name of the server machine.

-P port, --port=port
>   The network port number to use.

--secure
>   Enable network security checks which reduce database performance.

--skip-name-resolve
>   Use only IP numbers (not names) for connections. This increases network performance.

--skip-networking
>   Disable network connections and allow only local access.

--skip-thread-priority
>   Give all threads the same priority.

-S, --skip-new
>   Do not enable new (and possibly unsafe) routines.

-Sg
>   Disable access checking and allow all users full access to all databases.

-Sl
>   Do not perform thread locking.

--socket=file
>   The filename of the Unix socket

-T, --exit-info
>   Display debugging information when shutting down the server

--use-locking
>   Enable thread locking

-v, -V, --version
>   Display version information

mysqldump

```
mysqldump [options] database [table]
```

Outputs the contents of the given database (or table within a database) as a series of ANSI SQL commands. This command is handy for breaking up a database; use the -1 and -opt options.

Options

-?, --help

Display usage information.

-# debuglevel, --debug=debuglevel

Set the debugging level. A list of all of the available options can be found at *http://www.turbolift.com/mysql/appendixC.html.*

--add-drop-table

Include a DROP TABLE statement before every CREATE TABLE.

--add-locks

Add LOCK TABLE statements around the data insertion statements.

--allow-keywords

Output column names that are also reserved keywords. This is not normally desirable as the column may conflict with the keyword.

-c, --compleat-insert

Output complete INSERT statements.

-C, --compress

Use data compression in the connection with the server.

--delayed

Use the INSERT DELAYED statement to insert rows.

-d, --no-data

Do not dump the data, just the table creation statements.

-e, --extended-insert

Uses the multiple-value form of the INSERT statement which can speed up data insertion.

-f, --force

Do not exit if an error is encountered.

-F, --flush-logs

Flush buffered log data before dumping the table(s).

--fields-enclosed-by=delimeter

When dumping with –T, this delimiter is placed on both sides of each field.

--fields-escaped-by=delimeter

> When dumping with –T, this delimiter is placed before any special character as an escape character.

--fields-terminated-by=delimeter

> When dumping with –T, this delimiter is used after every field (default is tab).

-h hostname, --host=hostname

> Connect to a database server on a remote host.

-l, --lock-tables

> Lock the tables before dumping.

--lines-terminated-by=delimeter

> When dumping with –T, this delimiter is used after every line.

-t, --no-create-info

> Do not dump the table creation statements, just the data.

-O variable=value, --set-variable variable=value

> Set an option variable. See Chapter 16 for a full list of usable variables.

--opt

> Adds the most common and useful command line options: --add-drop-table, --add-locks, --extended-insert, --quick, and --use-locks.

-p [password], --password[=password]

> The password used to connect to the database server. If no argument is given, the password is asked from the command line.

-P port, --port=port

> The port used to connect to a remove database server.

-q, --quick

> Display all data immediately, without buffering.

-S file, --socket=file

> The Unix socket used to connect to the local server.

-T directory, --tab=directory

> Generates a tab-separated file with the table data along with a file containing the SQL table creation statements. The files are outputted to the given directory.

-u username, --user=username

> Username used to connect to the database server.

-v, --verbose

> Display information about the state of the process while dumping the data.

-V, --version

> Display version information.

-w statement, --where=statement

> Outputs only the rows that satisfy the given SQL WHERE clause.

mysqlimport

```
mysqlimport [options] database [file]
```

Reads a file of data in a variety of common formats (such as comma delimited or fixed width) and inserts the data into a database. A table with the same name as the file must exist in the database with enough columns of the appropriate type to store the data.

Options

-?, --help

> Display usage information.

-# debuglevel, --debug=debuglevel

> Set the debugging level. A list of all of the available options can be found at *http://www.turbolift.com/mysql/appendixC.html*.

-d, --delete

> Delete all data currently in the table before inserting the new data.

-f, --force

> Do not exit if an error is encountered.

--fields-terminated-by=string

> Indicates that the fields in the data file are terminated by a string.

--fields-enclosed-by=string

> Indicates that the fields in the data file are enclosed by a string.

--fields-optionally-enclosed-by=string

> Indicates that the fields in the data file could also be enclosed by another string.

--fields-escaped-by=string

> The string used as escape characters in the data file.

-h hostname, --host=hostname

> Connect to a database server on a remote host.

-I, --ignore

> Ignore the new data if it conflicts with an existing unique key.

-l, --lock-tables

> Lock the tables before inserting the data.

-p [password], --password[=password]

> Password used to connect to the database server. If no argument is given, the password is asked from the command line.

-P port, --port=port

> Port used to connect to a remove database server.

-r, --replace

> If the new data conflicts with an existing unique key, replace the old data.

-s, --silent

> Suppress some output.

-S file, --socket=file

> The Unix socket used to connect to the local database server.

-u username, --user=username

> The username used to connect to the database server.

-v, --verbose

> Display information about the process while inserting the data.

-V, --version

> Display version information.

mysqlshow

```
mysqlshow [options] [database] [table] [field]
```

Displays the layout of the requested database, table or field. If no argument is given, a list of all of the databases is given. With one argument the layout of the given database is show. With two arguments, a table within the database is displayed. If all three arguments are present, the information about a specific field within a table is presented.

Options

-?, --help

> Display usage information.

-# debuglevel, --debug=debuglevel

> Set the debugging level. A list of all of the available options can be found at *http://www.turbolift.com/mysql/appendixC.html*.

-h hostname, --host=hostname

> Connect to a remote database server.

-k, --keys

> Display the keys of a table.

-p [password], --password[=password]

> Password used to connect to the database server. If no argument is given, the password is asked from the command line.

-P port, --port=port

> Port used to connect to a remote database server.

-S file, --socket=file
>   The Unix socket used to connect to the local database server.

-u username, --user=username
>   Username used to connect to the database server.

-V, --version
>   Display version information.

mSQL Utilities

msql

```
msql [options] database
```

The mSQL command line monitor. This program is the most basic way to communicate with the mSQL server. SQL commands can be typed directly on the command line and the results are displayed on the screen. Statements can continue over multiple lines. No action is taken until a line ending with a command is entered.

Commands

\e Edit the previous statement using the default editor.

\g Submit statement to the database server.

\p Display the current statement.

\q Exit the program.

Options
-f file
>   Use an alternate configuration file.

-h hostname
>   Connect to the database server on a remote host.

msql2d

```
msql2d [options]
```

The mSQL server daemon. All other programs interact with the database through this server, so it should be left running at all times (except when down for maintenance).

Options
-f file
>   Use an alternate configuration file.

msqladmin

```
msqladmin [options] command
```

Performs operations that affect the database server as a whole. This utility is used to shut down the database server, add and delete entire databases, and other administrative functions.

Commands
copy database newdatabase

Create an exact duplicate of a database under a different name.

create database

Create a new blank database.

drop database

Remove a database and destroy its contents.

move database newdatabase

Rename a database.

reload

Reread the configuration files.

shutdown

Terminate the database server.

stats

Display statistics about the database server. This shows who is currently connected to the server, what database they are using and how many queries they have sent, among other things.

version

Display the version information for the database server.

Options
-f file

Use an alternate configuration file.

-h hostname

Connect to a database server on a remote host.

-q   Do not ask for verification of commands.

msqldump

```
msqldump [options] database [table]
```

Outputs the contents of the given database (or table within a database) as a series of ASCII SQL commands.

Options

-c   Output complete INSERT statements.

-f file

Use an alternate configuration file.

-h hostname

Connect to a database server on a remote host.

-t   Dump only the table creation statements; do not dump the data.

-w statement

Use an SQL WHERE clause to limit the data outputted.

-v   Display status information while dumping the data.

msqlexport

msqlexport [*options*] database table

Outputs the contents of the given table in ASCII delimited format.

Options

-e character

Use **character** to escape any of the delimiter characters found in the data.

-h hostname

Connect to a database server on a remote host.

-q character

The character used to surround each data value.

-s character

The character used to delimit the data.

-v   Display status information while dumping the data.

msqlimport

msqlimport [*options*] database table

Reads an ASCII delimited file and inserts the data into the given table.

Options

-e character

The character used to as an escape character in the data.

-h hostname

Connect to a database server on a remote host.

-q character

The character used to surround each data value.

-s character
> The character used to delimit the data.

-v Display status information while dumping the data.

relshow

```
relshow [options] [database] [table] [index|_seq]
```

Displays the layout of the requested database, table, index, or sequence. If no argument is given, a list of all of the databases is given. With one argument, the layout of the given database is shown. With two arguments, a table within the database is displayed. If all three arguments are present, the third argument must be an index within the given table, or _seq, in which case information about the sequence on the table is shown.

Options
-f file
> Use an alternate configuration file.

-h hostname
> Connect to a database server on a remote host.

18

PHP and Lite Reference

PHP

The following is the quick reference guide to PHP. This list is complete as of PHP 3. The functions that work with MySQL and mSQL are covered, but those specific to other database servers—such as Ababas D, dbm, Oracle, and PostgreSQL—are omitted.

abs

```
$pos_num = abs($number);
```

Returns the absolute value of **number**.

addslashes

```
$escaped_string = addslashes($string);
```

Returns a copy of **string** with any $ \ or ' characters escaped.

asort

```
$sorted_array = asort($array);
```

Returns a sorted copy of the associative array **array**. **asort** works only on associative arrays. Use **sort** to sort regular arrays. If the first member of the array is a number the returned array will.be sorted numerically, otherwise the returned array will be sorted alphabetically.

bindec

```
$decimal = bindec($binary);
```

Returns the decimal equivalent of **binary**.

ceil

```
$higher_integer = ceil($number);
```

Rounds **number** to the next highest integer and returns that as a floating point value.

chdir

```
chdir($directory);
```

Changes the current working directory to **directory**.

chgrp

```
chgrp($file,$group);
```

Changes the file **file** to belong to the group **group**.

chimed

```
chimed($file,$permissions);
```

Changes the file to have the permissions **permissions**. The permissions argument must be given as an octal value.

chown

```
chown($file, $owner);
```

Changes the file to belong to the owner **owner**. This function takes effect only if the PHP binary is running as root, which is not generally recommended.

chop

```
$stripped_string = chop($string);
```

Returns **string** with all trailing new lines, spaces, and tabs removed.

chr

```
$character = chr($number);
```

Returns the character that corresponds to the ASCII value of **number**. Hexadecimal and octal numbers are denoted with the usual 0xff and 077 respectively. All other numbers are considered decimal.

clearstack

```
clearstack();
```

Empties the current stack. This function is a kludge designed to circumvent a limitation in the design of PHP. If you have a user-defined function that contains a large loop, you may run into stack space problems. If this happens, call this function inside the loop. The drawback of doing this is that your function cannot be called within another function. The output of your function has to be saved to a variable which then can be used as you wish.

clearstatcache

```
clearstatcache();
```

Empties the cache used for any functions that access information about files. Because accessing file information can take a relatively long time, this information is stored in a cache by PHP. If you want to be sure you are getting the most current (i.e., noncached) information about a file, call this function before retrieving the information.

closedir

```
closedir($directory);
```

Closes a directory opened with **opendir**.

closelog

```
closelog();
```

Stops all logging done via **syslog**.

cos

```
$result = cos($number);
```

Returns the cosine of **number**.

count

```
$number = count($array);
```

Returns the number of elements in **array**. If **array** is a nonarray variable, the function returns 1 (because a variable looks like an array with only one element). If **array** is not defined, 0 is returned.

crypt

```
$encrypted_string = crypt($string);
$encrypted_string = crypt($string, $salt);
```

Returns an encrypted version of **string**. The encryption is the standard Unix DES encryption as used in Unix passwords and the like. An optional two-character salt can be provided.

date

```
$formatted_date = date($format,$time);
```

Returns **time** (a standard Unix time as given by the Time function) formatted with **format**. The returned value is the same as **format** except that the following characters are replaced with the appropriate value:

A   AM/PM

a   am/pm

D   Day (eg., Sun)

d   Day (eg., 13)

F   Month (eg., February)

H   Hours in 24 hour format (eg., 17)

h   Hours in 12 hour format (eg., 5)

i   Minutes (eg., 30)

l   Day (eg., Sunday)

M   Month (eg., Feb)

m   Month (eg., 02)

s   Seconds (eg., 27)

Y   Year (eg., 1998)

y   Year (eg., 98)

U   Seconds since epoch (eg., 803537321)

z   Day of the year (eg., 154)

dblist

```
$db_info = dblist();
```

Returns a list of the databases supported by PHP.

decbin

```
$binary = decbin($decimal);
```

Returns the binary equivalent of **decimal**.

dexhex

```
$hex = dechex($decimal);
```

Returns the hexadecimal equivalent of **decimal**.

decoct

```
$octal = decoct($decimal);
```

Returns the octal equivalent of **decimal**.

doubleval

```
$double = doubleval($variable);
```

Returns **variable** as a floating point number.

echo

```
echo [format_string] expression [, expression ...]
```

This is not a true function but rather PHP's built-in version of the C `printf` function. In its simplest form, **echo** simply prints out **expression**. Up to 5 expressions can be given, each of which are printed out in turn. In addition, a format string can be provided. The format string is in the same style as C or Perl's `printf` function.

end

```
end($array);
```

Sets the internal pointer of **array** to the end of the array.

ereg

```
$result = ereg($expression, $string);
$result = ereg($expression, $string, $match_array);
```

Returns a true value if **string** matches the regular expression **expression**. If an array is provided as the third argument, the values matched in the string are placed in the array.

eregi

```
$result = eregi($expression, $string);
$result = eregi($expression, $string, $match_array);
```

Identical to *eregi* except that case is ignored for the purposes of matching.

ereg_replace

```
ereg_replace($expression, $replacement_string, $string);
```

Replaces all parts of **string** that match **expression** with **replacement_string**.

eregi_replace

```
eregi_replace($expression, $replacement_string, $string);
```

Identical to **ereg_replace** except that case is ignored for the purposes of matching.

escapeshellcmd

```
$safe_string = escapeshellcmd($string);
```

Returns a copy of **string** with its characters escaped so that it is safe for use with *exec* or *system*.

eval

```
eval($string);
```

Evaluates the contents of **string** as if it were a PHP script. Variable substitution is done on the string so if you want to use a variable in the "miniscript" you should escape it.

exec

```
$last_line = exec($command);
$last_line = exec($command, $output_array);
$last_line = exec($command, $output_array, $return_code);
```

Executes **command** as a Unix command in a subshell. Only the last line of the command output is returned. If an array is provided as the second argument, all of the lines of output from the command are placed in the array. If a third argument is present, the return code from the command is placed in that variable.

exit

```
exit();
```

Ends all parsing of the HTML file.

exp

```
$result = exp($number);
```

Returns the number *e* raised to the **number** power.

fclose

```
fclose($fd);
```

Closes a file opened by **fopen**.

feof

```
$result = feof($fd);
```

Returns true if the file descriptor **fd** is at the end of the file.

fgets

```
$line = fgets($fd, $max_bytes);
```

Returns the next line (up to **max_bytes** in length) from the file referred to by **fd**.

fgetss

```
$line = fgetss($fd, $max_bytes);
```

Identical to **fgets** except that it attempts to strip all HTML and PHP tags from the input.

file

```
$array = file($filename);
```

Returns an array containing every line in the file **filename**.

fileatime

```
$time = fileatime($filename);
```

Returns (in standard Unix time format) the last time **filename** was accessed. If this information cannot be obtained for whatever reason, the function returns −1.

filectime

```
$time = filectime($filename);
```

Returns (in standard Unix time format) the last time **filename**'s status was changed. If this information cannot be obtained for whatever reason, the function returns −1.

filegroup

```
$group_id = filegroup($filename);
```

Returns the group ID of filename's group. If this information cannot be obtained for whatever reason, the function returns −1.

fileinode

```
$inode = fileinode($filename);
```

Returns the inode of **filename**. If this information cannot be obtained for whatever reason, the function returns −1.

filemtime

```
$time = filemtime($filename);
```

Returns (in standard Unix time format) the last time **filename** was modified. If this information cannot be obtained for whatever reason, the function returns –1.

fileowner

```
$owner = fileowner($filename);
```

Returns the ID of the owner of the file. If this information cannot be obtained for whatever reason, the function returns –1.

fileperms

```
$permissions = fileperms($filename);
```

Returns the permissions of **filename**. If this information cannot be obtained for whatever reason, the function returns –1.

filesize

```
$size = filesize($filename);
```

Returns the size of **filename** in bytes. If this information cannot be obtained for whatever reason, the function returns –1.

filetype

```
$type = filetype($filename);
```

Returns one of the following, indicating the type of **filename**: **dir**, **file**, **fifo**, **char**, **block**, or **link**.

floor

```
$lower_integer = floor($number);
```

Rounds **number** to the next lowest integer and returns that as a floating point value.

flush

```
flush();
```

Flushes the buffer on the standard output so that the end user immediately sees all of the output so far.

fopen

```
$fd = fopen($filename, $mode);
```

Opens the file filename in the mode mode and returns a file descripter associated with the open file. As with the C function **fopen**, the mode is one of "r", "r+", "w", "w+", "a", "a+". The function returns –1 if the file could not be opened.

fputs

```
fputs($fd, $string);
```

Writes **string** to the file associated with **fd**, followed by a newline.

fpassthru

```
fpassthru($fd);
```

Directly prints all of the remaining data in the file associated with **fd**.

fseek

```
fseek($fd, $position);
```

Positions the file associated with **fd** to **position** bytes from the beginning of the file.

fsockopen

```
$fd = fsockopen($hostname,$port);
```

Opens a connection with **hostname** on port **port** and returns a file descriptor associated with the open connection. If the port number is 0, the hostname will be considered the filename of a Unix-style socket file on the local host. In the case of an error, the function returns the following: -3 if the socket could not be created, -4 if the hostname could not be resolved, -5 if the connection was refused or timed out, -6 if the fdopen( ) call failed, or -7 if the setvbuf( ) call failed.

ftell

```
$position = ftell($fd);
```

Returns the position of the pointer in the file associated with **fd**. This value can be used as an argument to **fseek**.

getaccdir

```
$directory = getaccdir();
```

Returns the directory where the PHP configuration files are held.

getenv

```
$value = getenv($variable);
```

Returns the value of the environment variable `variable`.

gethostbyname

```
$address = gethostbyname($hostname);
```

Returns the IP address of `hostname`.

gethostbyaddr

```
$hostname = gethostbyaddr($address);
```

Returns the hostname of the machine with the IP address `address`.

getimagesize

```
$file_info_array = getimagesize($filename);
```

Returns an array of information about the image in the file `filename`. The first element of the array is the width of the image, the second is the height, and the third is the type of the image. GIF, JPG, and PNG images are currently recognized. The fourth element is a string of the format "width=xxx height=yyy" which can be used directly in an HTML `<IMG>` tag.

getlastaccess

```
$time = getlastaccess();
```

Returns (in standard Unix time format) the date and time the page was last accessed. This function works only if PHP was compiled with access logging enabled.

getlastbrowser

```
$browser = getlastbrowser();
```

Returns the identification string of the last browser to access the page. This function works only if PHP was compiled with access logging enabled.

getlastemail

```
$email = getlastemail();
```

Returns the e-mail address of the last person to access the page. This function works only if PHP was compiled with access logging enabled.

getlasthost

```
$host = getlasthost( );
```

Returns the hostname of the last machine to access the page. This function works only if PHP was compiled with access logging enabled.

getlastmod

```
$time = getlastmod( );
```

Returns the time (in standard Unix time format) that the page was last modified. This function works only if PHP was compiled with access logging enabled.

getlastref

```
$url = getlastref( );
```

Returns the URL of the referring page of the last visitor to the page. This function works only if PHP was compiled with access logging enabled.

getlogdir

```
$directory = getlogdir( );
```

Returns the directory that contains the PHP log files.

getmyinode

```
$inode = getmyinode( );
```

Returns the inode of the HTML file that contains the current PHP script.

getmypid

```
$pid = getmypid( );
```

Returns the process ID number of the current PHP process.

getmyuid

```
$id = getmyuid( );
```

Returns the user ID of the owner of the HTML file that contains the current PHP script.

getrandmax

```
$number = getrandmax( );
```

Returns the largest possible number that will be returned by **rand**.

getstartlogging

```
$time = getstartlogging();
```

Returns the time (in standard Unix format) that logging began on the HTML file containing the current PHP script.

gettoday

```
$hits = gettoday();
```

Returns the number of hits the page has received since midnight at the beginning of the current day.

gettotal

```
$hits = gettotal();
```

Returns the total number of hits the page has received since logging was started on the page.

gettype

```
$type = gettype($variable);
```

Returns one of "integer," "double," or "string," indicating the type of **variable**.

gmdate

```
$formatted_date = gmdate($format, $time);
```

Identical to Date except that it uses Greenwich Mean time to calculate the values instead of the local time.

header

```
header($header_string);
```

Outputs **header_string** as the HTTP header of the document. This function must be used before any HTML in the file and before any PHP commands which generate output.

hexdec

```
$decimal = hexdec($hex);
```

Returns the decimal equivalent of **hex**.

htmlspecialchars

```
$html_string = htmlspecialchars($string);
```

Returns string, replacing any special characters (including <, >, &, " and all ASCII characters from 160 to 255) with their HTML entity codes.

imagearc

```
imagearc($image, $cx, $cy, $width, $height, $start, $end, $color);
```

Draws a partial ellipse in **image** with the color **color**. The ellipse has the center (cx, cy) width **width**, height **height**, begins at **start** degrees, and ends at **end** degrees.

imagechar

```
imagechar($image, $size, $x, $y, $character, $color);
```

Draws **character** in image with the color **color** with the font size **size**. The top left of **character** is at the point (x, y).

imagecharup

```
imagecharup($image, $size, $x, $y, $character, $color);
```

Identical to **imagechar** except that the character is drawn vertically with the bottom left at (x, y).

imagecolorallocate

```
$color = imagecolorallocate($image, $red, $green, $blue);
```

Returns a color for use with the image **image** using the RGB components specified.

imagecolortransparent

```
imagecolortransparent($image, $color);
```

Sets **color** as the transparent color for **image**.

imagecopyresized

```
imagecopyresized($dest_image, $src_image, $dest_x, $dest_y, $src_x, $src_y,
    $dest_width, $dest_heigth, $src_width, $src_heigth);
```

Copies a rectangular portion from **src_image** and pastes it into **dest_image**, resizing if necessary. The arguments **dest_x** and **dest_y** are the coordinates of the top left of the rectangle for the destination image, and **dest_height** and dest_width are the height and width. The arguments src_x, src_y, src_width, and src_heigth are the corresponding values for the source image.

imagecreate

```
$image = imagecreate($width, $height);
```

Returns an image indentifier representing a new image with the specified height and width.

imagecreatefromgif

```
$image = imagecreatefromgif($filename);
```

Returns an image indentifier representing the image contained in the file filename.

imagedestroy

```
imagedestroy($image);
```

Frees any resources occupied by image.

imagefill

```
imagefill($image, $x, $y, $color);
```

Flood fills image with the color color starting at the point (x, y).

imagefilledpolygon

```
imagefilledpolygon($image, $points_array, $num_points, $color);
```

Creates a polygon in image filled with the color color. The second argument is an array of the points of the polygon. The first two elements of the array are the x and y values of the first point. The next two elements are the value of the next point, and so on. The third argument is the number of points in the polygon.

imagefilledrectangle

```
imagefilledrectangle($image, $x1, $y1, $x2, $y2, $color);
```

Creates a rectangle in image filled with the color *color*. The arguments x1 and y1 form the top left point of the rectangle and x2 and y2 form the bottom right.

imagefilltoborder

```
imagefilltoborder($image, $x, $y, $border, $color);
```

Identical to imagefill except that the fill stops where the color border is encountered.

imagegif

```
imagegif($image);
imagegif($image, $filename);
```

Outputs the contents of **image** as a GIF image. If a second argument is present the GIF is written to that filename, otherwise the output is sent straight to the browser.

imageinterlace

```
imageinterlace($image, $interlace);
```

Toggles the interlace bit of **image** to the value of **interlace**, which should be 1 (for on) or 0 (for off).

imageline

```
imageline($image, $x1, $y1, $x2, $y2, $color);
```

Creates a line in **image** of color **color** from the point (x1, y2) to (x2, y2).

imagepolygon

```
imagepolygon($image, $points, $numpoints, $color);
```

Identical to **imagefilledpolygon** except that the polygon is not filled.

imagerectangle

```
imagerectangle($image, $x1, $y1, $x2, $y2, $color);
```

Identical to **imagefilledrectangle** except that the rectangle is not filled.

imagesetpixel

```
imagesetpixel($image, $x, $y, $color);
```

Draws a single point on **image** at (x, y) of color **color**.

imagestring

```
imagestring($image, $size, $x, $y, $string, $color);
```

Identical to **imagechar** except that it outputs the entire string **string**.

imagestringup

```
imagestringup($image, $size, $x, $y, $string, $color);
```

Identical to **imagecharup** except that it outputs the entire string **string**.

imagesx

```
$x_size = imagesx($image);
```

Returns the width of **image** in pixels.

imagesy

```
$y_size = imagesy($image);
```

Returns the height of **image** in pixels.

include

```
include($filename);
```

Includes the file **filename** in the current page. Full PHP parsing is done on the included file. PHP searches each of the directories in the environment variable **PHP_INCLUDE_PATH** for **filename**.

initsyslog

```
initsyslog();
```

Prepares the system for **syslog** logging. After calling this function you can use **syslog** to generate log entries.

intval

```
$integer = intval($variable);
```

Returns the contents of **variable** as an integer.

isset

```
$defined = isset($variable);
```

Returns 1 if **variable** is defined, 0 otherwise.

key

```
$key = key($array);
```

Returns the key of the next element in **array**. For an associative array, it returns the name of the key. For a regular array it returns the number of the element.

link

```
link($target, $filename);
```

Creates a hard link from **filename** to **target**.

linkinfo

```
$info = linkinfo($filename);
```

Returns a true value if the link filename exists (but not necessarily the file to which the link points). The function returns –1 in case of an error.

log

```
$result = log($number);
```

Returns the natural logarithm of number.

log10

```
$result = log10($number);
```

Returns the base 10 logarithm of number.

logas

```
logas($filename);
```

Logs the hit on the current page as a hit on filename instead of the filename of the page.

mail

```
mail($to, $subject, $message);
mail($to, $subject, $message, $headers);
```

Sends an e-mail message to to with the subject subject and message as the body, If a forth argument is provided it is appended to the headers of the message.

max

```
$maximum = max($array);
```

Returns the largest value in array. If array contains strings, it returns the element that is last alphabetically.

md5

```
$hash = md5($string);
```

Returns the MD5 hash of string.

microtime

```
$ms = microtime();
```

Returns a string that contains the fractional part of the current second (expressed as a decimal) followed by the standard Unix time.

min

```
$minimum = min($array);
```

Returns the minimum value in **array**. If array contains strings, it returns the element that is first alphabetically.

mkdir

```
mkdir($directory, $mode);
```

Creates the directory **directory** with the given mode. The mode must be an octal value.

mktime

```
$time = mktime($hour,$minute,$second,$month,$day,$year);
```

Returns a time in standard Unix time format based on the parameters given. If there are less than six parameters, the rightmost parameters are assumed to be the current value (e.g., if four parameters are given, the current day and year are used).

msql

mysql

```
$result = msql($database, $query);
$result = mysql($database, $query);
```

Sends the query **query** to the mSQL/MySQL database **database**. For a non-SELECT statement the function returns 0 for mSQL 1.x and MySQL and the number of affected rows for mSQL 2.x. For a SELECT statement the function returns a result identifier to be used with other **msql_*** functions. In the case of an error the function returns −1.

mysql_affected_rows

```
$num_rows = mysql_affected_rows();
```

Returns the number of rows affected by the last INSERT, UPDATE, or DELETE statement.

msql_close

mysql_close

```
msql_close();
mysql_close();
```

Closes the connection to the mSQL/MySQL database server.

msql_connect

mysql_connect

```
msql_connect($hostname);
mysql_connect($hostname);
mysql_connect($hostname, $username);
mysql_connect($hostname, $username, $password);
```

Creates a connection with the mSQL/MySQL database server at hostname. A connection to the server on the local host is made with m(y)sql_connect("localhost"). If no connection exists at the time of the first call to m(y)sql, a connection is automatically made to the localhost. With MySQL an optional username or username/password combination may be given. If PHP is being run in its enhanced security mode (called SAFE MODE), the username must be either the owner of the HTML document or the owner of the web server process.

msql_createdb

mysql_createdb

```
msql_createdb($database);
mysql_createdb($database);
```

Creates the given database.

msql_dbname

mysql_dbname

```
$db = msql_dbname($result, $i);
$db = mysql_dbname($result, $i);
```

Returns the name of the database stored in the ith field of the result returned by a call to m(y)sql_listdbs.

msql_dropdb

mysql_dropdb

```
msql_dropdb($database);
mysql_dropdb($database);
```

Removes **database** and all tables within it.

msql_fieldflags

mysql_fieldflags

```
$flags = msql_fieldflags($result, $i);
$flags = mysql_fieldflags($result, $i);
```

Returns the flags belonging to the **i**th field of **result**. The returned value can be one of "primary key", "not null", "not null primary key" or "".

msql_fieldlen

mysql_fieldlen

```
$length = msql_fieldlen($result, $i);
$length = mysql_fieldlen($result, $i);
```

Returns the length of the ith field of **result**.

msql_fieldname

mysql_fieldname

```
$name = msql_fieldname($result, $i);
$name = mysql_fieldname($result, $i);
```

Returns the column name of the **i**th field of **result**.

msql_fieldtype

mysql_fieldtype

```
$type = msql_fieldtype($result, $i);
$type = mysql_fieldtype($result, $i);
```

Returns the type of the **i**th of **result** (i.e. "char", "real", etc.).

msql_freeresult

mysql_freeresult

```
msql_freeresult($result);
mysql_freeresult($result);
```

Frees the memory associated with a mSQL/MySQL result. All memory is automatically freed at the end of the script, so use this function only if your script is taking up too much memory.

mysql_insert_id

```
$id_num = mysql_insert_id();
```

Returns the ID number used for the last INSERT statement that contained an auto_ increment field.

msql_listdbs

mysql_listdbs

```
$result = msql_listdbs();
$result = mysql_listdbs();
```

Returns a result pointer containing the names of all of the databases available on the mSQL/MySQL server. The **m(y)sql_dbname** function can retrieve values from the pointer.

msql_listfields

mysql_listfields

```
$result = msql_listfields($database, $table);
$result = mysqllistfields($database, $table);
```

Returns a result pointer to information about the fields of the table **table** within **database**. The functions **m(y)sql_fieldflags**, **m(y)sql_fieldlen**, **m(y)sql_ fieldname**, and **m(y)sql_fieldtype** can retrieve data from the pointer.

msql_listtables

mysql_listtables

```
$result = msql_listtables($database);
$result = mysql_listtables($database);
```

Returns a result pointer containing the names of all of the tables within **database**. The **m(y)sql_tablename** function can retrieves values from the pointer.

msql_numfields

mysql_numfields

```
$num_fields = msql_numfields($result);
$num_fields = mysql_numfields($result);
```

Returns the number of fields within `result`.

msql_numrows

msql_numrows

```
$num_rows = msql_numrows($result);
$num_rows = mysql_numrows($result);_
```

Returns the number of rows within `result`.

msql_regcase

```
$new_string = msql_regcase($string);
```

Returns a copy of `string` which has been transformed into a regular expression that will perform a case-insensitive match in a mSQL statement.

msql_result

mysql_result

```
$result_string = msql_result($result, $i, $field);
$result_string = mysql_result($result, $I, $field);
```

Returns an entry from the field `field` in the `i`th row of `result`. The argument `field` is the name of the field column and can be specified as `table.field` for results that involved joined tables. Any MySQL internal functions which can affect SELECT results can be included in the `field` argument, for instance, `mysql_result $result, $i, "length($field)")`.

msql_tablename

mysql_tablename

```
$name = msql_tablename($result, $i);
$name = mysql_tablename($result, $i);
```

Returns the name of the table stored in the `i`th field of the result returned by a call to `m(y)sql_listtables`.

next

```
next($array);
```

Moves the pointer of **array** to the next element and returns that element.

octdec

```
$decimal = octdec($octal);
```

Returns the decimal equivalent of **octal**.

opendir

```
opendir($directory);
```

Opens a directory for use with the **readdir** function. You should close the directory with **closedir** when you are finished with it.

openlog

```
openlog($ident, $options, $facility);
```

Opens the system log for writing. This function should be called after **initlog** and before the first **syslog** call. The arguments are the same as the Unix **openlog** system call. The value of ident is prepended to each log message and is usually the name of the program. The value of options can be any of the following: LOG_CONS (log to the console if there is an error with the standard procedure), LOG_NDELAY (open the log connection immediately instead of at the time of the first log message), LOG_PERROR (log to stderr as well), LOG_PID (include the process PID with each log message). Options can be combined with bitwise OR (e.g. (LOG_DELAY|LOG_PERROR|LOG_PID)). Facility is one of the system-defined log levels (e.g. LOG_SYSLOG, LOG_USER, LOG_KERN, etc.).

ord

```
$number = ord($character);
```

Returns the ASCII value of **character**.

parse_str

```
parse_str($string);
```

Parses a URL encoded string of the format `"variable1=value1&variable2=value2"` and initializes variables with the appropriate values. The PHP program automatically performs this function with incoming form data at the beginning of every script.

passthru

```
passthru($command);
passthru($command, $return_value);
```

Executes the external command **command** and sends all of the output directory to the browser. If a second argument is present, the return value of the command is placed there.

pclose

```
pclose($fd);
```

Closes a pipe opened with **popen**.

phpinfo

```
phpinfo();
```

Prints an informational page that's useful when debugging the PHP setup. This is the same page that is printed if you add "?info" to any PHP URL, or if you access the PHP binary directly (i.e., *http://www.myserver.com/cgi-bin/php*).

phpversion

```
$version = phpversion();
```

Returns the version of PHP that is currently running.

popen

```
$fd = popen($command, $mode);
```

Runs the external command **command** and either sends data to the command (if **mode** is "w") or reads data from the command (if **mode** is "r"). You must close any file descriptors opened in this manner with **pclose**.

pos

```
$position = pos($array['element']);
```

Returns the numerical position of **array['element']** within the associative array **array**.

pow

```
$result = pow($x, $y);
```

Returns **x** raised to the power **y**.

prev

```
$element = prev($array);
```

Moves the internal pointer of **array** to the previous element and returns that element.

putenv

```
putenv($string);
```

Puts **string** into the local environment. Note that the environment is destroyed at the end of the script, so this function is really useful only when external programs are called within the script.

quotemeta

```
$quoted_string = quotemeta($string);
```

Returns **string** with all special characters escaped so that it is safe to use within a regular expression.

rand

```
$number = rand();
```

Returns a random number between 0 and the system-defined number **RANDMAX**. You should seed the random number generator with **srand** once and only once at the beginning of your script.

readdir

```
$file = readdir();
```

Returns the next directory entry in the current open directory and advances the directory pointer. Repeated calls to this function will return the next directory entry until there are no more left.

readfile

```
$filesize = readfile($filename);
```

Outputs the contents of **filename** directly to the browser and returns the size of the file. This function is safe to use on binary files such as images.

readlink

```
$filename = readline($link);
```

Returns the path of the real file referenced by **link**. In case of error the function returns −1.

reg_match

```
$result = reg_match($expression, $string);
$result = reg_match($expression, $string, $array);
```

Identical to *ereg*. This function is included only for backwards compatibility with older versions of PHP.

reg_replace

```
reg_replace($expression, $replacement, $string);
```

Identical to *ereg_replace*. This function is included only for backwards compatibility with older versions of PHP.

reg_search

```
$partial_string = reg_search($expression, $string);
$partial_string = reg_search($expression, $string, $array);
```

Identical to *ereg* except that the portion of **string** after the first match is returned. If there is no match, the function returns an empty string. This function is included only for backwards compatibility with older versions of PHP.

rename

```
rename($oldfile, $newfile);
```

Renames **oldfile** to **newfile**.

reset

```
reset($array);
```

Moves the internal pointer of **array** to the first element and returns that element.

return

```
return($value);
```

Exits the current user-defined function and returns **value**.

rewind

```
rewind($fd);
```

Moves the file pointer for **fd** to the beginning of the file.

rewinddir

```
rewinddir();
```

Moves the current directory pointer to the beginning of the directory.

rmdir

```
rmdir($directory);
```

Deletes `directory` if it is empty.

rsort

```
$sorted_array = rsort($array)
```

Returns a sorted copy of the nonassociative array **array** in descending order. If the first member of the array is a number, the returned array will be sorted numerically, otherwise the returned array will be sorted alphabetically.

setcookie

```
setcookie($name);
setcookie($name, $value, $expire, $path, $domain, $secure);
```

Sends a cookie with the given attributes to the browser. If only **name** is present, that cookie with that name is deleted from the browser. Any argument may be left out or replaced with `""` (or 0 in the case of **expire** and **secure**) to be skipped.

seterrorreporting

```
seterrorreporting($value);
```

If **value** is 0, all errors will be disabled, otherwise errors are reported as normal.

setlogging

```
setlogging($value);
```

If **value** is nonzero, access logging for the current page will be enabled, otherwise it will be disabled.

setshowinfo

```
setshowinfo($value);
```

If **value** is nonzero, an informational footer will be printed at the bottom of the page.

settype

```
settype($variable, $type);
```

Sets the type of **variable** to **type**, which can be **integer**, **double**, or **string**.

shl

```
$value = shl($number, $b);
```

Returns the value of **number** shifted **b** bits to the left.

shr

```
$value = shr($number, $b);
```

Returns the value of **number** shifted **b** bits to the right.

sin

```
$value = sin($number);
```

Returns the sine of **number** (in radians).

sleep

```
sleep($seconds);
```

Stops the processing of the page for **seconds** seconds.

sort

```
$sorted_array = sort($array)
```

Returns a sorted copy of the nonassociative array **array** in ascending order. If the first member of the array is a number, the returned array will be sorted numerically, otherwise the returned array will be sorted alphabetically.

soundex

```
$soundex_key = soundex($string);
```

Returns the soundex key of **string**.

sprintf

```
$string = sprintf($format, $arg, [$arg, $arg, ...]);
```

Returns format with each C **printf**-style variable indicator replaced with the appropriate **arg**. Up to 5 arguments can be provided.

sqrt

```
$value = sqrt($number);
```

Returns the square root of **number**.

srand

```
srand($integer);
```

Seeds the random number generator with the value **integer**. This function should be called once and only once at the beginning of any script where you use the **rand** function.

strcbr

strstr

```
$substring = strchr($string, $value);
$substring = strstr($string, $value);
```

Returns the portion of **string** that occurs starting after the first instance of **value**. The **strchr** and **strstr** functions are identical and are both included for the purposes of completeness.

strtr

```
strtr($string, $set1, $set2);
```

Translates all characters in **string** that are in **set1** to the corresponding character in **set2**. If **set1** is longer than **set2**, the last character in **set2** is used for the extra characters in **set1**. If **set2** is longer than **set1**, the extra characters in **set2** are ignored.

stripslashes

```
$plain_string = stripslashes($escaped_string);
```

Removes all escape characters from **escaped_string**.

strlen

```
$length = strlen($string);
```

Returns the length of **string**.

strrcbr

```
$substring = strrchr($string, $character);
```

Searches string backwards for character. The function returns the portion of **string** from the first occurrence of **character** it finds to the end of the string. An empty string is returned if **character** is not found.

strtok

```
$substring = strtok($string, $characters);
$substring = strtok($characters);
```

Splits **string** up into substrings using any of the characters in **characters** as delimiters. After the first call to **strtok**, omit the string argument in subsequent calls to return each successive substring until the end of **string** is reached.

strtolower

```
$lc_string = strtolower($string);
```

Returns **string** with all characters converted to lower case.

strtoupper

```
$uc_string = strtoupper($string);
```

Returns **string** with all characters converted to upper case.

strval

```
$string = strval($variable);
```

Returns **variable** as a string value.

substr

```
$substring = substr($string, $start, $length);
```

Returns the portion of **string** that begins at character **start** (0 is the first character) and continues for **length** characters.

symlink

```
symlink($target, $filename);
```

Creates a symbolic link from **filename** to **target**.

syslog

```
syslog($level, $message);
```

Logs **message** to the system logs at the level **level**.

system

```
$results = system($command);
$results = system($command, $return_value);
```

Executes the external command **command** and returns all output. If a second argument is provided, the return value of the command is placed there.

tan

```
$value = tan($number);
```

Returns the tangent of **number** (in radians).

tempnam

```
$filename = tempnam($path, $prefix);
```

Returns a filename, prepended with **prefix**, that will be unique in the directory specified by **path**.

time

```
$time = time( );
```

Returns the current time in Unix standard time format (the number of seconds since Jan 1, 1970).

umask

```
$umask = umask( );
umask($umask);
```

Returns the current umask if no argument is specified. Sets the umask to **umask** (which must be an octal number) if an argument is present.

uniqid

```
$result = uniqid( );
```

Returns a value that is guaranteed to be unique compared to other values returned by repeated calls.

unlink

```
unlink($filename);
```

Deletes the specified file.

unset

```
unset($variable);
```

Undefines the specified variable, which may be an element of an array. When performed on an array, it erases the entire array.

urldecode

```
$decoded_string = urldecode($string);
```

Returns a copy of string that has all URL escape codes translated into their values. This is done automatically with all incoming form data.

urlencode

```
$encoded_string = urlencode($string);
```

Returns a copy of string that has all special characters URL encoded.

usleep

```
usleep($ms);
```

Stops the parsing of the script for **ms** microseconds.

virtual

```
virtual($filename);
```

Includes `filename` exactly as if the tag `<!--#include virtual="$filename" -->` were present in a standard HTML file. This function is useful only in conjunction with the Apache web server.

Lite

Lite is the scripting language used by W3-mSQL. In syntax, it is similar to C and even more to Perl. In fact, many Lite scripts are syntactically indistinguishable from Perl scripts. Lite, however, lacks many of the advanced features of Perl.

Below is a quick reference of the standard Lite functions that are available when using W3-mSQL.

chdir

```
$result = chdir($path)
```

Changes directory to the specified path. If the operation is unsuccessful, a negative integer is returned.

chmod

```
$result = chmod($filename, $mode)
```

Changes the mode of the specified file to **mode**. If the operation is unsuccessful, a negative integer is returned. The value **mode** can be given as a decimal, octal or hexadecimal value.

chop

`$string = chop($string)`

Returns the string with the last character removed. This is handy for removing newlines from the end of strings read with **readln**.

close

`close ($fd)`

Closes the file associated with the file descriptor.

ctime

`$time = ctime($time)`

Converts **time**, which is some number of seconds since the epoch, into the common Unix text representation of the time.

echo

`echo($string)`

Prints the given string. Any variables in the string will be replaced with the values of the variables.

fprintf

`fprintf($fd, $string [, arg ...])`

Works like the C (or Perl) function of the same name. The first argument is a file descriptor. The formatted string is printed to the file associated with the file descriptor.

getbostbyaddr

`$hostinfo = gethostbyaddr($address)`

Returns the same array as **gethostbyname()** for given IP number. The IP should be given as a decimal string, as in "127.0.0.1". In the official W3-mSQL documentation, this function is referred to as both **gethostbyaddr** and **gethostbyaddress**. At the time of this writing **gethostbyaddress** is incorrect and does not exist as a function in W3-mSQL.

getbostbyname

`$hostinfo = gethostbyname($host)`

Returns an array of information about the given host. The first element of the array is the name of the host and the second is the IP number.

getpid

```
$pid = getpid()
```

Returns the process ID of the Lite program.

getpwnam

```
$entry = getpwnam($username)
```

Returns an array of information about the user with the username **username**. The fields of the array are as follows:

1. Username
2. Password
3. UID
4. GID
5. GECOS (Full name and other optional information)
6. Home directory
7. Shell

getpwuid

```
$entry = getpwuid($UID)
```

Returns an array identical to that of **getpwnam** for the user with the user ID $UID.

includeFile

```
includeFile($filename)
```

This function includes the file **filename** into the output of the program. The file is not modified or parsed in any way.

kill

```
$result = kill($pid, $signal)
```

Sends the signal **signal** to the process **pid**. If the operation is unsuccessful, a negative integer is returned.

link

```
$result = link($file, $newlinkname)
```

Creates a 'hard' link from **file** to **newlinkname**. If the operation is unsuccessful, a negative integer is returned.

mkdir

```
$result = mkdir($directoryname)
```

Creates a directory with the given name. If the operation is unsuccessful, a negative integer is returned.

msqlConnect

```
$socket = msqlConnect($host)
```

Connects to the mSQL server on the host **host**. The return value is the socket number used in a subsequence communication with the database server. If unsuccessful, a negative integer is returned.

msqlClose

```
msqlClose($socket)
```

Terminates the connection identified by **socket**.

msqlDataSeek

```
msqlDataSeek($result, $location)
```

This places the 'pointer' for **result** immediately before the row **location**. Setting the location to 0 puts the pointer at the beginning of the data. The next call to **msqlFetchRow** will retrieve the row after **location**.

msqlEncode

```
$string = msqlEncode($string)
```

This function returns a copy of **string** that is safely encoded for use in a mSQL query.

msqlFetchRow

```
$row = msqlFetchRow($result)
```

This function returns the next row of available data in **result** as an array.

msqlFieldSeek

```
msqlFieldSeek($result, $location)
```

This changes the 'pointer' of a result generated by **msqlInitFieldList** in the same way that **msqlDataSeek** effects results from **msqlStoreResult**.

msqlFreeResult

```
msqlFreeResult($result)
```

This frees any memory used by a result retrieved with **msqlStoreResult**. This function must be called for each result when you are finished with it.

msqlInitFieldList

```
$result = msqlInitFieldList($socket, $database, $table)
```

This creates a table of information about the table **table** in the database **database** on the server indicated by **socket**.

msqlListDBs

```
$databases = msqlListDBs($socket)
```

Returns an array of the names of all of the databases available on the server indicated by **socket**.

msqlListField

```
$tableinfo = msqlListField($result)
```

Returns an array of information about the next field in the table generated from **msqlInitFieldList**, indicated by **result**. Each successive call to **msqlListField** produces a new array until there are no more fields left. The array consists of the following fields:

0   Field Name

1   Table Type

2   Type

3   Length

4   Flags

msqlListTables

```
$tables = msqlListTables($socket, $database)
```

Returns an array of the names of the tables available on **database** on the server indicated by **socket**.

msqlNumRows

```
msqlNumRows($result)
```

Returns the number of rows of data contained in the result **result**.

msqlQuery

```
$result = msqlQuery($socket, $query)
```

This attempts to send to query **query** to the connection **socket**. If the query was not successfully executed, a negative integer is returned.

msqlSelectDB

```
$result = msqlSelectDB($socket, $database)
```

This function attempts to set the connection **socket** to use the database **database**. If unsuccessful, a negative integer is returned.

msqlStoreResult

```
$result = msqlStoreResult
```

Retrieves any data that was produced by the last **msqlQuery** call and stores it for access and manipulation.

open

```
$fd = open($file, $mode)
```

This function opens the given file using the given mode and associates a file descriptor with the file. The defined modes are as follows:

> Open the file for writing.

< Open the file for reading.

<> Open the file for reading or writing.

<P Create a named pipe and open it for reading.

>P Create a named pipe and open it for writing.

<| Execute the file as a command and read the output.

>| Execute the file as a command and write to the process.

pid

```
$pid = getppid()
```

Returns the process ID of the process that is the parent of the Lite program.

printf

```
printf($string [, arg, ... ])
```

This works like the C (or Perl) function of the same name. Variables in the string are not substituted; standard C '**%s**' format must be used to insert variables into the string.

read

```
$data = read($fd, $length)
```

Read **length** number of bytes from the specified file descriptor.

readln

```
$line = readln($fd)
```

Read the next line from the specified file descriptor.

readtok

```
$data = readtok($fd, $token)
```

Read data from the specified file descriptor until the token is encountered. Only the first character of **token** is used.

rename

```
$result = rename($oldname, $newname)
```

This attempts to rename of the specified file (or directory) from **oldname** to **newname**. If the operation is unsuccessful, a negative integer is returned.

rmdir

```
$result = rmdir($path)
```

This attempts to remove the given directory. If the operation is unsuccessful, a negative integer is returned.

setContentType

```
setContentType($string)
```

This function overrides the default content type of HTML page containing the script and uses **string** in its place. This function must be the very first line in the document to work. Not even a blank line can precede it.

sleep

```
sleep($time)
```

This stops the program for **time** number of seconds.

split

```
$strings = split($string, $token)
```

Splits the given string by the token character into an array of strings.

stat

```
$stat = stat($file)
```

Returns an array of information about **file**. The elements of the array are as follows:

1. Inode number
2. File mode
3. Number of links to file
4. UID
5. GID
6. Size of file
7. Atime
8. Mtime
9. Ctime
10. Block size of file system (in bytes)
11. Number of file system block used

strftime

```
$time = strftime($format, $time)
```

This converts a Unix time into a text representation of the time using **format** as a guide. Any of the following sequences in **format** are replaced with their corresponding value:

%a Day of week, using locale's abbreviated weekday names

%A Day of week, using locale's full weekday names

%b Month, using locale's abbreviated month names

%B Month, using locale's full month names

%d Day of month (01–31)

%D Date as %m/%d/%y

%e Day of month (1–31 with single digits preceded by a space)

%H Hour (00–23)

%I Hour (00–12)

%j Day of year (001–366)

%k Hour (0–23, blank padded)

%l hour (1–12, blank padded)

%*m* Month number (01–12)

%*M* Minute (00–59)

%*p* AM or PM

%*S* Seconds (00–59)

%*T* Time as %H:%M:%S

%*U* Week number in year (01–52)

%*w* Day of week (0–6, Sunday being 0)

%*y* Year within the century (00–99)

%*Y* Year including century (e.g., 1999)

strseg

```
$string = strseg($string, $start, $end)
```

Returns the substring of the given string which starts at `start` characters and ends at `end` characters from the beginning of the string.

sub

```
$string = sub($string, $expr1, $expr2)
```

This substitutes any occurrences of `expr1` in `string` with `expr2`. The values of `expr1` and `expr2` may differ in length; `string` will be lengthened or shortened automatically.

substr

```
$string = substr($string1, $regexp, $string2)
```

This finds the substrings of `string1` that match the regular expression `regexp`. For each part of the regular expression enclosed in parenthesis that matches, the corresponding variable $1, $2, $3, etc. is set with the value of the match. The value of `string2` is returned with variables (including $1, $2, $3, etc.) expanded.

symlink

```
$result = symlink($file, $newlinkname)
```

This attempts to create a symbolic link from `file` to `newlinkname`. This function is only supported on some operating systems. If the operation is unsuccessful, a negative integer is returned.

system

```
$result = system($command)
```

This function spawns a shell and executes **command**. Any output of the command is redirected to the output of the program.

test

```
$result = test($test, $filename)
```

This performs the test **test** on the file **filename**. If the test is successful, 1 is returned, otherwise 0 is returned. The available tests are as follows:

b   Block mode device

c   Character mode device

d   Directory

p   Named pipe

s   Nonempty regular file

f   Regular file

u   Setuid file

g   Setgid file

time

```
$time = time()
```

Returns the number of seconds since the epoch (00:00:00 GMT, Jan. 1, 1970).

time2unixtime

```
$time = time2unixtime($sec, $min, $hour, $day, $month, $year)
```

This converts the values for a time into the Unix form of the time (which is the number of seconds since the epoch).

tr

```
$string = tr($string, $list1, $list2)
```

Substitutes all of the characters in **list1** that exist in **string** with the equivalent character in **list2** (e.g., `tr("Robby","oy","ai")` would return the string "Rabbi"). The list of characters can contain a range of characters separated with `"-"`. For instance, `tr("e.e. cummings", "a-z," "A-Z")` will return the string "E. E. CUMMINGS."

truncate

```
$result = truncate($file, $length)
```

This attempts to truncate the given file to **length** bytes. This is usually used to create a zero-length file. If the operation is unsuccessful, a negative integer is returned.

umask

```
umask($mask)
```

This sets the umask of the current process to **mask**. The value **mask** can be given in decimal, octal, or hexadecimal.

*unixtime2**

```
$year = unixtime2year($time)
$month = unixtime2month($time)
$day = unixtime2day($time)
$hour = unixtime2hour($time)
$min = unixtime2min($time)
$sec = unixtime2sec($time)
```

These functions take a Unix time value and return the requested value. For example, **unixtime2day(time())**, would return the current day of the month (a value between 1 and 31).

unlink

```
$result = unlink("filename")
```

This deletes the specified file. If the operation is unsuccessful, a negative integer is returned.

urlEncode

```
$string = urlEncode($string)
```

This function returns a copy of **string** that is safely encoded for insertion into a URL.

19

C Reference

MySQL C API

The MySQL C API uses several defined datatypes beyond the standard C types. These types are defined in the 'mysql.h' header file that must be included when compiling any program that uses the MySQL library.

Datatypes

MYSQL

A structure representing a connection to the database server. The elements of the structure contain the name of the current database and information about the client connection among other things.

MYSQL_FIELD

A structure containing all of the information concerning a specific field in the table. Of all of the types created for MySQL, this is the only one whose member variables are directly accessed from client programs. Therefore it is necessary to know the layout of the structure:

char *name

The name of the field.

char *table

The name of the table containing this field. For result sets that do not correspond to real tables, this value is null.

char *def

The default value of this field, if one exists. This value will always be null unless `mysql_list_fields` is called, after which this will have the correct value for fields that have defaults.

enum enum_field_types type

> The type of the field. The type is one of the MySQL SQL datatypes.

unsigned int length

> The size of the field based on the field's type.

unsigned int max_length

> If accessed after calling `mysql_list_fields`, this contains the length of the maximum value contained in the current result set.

unsigned int flags

> Zero or more option flags. The following flags are currently defined:

> NOT_NULL_FLAG
>
>> If defined, the field cannot contain a NULL value.

> PRI_KEY_FLAG
>
>> If defined, the field is a primary key.

> UNIQUE_KEY_FLAG
>
>> If defined, the field is part of a unique key.

> MULTIPLE_KEY_FLAG
>
>> If defined, the field is part of a key.

> BLOB_FLAG
>
>> If defined, the field is of type `BLOB` or `TEXT`.

> UNSIGNED_FLAG
>
>> If defined, the field is a numeric type with an unsigned value.

> ZEROFILL_FLAG
>
>> If defined, the field was created with the `ZEROFILL` flag.

> BINARY_FLAG
>
>> If defined, the field is of type `CHAR` or `VARCHAR` with the `BINARY` flag.

> ENUM_FLAG
>
>> If defined, the field is of type `ENUM`.

> AUTO_INCREMENT_FLAG
>
>> If defined, the field has the `AUTO_INCREMENT` attribute.

> TIMESTAMP_FLAG
>
>> If defined, the field is of type `TIMESTAMP`.

unsigned int decimals

> When used with a numeric field, it lists the number of decimals used in the field.

> The following macros are provided to help examine the `MYSQL_FIELD` data:

IS_PRI_KEY*(flags)*

Returns true if the field is a primary key.

IS_NOT_NULL*(flags)*

Returns true if the field is defined as NOT NULL.

IS_BLOB*(flags)*

Returns true if the field is of type BLOB or TEXT.

IS_NUM(type)

Returns true if the field type is numeric.

MYSQL_FIELD_OFFSET

A numerical type indicating the position of the "cursor" within a row.

MYSQL_RES

A structure containing the results of a SELECT (or SHOW) statement. The actual output of the query must be accesses through MYSQL_ROW elements of this structure.

MYSQL_ROW

A single row of data returned from a SELECT query. Output of all MySQL data types are stored in this type (as an array of character strings).

my_ulonglong

A numerical type used for MySQL return values. The value ranges from 0 to 1.8E19, with -1 used to indicate errors.

mysql_affected_rows

```
my_ulonglong mysql_affected_rows(MYSQL *mysql)
```

Returns the number of rows affected by the most recent query. When used with a non-SELECT query, it can be used after the mysql_query call that sent the query. With SELECT, this function is identical to mysql_num_rows.

Example

```
/* Insert a row into the people table */
mysql_query(&mysql, "INSERT INTO people VALUES ('', 'Illyana Rasputin', 16)";
num = mysql_affected_rows(&mysql);
/* num should be 1 if the INSERT (of a single row) was successful, and -1 if
   there was an error */
```

mysql_close

```
void mysql_close(MYSQL *mysql)
```

Ends a connection to the database server. If there is a problem when the connection is broken, the error can be retrieved from the mysql_err function.

Example

```
mysql_close(&mysql);
/* The connection should now be terminated */
```

mysql_connect

```
MYSQL *mysql_connect(MYSQL *mysql, const char *host, const char *user,
const char *passwd)
```

Creates a connection to a MySQL database server. The first parameter must be a predeclared **MYSQL** structure. The second parameter is the hostname or IP address of the MySQL server. If the host is an empty string or `localhost`, a connection will be made to the MySQL server on the same machine. The final two parameters are the username and password used to make the connection. The password should be entered as plain text, not encrypted in any way. The return value is the MYSQL structure passed as the first argument, or NULL if the connection failed. (Because the structure is contained as an argument, the only use for the return value is to check if the connection succeeded.)

This function has been deprecated in the newer releases of MySQL and the **mysql_real_connect** function should be used instead.

Example

```
/* Create a connection to the local MySQL server using the name "bob" and
   password "mypass" */
MYSQL mysql;
if(!mysql_connect(&mysql, "", "bob", "mypass")) {
            printf("Connection error!\n");
            exit(0);
}
/* If we've reached this point we have successfully connected to the database
   server. */
```

mysql_create_db

```
int mysql_create_db(MYSQL *mysql, const char *db)
```

Creates an entirely new database with the given name. The return value is zero if the operation was successful and nonzero if there was an error.

This function has been deprecated in the newer releases of MySQL. MySQL now supports the **CREATE DATABASE** SQL statement. This should be used, via the *mysql_query* function, instead.

Example

```
/* Create the database 'new_database' */
result = mysql_create_db(&mysql, "new_database");
```

mysql_data_seek

```
void mysql_data_seek(MYSQL_RES *res, unsigned int offset)
```

Moves to a specific row in a group a results. The first argument is the MYSQL_RES structure that contains the results. The second argument is the row number you wish to seek to. The first row is 0. This function only works if the data was retrieved using mysql_store_result.

Example

```
/* Jump to the last row of the results */
mysql_data_seek(results, mysql_num_rows(results)-1);
```

mysql_debug

```
mysql_debug(char *debug)
```

Manipulates the debugging functions if the client has been compiled with debugging enabled. MySQL uses the Fred Fish debugging library, which has far too many features and options to detail here.

Example

```
/* This is a common use of the debugging library. It keeps a trace of the
   client program's activity in the file "debug.out" */
mysql_debug("d:t:O,debug.out");
```

mysql_drop_db

```
int mysql_drop_db(MYSQL *mysql, const char *db)
```

Destroys the database with the given name. The return value is zero if the operation was successful and nonzero if there was an error.

 This function has been deprecated in the newer releases of MySQL. MySQL now supports the DROP DATABASE SQL statement. This should be used, via the mysql_query function, instead.

Example

```
/* Destroy the database 'old_database' */
result = mysql_drop_db(&mysql, "old_database");
```

mysql_dump_debug_info

```
int mysql_dump_debug_info(MYSQL *mysql)
```

This function causes the database server to enter debugging information about the current connection into its logs. You must have Process privilege in the current connection to use this function. The return value is zero if the operation succeeded and nonzero in the case of an error.

Example

```
result = mysql_dump_debug_info(&mysql);
/* The server's logs should now contain information about this connection */
```

mysql_eof

```
my_bool mysql_eof(MYSQL_RES *result)
```

Returns a nonzero value if there is no more data in the group of results being examined. If there is an error in the result set, zero is returned. This function only works of the result set was retrieved with the **mysql_use_result** function.

Example

```
/* Read through the results until no more data comes out */
while((row = mysql_fetch_row(results)))
{
        /* Do work */
}

if(!mysql_eof(results))
{
    printf("Error. End of results not reached.\n");
```

mysql_errno

```
unsigned int mysql_errno(MYSQL *mysql)
```

Returns the error number of the last error associated with the current connection. If there have been no errors in the connection, the function returns zero.

Example

```
error = mysql_errno(&mysql);
printf("The last error was number %d\n", error);
```

mysql_error

```
char *mysql_error(MYSQL *mysql)
```

Returns the error message of the last error associated with the current connection. If there have been no errors in the connection, the function returns an empty string.

Example

```
printf("The last error was '%s'\n", mysql_error(&mysql));
```

mysql_escape_string

```
unsigned int mysql_escape_string(char *to, const char *from, unsigned int length)
unsigned int mysql_escape_string(char *to, const char *from)
```

Encodes a string so that it is safe to insert it into a MySQL table. The first argument is the receiving string, which must be at least one character greater than twice the length of the second argument, the original string. (That is, to >= from*2+1.) If a third argument is present, only that many bytes are copied from the originating string before encoding it. The function returns the number of bytes in the encoded string, not including the terminating null character.

Example

```
char name[15] = "Bob Marley's";
char enc_name[31];
mysql_escape_string(enc_name, name);
/* enc_name will now contain "Bob Marley\'s" (the single quote is escaped).
```

mysql_fetch_field

```
MYSQL_FIELD *mysql_fetch_field(MYSQL_RES *result)
```

Returns a **MYSQL_FIELD** structure describing the current field of the given result set. Repeated calls to this function will return information about each field in the result set until there are no more fields left, and then it will return a null value.

Example

```
MYSQL_FIELD *field;

while((field = mysql_fetch_field(results)))
{
    /* You can examine the field information here */
}
```

mysql_fetch_field_direct

```
MYSQL_FIELD * mysql_fetch_field_direct(MYSQL_RES * result, unsigned int fieldnr)
```

This function is the same as **mysql_fetch_field**, except that you specify which field you wish to examine, instead of cycling through them. The first field in a result set is 0.

Example

```
MYSQL_FIELD *field;

/* Retrieve the third field in the result set for examination */
field = mysql_fetch_field_direct(results, 2);
```

mysql_fetch_fields

```
MYSQL_FIELD *mysql_fetch_fields(MYSQL_RES * result)
```

The function is the same as **mysql_fetch_field**, except that it returns an array of MYSQL_FIELD structures containing the information for every field in the result set.

Example

```
MYSQL_FIELD *field;
MYSQL_FIELD *fields;

/* Retrieve all the field information for the results */
fields = mysql_fetch_fields(results);
/* Assign the third field to 'field' */
field = fields[2];
```

mysql_fetch_lengths

```
unsigned long *mysql_fetch_lengths(MYSQL_RES *result)
```

Returns an array of the lengths of each field in the current row. A null value is returned in the case of an error. You must have fetch at least one row (with **mysql_fetch_row**) before you can call this function. This function is the only way to determine the lengths of variable length fields, such as BLOB and VARCHAR, before you use the data.

Example

```
unsigned long *lengths;

row = mysql_fetch_row(results);
lengths = mysql_fetch_lengths(results);
printf("The third field is %d bytes long\n", lengths[2]);
```

mysql_fetch_row

```
MYSQL_ROW mysql_fetch_row(MYSQL_RES *result)
```

Retrieves the next row of the result and returns it as a MYSQL_ROW structure. A null value is returned if there are no more rows or there is an error. In the current implementation, the MYSQL_ROW structure is an array of character strings that can be used to represent any data.

Example

```
MYSQL_ROW row;

row = mysql_fetch_row(results);
printf("The data in the third field of this row is: %s\n", row[2]);
```

mysql_field_seek

MYSQL_FIELD_OFFSET mysql_field_seek(MYSQL_RES *result, MYSQL_FIELD_OFFSET offset)

Seeks to the given field of the current row of the result set. The position set by this function is used when **mysql_fetch_field** is called. The MYSQL_FIELD_OFFSET value passed should be the return value of a **mysql_field_tell** call (or another **mysql_field_seek**). Using the value 0 will seek to the beginning of the row. The return value is the position of the cursor before the function was called.

Example

```
MYSQL_FIELD field;

/* Seek back to the beginning of the row */
old_pos = mysql_field_seek(results, 0);
/* Fetch the first field of the row */
field = mysql_field_field(results);
/* Go back to where you where */
mysql_field_seek(results, old_pos);
```

mysql_field_tell

MYSQL_FIELD_OFFSET mysql_field_tell(MYSQL_RES *result)

Returns the value of the current field position within the current row of the result set. This value is used with **mysql_field_seek**.

Example

```
MYSQL_FIELD field1, field2, field3;

/* Record my current position */
old_pos = mysql_field_tell(results);
/* Fetch three more fields */
field1 = mysql_field_field(results);
field2 = mysql_field_field(results);
field3 = mysql_field_field(results);
/* Go back to where you where */
mysql_field_seek(results, old_pos);
```

mysql_free_result

void mysql_free_result(MYSQL_RES *result)

Frees the memory associated with a **MYSQL_RES** structure. This must be called whenever you are finished using this type of structure or else memory problems will occur.

Example

```
MYSQL_RES *results;
/* Do work with results */
mysql_free_result(results);
```

mysql_get_client_info

```
char *mysql_get_client_info(void)
```

Returns a string with the MySQL library version used by the client program.

Example

```
printf("This program uses MySQL client library version %s\n",
       mysql_get_client_info()));
```

mysql_get_host_info

```
char *mysql_get_host_info(MYSQL *mysql)
```

Returns a string with the hostname of the MySQL database server and the type of connection used (e.g., Unix socket or TCP).

Example

```
printf("Connection info: %s", mysql_get_host_info(&mysql));
```

mysql_get_proto_info

```
unsigned int mysql_get_proto_info(MYSQL *mysql)
```

Returns the MySQL protocol version used in the current connection as an integer.

Example

```
printf("This connection is using MySQL connection protocol ver. %d\n",
       mysql_get_proto_info());
```

mysql_get_server_info

```
char *mysql_get_server_info(MYSQL *mysql)
```

Returns a string with the version number of the MySQL database server used by the current connection.

Example

```
printf("You are currently connection to MySQL server version %s\n",
       mysql_get_server_info(&mysql);
```

mysql_info

```
char *mysql_info(MYSQL *mysql)
```

Returns a string containing information about the most recent query, if the query was of a certain type. Currently, the following SQL queries supply extra information via this function: INSERT INTO (when used with a SELECT clause); LOAD DATA INFILE; ALTER TABLE; INSERT INTO TABLE (when used with multiple records). If the last query had no additional information (e.g., it was not one of the above queries), this function returns a null value.

Example

```
/* We just sent LOAD DATA INFILE query reading a set of record from a file
into
    an existing table */
printf("Results of data load: %s\n", mysql_info(&mysql));
```

mysql_init

```
MYSQL *mysql_init(MYSQL *mysql)
```

Initializes a MYSQL structure used to create a connection to a MySQL database server. This, along with mysql_real_connect, is currently the approved way to initialize a server connection. You pass this function a MYSQL structure that you declared, or a null pointer, in which case a MYSQL structure will be created and returned. Structures created by this function will be properly freed when mysql_close is called. A null value is returned if there is not enough memory to initialize the structure.

Example

```
MYSQL mysql;

if (!mysql_init(&mysql)) {
        printf("Error initializing MySQL client\n");
        exit(1);
}
```

mysql_insert_id

```
my_ulonglong mysql_insert_id(MYSQL *mysql)
```

Returns the last number generated for an AUTO_INCREMENT field. This function is usually used immediately after a value is inserted into an AUTO_INCREMENT field, to determine the value that was inserted.

Example

```
/* We just inserted an employee record with automatically generated ID into
    a table */
id = mysql_insert_id(&mysql);
printf("The new employee has ID %d\n", id);
```

mysql_kill

```
int mysql_kill(MYSQL *mysql, unsigned long pid)
```

Attempts to kill the MySQL server thread with the specified Process ID. This function returns zero if the operation was successful and nonzero on failure. You must have Process privileges in the current connection to use this function.

Example

```
/* Kill thread 4 */
result = mysql_kill(&mysql, 4);
```

mysql_list_dbs

```
MYSQL_RES *mysql_list_dbs(MYSQL *mysql, const char *wild)
```

Returns a MYSQL_RES structure containing the names of all existing databases that match the pattern given by the second argument. This argument may be any standard SQL regular expression. If a null pointer is passed instead, all databases are listed. Like all MYSQL_RES structures, the return value of this function must be freed with mysql_free_result. This function returns a null value in the case of an error.

Example

```
MYSQL_RES databases;
databases = mysql_list_dbs(&mysql, (char *)NULL);
/* 'databases' now contains the names of all of the databases in the
    MySQL server */
```

mysql_list_fields

```
MYSQL_RES *mysql_list_fields(MYSQL *mysql, const char *table, const char *wild)
```

Returns a MYSQL_RES structure containing the names of all existing fields in the given table that match the pattern given by the third argument. This argument may be any standard SQL regular expression. If a null pointer is passed instead, all fields are listed. Like all MYSQL_RES structures, the return value of this function must be freed with *mysql_free_result*. This function returns a null value in the case of an error.

Example

```
MYSQL_RES fields;
fields = mysql_list_fields(&mysql, "people", "address%");
/* 'fields' now contains the names of all fields in the 'people' table
    that start with 'address' */
```

mysql_list_processes

```
MYSQL_RES *mysql_list_processes(MYSQL *mysql)
```

Returns a MYSQL_RES structure containing the information on all of the threads currently running on the MySQL database server. This information contained here can be used with mysql_kill to remove faulty threads. Like all MYSQL_RES structures, the return value of this function must be freed with mysql_free_result. This function returns a null value in the case of an error.

Example

```
MYSQL_RES threads;
threads = mysql_list_processes(&mysql);
```

mysql_list_tables

```
MYSQL_RES *mysql_list_tables(MYSQL *mysql, const char *wild)
```

Returns a **MYSQL_RES** structure containing the names of all existing tables in the current database that match the pattern given by the second argument. This argument may be any standard SQL regular expression. If a null pointer is passed instead, all tables are listed. Like all **MYSQL_RES** structures, the return value of this function must be freed with **mysql_free_result**. This function returns a null value in the case of an error.

Example

```
MYSQL_RES tables;
tables = mysql_list_tables(&mysql, "p%");
/* 'tables' now contains the names of all tables in the current database
    that start with 'p' */
```

mysql_num_fields

```
unsigned int mysql_num_fields(MYSQL_RES *result)
```

Returns the number of fields contained in each row of the given result set.

Example

```
num_fields = mysql_num_fields(results);
printf("There are %d fields in each row\n", num_fields);
```

mysql_num_rows

```
int mysql_num_rows(MYSQL_RES *result)
```

Returns the number of rows of data in the result set. This function is only accurate if the result set was retrieved with **mysql_store_result**. If **mysql_use_result** was used, the value returned by this function will be the number of rows accessed so far.

Example

```
num_rows = mysql_num_rows(results);
printf("There were %d rows returned\n", num_rows);
```

mysql_ping

```
int mysql_ping(MYSQL *mysql)
```

Checks to see if the connection to the MySQL server is still alive. If it is not, the client will attempt to reconnect automatically. This function returns zero if the connection is alive and nonzero in the case of an error.

Example

```
while(mysql_ping(&mysql)) printf("Error, attempting reconnection...\n");
```

mysql_query

```
int mysql_query(MYSQL *mysql, const char *query)
```

Executes the SQL query given in the second argument. If the query contains any binary data (particularly the null character), this function cannot be used and `mysql_real_query` should be used instead. The function returns zero if the query was successful and nonzero in the case of an error.

Example

```
error = mysql_query(&mysql, "SELECT * FROM people WHERE name like 'Bill%'");
if (error) {
    printf("Error with query!\n");
    exit(1);
}
```

mysql_real_connect

```
MYSQL *mysql_real_connect(MYSQL *mysql, const char *host, const char *user,
const char *passwd, const char *db, uint port, const char *unix_socket,
uint client_flag)
```

Creates a connection with a MySQL database server. There are eight arguments to this function:

- An initialized MYSQL structure, created with `mysql_init`.

- The hostname or IP address of the MySQL database server (use an empty string or `localhost` to connect to the local MySQL server over a Unix socket).

- The username used to connect to the database server (an empty string may be used assuming the Unix login name of the person running the client).

- The password used to authenticate the given user. If an empty string is used, only users with no passwords are checked for authentication.

- The initial database selected when you connect (an empty string may be used to not initially choose a database).

- The port used to remotely connect to a MySQL database server over TCP (0 may be used to accept the default port).

- The filename of the Unix socket used to connect to a MySQL server on the local machine (an empty string may be used to accept the default socket).

- Zero or more of a set of flags used under special circumstances:

  CLIENT_FOUND_ROWS

  > When using queries that change tables, returns the number of rows found in the table, not the number of rows affected.

CLIENT_NO_SCHEMA

Prevent the client from using the full `database.table.column` form to specify a column from any database.

CLIENT_COMPRESS

Use compression when communicating with the server.

CLIENT_ODBC

Tell the server the client is an ODBC connection.

Example

```
/* Connect to the server on the local host with standard options. */
if (! mysql_real_connect(&mysql, "localhost", "bob", "mypass", "", 0, "", 0))
{ print "Error connecting!\n";
  exit(1);
}
```

mysql_real_query

```
int mysql_real_query(MYSQL *mysql, const char *query, unsigned int length)
```

Executes the SQL query given in the second argument. The length of the query must be given in the third argument. By supplying the length, you can use binary data, including null characters, in the query. This function is also faster than `mysql_query`. The function returns zero if the query was successful and nonzero in the case of an error.

Example

```
error = mysql_real_query(&mysql, "SELECT * FROM people WHERE name like
'Bill%'",
        44);
if (error) {
    printf("Error with query!\n");
    exit(1);
}
```

mysql_reload

```
int mysql_reload(MYSQL *mysql)
```

Reloads the permission tables on the MySQL database server. You must have Reload permissions on the current connection to use this function. If the operation is successful, zero is returned otherwise a nonzero value is returned.

Example

```
result = mysql_reload(&mysql);
```

mysql_row_tell

unsigned int mysql_row_tell(MYSQL_RES *result)

Returns the value of the cursor used as **mysql_fetch_row** reads the rows of a result set. The return value of this function can used with **mysql_row_seek** to jump to a specific row in the result set.

Example

```
saved_pos = mysql_row_tell(results);
/* I can now jump back to this row at any time */
```

mysql_select_db

int mysql_select_db(MYSQL *mysql, const char *db)

Changes the current database. The user must have permission to access the new database. The function returns zero if the operation was successful and nonzero in the case of an error.

Example

```
result = mysql_select_db(&mysql, "newdb");
```

mysql_shutdown

int mysql_shutdown(MYSQL *mysql)

Shutdown the MySQL database server. The user must have Shutdown privileges on the current connection to use this function. The function returns zero if the operation was successful and nonzero in the case of an error.

Example

```
result = mysql_shutdown(&mysql);
```

mysql_stat

char *mysql_stat(MYSQL *mysql)

Returns information about the current operating status of the database server. This includes the uptime, the number of running threads, and the number of queries being processed, among other information.

Example

```
printf("Server info\n-----------\n%s\n", mysql_stat(&mysql));
```

mysql_store_result

MYSQL_RES *mysql_store_result(MYSQL *mysql)

Reads the entire result of a query and stores in a **MYSQL_RES** structure. Either this function or **mysql_use_result** must be called to access return information from a query. You must call `mysql_free_result` to free the `MYSQL_RES` structure when you are done with it. The function returns a null value in the case of an error.

Example

```
MYSQL_RES results;
mysql_query(&mysql, "SELECT * FROM people");
results = mysql_store_result(&mysql);
/* 'results' now contains all of the information from the 'people' table */
```

mysql_thread_id

```
unsigned long mysql_thread_id(MYSQL * mysql)
```

Returns the thread ID of the current connection. This value can be used with *mysql_kill* to terminate the thread in case of an error.

Example

```
thread_id = mysql_thread_id(&mysql);
```

mysql_use_result

```
MYSQL_RES *mysql_use_result(MYSQL *mysql)
```

Reads the result of a query row by row and allows access to the data through a `MYSQL_RES` structure. Either this function or `mysql_use_result` must be called to access return information from a query. Because this function does not read the entire data set at once, it is faster and more memory efficient than `mysql_store_result`. However, when using this function you must read all of the rows of the dataset from the server or else the next query will receive the left over data. Also, you can not run any other queries until you are done with the data in this query. You must call `mysql_free_result` to free the `MYSQL_RES` structure when you are done with it. The function returns a null value in the case of an error.

Example

```
MYSQL_RES results;
mysql_query(&mysql, "SELECT * FROM people");
results = mysql_store_result(&mysql);
/* 'results' will now allow access (using mysql_fetch_row) to the table
   data, one row at a time */
```

mSQL C API

The mSQL C API has remained relatively stable between mSQL Versions 1 and 2. However, several new functions have been added, and there have been a few changes in the existing function. Wherever a function or feature can only be used with mSQL 2, it is noted.

Datatypes

The mSQL C API uses a few defined datatypes beyond the standard C types. These types are defined in the 'msql.h' header file that must be included when compiling any program that uses the MySQL library.

m_result

A structure containing the results of a SELECT (or SHOW) statement. The actual output of the query must be accessed through m_row elements of this structure.

m_row

A single row of data returned from a SELECT query. Output of all mSQL datatypes are stored in this type (as an array of character strings).

m_field

A structure containing all of the information concerning a specific field in the table. The elements of the **m_field** structure can be directly examined and are as follows:

*char *name*

The name of the field.

*char *table*

The name of the table containing the field. This is a null value if the result set does not correspond to a real table.

int type

The type of the field. This is an integer corresponding to the mSQL SQL datatypes defined in the *msql.h* header file.

int length

The byte length of the field.

int flags

Zero or more option flags. The flags are accessed through the following macros:

IS_PRI_KEY(flags)

Returns true if the field is a primary key.

IS_NOT_NULL(flags)

Returns true if the field is defined as NOT NULL.

msqlConnect

```
int msqlConnect ( char *host )
```

Creates a connection to the mSQL server whose hostname or IP address is given. If a null value is passed as the argument, the connection is made to the mSQL server on the local host using Unix sockets. The return value is a database handle used to communicate with the database server. In the case of an error, -1 is returned.

Example

```
/* Create a connection to the database server on the local host */
dbh = msqlConnect( (char *)NULL );
if (dbh == -1) {
    print "Error connecting!\n";
    exit(1);
}
```

msqlSelectDB

```
int msqlSelectDB ( int sock , char *dbName )
```

Chooses a database for the specified connection. A database must be chosen before any queries are sent to the database server. In the case of an error, -1 is returned.

Example

```
/* Select the "mydatabase" database */
result = msqlSelectDB( dbh, "mydatabase" );
if (result == -1) {
    print "Error selecting database!\n";
    exit(1);
}
```

msqlQuery

```
int msqlQuery( int sock , char *query )
```

Executes the given SQL query. In mSQL 2, the return value is the number of rows affected by the query (or selected by a **SELECT** query). In mSQL 1, zero is returned upon success. In both versions, in the case of an error, -1 is returned.

Example

```
rows_returned = msqlQuery( dbh, "SELECT * FROM people" );
```

msqlStoreResult

```
m_result *msqlStoreResult()
```

Stores the result of a **SELECT** query. This function is called immediately after calling `msqlQuery` with an SQL **SELECT** query. The results of the query are then stored in the `m_result` structure. Only after this function has been called, can other queries be sent to the database server. Every `m_result` structure must be freed using `msqlFreeResult` when you are finished with it.

Example

```
m_result *results;
```

```
rows_returned = msqlQuery( dbh, "SELECT * FROM people" );
results = msqlStoreResult();
/* Other queries may now be submitted and the data from this query can be
   accessed through 'results' */
```

msqlFreeResult

```
void msqlFreeResult ( m_result *result )
```

Frees the memory associated with an **m_result** structure.

Example

```
m_result *results;

rows_returned = msqlQuery( dbh, "SELECT * FROM people" );
results = msqlStoreResult();

/* Do work */

msqlFreeResult(results);
```

msqlFetchRow

```
m_row msqlFetchRow ( m_result *result )
```

Retrieves a single row of data from a result set. This data is placed in an **m_row** structure, which is an array of character strings. With each successive call to **msqlFetchRow**, another row is returned until there are no more rows left, then a null value is returned.

Example

```
m_result *results;
m_row *row;

rows_returned = msqlQuery( dbh, "SELECT * FROM people" );
results = msqlStoreResult();
row = msqlFetchRow(results);
printf("The third field of the first row of the table is: %s\n", row[2]);
```

msqlDataSeek

```
void msqlDataSeek ( m_result *result, int pos )
```

Sets the cursor that tells **msqlFetchRow** which row to fetch next. Setting a position of 0 will move the cursor to the beginning of the data. Setting the cursor to a position past the last row of data will place the cursor at the end of the data.

Example

```
m_result *results;
m_row *row;

rows_returned = msqlQuery( dbh, "SELECT * FROM people" );
```

```
results = msqlStoreResult();
row = msqlFetchRow(results);
/* Now go back to the beginning */
msqlDataSeek(results, 0);
```

msqlNumRows

```
int msqlNumRows ( m_result *result )
```

Returns the number of rows in the result set.

Example

```
rows_returned = msqlQuery( dbh, "SELECT * FROM people" );
results = msqlStoreResult();
rows = msqlNumRows(results);
```

msqlFetchField

```
m_field *msqlFetchField ( m_result *result )
```

Returns the information about the fields in the result set. Each successive call to **msqlFetchField** will return a **m_field** structure for the next field until there are no more fields left, then a null value will be returned.

Example

```
m_field *field;

rows_returned = msqlQuery( dbh, "SELECT * FROM people" );
results = msqlStoreResult();
field = msqlFetchField(results);
/* 'field' now contains information about the first field in the result set
*/
field = msqlFetchField(results);
/* 'field' now contains information about the second field in the result set
*/
```

msqlFieldSeek

```
void msqlFieldSeek ( m_result *result , int pos )
```

Sets the cursor that tells **msqlFetchField** which field to fetch next. Setting a position of 0 will move the cursor to the beginning of the fields. Setting the cursor to a position past the last field places the cursor just past the last field.

Example

```
m_result *results;
m_field *field;

rows_returned = msqlQuery( dbh, "SELECT * FROM people" );
results = msqlStoreResult();
field = msqlFetchField(results);
/* Now go back to the beginning */
msqlFieldSeek(results, 0);
```

msqlNumFields

```
int msqlNumFields ( m_result *result )
```

Returns the number of fields in the result set.

Example

```
rows_returned = msqlQuery( dbh, "SELECT * FROM people" );
results = msqlStoreResult();
fields = msqlNumFields(results);
```

msqlClose

```
int msqlClose ( int sock )
```

Closes the connection to the mSQL database server.

Example

```
dbh = msqlConnect( (char *)NULL );
/* Do work */
msqlClose(dbh);
```

msqlListDBs

```
m_result *msqlListDBs ( int sock )
```

Returns an **m_result** structure containing the names of all of the databases available in the database server. Like all **m_result** structures, the return value of this function must be freed with **msqlFreeResult** when you are done with it.

Example

```
databases = msqlListDBs(dbh);
/* 'databases' now contains the names of all of the databases on the server
*/
```

msqlListTables

```
m_result *msqlListTables ( int sock )
```

Returns an **m_result** structure containing the names of all of the tables in the current database. Like all **m_result** structures, the return value of this function must be freed with **msqlFreeResult** when you are done with it.

Example

```
tables = msqlListTables(dbh);
/* 'tables' now contains the names of all of the tables in the
   current database */
```

msqlListFields

```
m_result *msqlListFields ( int sock , char *tableName )
```

Returns an m_result structure containing the names of all of the fields in the given table. Like all m_result structures, the return value of this function must be freed with msqlFreeResult when you are done with it.

Example

```
fields = msqlListFields(dbh, "people");
/* 'fields' now contains the names of all of the fields in the
    'people' table */
```

msqlListIndex

```
m_result *msqlListIndex ( int sock , char *tableName , char *index )
```

Returns an m_result structure containing information about the given index. The returned result set will contain the type of index (currently, 'avl' is the only supported type), and the names of the fields contained in the index. Like all m_result structures, the return value of this function must be freed with msqlFreeResult when you are done with it.

Example

```
index = msqlListIndex(dbh, "people", "idx1");
/* 'index' now contains the information about the 'idx1' index in the
'people'
    table */
```

20

Python Reference

There are actually a handful of Python modules running around that support database access against MySQL and mSQL. They are very similar in most respects. This chapter provides the API specification for two common modules. It is, however, important to note an approaching unification of Python database APIs under a single API being specified by the Python Database SIG. mSQL currently has no support for this API.

Module: MySQL

The entry point into the `MySQL` module is via the `MySQL.connect()` method. The return value from this method represents a connection to a MySQL database that you can use for all of your MySQL operations.

Method: MySQL.connect( )

Signature

```
connection = MySQL.connect(host)
```

Synopsis

Connects to the MySQL database engine on the specified server. If you call `connect()` with no arguments, it will connect you to the MySQL database engine on the local machine. It returns a Python object representing a connection to a MySQL database.

Example

```
conn = MySQL.connect('carthage.imaginary.com');
```

Method: connection.selectdb( )

Signature

```
connection.selectdb(database)
```

Synopsis

Selects the database against which you intend to operate.

Example

```
connection.selectdb('test');
```

Method: connection.do( )

Signature

```
results = connection.do(sql)
```

Synopsis

Sends the specified SQL statement to the currently selected database for execution. The results are returned as a list of lists where each list represents a single row. The method is also used for updates—you just do not process the return value.

Example

```
results = conn.do('SELECT title, year FROM movies');
row1 = results[0];
```

Method: connection.query( )

Signature

```
statement_handle = connection.query(sql)
```

Synopsis

Like the do( ) method, this method sends the specified SQL statement to the currently selected database. Unlike the do( ) method, this method returns a statement handler object that encapsulates data about the results of the SQL query as well as the results themselves.

Example

```
hndl = conn.query('SELECT title, year FROM movies');
```

Method: statement_handle.affectedrows( )

Signature

```
rowcount = statement_handle.affectedrows()
```

Synopsis

Assuming the results of the SQL represented by this statement handler came from
an UPDATE, DELETE, or INSERT, this method returns the number of rows actually
modified by that statement.

Example

```
rowcount = hndl.affectedrows()
```

Method: statement_handle.numrows( )

Signature

```
rowcount = statement_handle.numrows()
```

Synopsis

Assuming the results of the SQL represented by this statement handler came from
a SELECT, this method provides the number of rows in the result set.

Example

```
rowcount = hndl.numrows()
```

Method: statement_handle.fields( )

Signature

```
list = statement_handle.fields()
```

Synopsis

Provides meta-information about the columns in the results returned by this query.
The list is actually a list of lists. Each member of the returned list is a list of meta-
information about a specific column. In other words, the returned list will have
one member for each column in the result set. The first member of the list represents the first column, the second member the second column, and so on.

The meta-data for each column is a list of five elements:

*   A string containing the column name

*   A string containing the name of the table from which the column came

*   A string with the name of the SQL datatype for the column

*   An int containing the size of the column

*   A string containing the column modifies such as NOTNULL

Example

```
flds = hndl.fields();
for column in flds:
```

```
name = column[0];
table = column[1];
type = column[2];
size = columns[3];
mods = column[4];
```

Method: statement_handle.fetchrows()

Signature

```
list = statement_handle.fetchrows(rownum)
```

Synopsis

Fetches the row values of the specified row number associated with the result set represented by the statement handler. If you pass -1 as an argument, this method will return a list of all the rows. For each row in the list, a row is represented by a list whose number of elements equals the number of columns in the result set. The first element represents the first column value, the second element the second column, and so on.

Example

```
rows = hndl.fetchrows(-1);
for row in rows:
    col1 = row[0];
    col2 = row[1];
```

Method: connection.listdbs()

Signature

```
dbs = connection.listdbs()
```

Synopsis

Provides a Python list of databases available on the database server.

Example

```
dbs = conn.listdbs()
```

Method: connection.listtables()

Signature

```
tables = connection.listtables();
```

Synopsis

Provides a Python list of tables stored in the selected database.

Example
```
tables = conn.listtables();
```

Module: mSQL

The mSQL module is very similar to the MySQL one. The entry point into the module is via the mSQL.connect() method. The return value from this method represents a connection to an mSQL database that you can use for all of your mSQL operations.

Method: mSQL.connect()

Signature
```
connection = mSQL.connect()
connection = mSQL.connect(host)
```

Synopsis

Connects to the mSQL database engine on the specified server. If you call connect with no arguments, the method connects to the database engine on the local machine. It returns an mSQL connection handle that you can use for database access.

Example
```
connection = mSQL.connect('carthage.imaginary.com')
```

Method: connection.selectdb()

Signature
```
connection.selectdb(database)
```

Synopsis

Selects the name of the database for your connection to use. Any further operations on that connection will work against that database unless you later select a new database.

Example
```
connection.selectdb('test');
```

Method: connection.query()

Signature
```
results = connection.query(sql)
```

Synopsis

Sends the specified SQL statement to the currently selected database for execution. The results are returned as a list of tuples, where each tuple represents a row. This method is also used for updates—you just do not process the return value.

Example
```
results = conn.query('SELECT title, year FROM movies');
row1 = results[0];
```

Method: connection.listdbs( )

Signature
```
dbs = connection.listdbs()
```

Synopsis

Provides a Python list of databases available on the server.

Example
```
dbs = conn.listdbs()
```

Method: connection.listtables( )

Signature
```
connection.listtables()
```

Synopsis

Provides a Python list of tables stored in the selected database.

Example
```
tables = conn.listtables()
```

Attribute: connection.serverinfo

Synopsis

Returns the version number of the mSQL instance to which you are currently connected.

Example
```
info = connection.serverinfo;
```

Attribute: connection.hostname

Synopsis

Returns the name of the server on which the mSQL instance is running.

Example

```
host = connection.hostname
```

21

Perl Reference

Installation

To use the mSQL and MySQL interfaces to DataBase Dependent/DataBase Independent (DBI/DBD) or to the MsqlPerl and MysqlPerl modules, you must have the following:

Perl 5

You must have a working copy of Perl 5 on your system. At the time of this writing, the newest release of Perl was 5.005_02. You should have at least Perl 5.004 since earlier versions of Perl contained security related bugs. For more information about Perl, including download sites, see *http://www.perl.com*.

DBI

The DataBase Independent portion of the DBI/DBD module can be downloaded from the Comprehensive Perl Archive Network (CPAN). At the time of this writing, the most recent version is DBI-0.90. You can find it at *http://www.perl.com/CPAN/authors/id/TIMB/DBI/DBI-1.06.tar.gz*.

Data::ShowTable

Data::ShowTable is a module that simplifies the act of displaying large amounts of data. The Msql-Mysql modules require this. The most recent version is Data-ShowTable-3.3 and it can be found at *http://www.perl.com/CPAN/authors/id/AKSTE/Data-ShowTable-3.3.tar.gz*.

mSQL and/or MySQL

Chapter 3, *Installation*, contains information about how to obtain and install the mSQL and MySQL database servers.

C compiler and related tools

The MsqlPerl and MysqlPerl modules require an ANSI compliant C compiler as well some common related tools (such as *make, ld*, etc.). The tools that built the copy of Perl you are using should be sufficient. If you have no such tools, the GNU C compiler (along with all necessary supporting programs) is available free at *ftp://ftp.gnu.org/pub/gnu/*.

The current maintainer of the Msql-Mysql modules is Jochen Wiedmann, who has the CPAN author ID of JWIED. Therefore, the current release of the Msql-Mysql modules can always be found at *http://www.perl.com/authors/id/JWIED*. At the time of this writing, the current version *is Msql-Mysql-modules-1.2017.tar.gz*.

After you have downloaded the package, uncompress and untar it into a directory.

```
tar xvzf Msql-Mysql-modules-1.2017.tar.gz
cd Msql-Mysql-modules-1.2017
```

Inside the distribution directory is the file *INSTALL*, which gives several installation hints. The first step is to execute the *Makefile.PL* file:

```
perl Makefile.PL
```

This command starts by asking whether you want to install the modules for mSQL, MySQL or both. You can install the modules for whichever database server that you have installed.

After some system checking, the program then asks for the location of your mSQL installation. This is the directory that contains the *lib* and *include* subdirectories that have the mSQL library and include files. By default it is */usr/local/Hughes*, but be sure to double check this, as many systems use */usr/local or even /usr/local/Minerva*.

Next the installation script asks for the location of MySQL. As with mSQL, this is the directory that contains the appropriate *lib* and *include* subdirectories. By default it is */usr/local*. This is the correct location for most installations, but you should double check in case it is located elsewhere.

At this point, the installation script creates the appropriate makefiles and exits. The next step is to run *make* to compile the files.

```
make
```

If your Perl, mSQL, and/or MySQL are all installed correctly, the make should run without errors. When it is finished, all of the modules have been created and all that is left is to test and install them.

```
make test
```

While this is running, a series of test names will scroll down your screen. All of them should end with . . . ok. Finally, you need to install the modules.

> **make install**

You need to have permission to write to the Perl installation directory to install the modules. In addition, you need to have permission to write to your system binary directory (usually */usr/local/bin* or */usr/bin*) to install the supporting programs that come with the module (*pmsql, pmysql,* and *dbimon*).

DBI.pm API

The DBI API is the standard database API in Perl. So while MsqPerl and MysqlPerl may be more common in legacy code, all new code should be written with DBI.

use

```
use DBI;
```
   This must be declared in every Perl program that uses the DBI module.

DBI::available_drivers

```
@available_drivers = DBI->available_drivers;
@available_drivers = DBI->available_drivers($quiet);
```

`DBI::available_drivers` returns a list of the available DBD drivers. The function does this by searching the Perl distribution for DBD modules. Unless a true value is passed as the argument, the function will print a warning if two DBD modules of the same name are found in the distribution. In the current Msql-Mysql modules distribution, the driver for mSQL is named 'mSQL' and the driver for MySQL is named 'mysql'.

Example

```
use DBI;

my @drivers = DBI->available_drivers;
print "All of these drivers are available:\n" . join("\n",@drivers) .
            "\nBut we're only interested in mSQL and mysql. :)\n";
```

DBI::bind_col

```
$result = $statement_handle->bind_col($col_num, \$col_variable, \%unused);
```

`DBI::bind_col` binds a column of a **SELECT** statement with a Perl variable. Every time that column is accessed or modified, the value of the corresponding variable changes to match. The first argument is the number of the column in the statement, where the first column is number 1. The second argument is a reference to the Perl variable to bind to the column. The optional third argument is a reference to a hash of attributes. This is unused in DBD::mysql and DBD::mSQL. The function returns an undefined value **undef** if the binding fails for some reason.

Example

```
use DBI;
my $db = DBI->connect('DBI:mSQL:mydata',undef,undef);
my $query = "SELECT name, date FROM myothertable";
my $myothertable_output = $db->prepare($query);

my ($name, $date);
$myothertable_output->bind_col(1,\$name,undef);
$myothertable_output->bind_col(2,\$date,undef);
# $name and $date are now bound to their corresponding fields in the outout.

$myothertable_output->execute;
while ($myothertable_output->fetch) {
        # $name and $date are automatically changed each time.
                print "Name: $name Date: $date\n";
}
```

DBI::bind_columns

```
$result = $statement_handle->bind_columns(\%unused, @list_of_refs_to_vars);
```

DBI::bind_columns binds an entire list of scalar references to the corresponding field values in the output. The first argument to the function is a reference to a hash of attributes, as in **DBI::bind_col**. DBD::mSQL and DBD::mysql do not use this argument. Each following argument must be a reference to a scalar. Optionally, the scalars can be grouped into a \($var1, $var2) structure which has the same effect. There must be exactly as many scalar references as there are fields in the output or the program will die.

Example

```
use DBI;
my $db = DBI->connect('DBI:mSQL:mydata',undef,undef);
my $query = "SELECT name, date FROM myothertable";
my $myothertable_output = $db->prepare($query);

my ($name, $date);
$myothertable_output->bind_columns(undef, \($name, $date));
# $name and $date are now bound to their corresponding fields in the outout.

$myothertable_output->execute;
while ($myothertable_output->fetch) {
        # $name and $date are automatically changed each time.
                print "Name: $name Date: $date\n";
}
```

DBI::bind_param

```
$result = $statement_handle->bind_param($param_number, $bind_value);
$result = $statement_handle->bind_param($param_number, $bind_value, $bind_type);
$result = $statement_handle->bind_param($param_number, $bind_value, \%bind_type);
```

`DBI::bind_param` substitutes real values for the '?' placeholders in statements (see `DBI::prepare`). The first argument is the number of the placeholder in the statement. The first placeholder (from left to right) is 1. The second argument is the value with which to replace the placeholder. An optional third parameter can be supplied which determines the type of the value to be substituted. This can be supplied as a scalar or as a reference to a hash of the form `{ TYPE => &DBI::SQL_TYPE }` where 'SQL_TYPE' is the type of the parameter. As of the time of this writing the (undocumented) SQL types supported by DBI are SQL_CHAR, SQL_NUMERIC, SQL_DECIMAL, SQL_INTEGER, SQL_SMALLINT, SQL_FLOAT, SQL_REAL, SQL_DOUBLE, and SQL_VARCHAR. It is not documented how these correspond to the actual types used by DBD::mSQL and DBD::Mysql. However, Table 21-1 contains a list of the corresponding types as of the time of this writing. The function returns `undef` if the substitution is unsuccessful.

Table 21-1. Corresponding SQL Types

DBI	MSQL	MySQL
SQL_CHAR	CHAR_TYPE IDENT_TYPE NULL_TYPE DATE_TYPE MONEY_TYPE TIME_TYPE IDX_TYPE SYSVAR_TYPE ANY_TYPE	FIELD_TYPE_CHAR FIELD_TYPE_DATE FIELD_TYPE_DATETIME FIELD_TYPE_NULL FIELD_TYPE_TIMESTAMP FIELD_TYPE_TIME
SQL_NUMERIC		FIELD_TYPE_LONG FIELD_TYPE_LONGLONG FIELD_TYPE_SHORT
SQL_DECIMAL		FIELD_TYPE_DECIMAL
SQL_INTEGER	INT_TYPE	FIELD_TYPE_INT24
SQL_SMALLINT	UINT_TYPE	FIELD_TYPE_INT24
SQL_FLOAT		FIELD_TYPE_FLOAT
SQL_REAL	REAL_TYPE LAST_REAL_TYPE	FIELD_TYPE_DOUBLE
SQL_DOUBLE		FIELD_TYPE_DOUBLE

Table 21-1. Corresponding SQL Types (continued)

DBI	MSQL	MySQL
SQL_VARCHAR	TEXT_TYPE	FIELD_TYPE_TINY_BLOB
		FIELD_TYPE_MEDIUM_BLOB
		FIELD_TYPE_BLOB
		FIELD_TYPE_LONG_BLOB
		FIELD_TYPE_VAR_STRING
		FIELD_TYPE_STRING

Example

```
use DBI;
my $db = DBI->connect('DBD:msql:mydata','me','mypass');
my $statement = $db->prepare(
"SELECT name, date FROM myothertable WHERE name like ? OR name like ?");

$statement->bind_param(1,'J%','SQL_CHAR');
$statement->bind_param(2,'%oe%', { TYPE => &DBI::SQL_CHAR });
# The statement will now be:
# SELECT name, date FROM myothertable WHERE name like 'J%' or name like
'%oe%'
```

DBI::connect

```
$db = DBI->connect($data_source, $username, $password);
$db = DBI->connect($data_source, $username, $password, \%attributes);
```

DBI::connect requires at least three arguments, with an optional fourth, and returns a handle to the requested database. It is through this handle that you perform all of the transactions with the database server. The first argument is a data source. A list of available data sources can be obtained using DBI::data_sources. For mSQL and MySQL the format of the data sources is 'DBI:mSQL:$database:$hostname:$port' and 'DBI:mysql:$database:$hostname:$port' respectively. You may leave the ':$port' extension off to connect to the standard port. Also, you may leave the ':$hostname:$port' extension off to connect to a server on the local host using a Unix-style socket. A database name must be supplied.

The second and third arguments are the username and password of the user connecting to the database. For mSQL, these should both be 'undef'. If they are 'undef' for MySQL, the user running the program must have permission to access the requested databases.

The final argument is optional and is a reference to an associative array. Using this hash you may preset certain attributes for the connection. Currently, the only supported attributes are PrintError, RaiseError, and AutoCommit. These can be set to 0 for off and some true value for on. The defaults for PrintError and AutoCommit are on and the default for RaiseError is off. Because mSQL and MySQL both do not currently support transactions, the AutoCommit attribute must be set to on (see Attributes for more details).

If the connection fails, an undefined value **undef** is returned and the error is placed in $DBI::errstr.

Example

```
use DBI;

my $db1 = DBI->connect('DBI:mSQL:mydata',undef,undef);
# $db1 is now connected to the local mSQL server using the database 'mydata'.

my $db2 = DBI->connect('DBI:mysql:mydata:myserver.com','me','mypassword');
# $db2 is now connected to the MySQL server on the default port of
# 'myserver.com' using the database 'mydata'. The connection was made with
# the username 'me' and the password 'mypassword'.

My $db3 = DBI->connect('DBI:mSQL:mydata',undef,undef, {
            RaiseError => 1
});
# $db3 is now connected the same way as $db1 except the 'RaiseError'
# attribute has been set to true.
```

DBI::data_sources

```
@data_sources = DBI->data_sources($dbd_driver);
```

DBI::data_sources takes the name of a DBD module as its argument and returns all of the available databases for that driver in a format suitable for use as a data source in the **DBI::connect** function. The program will die with an error message if an invalid DBD driver name is supplied. In the current Msql-Mysql modules distribution, the driver for mSQL is named 'mSQL' and the driver for MySQL is named 'mysql'.

Example

```
use DBI;

my @msql_data_sources = DBI->data_sources('mSQL');
my @mysql_data_sources = DBI->data_sources('mysql');
# Both DBD::mSQL and DBD::mysql had better be installed or
# the program will die.

print "mSQL databases:\n" . join("\n",@msql_data_sources) . "\n\n";
print "MySQL databases:\n" . join("\n",@mysql_data_sources) . "\n\n";
```

DBI::do

```
$rows_affected  = $db->do($statement);
$rows_affected  = $db->do($statement, \%unused);
$rows_affected  = $db->do($statement, \%unused, @bind_values);
```

DBI::do directly performs a non-SELECT SQL statement and returns the number of rows affected by the statement. This is faster than a DBI::prepare/DBI:: execute pair which requires two function calls. The first argument is the SQL statement itself. The second argument is unused in DBD::mSQL and DBD::mysql, but can hold a reference to a hash of attributes for other DBD modules. The final argument is an array of values used to replace 'placeholders,' which are indicated with a '?' in the statement. The values of the array are substituted for the placeholders from left to right. As an additional bonus, DBI::do will automatically quote string values before substitution.

Example

```
use DBI;
my $db = DBI->connect('DBI:mSQL:mydata',undef,undef);

my $rows_affected = $db->do("UPDATE mytable SET name='Joe' WHERE
name='Bob'");
print "$rows_affected Joe's were changed to Bob's\n";

my $rows_affected2 = $db->do("INSERT INTO mytable (name) VALUES (?)",
                {}, ("Sheldon's Cycle"));
# After quoting and substitution, the statement:
# INSERT INTO mytable (name) VALUES ('Sheldon's Cycle')
# was sent to the database server.
```

DBI::disconnect

```
$result  = $db->disconnect;
```

DBI::disconnect disconnects the database handle from the database server. With mSQL and MySQL, this is largely unnecessary because the databases do not support transactions and an unexpected disconnect will do no harm. However, databases that do support transactions need to be explicitly disconnected. Therefore, for portable code you should always call disconnect before exiting the program. If there is an error while attempting to disconnect, a nonzero value will be returned and the error will be set in $DBI::errstr.

Example

```
use DBI;
my $db1 = DBI->connect('DBI:mSQL:mydata',undef,undef);
my $db2 = DBI->connect('DBI:mSQL:mydata2',undef,undef);
...
$db1->disconnect;
# The connection to 'mydata' is now severed. The connection to 'mydata2'
# is still alive.
```

DBI::dump_results

```
$neat_rows = DBI::dump_results($statement_handle);
$neat_rows = DBI::dump_results($statement_handle, $maxlen);
$neat_rows = DBI::dump_results($statement_handle, $maxlen, $line_sep);
$neat_rows = DBI::dump_results($statement_handle, $maxlen, $line_sep,
        $field_sep);
$neat_rows = DBI::dump_results($statement_handle, $maxlen, $line_sep,
        $field_sep, $file_handle);
```

DBI::dump_results prints the contents of a statement handle in a neat and orderly fashion by calling DBI::neat_string on each row of data. This is useful for quickly checking the results of queries while you write your code. The only required argument is the statement handle to print out. If a second argument is present, it is used as the maximum length of each field in the table. The default is 35. A third argument is the string used to separate each line of data. The default is \n. The fourth argument is the string used to join the fields in a row. The default is a comma. The final argument is a reference to a filehandle glob. The results are printed to this filehandle. The default is STDOUT. If the statement handle cannot be read, an undefined value undef is returned.

Example

```
use DBI;
my $db = DBI->connect('DBI:mSQL:mydata',undef,undef);
my $query = "SELECT name, date FROM myothertable";
my $myothertable_output = $db->prepare($query);
$myothertable_output->execute;

print DBI::dump_results($myothertable_output);
# Print the output in a neat table.

open(MYOTHERTABLE, ">>myothertable");
print DBI::dump_results($myothertable_output,undef,undef,undef,\
*MYOTHERTABLE);
# Print the output again into the file 'myothertable'.
```

$DBI::err

```
$error_code  = $handle->err;
```

$DBI::err returns the error code for the last DBI error encountered. This error number corresponds to the error message returned from $DBI::errstr. The variable $DBI::err performs the same function. This function is available from both database and statement handles.

Example

```
use DBI;
my $db = DBI->connect('DBI:mysql:mydata','webuser','super_secret_squirrel');

# There is a parse error in this query...
```

```
my $output = $db->prepare('SLECT * from mydata');
$output->execute;

if (not $output) {
            print "Error $DBI:err: $DBI:errstr\n";
}
```

$DBI::errstr

```
$error = $handle->errstr;
```

$DBI::errstr returns the error message for the last DBI error encountered. The value remains until the next error occurs, at which time it is replaced. If no error has occurred during your session, the function returns undef. The variable $DBI::errstr performs the same function. This function is available from both database and statement handles.

Example

```
Use DBI;
my $db = DBI->connect('DBI:mysql:mydata','webuser','super_secret_squirrel');
...
my $error = $db->errstr;
warn("This is your most recent DBI error: $error");
```

DBI::execute

```
$rows_affected = $statement_handle->execute;
$rows_affected = $statement_handle->execute(@bind_values);
```

DBI::execute executes the SQL statement held in the statement handle. For a non-SELECT query, the function returns the number of rows affected. The function returns '-1' if the number of rows is not known. For a SELECT query, some true value is returned upon success. If arguments are provided, they are used to fill in any placeholders in the statement (see DBI::prepare).

Example

```
use DBI;
my $db = DBI->connect('DBI:mSQL:mydata',undef,undef);
my $statement_handle = $db->prepare("SELECT * FROM mytable");
my $statement_handle2 = $db->prepare("SELECT name, date FROM myothertable
    WHERE name like ?");

$statement_handle->execute;
# The first statement has now been performed. The values can now be accessed
# through the statement handle.

$statement_handle->execute("J%");
# The second statement has now been executed as the following:
# SELECT name, date FROM myothertable WHERE name like 'J%'
```

DBI::fetchall_arrayref

```
$ref_of_array_of_arrays = $statement_handle->fetchall_arrayref;
```

DBI::fetchall_arrayref returns all of the remaining data in the statement handle as a reference to an array. Each row of the array is a reference to another array that contains the data in that row. The function returns an undefined value **undef** if there is no data in the statement handle. If any previous DBI::fetchrow_* functions were called on this statement handle, DBI::fetchall_arrayref returns all of the data after the last DBI::fetchrow_* call.

Example

```
use DBI;
my $db = DBI->connect('DBI:mSQL:mydata',undef,undef);
my $query = "SELECT name, date FROM myothertable";
my $output = $db->prepare($query);
$output->execute;

my $data = $output->fetchall_arrayref;
# $data is not a reference to an array of arrays. The each element of the
# 'master' array is itself an array that contains a row of data.

print "The fourth date in the table is: " . $data->[3][1] . "\n";
# Element 3 of the 'master' array is an array containing the fourth row of
# data.
# Element 1 of that array is the date.
```

DBI::fetchrow_array

```
@row_of_data = $statement_handle->fetchrow;
```

DBI::fetchrow returns the next row of data from a statement handle generated by DBI::execute. Each successive call to DBI::fetchrow returns the next row of data. When there is no more data, the function returns an undefined value **undef**. The elements in the resultant array are in the order specified in the original query. If the query was of the form **SELECT * FROM . . .**, the elements are ordered in the same sequence as the fields were defined in the table.

Example

```
use DBI;
my $db = DBI->connect('DBI:mSQL:mydata',undef,undef);
my $query = "SELECT name, date FROM myothertable WHERE name LIKE 'Bob%'";
my $myothertable_output = $db->prepare($query);
$myothertable_output->execute;

my ($name, $date);

# This is the first row of data from $myothertable_output.
($name, $date) = $myothertable_output->fetchrow_array;
# This is the next row...
($name, $date) = $myothertable_output->fetchrow_array;
```

```
# And the next...
my @name_and_date = $myothertable_output->fetchrow_array;
# etc...
```

DBI::fetchrow_arrayref, DBI::fetch

```
$array_reference = $statement_handle->fetchrow_arrayref;
$array_reference = $statement_handle->fetch;
```

`DBI:: fetchrow_arrayref` and its alias, `DBI::fetch`, work exactly like `DBI::fetchrow_array` except that they return a reference to an array instead of an actual array.

Example

```
use DBI;
my $db = DBI->connect('DBI:mSQL:mydata',undef,undef);
my $query = "SELECT name, date FROM myothertable WHERE name LIKE 'Bob%'";
my $myothertable_output = $db->prepare($query);
$myothertable_output->execute;

my $name1 = $myothertable_output->fetch->[0]
# This is the 'name' field from the first row of data.
my $date2 = $myothertable_output->fetch->[1]
# This is the 'date' from from the *second* row of data.
my ($name3, $date3) = @{$myothertable_output->fetch};
# This is the entire third row of data. $myothertable_output->fetch returns a
# reference to an array. We can 'cast' this into a real array with the @{}
# construct.
```

DBI::fetchrow_hashref

```
$hash_reference = $statement_handle->fetchrow_hashref;
```

`DBI::fetchrow_hashref` works exactly like `DBI::fetchrow_arrayref` except that it returns a reference to an associative array instead of a regular array. The keys of the hash are the names of the fields and the values are the values of that row of data.

Example

```
use DBI;
my $db = DBI->connect('DBI:mSQL:mydata',undef,undef);
my $query = "SELECT * FROM mytable";
my $mytable_output = $db->prepare($query);
$mytable_output->execute;

my %row1 = $mytable_ouput->fetchrow_hashref;
my @field_names = keys %row1;
# @field_names now contains the names of all of the fields in the query.
# This needs to be set only once. All future rows will have the same fields.
my @row1 = values %row1;
```

DBI::finish

```
$result = $statement_handle->finish;
```

DBI::finish releases all data in the statement handle so that the handle may be destroyed or prepared again. Some database servers require this in order to free the appropriate resources. DBD::mSQL and DBD::mysql do not need this function, but for portable code, you should use it after you are done with a statement handle. The function returns an undefined value **undef** if the handle cannot be freed.

Example

```
use DBI;
my $db = DBI->connect('DBI:mysql:mydata','me','mypassword');
my $query = "SELECT * FROM mytable";
my $mytable_output = $db->prepare($query);
$mytable_output->execute;
...
$mytable_output->finish;
# You can now reassign $mytable_output or prepare another statement for it.
```

DBI::func

```
$handle->func(@func_arguments, $func_name);
@dbs = $db->func("$hostname", '_ListDBs');
@dbs = $db->func("$hostname:$port", '_ListDBs');
@tables = $db->func('_ListTables');
$result = $drh->func( $database, '_CreateDB' );
$result = $drh->func( $database, '_DropDB' );
```

DBI::func calls specialized nonportable functions included with the various DBD drivers. It can be used with either a database or a statement handle depending on the purpose of the specialized function. If possible, you should use a portable DBI equivalent function. When using a specialized function, the function arguments are passed as a scalar first followed by the function name. DBD::mSQL and DBD::mysql implement the following functions:

_ListDBs

The _ListDBs function takes a hostname and optional port number and returns a list of the databases available on that server. It is better to use the portable function DBI::data_sources.

_ListTables

The _ListTables function returns a list of the tables present in the current database.

_CreateDB

The _CreateDB function takes the name of a database as its argument and attempts to create that database on the server. You must have permission to create databases for this function to work. The function returns –1 on failure and 0 on success.

_DropDB

> The _DropDB function takes the name of a database as its argument and attempts to delete that database from the server. This function does not prompt the user in any way, and if successful, the database will be irrevocably gone forever. You must have permission to drop databases for this function to work. The function returns –1 on failure and 0 on success.

Example

```
use DBI;
my $db = DBI->connect('DBI:mysql:mydata','me','mypassword');

my @tables = $db->func->('_ListTables');
# @tables now has a list of the tables in 'mydata'.
```

DBI::neat

```
$neat_string = DBI::neat($string);
$neat_string = DBI::neat($string, $maxlen);
```

DBI::neat takes as its arguments a string and an optional length. The string is then formatted to print out neatly. The entire string is enclosed in single quotes. All unprintable characters are replaced with periods. If the length argument is present, are characters after the maximum length are removed and the string is terminated with three periods (...). If no length is supplied, 400 is used as the default length.

Example

```
use DBI;

my $string = "This is a very, very, very long string with lots of stuff in
it.";
my $neat_string = DBI::neat($string,14);
# $neat_string is now: 'This is a very...
```

DBI::neat_list

```
$neat_string = DBI::neat_list(\@listref, $maxlen);
$neat_string = DBI::neat_list(\@listref, $maxlen, $field_seperator);
```

DBI::neat_list takes three arguments and returns a neatly formatted string suitable for printing. The first argument is a reference to a list of values to print. The second argument is the maximum length of each field. The final argument is a string used to join the fields. DBI::neat is called for each member of the list using the maximum length given. The resulting strings are then joined using the last argument. If the final argument is not present, a comma is used as the separator.

Example

```
use DBI;

my @list = ('Bob', 'Joe', 'Frank');
my $neat_string = DBI::neat_list(\@list, 3);
# $neat_string is now: 'Bob', 'Joe', 'Fra...
```

DBI::prepare

```
$statement_handle = $db->prepare($statement);
$statement_handle = $db->prepare($statement, \%unused);
```

DBI::prepare takes as its argument an SQL statement, which some database modules put into an internal compiled form so that it runs faster when DBI::execute is called. These DBD modules (not DBD::mSQL or DBD::mysql) also accept a reference to a hash of optional attributes. The mSQL and MySQL server do not currently implement the concept of "preparing," so DBI::prepare merely stores the statement. You may optionally insert any number of '?' symbols into your statement in place of data values. These symbols are known as "placeholders." The DBI::bind_param function is used to substitute the actual values for the placeholders. The function returns undef if the statement cannot be prepared for some reason.

Example

```
use DBI;
my $db = DBI->connect('DBI:mysql:mydata','me','mypassword');

my $statement_handle = $db->prepare('SELECT * FROM mytable');
# This statement is now ready for execution.

My $statement_handle = $db->prepare(
'SELECT name, date FROM myothertable WHERE name like ?');
# This statement will be ready for exececuting once the placeholder is filled
# in using the DBI::bind_param function.
```

DBI::quote

```
$quoted_string = $db->quote($string);
```

DBI::quote takes a string intended for use in an SQL query and returns a copy that is properly quoted for insertion in the query. This includes placing the proper outer quotes around the string.

Example

```
use DBI;
my $db1 = DBI->connect('DBI:mSQL:mydata',undef,undef);
my $db2 = DBI->connect('DBI:mysql:myotherdata','me','mypassword');
```

```
my $string = "Sheldon's Cycle";

my $qs1 = $db1->quote($string);
# $qs1 is: 'Sheldon\'s Cycle' (including the outer quotes)
my $qs2 = $db2->quote($string);
# $qs2 is: 'Sheldon's Cycle' (including the outer quotes)
# Both strings are now suitable for use in a statement for their respective
# database servers.
```

DBI::rows

```
$number_of_rows = $statement_handle->rows;
```

DBI::rows returns the number of rows of data contained in the statement handle. With DBD::mSQL and DBD::mysql, this function is accurate for all statements, including SELECT statements. For many other drivers which do not hold of the results in memory at once, this function is only reliable for non-SELECT statements. This should be taken into account when writing portable code. The function returns '-1' if the number of rows is unknown for some reason. The variable $DBI::rows provides the same functionality.

Example

```
use DBI;
my $db = DBI->connect('DBI:mSQL:mydata',undef,undef);
my $query = "SELECT name, date FROM myothertable WHERE name='Bob'";
my $myothertable_output = $db->prepare($query);
$myothertable_output->execute;

my $rows = $myothertable_output->rows;
print "There are $rows 'Bob's in 'myothertable'.\n";
```

DBI::state

```
$sql_error  = $handle->state;
```

DBI::state returns the SQLSTATE SQL error code for the last error DBI encountered. Currently both DBD::mSQL and DBD::mysql report 'S1000' for all errors. This function is available from both database and statement handles. The variable $DBI::state performs the same function.

Example

```
Use DBI;
my $db = DBI->connect('DBI:mysql:mydata','webuser','super_secret_squirrel');
...
my $sql_error = $db->state;
warn("This is your most recent DBI SQL error: $sql_error");
```

DBI::trace

```
DBI->trace($trace_level)
DBI->trace($trace_level, $trace_file)
$handle->trace($trace_level);
$handle->trace($trace_level, $trace_file);
```

`DBI::trace` is useful mostly for debugging purposes. If the trace level is set to 2, full debugging information will be displayed. Setting the trace level to 0 disables the trace. If `DBI->trace` is used, tracing is enabled for all handles. If `$handle->trace` is used, tracing is enabled for that handle only. This works for both database and statement handles. If a second argument is present for either `DBI->trace` or `$handle->trace`, the debugging information for all handles is appended to that file. You can turn on tracing also by setting the environment variable `DBI_TRACE`. If the environment variable is defined as a number (0 or 2, currently) tracing for all handles is enabled at that level. With any other definition, the trace level is set to 2 and the value of the environment variable is used as the filename for outputting the trace information.

Example

```
use DBI;
my $db1 = DBI->connect('DBI:mysql:mydata','webuser','super_secret_squirrel');
my $db2 = DBI->connect('DBI:mSQL:myotherdata',undef,undef);

DBI->trace(2);
# Tracing is now enabled for all handles at level 2.
$db2->trace(0);
# Tracing is now disabled for $db2, but it is still enabled for $db1
$db1->trace(2,'DBI.trace');
# Tracing is now enabled for all handles at level 2, with the output being
# sent to the file 'DBI.trace'.
```

DBI::commit, DBI::rollback, DBI::ping

```
$result = $db->commit;
$result = $db->rollback;
$result = $db->ping;
```

`DBI::commit` and `DBI::rollback` are useful only with database servers that support transactions. They have no effect when used with DBD::mSQL and DBD::mysql. `DBD::ping` attempts to verify if the database server is running. It is not implemented and has no effect with DBD::mSQL and DBD::mysql.

Attributes

```
$db->{AutoCommit}
$handle->{ChopBlanks}
$handle->{CompatMode}
$handle->{InactiveDestroy}
$handle->{LongReadLen}
$handle->{LongTruncOk}
$handle->{PrintError}
$handle->{RaiseError}
$handle->{Warn}
$statement_handle->{CursorName}
$statement_handle->{insertid} (MySQL only)
$statement_handle->{is_blob} (MySQL only)
$statement_handle->{is_key} (MySQL only)
$statement_handle->{is_not_null}
$statement_handle->{is_num}
$statement_handle->{is_pri_key} (MySQL and mSQL 1.x only)
$statement_handle->{length}
$statement_handle->{max_length} (MySQL only)
$statement_handle->{NAME}
$statement_handle->{NULLABLE}
$statement_handle->{NUM_OF_FIELDS}
$statement_handle->{NUM_OF_PARAMS}
$statement_handle->{table}
$statement_handle->{type}
```

The DBI.pm API defines several attributes that may be set or read at any time. Assigning a value to an attribute that can be set changes the behavior of the current connection in some way. Assigning any true value to an attribute will set that attribute on. Assigning 0 to an attribute sets it off. Some values are defined only for particular databases and are not portable. The following are attributes that are present for both database and statement handles.

`$db->{AutoCommit}`

This attribute affects the behavior of database servers that support transactions. For mSQL and MySQL, they must always be set to 'on' (the default). Attempting to change this will kill the program.

`$handle->{ChopBlanks}`

If this attribute is on, any data returned from a query (such as `DBI::fetchrow` call) will have any leading or trailing spaces chopped off. Any handles deriving from the current handle inherit this attribute. The default for this attribute is 'off.'

`$handle->{InactiveDestroy}`

This attribute is designed to enable handles to survive a 'fork' so that a child can make use of a parent's handle. You should enable this attribute in either the parent or the child but not both. The default for this attribute is 'off.'

$handle->{PrintError}

If this attribute is on, all warning messages will be displayed to the user. If this attribute is off, the errors are available only through $DBI::errstr. Any handles deriving from the current handle inherit this attribute. The default for this attribute is 'on.'

$handle->{RaiseError}

If this attribute is on, any errors will raise an exception in the program, killing the program if no '__DIE__' handler is defined. Any handles deriving from the current handle inherit this attribute. The default for this attribute is 'off.'

$handle->{Warn}

If this attribute is on, warning messages for certain bad programming practices (most notably holdovers from Perl 4) will be displayed. Turning this attribute off disables DBI warnings and should be used only if you are really confident in your programming skills. Any handles deriving from the current handle (such as a statement handle resulting from a database handle query) inherit this attribute. The default for this attribute is 'on.'

$statement_handle->{insertid}

This is a nonportable attribute that is defined only for DBD::mysql. The attribute returns the current value of the auto_increment field (if there is one) in the table. If no auto_increment field exists, the attribute returns undef.

$statement_handle->{is_blob}

This is a nonportable attribute which is defined only for DBD::mysql. The attribute returns a reference to an array of boolean values indicating if each of the fields contained in the statement handle is of a BLOB type. For a statement handle that was not returned by a SELECT statement, $statement_handle->{is_blob} returns undef.

$statement_handle->{is_key}

This is a nonportable attribute which is defined only for DBD::mysql. The attribute returns a reference to an array of boolean values indicating if each of the fields contained in the statement handle were defined as a KEY. For a statement handle that was not returned by a SELECT statement, $statement_handle->{is_key} returns undef.

$statement_handle->{is_not_null}

This is a nonportable attribute which is defined only for DBD::mSQL and DBD::mysql. The attribute returns a reference to a list of boolean values indicating if each of the fields contained in the statement handle are defined 'NOT NULL'. For a statement handle that was not returned by a SELECT statement, $statement_handle->{is_not_null} returns undef. The same effect of this attribute can be accomplished in a portable manner by using `$statement_handle->{NULLABLE}`.

`$statement_handle->{is_num}`

This is a nonportable attribute which is defined only for DBD::mSQL and DBD::mysql. The attribute returns a reference to an array of boolean values indicating if each of the fields contained in the statement handle is a number type. For a statement handle that was not returned by a SELECT statement, `$statement_handle->{is_num}` returns undef.

`$statement_handle->{is_pri_key}`

This is a nonportable attribute which is defined only for DBD::mSQL and DBD::mysql. When used with DBD::mSQL it has effect only in conjunction with mSQL 1.x servers, because mSQL 2.x does not use primary keys. The attribute returns a reference to a list of boolean values indicating if each of the fields contained in the statement handle is a primary key. For a statement handle that was not returned by a SELECT statement, `$statement_handle->{is_pri_key}` returns undef.

`$statement_handle->{length}`

This is a nonportable attribute which is defined only for DBD::mysql and DBD::mSQL. The attribute returns a reference to a list of the maximum possible length of each field contained in the statement handle. For a statement handle that was not returned by a SELECT statement, `$statement_handle->{length}` returns undef.

`$statement_handle->{max_length}`

This is a nonportable attribute which is defined only for DBD::mysql. The attribute returns a reference to a list of the actual maximum length of each field contained in the statement handle. For a statement handle that was not returned by a SELECT statement, `$statement_handle->{max_length}` returns undef.

`$statement_handle->{NAME}`

This attribute returns a reference to a list of the names of the fields contained in the statement handle. For a statement handle that was not returned by a SELECT statement, `$statement_handle->{NAME}` returns undef.

`$statement_handle->{NULLABLE}`

This attribute returns a reference to a list of boolean values indicating if each of the fields contained in the statement handle can have a NULL value. A field defined with 'NOT NULL' will have a value of 0 in the list. All other fields will have a value of 1. For a statement handle that was not returned by a SELECT statement, `$statement_handle->{NULLABLE}` returns undef.

`$statement_handle->{NUM_OF_FIELDS}`

This attribute returns the number of columns of data contained in the statement handle. For a statement handle that was not returned by a SELECT statement, `$statement_handle->{NUM_OF_FIELDS}` returns 0.

`$statement_handle->{NUM_OF_PARAMS}`

This attribute returns the number of "placeholders" in the statement handle. Placeholders are indicated with a '?' in the statement. The `DBI::bind_values` function is used to replace the placeholders with the proper values.

`$statement_handle->{table}`

This is a nonportable attribute which is defined only for DBD::mSQL and DBD::mysql. The attribute returns a reference to a list of the names of the tables accessed in the query. This is particularly useful in conjunction with a JOINed SELECT that uses multiple tables.

`$statement_handle->{type}`

This is a nonportable attribute which is defined only for DBD::mSQL and DBD::mysql. The attribute returns a reference to a list of the types of the fields contained in the statement handle. For a statement handle that was not returned by a SELECT statement, `$statement_handle->{max_length}` returns undef. The values of this list are integers that correspond to an enumeration in the mysql_com.h C header file found in the MySQL distribution. There is currently no method to access the names of these types from within DBI. But the types are accessible via the `&Mysql::FIELD_TYPE_*` function in Mysql.pm. There is also an undocumented attribute in DBD::mysql called `$statement_handle->{format_type_name}` which is identical to `$statement_handle->{type}` except that it returns the SQL names of the types instead of integers. *It should be stressed that this is an undocumented attribute and the author of* DBD::mysql *has stated his intention to remove it should DBI implement the same functionality.*

`$statement_handle->{CursorName}`
`$handle->{LongReadLen}`
`$handle->{LongTruncOk}`
`$handle->{CompatMode}`

All of these attributes are unsupported in DBD::mSQL and DBD::mysql. Assigning to them will do nothing and reading them will return a 0 or undef. The exception is `$statement_handle->{CursorName}`. Currently, accessing this attribute in any way will cause the program to die.

Example

```
use DBI;
my $db = DBI->connect('mysql:mydata','me','mypassword');

$db->{RAISE_ERROR} = 1;
```

```
# Now, any DBI/DBD errors will kill the program.

my $statement_handle = $db->prepare('SELECT * FROM mytable');
$statement_handle->execute;

my @fields = @{$statement_handle->{NAME}};
# @fields now contains an array of all of the field names in 'mytable'.
```

Msql.pm API

use Msql

```
use Msql;
```
    This must be declared in every Perl program that uses the Msql.pm module.

Msql::connect

```
$db = Msql->connect;
$db = Msql->connect($host);
$db = Msql->connect($host, $database);
```

Establishes a connection between your Perl program and the Msql server. There are three versions of the function. With no arguments, a connection is made to the Msql Unix socket on the local host with no database defined. This is the most efficient connection. If one scalar argument is present, that argument is taken to be the hostname or IP address of the mSQL server. A connection is then made to that server with no database set. If two scalar arguments are present, the first is taken to be the host of the mSQL server and the second is the name of the desired database. The program then makes a connection to the given server and selects the given database. The value returned is a reference to an object called the "database handle." All communication with the database server itself takes places through this object. If the connection fails for any of the above cases, **undef** is returned and the error is placed in **$Msql::db_errstr**.

Example

```
use Msql;

# Connect to the localhost Unix socket
my $db = Msql->connect;

# Or...
# Connect to host 'www.myserver.com' with no database defined
my $db = Msql->connect('www.myserver.com');

# Or...
# Connect to host 'www.myserver.com' and select database 'mydata'
my $db = Msql->connect('www.myserver.com','mydata');
```

Msql::createdb

```
$result = $db->createdb($database);
```

`Msql::createdb` takes as its argument the name of a database to create. It then sends the creation request to the mSQL server. The command is sent as the same user running the CGI program. Thus, to work in a CGI program, the program must be run as a user with the right to create a new database. The function returns −1 on failure and 0 on success.

Example

```
use Msql;
my $db = Msql->connect;
my $my_new_database = 'mynewdata';
my $result = $db->createdb($my_new_database);
die "Database was not created!" if $result == -1;
print "$my_new_database has been created.\n";
```

Msql::database

```
$database = $db->database;
```

`Msql::database` returns the name of the current database as a scalar. The function returns `undef` if no database has been selected.

Example

```
use Msql;
my $db = Msql->connect('www.myserver.com','mydata');

my $database = $db->database;

print "This should say 'mydata': $database\n";
```

Msql::dropdb

```
$result = $db->dropdb($database);
```

`Msql::dropdb` takes as its argument the name of a database to destroy. It then sends the destruction request to the mSQL server. The command is sent as the same user running the CGI program. Thus, to work in a CGI program, the program must be run as a user with the right to destroy the database. The function returns −1 on failure and 0 on success. This function does not ask for any confirmation and the results are permanent. Thus, this function should be used with the most extreme caution.

Example

```
use Msql;
my $db = Msql->connect;
my $result = $db->dropdb('mydata');
die "Command failed!" if result == -1;
print "'mydata' is now gone forever.\n";
```

Msql::errmsg

```
$error = $db->errmsg;
```

`Msql::errmsg` returns the last error encountered by your session with the mSQL server. The value remains until the next error occurs, at which time it is replaced. If no error has occurred during your session, the function returns **undef**.

Example

```
use Msql;
my $db = Msql->connect;
...
my $error = $db->errmsg;
warn("This is your most recent mSQL error: $error");
```

Msql::getsequenceinfo

```
($step, $value) = $db->getsequenceinfo($table);
```

`Msql::getsequenceinfo` takes the name of a table as its argument. It returns the step and value of the sequence defined on the table, if any. If there is no sequence defined on the given table, an undefined value **undef** is returned and an error is placed in `Msql::errmsg`.

Example

```
use Msql;
my $db = Msql->connect;
my ($step, $value) = $db->getsequenceinfo('mytable');
die "There is no sequence on mytable" if not $step;
print "mystep has a sequence with a value of $value and a step of $step\n";
```

Msql::host

```
$host = $db->host;
```

`Msql::host` returns the hostname of the database server as a scalar. There is no guarantee that the function will return the canonical name of the server or even a fully qualified domain name. In fact, although not documented, it appears that `Msql::host` returns the same string given to the server in the `Msql::connect` call. This is true even to the point that `Msql::host` returns **undef** if you use the no-argument form of `Msql::connect`.

Example

```
use Msql;
my $db = Msql->connect('www.myserver.com');

my $host = $db->host;

print "You'll probably see 'www.myserver.com': $host\n";
```

Msql::listdbs

```
@databases = $db->listdbs;
```

`Msql::listdbs` returns an array of the databases available on the server. If there are no databases on the server, it returns an empty array.

Example

```
use Msql;
my $db = Msql->connect;

my @databases = $db->listdbs;
print "Available databases:\n\n" . join("\n",@databases);
```

Msql::listfields

```
$fields = $db->listfields($table);
```

`Msql::listfields` takes as an argument the name of a table in the current database. It returns a reference to an object which contains the names of all of the fields, as well as some other information. This reference is known as a statement handle. You can access the information in a statement handle using any of the following functions: `Msql::Statement::as_string`, `Msql::Statement::listindices` (mSQL 2.0 only), `Msql::Statement::numfields`, `Msql::Statement::table`, `Msql::Statement::name`, `Msql::Statement::type`, `Msql::Statement::isnotnull`, `Msql::Statement::isprikey`, `Msql::Statement::isnum`, and `Msql::Statement::length`. If the table does not exist, the function returns an undefined value `undef`, and the error is placed in `Msql::errmsg`. See `Msql::Statement::fetchhash` for a technique that makes this function somewhat obsolete.

Example

```
use Msql;
my $db = Msql->connect;
$db->selectdb('mydata');

my $fields = $db->listfields('mytable');
warn ("Problem with 'mytable': " . $db->errmsg) if (not $fields);
# $fields is now a reference to all of the fields in the table 'mytable'.
print "mytable contains the following fields:\n";
print $fields->as_string;
```

Msql::listindex

```
@index_handles = $db->listindex($table,$index);
```

`Msql::listindex` accepts the names of a table and the name of an index as its arguments and returns an array of statement handles containing information about each of the indices. Although this function is documented as returning an array of statement handles, we can find no case where more than one statement handle would be returned. Therefore it is probably safe to treat this function as returning a scalar statement handle. The statement handle is of the same style as a statement handle returned by `Msql::query` and can be accessed by the same functions. If the index does not exist, an undefined value **undef** is returned. The table of data returned about the index has one column, which has the title "Index". The first row is the type of index, which in mSQL 2.0 is always "avl". The other rows are the names of the fields that comprise the index. This function is valid only with mSQL 2.0 or greater database servers.

Example

```
use Msql;
my $db = Msql->connect;
$db->selectdb('mydata');
my $mytable_fields = $db->listfields('mytable');
my @indices = $mytable_fields->listindices;
# I now know the names of all of the indices.

foreach (@indices) {
    my $index_info_handle = $db->listindex('mytable',$_);
    my (@index_info) = $index_info_handle->fetchcol(0);
    my $type_of_index = shift(@index_info);
    # $type_of_index now contains the type of the index (probably 'avl')
    # and @index_info now contains a list of the fields in the index.
```

Msql::listtables

```
@tables = $db->listtables;
```

`Msql::listtables` returns an array of the tables available in the current database. If the database has no tables, the function returns an empty array.

Example

```
use Msql;
my $db = Msql->connect;

my @tables = $db->listtables;
my $database = $db->database;
print "$database has the following tables:\n\n"
                . join("\n",@tables);
```

Msql::query

```
$query_output = $db->query($sql_statement);
```

`Msql::query` is the most important and most frequently used function in the Msql.pm API. It is through this function that you actually send the SQL queries to the database server. The function takes a scalar string containing an SQL query as an argument. If the query is a **SELECT** statement, the function returns a statement handle containing the results of the query. Otherwise, the function returns the number of rows that were affected by the query. The statement handle can be accessed by the same functions listed for `Msql::listfields` (except for `Msql::Statement::listindices`) as well as the following: `Msql::Statement::fetchrow`, `Msql::Statement::fetchcol`, `Msql::Statement::fetchhash`, `Msql::Statement::numrows`, `Msql::Statement::maxlength`, and `Msql::Statement::dataseek`. If the query is unsuccessful for any reason, an undefined value `undef` is returned and the error is placed in `Msql::errmsg`. Each statement handle contains the output of a separate query. Therefore, you can send as many queries as your system can handle and then deal with each of the statement handles at your leisure.

Example

```
use Msql;
my $db = Msql->connect;
$db->selectdb('mydata');

my $query1 = "SELECT * FROM mytable";
my $query2 = "SELECT name, date FROM myothertable WHERE name LIKE 'Bob%'";
my $query3 = "UPDATE myothertable SET name='Bob' WHERE name='Joe'";

my $mytable_output = $db->query($query1);
my $myothertable_output = $db->query($query2);
my $myothertable_input = $db->query($query3);

# $mytable_output contains the results of the query on 'mytable'
# $myothertable_output contains the results of the query on 'myothertable'
print "The update on 'myothertable' affected $myothertable_input names\n";
```

$Msql::QUIET

The `$Msql::QUIET` variable, when true, turns off error reporting when the `-` option is used in Perl. Otherwise, all MsqlPerl errors will be automatically sent to STDERR. The variable can be reset at any time. The *-w* error reporting feature is so useful that setting `$Msql::QUIET` is not recommended.

Example

```
use Msql;

# Turn off error reporting. This has an effect only if the script is being
# run with '-w'.
$Msql::QUIET = 1;

# Do noisy section...

# Turn error reporting back on.
$Msql::QUIET = undef;
```

Msql::quote

```
$quoted_string = $db->quote($string);
$truncated_quoted_string = $db->quote($string,$length);
```

Msql::quote takes as its argument a scalar string. It returns the same string quoted so that it is safe for insertion into a **CHAR** or **TEXT** field in the database. More specifically, it surrounds the string with single quotes, and uses backslashes to escape any single quotes already in the string. If a second argument is present, the result is truncated to be that many characters long.

Example

```
    use Msql;
    my $db = Msql->connect;

    my $string = "This is a field's value";

    my $qstring = $db->quote($string);

    print qq%This now says "'This is a field\\'s value'" : $qstring\n%;
```

Msql::selectdb

```
$db->selectdb($database);
```

Msql::selectdb selects a database from the database server. If the selection fails, the error is placed in **Msql::errmsg**. The only effective way to test for the success of this function is to examine the value of **$db->database** and compare it to the database to which you intended to connect. You may switch databases at any time during your program.

Example

```
    use Msql;
    my $db = Msql->connect;

    $db->selectdb('mydata');
    # The database is now 'mydata'
    if ($db->database ne 'mydata') {
                warn('AWOOOGA! The database wasn't properly selected!');
    }
    ...
    $db->selectdb('myotherdata');
    # The database is now 'myotherdata'
```

Msql::shutdown

```
$result = $db->shutdown;
```

Msql::shutdown sends a shutdown command to the mSQL server. The command is sent as the user is running the program. Thus, to work in a CGI program, the program must be run as a user with the right to shutdown the database. The function returns –1 on failure and 0 on success.

Example

```
use Msql;
my $db = Msql->connect;
# Time to shutdown the database...
my $result = $db->shutdown;
die "Command failed!" if $result == -1;
print "The server has been stopped.\n";
```

Msql::Statement::as_string

```
$formatted_table = $statement_handle->as_string;
```

Msql::Statement::as_string returns the data contained in the statement handle in a neatly formatted ASCII table. The table is similar to the ones used by the *msql* monitor. The *pmsql* program supplied with the *Msql.pm* module uses this function to generate its tables.

Example

```
use Msql;
my $db = Msql->connect;
$db->selectdb('mydata');
my $query = "SELECT * FROM mytable";
my $mytable_output = $db->query($query);

print "My Table:\n", $mytable_output->as_string;
# This prints the entire table in a fashion much cleaner than the
# Msql::Statement::fetchhash example.
```

Msql::Statement::dataseek

```
$statement_handle->dataseek($row_number);
```

Msql::Statement::dataseek takes the number of a row as its argument. The function resets the data so that the next call to Msql::Statement::fetchrow or Msql::Statement::fetchhash will return the information in that row. If a row number is supplied that is beyond the range of the table, the pointer is placed at the end of the table so that the next access will return an undefined value undef. The first row of the table is row number 0.

Example

```
use Msql;
my $db = Msql->connect;
$db->selectdb('mydata');
my $query = "SELECT name, date FROM myothertable";
my $myothertable_output = $db->query($query);

my @names = $myothertable_output->fetchcol(0);
my @dates = $myothertable_output->fetchcol(1);
# The pointer is now at the end of the table.
```

```
$myothertable_output->dataseek(0);
# The pointer is now reset to the beginning of the table.

print "This is the first row of data: ", $myothertable_output->fetchrow, "\n".
```

Msql::Statement::fetchcol

```
@column_of_data = $statement_handle->fetchcol($column_number);
```

`Msql::Statement::fetchcol` takes the number of a column as its argument and
returns an array of all of the values in that column. Multiple calls return all columns in the same order, so that all of the values with a certain element number
refer to the same row. The first output column is numbered 0. To perform this call,
the module must read the entire table. Therefore, if you want to continue examining the table after using this function you have to reset the data using `Msql::`
`Statement::dataseek`. An undefined value is returned. The function returns
`undef` if an invalid column number is provided.

Example

```
use Msql;
my $db = Msql->connect;
$db->selectdb('mydata');
my $query = "SELECT name, date FROM myothertable WHERE name LIKE 'Bob%'";
my $myothertable_output = $db->query($query);

my @names = $myothertable_output->fetchcol(0);
# @names now contains all of the names.
my @dates = $myothertable_output->fetchcol(1);
# @dates now contains all of the dates.
for (0..$#names) {
    print "Row $_: $names[$_], $dates[$_]\n";
}
```

Msql::Statement::fetchhash

```
%hash = $statement_handle->fetchhash;
```

`Msql::Statement::fetchhash` returns the current row of the statement handle
as an associative array (or hash). The keys of the hash are the names of the fields
and the values are the data values for the current row. Each successive call to the
function returns the next row of data. When there is no more data, the function
returns an undefined value `undef`.

Example

```
use Msql;
my $db = Msql->connect;
$db->selectdb('mydata');
my $query = "SELECT * FROM mytable";
my $mytable_output = $db->query($query);
my %first_data_row = $mytable_output->fetchhash;
```

```
my @fields = keys %first_data_row;
# @fields now contains all of the field names. Therefore there is never
really
# any need to use Msql::listfields, since we can get that information along
# with a lot more through the statement handle returned from Msql::query.

my (%data_row);
print join("", @fields), "\n';
print "-"x70;
print join("", values(%first_data_row);
print join("", values(%data_row)) while %data_row = $mytable_output->
fetchhash;
# This prints a complete dump of the table. (Albeit in a very misaligned
format.
```

Msql::Statement::fetchrow

```
@row_of_data = $statement_handle->fetchrow;
```

`Msql::Statement::fetchrow` returns the next row of data from a statement handle generated by *Msql::query*. Each successive call to `Msql::Statement::fetchrow` returns the next row of data. When there is no more data, the function returns an undefined value **undef**. The elements in the resultant array are in the order specified in the original query. If the query was of the form SELECT * FROM . . ., the elements are ordered in the same sequence that the fields were defined in the table.

Example

```
use Msql;
my $db = Msql->connect;
$db->selectdb('mydata');
my $query1 = "SELECT * FROM mytable";
my $query2 = "SELECT name, date FROM myothertable WHERE name LIKE 'Bob%'";
my $mytable_output = $db->query($query1);
my $myothertable_output = $db->query($query2);
my $i = 0;

# This will keep reading the rows of data until there
# are no more left.
while (my(@mytable_rows)=$mytable_output->fetchrow) {
    print "Row ".$i++.": ".join(', ',@mytable_rows)."\n";
    # Unless I know something about the structure of 'mytable'
    # I have no idea how many elements are in @mytable_rows or
    # what order they are in.
}

my ($name, $date);

# This is the first row of data from $myothertable_output.
($name, $date) = $myothertable_output->fetchrow;
# This is the next row...
($name, $date) = $myothertable_output->fetchrow;
```

```
# And the next...
my @name_and_date = $myothertable_output->fetchrow;
# etc...
```

Msql::Statement::isnotnull

```
@not_null  = $statement_handle->isnotnull;
```

`Msql::Statement::isnotnull` returns a list of boolean values indicating if each of the columns of data contained in the statement handle have been defined as 'NOT NULL'. When called in a scalar context the function returns a reference to an array.

Example

```
use Msql;
my $db = Msql->connect;
$db->selectdb('mydata');
my $output = $db->query("select * from mydata");
my @names = $output->name;

my @not_null = $output->isnotnull;
for (0..$#not_null) {
                 print "$names[$_] is not null\n" if $not_null[$_];
}
```

Msql::Statement::isnum

```
@numbers  = $statement_handle->isnum;
```

`Msql::Statement::isnum` returns a list of boolean values indicating if each of the columns of data contained in the statement handle is a numerical value. When called in a scalar context, the function returns a reference to an array. Numerical values include types, such as 'INT' and 'REAL', but do not include a 'CHAR' or 'TEXT' field that contains numbers.

Example

```
use Msql;
my $db = Msql->connect;
$db->selectdb('mydata');
my $output = $db->query("select name, date from myothertable");

print "Name is a number" if $output->isnum->[0];
print "Date is a number" if $output->isnum->[1];
```

Msql::Statement::isprikey

```
@primary_key  = $statement_handle->isprikey;
```

`Msql::Statement::isprikey` returns a list of boolean values indicating if each of the columns of data contained in the statement handle is a primary key. When called in a scalar context, the function returns a reference to an array. This function will always return a list of 0's when connected to a mSQL 2 server because mSQL 2 does not use primary keys. However, this function is useful with mSQL 1 servers, which do implement primary keys.

Example

```
use Msql;
my $db = Msql->connect;
$db->selectdb('mydata');
my $output = $db->query("select * from mytable");

my @prikeys = $output->isprikey;
my $number_of_prikeys = scalar @prikeys;
print "There are $number_of_prikeys primary keys in this statement handle. ".
    "There are at least this many different tables in the query as each
table".
    "can have only one primary key.\n";
```

Msql::Statement::length

```
@lengths = $statement_handle->length;
```

`Msql::Statement::length` returns a list of the maximum possible length of each of the columns of data contained in the statement handle. These values are the maximums defined when the table was created. When called in a scalar context, the function returns a reference to an array.

Example

```
use Msql;
my $db = Msql->connect;
$db->selectdb('mydata');
my $output = $db->query("select * from mytable");
my @types = $output->type;

my @lengths = $output->length;
for (0..$#types) {
    if ($types[$_] == &Msql::CHAR_TYPE and $lengths[$_] > 1000000) {
        print "You've got one mighty big CHAR field in that table!\";
    }
}
```

Msql::Statement::listindices

```
@indices = $statement_handle->listindices;
```

`Msql::Statement::listindices` returns the indices associated with any of the fields found in the statement handle. Because the function looks for field names directly, it is useful only with names returned from `Msql::listfields`. If no indices are found, an undefined value `undef` is returned. This function can only be used with mSQL 2.0, or greater, database servers.

Example

```
use Msql;
my $db = Msql->connect;
$db->selectdb('mydata');
my $mytable_fields = $db->listfields('mytable');

my @indices = $mytable_fields->listindices;
print "'mytable' contains these indices: " . join(", ",@indices) . "\n";
```

Msql::Statement::maxlength

```
@max_lengths  = $statement_handle->maxlength;
```

`Msql::Statement::maxlength` returns a list of the actual maximum length of each field contained in the table. When called in a scalar context, the function returns a reference to an array. Since the mSQL server does not provide this information directly, this function is implemented by reading the entire table and searching for the maximum value of each field. Thus, with mSQL this function can be resource heavy when used with queries that return large amounts of information.

Example

```
use Msql;
$db = Msql->connect;
$db->selectdb('mydata');
my $output = $db->query('select name, date from myothertable');

print "The longest name is " . $ouput->maxlength->[0] . " characters long.\
n";
```

Msql::Statement::name

```
@column_names  = $statement_handle->name;
```

`Msql::Statement::name` returns the names of the columns of data contained in the statement handle. When called in a scalar context the function returns a reference to an array. As with `Msql::Statement::table`, the scalar value of this list (as opposed to the value of the function when called in a scalar context) is identical to the value of `Msql::Statement::numfields`.

Example

```
use Msql;
my $db = Msql->connect;
$db->selectdb('mydata');
my $output = $db->query("select * from mytable");

my @column_names = $output->names;
# @column_names is now a list of the columns in 'mytable'
```

Msql::Statement::numfields

```
$number_of_fields = $statement_handle->numfields;
```

`Msql::Statement::numfields` returns the number of fields contained in a single row of the output stored in the statement handle. All output has at least one field, so this function will return a positive integer for any defined statement handle.

Example

```
use Msql;
my $db = Msql->connect;
$db->selectdb('mydata');
my $output = $db->query("select * from mytable");

my $numfields = $output->numfields;
my $numrows = $output->numrows;
print "There are $numfields field in each row of 'mytable'\n";
print "And there are $numrows rows of data. Thus, 'mytable'\n";
print "contains " . ($numfields*$numrows) . " cells of data.\n";
```

Msql::Statement::numrows

```
$number_of_rows = $statement_handle->numrows;
```

`Msql::Statement::numrows` returns the number of rows contained in the statement handle. If run on a statement handle that cannot contain any rows, such as one returned by `Msql::listfields`, the function returns the string 'N/A.' If the statement handle could contain rows but does not, such as one returned by a SELECT that does not match any fields, the function returns 0.

Example

```
use Msql;
my $db = Msql->connect;
$db->selectdb('mydata');
my $output = $db->query("select * from mytable");

my $numrows = $output->numrows;
print "There are $numrows rows of data in 'mytable'\n";
```

Msql::Statement::table

```
@tables  = $statement_handle->table;
```

`Msql::Statement::table` returns a list of the tables associated with each of the columns of data contained in the statement handle. When called in a scalar context, the function returns a reference to an array. (See `Msql::Statement::isnum` for an example of how to use the array reference.) One entry is present for each column of data even if only one table was used in the query. As a side effect, the scalar value of the array returned by `$statement_handle->table` is the same value as `$statement_handle->numfields`.

Example

```
use Msql;
my $db = Msql->connect;
$db->selectdb('mydata');
my $output = $db->query('select myothertable.name, myothertable.date,
    mythirdtable.name from myothertable, mythirdtable where myothertable.name
    = mythirdtable.name');

my @tables = $output->table;
# @tables now contains ('myothertable', 'myothertable', 'mythirdtable')
```

Msql::Statement::type

```
@column_types  = $statement_handle->type;
```

`Msql::Statement::type` returns the types of the columns of data contained in the statement handle. When called in a scalar context the function returns a reference to an array. The pure value of this array is not of much use to most users (in the current implementation it is a list of integers). Rather, the values can be compared to the built-in values defined in Msql.pm such as &Msql::CHAR_TYPE and &Msql::INT_TYPE. One method of accessing this data is to build an array matching readable names to the predefined types. This method was demonstrated in Chapter 10, *Perl*. Another method is demonstrated below.

Example

```
use Msql;
my $db = Msql->connect;
$db->selectdb('mydata');
my $output = $db->query("select name, date from myothertable");

my ($name_type, $date_type) = $output->type;
for ($name_type) {
    $_ eq &Msql::CHAR_TYPE and do { print 'name is a CHAR'; last; }
    $_ eq &Msql::INT_TYPE and do { print 'name is an INT'; last; }
    # etc...
}
# repeat for $date_type
```

Msql::sock

```
$sock = $db->sock;
```

`Msql::sock` returns a scalar containing the number of the socket used to connect with the mSQL server. This is generally useful only for real nuts and bolts programming.

Example

```
use Msql;
my $db = Msql->connect;
```

```
my $sock = $db->sock;

print "I am connected on socket $sock.\n";
```

Msql::*_TYPE

`Msql.pm` provides the following defined functions that correspond to the mSQL datatypes:

```
&Msql::CHAR_TYPE
&Msql::INT_TYPE
&Msql::REAL_TYPE
&Msql::IDENT_TYPE
&Msql::TEXT_TYPE
&Msql::IDX_TYPE
&Msql::NULL_TYPE
&Msql::DATE_TYPE
&Msql::UINT_TYPE
&Msql::MONEY_TYPE
&Msql::TIME_TYPE
&Msql::SYSVAR_TYPE
```

Example

```
use Msql;

%types = (
                'CHAR' => &Msql::CHAR_TYPE,
                'INT' => &Msql::INT_TYPE,
                'REAL' => &Msql::REAL_TYPE,
                'SYSVAR' => &Msql::SYSVAR_TYPE,
                'TIME' => &Msql::TIME_TYPE,
                'MONEY' => &Msql::MONEY_TYPE,
                'UINT' => &Msql::UINT_TYPE,
                'TEXT' => &Msql::TEXT_TYPE,
                'NULL' => &Msql::NULL_TYPE,
                'DATE' => &Msql::DATE_TYPE,
                'IDENT' => &Msql::IDENT_TYPE,
                'IDX' => &Msql::IDX_TYPE,
);
# $types{'CHAR'} is now an easily accessible alias for
# &Msql::CHAR_TYPE. Having the values in %types gives you access to all of
the
# handy hash functions such as keys() and values().
```

$Msql::VERSION

The `$Msql::VERSION` variable contains the version of the Msql.pm module.

Example

```
use Msql;

print "You are using Msql.pm version $Msql::VERSION.\n";
```

Mysql.pm API

The Mysql.pm API is identical to the Msql API (with "Msql" replaced with "Mysql" in all places) except for the following differences.

Mysql::connect

```
$db = Mysql->connect($host, $database, $user, $password);
```

In addition to the three connect methods that are identical to `Msql::connect`, `Mysql::connect` provides a fourth method that requires an additional password argument. The first argument is the hostname or IP address of the MySQL server. If `undef` is passed as this argument, the module connects to the Unix-style socket on the localhost. The second argument is the name of the initial database to select. This can always be changed later with `Mysql::selectdb`. You may also supply `undef` as the second argument to select no initial database. The third argument is the username of the user connecting to the database. To successfully connect, the username must exist in the MySQL access tables. The final argument is the password of the user.

Example

```
use Mysql;

$db = Mysql->connect(undef,'mydata','webuser','super_secret_squirrel');
# The database handle is now connected to the local MySQL server using the
# database 'mydata'. The user name 'webuser' was used to connect who had
# the password 'super_secret_squirrel'.
```

Mysql::errno

```
$error_number = $db->errno;
```

`Mysql::errno` returns the error number of the last error. This error number corresponds to the error message returned from `Msql::errmsg`.

Example

```
use Mysql;
my $db = Mysql->connect(undef,'mydata','webuser','super_secret_squirrel');

# There is a parse error in this query...
my $output = $db->query('SLECT * from mydata');

if (not $output) {
```

```
                              print "Error " . $output->errno . ": " . $output->errmsg . "\
     n";
     }
```

Mysql::FIELD_TYPE_*

In addition to the `Mysql::TYPE_*` datatype functions that are identical to the `Msql::TYPE_*` functions, *Mysql.pm* provides these extra datatype functions:

&Mysql::FIELD_TYPE_BLOB

&Mysql::FIELD_TYPE_CHAR

&Mysql::FIELD_TYPE_DECIMAL

&Mysql::FIELD_TYPE_DATE

&Mysql::FIELD_TYPE_DATETIME

&Mysql::FIELD_TYPE_DOUBLE

&Mysql::FIELD_TYPE_FLOAT

&Mysql::FIELD_TYPE_INT24

&Mysql::FIELD_TYPE_LONGLONG

&Mysql::FIELD_TYPE_LONG_BLOB

&Mysql::FIELD_TYPE_LONG

&Mysql::FIELD_TYPE_MEDIUM_BLOB

&Mysql::FIELD_TYPE_NULL

&Mysql::FIELD_TYPE_SHORT

&Mysql::FIELD_TYPE_STRING

&Mysql::FIELD_TYPE_TIME

&Mysql::FIELD_TYPE_TIMESTAMP

&Mysql::FIELD_TYPE_TINY_BLOB

&Mysql::FIELD_TYPE_VAR_STRING

Example

```
use Mysql;
my $db = Mysql->connect(undef,'mydata');
my $output = $db->query("SELECT name, data from myothertable");

if ($output->type->[0] = &Mysql::FIELD_TYPE_STRING) {
                print "Name is a STRING.\n";
}
```

Mysql::Statement::affectedrows

`$number_of_affected_rows  = $statement_handle->affectedrows;`

`Msql::Statement::affectedrows` returns the number of rows that were affected by the query. This function is useful since Mysql.pm returns a statement handle even on non-SELECT statements.

Example

```
use Mysql;
my $db = Mysql->connect(undef,'mydata');

my $output = $db->query("UPDATE mytable set name='bob' where name='joe'");
print $output->affectedrows . " rows were updated.\n";
```

Mysql::Statement::info

```
$info  = $sth->info;
```

`Mysql::Statement::info` returns extra results from certain queries that do not have specialized functions in *Mysql.pm*, such as `ALTER TABLE` and `LOAD DATA INFILE`. For example, when using `LOAD DATA INFILE`, `Mysql::Statement::info` returns the number of records inserted, the number deleted, the number skipped and the number of unparsable entries.

Example

```
use Mysql;
$db = Mysql->connect(undef,'mydata');

my $output = $db->query("LOAD DATA INFILE 'mydata.dat' INTO TABLE mytable");

my $info = $output->info($output);
print "LOAD DATA result: $info\n";
```

Mysql::Statement::insertid

```
$new_id  = $statement_handle->insertid;
```

`Mysql::Statement::insertid` returns the current value of the `auto_increment` field (if there is one) in the table. If there is no `auto_increment` field in the table, the function returns an undefined value `undef`.

Example

```
use Mysql;
my $db = Mysql->connect(undef,'mydata');

my $output = $db->query(
    "INSERT into mytable (id, name, date) VALUES ('','bob','today')";

my $new_id = $output->insertid;
print "Bob was entered with an ID number of $new_id.\n";
```

Mysql::Statement::isblob

```
@blobs  = $statement_handle->isblob;
```

`Mysql::Statement::isblob` returns a list of boolean values indicating if the fields contained in the statement handle are of a `BLOB` type. If called in a scalar context, the function returns a reference to an array.

Example

```
use Mysql;
$db = Mysql->connect(undef,'mydata');

my $output = $db->query('SELECT name, data from myothertable');

if ($output->isblob->[0]) {
                print "Name is a BLOB.\n";
} else {
                print "Name is not a BLOB.\n";
}
```

Mysql::query

Unlike *Msql.pm*, *Mysql.pm* returns a statement handle even with non-**SELECT** queries, such as **INSERT**, **UPDATE**, and **DELETE**.

Example

```
use Mysql;
my $db = Mysql->connect(undef,'mydata');

my $output = $db->query("UPDATE mytable set name='joe' where name='bob'");
# $output is a statement handle.
```

22

JDBC Reference

The `java.sql` package contains the entire JDBC API. It first became part of the core Java libraries with the 1.1 release. Classes new as of JDK 1.2 are indicated by the "Availability" header. Deprecated methods are preceded by a hash (#) mark. New JDK 1.2 methods in old JDK 1.1 classes are shown in bold. Figure 22-1 shows the entire `java.sql` package.

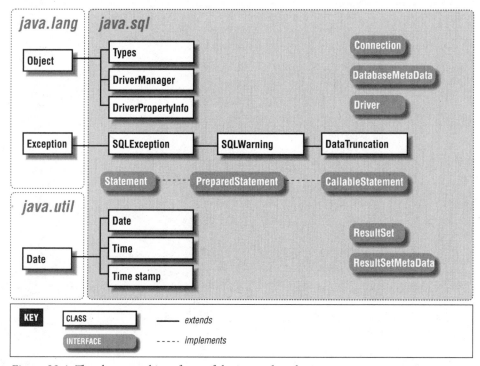

Figure 22-1. The classes and interfaces of the java.sql package

Array

Synopsis

Class Name: `java.sql.Array`
Superclass: None
Immediate Subclasses: None
Interfaces Implemented: None
Availability: New as of JDK 1.2

Description

The `Array` interface is a new addition to JDBC that supports SQL3 array objects. The default duration of a reference to a SQL array is for the life of the transaction in which it was created.

Class Summary

```
public interface Array {
    Object getArray() throws SQLException;
    Object getArray(Map map) throws SQLException;
    Object getArray(long index, int count)
        throws SQLException;
    Object getArray(long index, int count, Map map)
        throws SQLException;
    int getBaseType() throws SQLException;
    String getBaseTypeName() throws SQLException;
    ResultSet getResultSet() throws SQLException;
    ResultSet getResultSet(Map map) throws SQLException;
    ResultSet getResultSet(long index, int count)
        throws SQLException;
    ResultSet getResultSet(long index, int count,
                        Map map) throws SQLException
}
```

Object Methods

getArray()

```
public Object getArray() throws SQLException
public Object getArray(Map map) throws SQLException
public Object getArray(long index, int count)
    throws SQLException
public Object getArray(long index, int count, Map map)
    throws SQLException
```

Description: Place the contents of this SQL array into a Java language array or, instead, into the Java type specified by a provided Map. If a map is specified but no match is found in there, then the default mapping to a Java array is used. The two versions that accept an array index and element count enable you to place a subset of the elements in the array.

getBaseType( )
```
public int getBaseType() throws SQLException
```
Description: Provides the JDBC type of the elements of this array.

getBaseTypeName( )
```
public String getBaseTypeName() throws SQLException
```
Description: Provides the SQL type name for the elements of this array.

getResultSet( )
```
public ResultSet getResultSet() throws SQLException
public ResultSet getResultSet(Map map)
    throws SQLException
public ResultSet getResultSet(long index, int count)
    throws SQLException
public ResultSet getResultSet(long index, int count,
                              Map map)
    throws SQLException
```
Description: Provides a result set that contains the array's elements as rows. If appropriate, the elements are mapped using the type map for the connection, or the specified type map if you pass one. Each row contains two columns: the first column is the index number (starting with 1), and the second column is the actual value.

Blob

Synopsis

Class Name: `java.sql.Blob`
Superclass: None
Immediate Subclasses: None
Interfaces Implemented: None
Availability: New as of JDK 1.2

Description

The JDBC `Blob` interface represents a SQL BLOB. BLOB stands for "binary large object" and is a relational database representation of a large piece of binary data. The value of using a BLOB is that you can manipulate the BLOB as a Java object without retrieving all of the data behind the BLOB from the database. A BLOB object is only valid for the duration of the transaction in which it was created.

Class Summary
```
public interface Blob {
    InputStream getBinaryStream() throws SQLException;
    byte[] getBytes(long pos, int count)
        throws SQLException;
    long length() throws SQLException;
    long position(byte[] pattern, long start)
```

```
        throws SQLException;
    long position(Blob pattern, long start)
        throws SQLException;
}
```

Object Methods

getBinaryStream()

```
public InputStream getBinaryStream() throws SQLException
```

Description: Retrieves the data that makes up the binary object as a stream from the database.

getBytes()

```
public byte[] getBytes(long pos, int count)
    throws SQLException
```

Description: Returns the data that makes up the underlying binary object in part or in whole as an array of bytes. You can get a subset of the binary data by specifying a nonzero starting index or by specifying a number of bytes less than the object's length.

length()

```
public long length() throws SQLException
```

Description: Provides the number of bytes that make up the BLOB.

position()

```
public long position(byte[] pattern, long start)
    throws SQLException
public long position(Blob pattern, long start)
    throws SQLException
```

Description: Searches this Blob for the specified pattern and returns the byte at which the specified pattern occurs within this Blob. If the pattern does not occur, then this method will return -1.

CallableStatement

Synopsis

Class Name: `java.sql.CallableStatement`
Superclass: `java.sql.PreparedStatement`
Immediate Subclasses: None
Interfaces Implemented: None
Availability: JDK 1.1

Description

The `CallableStatement` is an extension of the `PreparedStatement` interface that provides support for SQL stored procedures. It specifies methods that handle the binding of output parameters. JDBC prescribes a standard form in which stored procedures should appear independent of the DBMS being used. The format is:

```
{? = call …}
{call …}
```

Each question mark is a place holder for an input or output parameter. The first syntax provides for a single result parameter. The second syntax has no result parameters. The parameters are referred to sequentially with the first question mark holding the place for parameter 1.

Before executing a stored procedure, all output parameters should be registered using the `registerOutParameter()` method. You then bind the input parameters using the various set methods, and then execute the stored procedure.

Class Summary

```java
public interface CallableStatement extends PreparedStatement {
    Array getArray(int index) throws SQLException;
    BigDecimal getBigDecimal(int index)
        throws SQLException;
    #BigDecimal getBigDecimal(int index, int scale)
        throws SQLException;
    Blob getBlob(int index) throws SQLException;
    boolean getBoolean(int index) throws SQLException;
    byte getByte(int index) throws SQLException;
    byte[] getBytes(int index) throws SQLException;
    Clob getClob(int index) throws SQLException;
    java.sql.Date getDate(int index, Calendar cal)
        throws SQLException;
    java.sql.Date getDate(int index) throws SQLException;
    double getDouble(int index) throws SQLException;
    float getFloat(int index) throws SQLException;
    int getInt(int index) throws SQLException;
    long getLong(int index) throws SQLException;
    Object getObject(int index) throws SQLException;
    Object getObject(int index, Map map)
        throws SQLException;
    Ref getRef(int index) throws SQLException;
    short getShort(int index) throws SQLException;
    String getString(int index) throws SQLException;
    java.sql.Time getTime(int index) throws SQLException;
    java.sql.Time getTime(int index, Calendar cal)
        throws SQLException;
    java.sql.Timestamp getTimestamp(int index)
        throws SQLException;
    java.sql.Timestamp getTimestamp(int index,
                                    Calendar cal)
        throws SQLException;
    void registerOutParameter(int index, int type)
        throws SQLException;
    void registerOutParameter(int index, int type,
                              int scale)
```

```
            throws SQLException;
        void registerOutParameter(int index, int type,
                                   String typename)
            throws SQLException;
        boolean wasNull() throws SQLException;
    }
```

Object Methods

getBigDecimal()

```
    public BigDecimal getBigDecimal(int index)
        throws SQLException
    #public BigDecimal getBigDecimal(int index, int scale)
        throws SQLException
```

Description: Returns the value of the parameter specified by the **index** parameter as a Java **BigDecimal** with a scale specified by the **scale** argument. The scale is a nonnegative number representing the number of digits to the right of the decimal. Parameter indices start at 1; parameter 1 is thus **index** 1.

getArray(), getBlob(), getBoolean(), getByte(), getBytes(), getClob(), getDouble(), getFloat(), getInt(), getLong(), getRef(), getShort(), and getString()

```
    public Array getArray(int index)
        throws SQLException
    public Blob getBlob(int index) throws SQLException
    public boolean getBoolean(int index) throws SQLException
    public byte getByte(int index) throws SQLException
    public byte[] getBytes(int index) throws SQLException
    public Clob getClob(int index) throws SQLException
    public double getDouble(int index) throws SQLException
    public float getFloat(int index) throws SQLException
    public int getInt(int index) throws SQLException
    public long getLong(int index) throws SQLException
    public Ref getRef(int index) throws SQLException
    public short getShort(int index) throws SQLException
    public String getString(int index) throws SQLException
```

Description: Returns the value of the parameter specified by the **index** argument as the Java datatype indicated by the method name.

getDate(), getTime(), and getTimestamp()

```
    public Date getDate(int index) throws SQLException
    public Date getDate(int index, Calendar cal)
        throws SQLException
    public Time getTime(int index) throws SQLException
    public Time getTime(int index, Calendar cal)
        throws SQLException
    public Timestamp getTimestamp(int index)
        throws SQLException
    public Timestamp getTimestamp(int index, Calendar cal)
        throws SQLException
```

Description: JDBC provides refinements on the basic java.util.Date object more suitable to database programming. These methods provide ways to access return values from a CallableStatement as a Date, Time, or Timestamp object. The new JDK 1.2 variants allow you to specify a Calendar.

getObject( )

```
public Object getObject(int index) throws SQLException
public Object getObject(int index, Map map)
    throws SQLException
```

Description: Like the other **getXXX()** methods, this method returns the value of the specified output parameter. In the case of **getObject()**, however, the JDBC driver chooses the Java class that corresponds to the SQL type registered for this parameter using **registerOutParameter()** or according to the specified type map.

registerOutParameter( )

```
public void registerOutParameter(int index, int type)
    throws SQLException
public void registerOutParameter(int index, int type,
                                 int scale)
    throws SQLException
public void registerOutParameter(int index, int type,
                                 String typename)
    throws SQLException
```

Description: Before executing any stored procedure using a **CallableStatement**, you must register each of the output parameters. This method registers the **java.sql.Type** of an output parameter for a stored procedure. The first parameter specifies the output parameter being registered and the second the **java.sql.Type** to register. The three-argument version of this method is for **BigDecimal** types that require a scale. You later read the output parameters using the corresponding **getXXX()** method or **getObject()**. The third version of this method is new to JDK 1.2 and provides a way to map **REF** SQL types or custom SQL types.

wasNull( )

```
public boolean wasNull() throws SQLException
```

Description: If the last value you read using a **getXXX()** call was SQL NULL, this method will return **true**.

Clob

Synopsis

Class Name: **java.sql.Clob**
Superclass: None
Immediate Subclasses: None
Interfaces Implemented: None
Availability: New as of JDK 1.2

Description

CLOB is a SQL3 type that stands for "character large object." Like a BLOB, a CLOB represents a very large chunk of data in the database. Unlike a BLOB, a CLOB represents text stored using some sort of character encoding. The point of a CLOB type as opposed to a CHAR or VARCHAR type is that CLOB data, like BLOB data, can be retrieved as a stream instead of all at once.

Class Summary

```
public interface Clob {
    InputStream getAsciiStream() throws SQLException;
    Reader getCharacterStream() throws SQLException;
    String getSubString(long pos, int count)
        throws SQLException;
    long length() throws SQLException;
    long position(String pattern, long start)
        throws SQLException;
    long position(Clob pattern, long start)
        throws SQLException;
}
```

Object Methods

getAsciiStream( )

```
public InputStream getAsciiStream() throws SQLException
```

Description: Provides access to the data that makes up this Clob via an ASCII stream.

getCharacterStream( )

```
public Reader getCharacterStream() throws SQLException
```

Description: Provides access to the data that makes up this Clob via a Unicode stream.

getSubString( )

```
public String getSubString(long pos, int count)
    throws SQLException
```

Description: Returns a substring of the Clob starting at the named position up to the number of character specified by the count value.

length( )

```
public long length() throws SQLException
```

Description: Provides the number of characters that make up the Clob.

position( )

```
public long position(String pattern, long start)
    throws SQLException;
public long position(Clob pattern, long start)
    throws SQLException;
```

Description: Searches the Clob for the specified pattern starting at the specified start point. If the pattern is found within the Clob, the index at which the pattern first occurs is returned. If it does not exist within the Clob, then this method returns -1.

Connection

Synopsis

Class Name: java.sql.Connection
Superclass: None
Immediate Subclasses: None
Interfaces Implemented: None
Availability: JDK 1.1

Description

The Connection class is the JDBC representation of a database session. It provides an application with Statement objects (and its subclasses) for that session. It also handles the transaction management for those statements. By default, each statement is committed immediately upon execution. You can use the Connection object to turn off this Autocommit feature for the session. In that event, you must expressly send commits, or any statements executed will be lost.

Class Summary

```
public interface Connection {
    static public final int TRANSACTION_NONE;
    static public final int TRANSACTION_READ_UNCOMMITTED;
    static public final int TRANSACTION_READ_COMMITTED;
    static public final int TRANSACTION_REPEATABLE_READ;
    static public final int TRANSACTION_SERIALIZABLE;

    void clearWarnings() throws SQLException;
    void close() throws SQLException;
    void commit() throws SQLException;
    Statement createStatement() throws SQLException;
    Statement createStatement(int type, int concur)
        throws SQLException;
    boolean getAutoCommit() throws SQLException;
    String getCatalog() throws SQLException;
    Map getTypeMap() throws SQLException;
    DatabaseMetaData getMetaData() throws SQLException;
    int getTransactionIsolation() throws SQLException;
    SQLWarning getWarnings() throws SQLException;
    boolean isClosed() throws SQLException;
    boolean isReadOnly() throws SQLException;
    String nativeSQL(String sql) throws SQLException;
    CallableStatement prepareCall(String sql)
        throws SQLException;
    CallableStatement prepareCall(String sql, int type,
                                  int concur)
        throws SQLException;
```

```
        PreparedStatement prepareStatement(String sql)
            throws SQLException;
        PreparedStatement prepareStatement(String sql,
                                           int type,
                                           int concur)
            throws SQLException;
        void rollback() throws SQLException;
        void setAutoCommit(boolean ac) throws SQLException;
        void setCatalog(String catalog) throws SQLException;
        void setReadOnly(boolean ro) throws SQLException;
        void setTransactionIsolation(int level)
            throws SQLException;
        void setTypeMap(Map map) throws SQLException;
    }
```

Class Attributes

TRANSACTION_NONE

`static public final int TRANSACTION_NONE`

Description: Transactions are not supported.

TRANSACTION_READ_UNCOMMITTED

`static public final int TRANSACTION_READ_UNCOMMITTED`

Description: This transaction isolation level allows uncommitted changes by one transaction to be readable by other transactions.

TRANSACTION_READ_COMMITTED

`static public final int TRANSACTION_READ_COMMITTED`

Description: This transaction isolation level prevents dirty reads from occurring. In other words, changes by a **TRANSACTION_READ_COMMITTED** transaction are invisible to other transactions until the transaction making the change commits those changes.

TRANSACTION_REPEATABLE_READ

`static public final int TRANSACTION_REPEATABLE_READ`

Description: This transaction isolation level prevents dirty reads and nonrepeatable reads. A nonrepeatable read is one where one transaction reads a row, a second transaction alters the row, and the first transaction rereads the row, getting different values the second time.

Object Methods

clearWarnings()

`public void clearWarnings() throws SQLException`

Description: Clears out all the warnings associated with this **Connection** so that `getWarnings()` will return null until a new warning is reported.

close()

`public void close() throws SQLException`

Description: This method manually releases all resources (such as network connections and database locks) associated with a given JDBC `Connection`. This method is automatically called when garbage collection occurs; however, it is best to manually close a `Connection` once you are done with it.

commit()

```
public void commit() throws SQLException
```

Description: This method makes permanent the changes created by all statements associated with this `Connection` since the last commit or rollback was issued. It should only be used when Autocommit is off. It does not commit changes made by statements associated with other `Connection` objects.

createStatement()

```
public Statement createStatement() throws SQLException
public Statement createStatement(int type, int concur)
    throws SQLException
```

Description: This method creates a `Statement` object associated with this `Connection` session. The no argument version of this method creates a `Statement` whose `ResultSet` instances are type forward-only and read-only concurrency.

getAutoCommit() and setAutoCommit()

```
public boolean getAutoCommit() throws SQLException
public void setAutoCommit(boolean ac)
    throws SQLException
```

Description: By default, all `Connection` objects are in Autocommit mode. With Autocommit mode on, each statement is committed as it is executed. An application may instead choose to manually commit a series of statements together as a single transaction. In this case, you use the `setAutoCommit()` method to turn Autocommit off. You then follow your statements with a call to `commit()` or `rollback()` depending on the success or failure of the transaction.

When in Autocommit mode, a statement is committed either when the statement completes or when the next statement is executed, whichever is first. For statements returning a `ResultSet`, the statement completes when the last row has been retrieved or the `ResultSet` has been closed. If a statement returns multiple result sets, the commit occurs when the last row of the last `ResultSet` object has been retrieved.

getCatalog() and setCatalog()

```
public String getCatalog() throws SQLException
public void setCatalog(String catalog) throws SQLException
```

Description: If a driver supports catalogs, then you use `setCatalog()` to select a subspace of the database with the specified catalog name. If the driver does not support catalogs, it will ignore this request.

getMetaData( )

```
public DatabaseMetaData getMetaData() throws SQLException
```

Description: The DatabaseMetaData class provides methods that describe a database's tables, SQL support, stored procedures, and other information relating to the database and this Connection, which are not directly related to executing statements and retrieving result sets. This method provides an instance of the DatabaseMetaData class for this Connection.

getTransactionIsolation( ) and setTransactionIsolation( )

```
public int getTransactionIsolation() throws SQLException
public void setTransactionIsolation(int level)
    throws SQLException
```

Description: Sets the Connection object's current transaction isolation level using one of the class attributes for the Connection interface. Those levels are called TRANSACTION_NONE, TRANSACTION_READ_UNCOMMITTED, TRANSACTION_READ_COMMITTED, and TRANSACTION_REPEATABLE_READ.

getTypeMap( ) and setTypeMap( )

```
public Map getTypeMap() throws SQLException
public void setTypeMap(Map map) throws SQLException
```

Description: You can use these methods to define or retrieve a custom mapping for SQL structured types and distinct types for all statements associated with this connection.

getWarnings( )

```
public SQLWarning getWarnings() throws SQLException
```

Description: Returns the first warning in the chain of warnings associated with this Connection object.

isClosed( )

```
public boolean isClosed() throws SQLException
```

Description: Returns true if the Connection has been closed.

isReadOnly( ) and setReadOnly( )

```
public boolean isReadOnly() throws SQLException
public void setReadOnly(boolean ro) throws SQLException
```

Description: Some databases can optimize for read-only database access. The setReadOnly() method provides you with a way to put a Connection into read-only mode so that those optimizations occur. You cannot call setReadOnly() while in the middle of a transaction.

nativeSQL( )

```
public String nativeSQL(String sql) throws SQLException
```

Description: Many databases may not actually support the same SQL required by JDBC. This method allows an application to see the native SQL for a given JDBC SQL string.

prepareCall( )

```
public CallableStatement prepareCall(String sql)
    throws SQLException
public CallableStatement prepareCall(String sql,
                                    int type,
                                    int concur)
    throws SQLException
```

Description: Given a particular SQL string, this method creates a `CallableStatement` object associated with this `Connection` session. This is the preferred way of handling stored procedures. The default (no argument) version of this method provides a `CallableStatement` whose `ResultSet` instances are type forward-only and read-only concurrency.

prepareStatement( )

```
public PreparedStatement prepareStatement(String sql)
    throws SQLException
public PreparedStatement prepareStatement(String sql,
                                        int type,
                                        int concur)
    throws SQLException
```

Description: Provides a `PreparedStatement` object to be associated with this `Connection` session. This is the preferred way of handling precompiled SQL statements. The default (no argument) version of this method provides a `PreparedStatement` whose `ResultSet` instances are type forward-only and read-only concurrency.

rollback( )

```
public void rollback() throws SQLException
```

Description: Aborts all changes made by statements associated with this Connection since the last time a commit or rollback was issued. If you want to make those changes at a later time, your application will have to reexecute the statements that made those changes. This should be used only when auto-commit is off.

DatabaseMetaData

Synopsis

Class Name: `java.sql.DatabaseMetaData`
Superclass: None
Immediate Subclasses: None
Interfaces Implemented: None
Availability: New as of JDK 1.1

Description

This class provides a lot of information about the database to which a `Connection` object is connected. In many cases, it returns this information in the form of JDBC `ResultSet` objects. For databases that do not support a particular kind of metadata, `DatabaseMetaData` will throw an SQLException.

`DatabaseMetaData` methods take string patterns as arguments where specific tokens within the `String` are interpreted to have a certain meaning. `%` matches any substring of 0 or more characters and `_` matches any one character. You can pass null to methods in place of string pattern arguments; this means that the argument's criteria should be dropped from the search.

Class Summary

```
public interface DatabaseMetaData {
    static public final int bestRowTemporary;
    static public final int bestRowTransaction;
    static public final int bestRowSession;
    static public final int bestRowUnknown;
    static public final int bestRowNotPseudo;
    static public final int bestRowPseudo;
    static public final int columnNoNulls;
    static public final int columnNullable;
    static public final int columnNullableUnknown;
    static public final int importedKeyCascade;
    static public final int importedKeyRestrict;
    static public final int importedKeySetNull;
    static public final int importedKeyNoAction;
    static public final int importedKeySetDefault;
    static public final int importedKeyInitiallyDeferred;
    static public final int importedKeyInitiallyImmediate;
    static public final int importedKeyNotDeferrable;
    static public final int procedureResultUnknown;
    static public final int procedureNoResult;
    static public final int procedureReturnsResult;
    static public final int procedureColumnUnknown;
    static public final int procedureColumnIn;
    static public final int procedureColumnOut;
    static public final int procedureColumnReturn;
    static public final int procedureColumnResult;
    static public final int procedureNoNulls;
    static public final int procedureNullable;
    static public final int procedureNullableUnknown;
    static public final short tableIndexStatistic;
    static public final short tableIndexClustered;
    static public final short tableIndexHashed;
    static public final short tableIndexOther;
    static public final int typeNoNulls;
    static public final int typeNullable;
    static public final int typeNullableUnknown;
    static public final int typePredNone;
    static public final int typePredChar;
```

```
static public final int typePredBasic;
static public final int typeSearchable;
static public final int versionColumnUnknown;
static public final int versionColumnNotPseudo;
static public final int versionColumnPseudo;

boolean allProceduresAreCallable()
    throws SQLException;
boolean allTablesAreSelectable() throws SQLException;
boolean dataDefinitionCausesTransactionCommit()
    throws SQLException;
boolean dataDefinitionIgnoredInTransactions()
    throws SQLException;
ResultSet getBestRowIdentifier(String catalog,
    String schema, String table, int scope,
    boolean nullable)
    throws SQLException;
ResultSet getCatalogs() throws SQLException;
String getCatalogSeparator() throws SQLException;
String getCatalogTerm() throws SQLException;
ResultSet getColumnPriveleges(String catalog,
        String spat, String table,
        String cpat) throws SQLException;
ResultSet getColumns(String catalog,
        String spat, String tpat,
        String cpat) throws SQLException;
ResultSet getCrossReference(String primaryCatalog,
        String primarySchema, String primaryTable,
        String foreignCatalog, String foreignSchema,
        String foreignTable) throws SQLException;
String getDatabaseProductName() throws SQLException;
String getDatabaseProductVersion()
    throws SQLException;
int getDefaultTransactionIsolation()
    throws SQLException;
int getDriverMajorVersion();
int getDriverMinorVersion();
String getDriverName() throws SQLException;
String getDriverVersion() throws SQLException;
ResultSet getExportedKeys(String catalog,
    String schema, String table)
    throws SQLException;
String getExtraNameCharacters() throws SQLException;
String getIdentifierQuoteString() throws SQLException;
ResultSet getImportedKeys(String catalog,
    String schema, String table) throws SQLException;
ResultSet getIndexInfo(String catalog,
    String schema, String table, boolean unique,
    boolean approximate) throws SQLException;
int getMaxBinaryLiteralLength() throws SQLException;
int getMaxCatalogNameLength() throws SQLException;
int getMaxCharLiteralLength() throws SQLException;
int getMaxcnameLength() throws SQLException;
int getMaxColumnsInGroupBy() throws SQLException;
```

```
int getMaxColumnsInIndex() throws SQLException;
int getMaxColumnsInOrderBy() throws SQLException;
int getMaxColumnsInSelect() throws SQLException;
int getMaxColumnsInTable() throws SQLException;
int getMaxConnections() throws SQLException;
int getMaxIndexLength() throws SQLException;
int getMaxProcedureNameLength()
    throws SQLException;
int getMaxRowSize() throws SQLException;
int getMaxRowSizeIncludeBlobs()
    throws SQLException;
int getMaxSchemaNameLength() throws SQLException;
int getMaxStatementLength() throws SQLException;
int getMaxStatements() throws SQLException;
int getMaxTableNameLength() throws SQLException;
int getMaxTablesInSelect() throws SQLException;
int getMaxUserNameLength() throws SQLException;
String getNumericFunctions() throws SQLException;
ResultSet getPrimaryKeys(String catalog,
    String schema, String table) throws SQLException;
ResultSet getProcedureColumns(String catalog,
    String schemePattern, String procedureNamePattern,
    String cnamePattern) throws SQLException;
String getProcedureTerm() throws SQLException;
ResultSet getProcedures(String catalog,
    String schemaPattern, String procedureNamePattern)
    throws SQLException;
public abstract ResultSet getSchemas() throws SQLException;
public abstract String getSchemaTerm() throws SQLException;
String getSearchStringEscape() throws SQLException;
String getSQLKeywords() throws SQLException;
String getStringFunctions() throws  SQLException;
String getSystemFunctions() throws SQLException;
ResultSet getTablePrivileges(String catalog,
    String schemaPattern, String tableNamePattern)
    throws SQLException;
ResultSet getTableTypes() throws SQLException;
ResultSet getTables(String catalog,
    String schemaPattern, String tableNamePattern,
    String types[]) throws SQLException;
String getTimeDateFunctions() throws SQLException;
ResultSet getTypeInfo() throws SQLException;
String getURL() throws SQLException;
String getUserName() throws SQLException;
ResultSet getVersionColumns(String catalog,
    String schema, String table) throws SQLException;
boolean isCatalogAtStart() throws SQLException;
boolean isReadOnly() throws SQLException;
boolean nullPlusNonNullIsNull() throws SQLException;
boolean nullsAreSortedHigh() throws SQLException;
boolean nullsAreSortedLow() throws SQLException;
boolean nullsAreSortedAtStart() throws SQLException;
boolean nullsAreSortedAtEnd() throws SQLException;
boolean storesLowerCaseIdentifiers()
```

```
        throws SQLException;
boolean storesLowerCaseQuotedIdentifiers()
    throws SQLException;
boolean storesMixedCaseIdentifiers()
    throws SQLException;
boolean storesMixedCaseQuotedIdentifiers()
    throws SQLException;
boolean storesUpperCaseIdentifiers()
    throws SQLException;
boolean storesUpperCaseQuotedIdentifiers()
    throws SQLException;
boolean supportsAlterTableWithAddColumn()
    throws SQLException;
boolean supportsAlterTableWithDropColumn()
    throws SQLException;
boolean supportsANSI92FullSQL() throws SQLException;
boolean supportsANSI92IntermediateSQL()
    throws SQLException;
boolean supportsCatalogsInDataManipulation()
    throws SQLException;
boolean suppportsCatalogsInIndexDefinitions()
    throws SQLException;
boolean supportsCatalogsInPrivelegeDefinitions()
    throws SQLException;
boolean supportsCatalogsInProcedureCalls()
    throws SQLException;
boolean supportsCatalogsInTableDefinitions()
    throws SQLException;
boolean supportsColumnAliasing() throws SQLException;
boolean supportsConvert() throws SQLException;
boolean supportsConvert(int fromType, int toType)
    throws SQLException;
boolean supportsCoreSQLGrammar() throws SQLException;
boolean supportsCorrelatedSubqueries()
    throws SQLException;
boolean
supportsDataDefinitionAndDataManipulationTransactions()
    throws SQLException;
boolean supportsDataManipulationTransactionsOnly()
    throws SQLException;
boolean supportsDifferentTableCorrelationNames()
    throws SQLException;
boolean supportsExpressionsInOrderBy()
    throws SQLException;
boolean supportsExtendedSQLGrammar()
    throws SQLException;
boolean supportsFullOuterJoins() throws SQLException;
boolean supportsGroupBy() throws SQLException;
boolean supportsGroupByBeyondSelect()
    throws SQLException;
boolean supportsGroupByUnrelated()
    throws SQLException;
boolean supportsIntegrityEnhancementFacility()
    throws SQLException;
```

```
boolean supportsLikeEscapeClause()
    throws SQLException;
boolean supportsLimitedOuterJoins()
    throws SQLException;
boolean supportsMinimumSQLGrammar()
    throws SQLException;
boolean supportsMixedCaseIdentifiers()
    throws SQLException;
boolean supportsMixedCaseQuotedIdenfitiers()
    throws SQLException;
boolean supportsMultipleResultSets()
    throws SQLException;
boolean supportsMultipleTransactions()
    throws SQLException;
boolean supportsNonNullableColumns()
    throws SQLException;
boolean supportsOpenCursorsAcrossCommit()
    throws SQLException;
boolean supportsOpenCursorsAcrossRollback()
    throws SQLException;
boolean supportsOpenStatementsAcrossCommit()
    throws SQLException;
boolean supportsOpenStatementsAcrossRollback()
    throws SQLException;
boolean supportsOrderByUnrelated()
    throws SQLException;
boolean supportsOuterJoins() throws SQLException;
boolean supportsPositionedDelete()
    throws SQLException;
boolean supportsPositionedUpdate()
    throws SQLException;
boolean supportsSchemasInDataManipulation()
    throws SQLException;
boolean supportsSchemasInIndexDefinitions()
    throws SQLException;
boolean supportsSchemasInPrivelegeDefinitions()
    throws SQLException;
boolean supportsSchemasInProcedureCalls()
    throws SQLException;
boolean supportsSchemasInTableDefinitions()
    throws SQLException;
boolean supportsSelectForUpdate()
    throws SQLException;
boolean supportsStoredProcedures()
    throws SQLException;
boolean supportsSubqueriesInComparisons()
    throws SQLException;
boolean supportsSubqueriesInExists()
    throws SQLException;
boolean supportsSubqueriesInIns()
    throws SQLException;
boolean supportsSubqueriesInQuantifieds()
    throws SQLException;
boolean supportsTableCorrelationNames()
```

```
        throws SQLException;
boolean supportsTransactionIsolationLevel(int level)
        throws SQLException;
boolean supportsTransactions() throws SQLException;
boolean supportsUnion() throws SQLException;
boolean supportsUnionAll() throws SQLException;
boolean usesLocalFilePerTable()
        throws SQLException;
boolean usesLocalFiles() throws SQLException;
}
```

Date

Synopsis

Class Name: `java.sql.Date`

Superclass: `java.util.Date`

Immediate Subclasses: None

Interfaces Implemented: None

Availability: JDK 1.1

Description

This class deals with a subset of functionality found in the `java.util.Date` class. It specifically worries only about days and ignores hours, minutes, and seconds.

Class Summary

```
public class Date extends java.util.Date {
    static public Date valueOf(String s);
    #public Date(int year, int month, int day);
    public Date(long date);
    public void setTime(long date);
    public String toString();
}
```

Class Methods

valueOf()

```
static public Date valueOf(String s)
```

Description: Given a `String` in the form of **yyyy-mm-dd**, this will return a corresponding instance of the `Date` class representing that date.

Object Constructors

Date()

```
public Date(long date)
#public Date(int year, int month, int day)
```

Description: Constructs a new `Date` instance. The proper way to construct a `Date` is to use the new JDK 1.2 `Date(long)` constructor. The date argument specifies the number of milliseconds since 1 January 1970 00:00:00 GMT. A negative number represents the milliseconds before that date. The second, deprecated constructor naturally should never be used since it is ambiguous with respect to calendar and time zone.

Object Methods
setTime()

```
public void setTime(long date)
```

Description: Sets the time represented by this Date object to the specified number of milliseconds since 1 January 1970 00:00:00 GMT. A negative number represents the milliseconds before that date.

toString()

```
public String toString()
```

Description: Provides a `String` representing this `Date` in the form `yyyy-mm-dd`.

Driver

Synopsis

Class Name: `java.sql.Driver`
Superclass: None
Immediate Subclasses: None
Interfaces Implemented: None
Availability: JDK 1.1

Description

This class represents a specific JDBC implementation. When a `Driver` is loaded, it should create an instance of itself and register that instance with the `DriverManager` class. This allows applications to create instances of it using the `Class.forName()` call to load a driver.

The `Driver` object then provides the ability for an application to connect to one or more databases. When a request for a specific database comes through, the `DriverManager` will pass the data source request to each `Driver` registered as a URL. The first `Driver` to connect to the data source using that URL will be used.

Class Summary

```
public interface Driver {
    boolean acceptsURL(String url) throws SQLException;
    Connection connect(String url, Properties info)
        throws SQLException;
    int getMajorVersion();
    int getMinorVersion();
    DriverPropertyInfo[] getPropertyInfo(String url,
                                         Properties info)
```

```
    throws SQLException;
boolean jdbcCompliant();
}
```

Object Methods

acceptsURL()

```
public boolean acceptsURL(String url) throws SQLException
```

Description: Returns **true** if the specified URL matches the URL subprotocol used by this driver.

connect()

```
public Connection connect(String url, Properties info)
    throws SQLException
```

Description: This method attempts a connect using the specified URL and **Property** information (usually containing the user name and password). If the URL is not right for this driver, **connect()** simply returns **null**. If it is the right URL, but an error occurs during the connection process, an **SQLException** should be thrown.

getMajorVersion()

```
public int getMajorVersion()
```

Description: Returns the major version number for the driver.

getMinorVersion()

```
public int getMinorVersion()
```

Description: Returns the minor version number for the driver.

getPropertyInfo()

```
public DriverPropertyInfo[] getPropertyInfo(String url,
                                  Properties info)
    throws SQLException;
```

Description: This method allows GUI-based RAD environments to find out which properties the driver needs on connect so that it can prompt a user to enter values for those properties.

jdbcCompliant()

```
public boolean jdbcCompliant()
```

Description: A Driver can return true here only if it passes the JDBC compliance tests. This means that the driver implementation supports the full JDBC API and full SQL 92 Entry Level.

DriverManager

Synopsis

    Class Name: `java.sql.DriverManager`

    Superclass: `java.lang.Object`

    Immediate Subclasses: None

    Interfaces Implemented: None

    Availability: JDK 1.1

Description

The `DriverManager` holds the master list of registered JDBC drivers for the system. Upon initialization, it loads all classes specified in the `jdbc.drivers` property. You can thus specify any runtime information about the database being used by an application on the command line.

During program execution, other drivers may register themselves with the `DriverManager` by calling the `registerDriver()` method. The `DriverManager` uses a JDBC URL to find an application's desired driver choice when requests are made through `getConnection()`.

The `DriverManager` class is likely to disappear one day as the new JDBC 2.0 Standard Extension provides a much more application-friendly way of getting a database connection.

Class Summary

```
public class DriverManager {
    static void deregisterDriver(Driver driver)
        throws SQLException;
    static public synchronized Connection getConnection(String url,
        Properties info) throws SQLException;
    static public synchronized Connection getConnection(String url,
        String user, String password) throws SQLException;
    static public synchronized Connection getConnection(String url)
        throws SQLException;
    static public Driver getDriver(String url) throws SQLException;
    static public Enumeration getDrivers();
    static public int getLoginTimeout();
    #static public PrintStream getLogStream();
    static public PrintWriter getLogWriter();

    static public void println(String message);
    static public synchronized void registerDriver(Driver driver)
        throws SQLException;
    #static public void setLogStream(PrintStream out);
    static public void setLogWriter(PrintWriter out);
    static public void setLoginTimeout(int seconds);
}
```

Class Methods

deregisterDriver( )

```
static public void deregisterDriver(Driver driver) throws SQLException
```

Description: Removes a **Driver** from the list of registered drivers.

getConnection( )

```
static public synchronized Connection getConnection(String url,
       Properties info) throws SQLException
static public synchronized Connection getConnection(String url,
       String user, String password) throws SQLException
static public synchronized Connection getConnection(String url)
       throws SQLException
```

Description: Establishes a connection to the data store represented by the URL given. The **DriverManager** then looks through its list of registered **Driver** instances for one that will handle the specified URL. If none is found, it throws an **SQLException**. Otherwise it returns the **Connection** instance from the **connect()** method in the **Driver** class.

getDriver( )

```
static public Driver getDriver(String url) throws SQLException
```

Description: Returns a driver than can handle the specified URL.

getDrivers( )

```
static public Enumeration getDrivers()
```

Description: Returns a list of all registered drivers.

getLoginTimeout( ) and setLoginTimeout( )

```
static public int getLoginTimeout()
static public int setLoginTimeout()
```

Description: The login timeout is the maximum time in seconds that a driver can wait in attempting to log in to a database.

getLogStream( ) and setLogStream( )

```
#static public PrintStream getLogStream()
#static public void setLogStream(PrintStream out)
static public PrintWriter getLogWriter()
static public void setLogWriter(PrintWriter out)
```

Description: Sets the stream used by the **DriverManager** and all drivers. The **LogStream** variant is the old JDK 1.1 version and should be avoided in favor of log writers

println( )

```
static public void println(String message)
```

Description: Prints a message to the current log stream.

registerDriver( )

```
static public synchronized void registerDriver(Driver driver)
       throws SQLException
```

Description: This method allows a newly loaded `Driver` to register itself with the `DriverManager` class.

DriverPropertyInfo

Synopsis

Class Name: `java.sql.DriverPropertyInfo`
Superclass: `java.lang.Object`
Immediate Subclasses: None
Interfaces Implemented: None
Availability: JDK 1.1

Description

This class provides information required by a driver in order to connect to a database. Only development tools are likely ever to require this class. It has no methods, simply a list of public attributes.

Class Summary

```
public class DriverPropertyInfo {
    public String[] choices;
    public String description;
    public String name;
    public boolean required;
    public String value;
    public DriverPropertyInfo(String name, String value);
}
```

Object Attributes

choices

`public String[] choices`

Description: A list of choices from which a user may be prompted to specify a value for this property. This value can be null.

description

`public String description`

Description: A brief description of the property or null.

name

`public String name`

Description: The name of the property.

required

`public boolean required`

Description: Indicates whether or not this property must be set in order to make a connection.

value
```
public String value
```
Description: The current value of the property or null if no current value is set.

Object Constructors
DriverPropertyInfo()
```
public DriverPropertyInfo(String name, String value)
```
Description: Constructs a new **DriverPropertyInfo** object with the **name** and **value** attributes set to the specified parameters. All other values are set to their default values.

PreparedStatement

Synopsis
Class Name: `java.sql.PreparedStatement`
Superclass: `java.sql.Statement`
Immediate Subclasses: `java.sql.CallableStatement`
Interfaces Implemented: None
Availability: JDK 1.1

Description
This class represents a precompiled SQL statement.

Class Summary
```
public interface PreparedStatement extends Statement {
    void addBatch() throws SQLException;
    void clearParameters() throws SQLException;
    boolean execute() throws SQLException;
    ResultSet executeQuery() throws SQLException;
    int executeUpdate() throws SQLException;
    ResultSetMetaData getMetaData() throws SQLException;
    void setArray(int index, Array arr)
        throws SQLException;
    void setAsciiStream(int index, InputStream is,
        int length) throws SQLException;
    void setBigDecimal(int index, BigDecimal d)
        throws SQLException;
    void setBinaryStream(int index, InputStream is,
        int length) throws SQLException;
    void setBlob(int index, Blob b) throws SQLException;
    void setBoolean(int index, boolean b)
        throws SQLException;
    void setByte(int index, byte b) throws SQLException;
    void setBytes(int index, byte[] bts)
        throws SQLException;
    void setCharacterStream(int index, Reader rdr,
        int length) throws SQLException;
```

```
      void setClob(int index, Clob c) throws SQLException;
      void setDate(int index, Date d) throws SQLException;
      void setDate(int index, Date d, Calendar cal)
          throws SQLException;
      void setDouble(int index, double x)
          throws SQLException;
      void setFloat(int index, float f) throws SQLException;
      void setInt(int index, int x) throws SQLException;
      void setLong(int index, long x) throws SQLException;
      void setNull(int index, int type) throws SQLException;
      void setNull(int index, int type, String tname)
          throws SQLException;
      void setObject(int index, Object ob)
          throws SQLException;
      void setObject(int index, Object ob, int type)
          throws SQLException;
      void setObject(int index, Object ob, int type,
          int scale) throws SQLException;
      void setRef(int index, Ref ref) throws SQLException;
      void setShort(int index, short s) throws SQLException;
      void setString(int index, String str)
          throws SQLException;
      void setTime(int index, Time t) throws SQLException;
      void setTime(int index, Time t, Calendar cal)
          throws SQLException;
      void setTimestamp(int index, Timestamp ts)
          throws SQLException;
      void setTimestamp(int index, Timestamp ts, Calendar cal)
          throws SQLException;
      #void setUnicodeStream(int index, InputStream is,
          int length) throws SQLException;
  }
```

Object Methods

addBatch()

```
      public void addBatch() throws SQLException
```

Description: Adds a set of parameters to the batch for batch processing.

clearParameters()

```
      public abstract void clearParameters() throws SQLException
```

Description: Once set, a parameter value remains bound until either a new value is set for the parameter or until **clearParameters()** is called. This method clears all parameters associated with the **PreparedStatement**.

execute(), executeQuery(), and executeUpdate()

```
      public abstract boolean execute() throws SQLException
      public abstract ResultSet executeQuery() throws SQLException
      public abstract int executeUpdate() throws SQLException
```

Description: Executes the **PreparedStatement**. The first method, **execute()**, allows you to execute the **PreparedStatement** when you do not know if it is a query or an update. It returns true if the statement has result sets to process.

The executeQuery() method is used for executing queries. It returns a result set for processing.

The executeUpdate() statement is used for executing updates. It returns the number of rows affected by the update.

getMetaData()

```
public ResultSetMetaData getMetaData() throws SQLException;
```

Description: Retrieves the number, types, and properties of a ResultSet's columns.

setArray(), setAsciiStream(), setBigDecimal(), setBinaryStream(), setBlob(), setBoolean(), setByte(), setBytes(), setCharacterStream(), setClob(), setDate(), setDouble(), setFloat(), setInt(), setLong(), setNull(), setObject(), setRef(), setShort(), setString(), setTime(), setTimestamp(), and setUnicodeStream()

```
public void setArray(int index, Array arr)
    throws SQLException
public void setAsciiStream(int index, InputStream is,
    int length) throws SQLException
public void setBigDecimal(int index, BigDecimal d)
    throws SQLException
public void setBinaryStream(int index, InputStream is,
    int length) throws SQLException
public void setBlob(int index, Blob b)
    throws SQLException
public void setBoolean(int index, boolean b)
    throws SQLException
public void setByte(int index, byte b)
    throws SQLException
public void setBytes(int index, byte[] bts)
    throws SQLException
public void setCharacterStream(int index, Reader rdr,
    int length) throws SQLException
public void setClob(int index, Clob c)
    throws SQLException
public void setDate(int index, Date d)
    throws SQLException
public void setDate(int index, Date d, Calendar cal)
    throws SQLException
public void setDouble(int index, double d)
    throws SQLException
public void setFloat(int index, float f)
    throws SQLException
public void setInt(int index, int x)
    throws SQLException
public void setLong(int index, long x)
    throws SQLException
public void setNull(int index, int type)
    throws SQLException
```

```
public void setNull(int index, int type, String tname)
    throws SQLException
public void setObject(int index, Object ob)
    throws SQLException
public void setObject(int index, Object ob, int type)
    throws SQLException
public void setObject(int index, Object ob, int type,
    int scale) throws SQLException
public void setRef(int index, Ref ref)
    throws SQLException
public void setShort(int index, short s)
    throws SQLException
public void setString(int index, String str)
    throws SQLException
public void setTime(int index, Time t)
    throws SQLException
public void setTime(int index, Time t, Calendar cal)
    throws SQLException
public void setTimestamp(int index, Timestamp ts)
    throws SQLException
public void setTimestamp(int index, Timestamp ts,
    Calendar cal) throws SQLException
#public void setUnicodeStream(int index, InputStream is,
    int length) throws SQLException
```

Description: Binds a value to the specified parameter.

Ref

Synopsis

Class Name: `java.sql.Ref`

Superclass: None

Immediate Subclasses: None

Interfaces Implemented: None

Availability: New as of JDK 1.2

Description

A `Ref` is a reference to a value of an SQL structured type in the database. You can dereference a `Ref` by passing it as a parameter to an SQL statement and executing the statement.

Class Summary

```
public interface Ref {
    String getBaseTypeName() throws SQLException;
}
```

Object Methods

getBaseTypeName()

```
public String getBaseTypeName() throws SQLException
```

Description: Provides the SQL structured type name for the referenced item.

ResultSet

Synopsis

Class Name: `java.sql.ResultSet`
Superclass: None
Immediate Subclasses: None
Interfaces Implemented: None
Availability: JDK 1.1

Description

This class represents a database result set. It provides an application with access to database queries one row at a time. During query processing, a `ResultSet` maintains a pointer to the current row being manipulated. The application then moves through the results sequentially until all results have been processed or the `ResultSet` is closed. A `ResultSet` is automatically closed when the `Statement` that generated it is closed, reexecuted, or used to retrieve the next `ResultSet` in a multiple result set query.

Class Summary

```
public interface ResultSet {
     static public final int CONCUR_READ_ONLY;
     static public final int CONCUR_UPDATABLE;
     static public final int FETCH_FORWARD;
     static public final int FETCH_REVERSE;
     static public final int FETCH_UNKNOWN;
     static public final int TYPE_FORWARD_ONLY;
     static public final int TYPE_SCROLL_INSENSITIVE;
     static public final int TYPE_SCROLL_SENSITIVE;
     boolean absolute(int row) throws SQLException;
     void afterLast() throws SQLException;
     void beforeFirst() throws SQLException;
     void cancelRowUpdates() throws SQLException;
     void clearWarnings() throws SQLException;
     void close() throws SQLException;
     void deleteRow() throws SQLException;
     int findColumn(String cname) throws SQLException;
     boolean first() throws SQLException;
     Array getArray(int index) throws SQLException;
     Array getArray(String cname) throws SQLException;
     InputStream getAsciiStream(int index)
          throws SQLException;
     InputStream getAsciiStream(String cname)
          throws SQLException;
     InputStream getBinaryStream(int index)
          throws SQLException;
     InputStream getBinaryStream(String cname)
```

```
           throws SQLException;
BigDecimal getBigDecimal(int index)
           throws SQLException;
#BigDecimal getBigDecimal(int index, int scale)
           throws SQLException;
BigDecimal getBigDecimal(String cname)
           throws SQLException;
#BigDecimal getBigDecimal(String cname, int scale)
           throws SQLException;
InputStream getBinaryStream(int index)
           throws SQLException;
InputStream getBinaryStream(String cname)
           throws SQLException;
Blob getBlob(int index) throws SQLException;
Blob getBlob(String cname) throws SQLException;
boolean getBoolean(int index) throws SQLException;
boolean getBoolean(String cname) throws SQLException;
byte getByte(int index) throws SQLException;
byte getByte(String cname) throws SQLException;
byte[] getBytes(int index) throws SQLException;
byte[] getBytes(String cname) throws SQLException;
Reader getCharacterStream(int index)
           throws SQLException;
Reader getCharacterStream(String cname)
           throws SQLException;
Clob getClob(int index) throws SQLException;
Clob getClob(String cname) throws SQLException;
int getConcurrency() throws SQLException;
String getCursorName() throws SQLException;
Date getDate(int index) throws SQLException;
Date getDate(int index, Calendar cal)
           throws SQLException;
Date getDate(String cname) throws SQLException;
Date getDate(String cname, Calendar cal)
           throws SQLException;
double getDouble(int index) throws SQLException;
double getDouble(String cname) throws SQLException;
int getFetchDirection() throws SQLException;
int getFetchSize() throws SQLException;
float getFloat(int index) throws SQLException;
float getFloat(String cname) throws SQLException;
int getInt(int index) throws SQLException;
int getInt(String cname) throws SQLException;
long getLong(int index) throws SQLException;
long getLong(String cname) throws SQLException;
ResultSetMetaData getMetaData() throws SQLException;
Object getObject(int index) throws SQLException;
Object getObject(int index, Map map)
           throws SQLException;
Object getObject(String cname) throws SQLException;
Object getObject(String cname, Map map)
           throws SQLException;
Ref getRef(int index) throws SQLException;
Ref getRef(String cname) throws SQLException;
```

```
int getRow() throws SQLException;
short getShort(int index) throws SQLException;
short getShort(String cname) throws SQLException;
Statement getStatement() throws SQLException;
String getString(int index) throws SQLException;
String getString(String cname) throws SQLException;
Time getTime(int index) throws SQLException;
Time getTime(int index, Calendar cal)
     throws SQLException;
Time getTime(String cname) throws SQLException;
Time getTime(String cname, Calendar cal)
     throws SQLException;
Timestamp getTimestamp(int index) throws SQLException;
Timestamp getTimestamp(int index, Calendar cal)
     throws SQLException;
Timestamp getTimestamp(String cname) throws SQLException;
Timestamp getTimestamp(String cname, Calendar cal)
     throws SQLException;
int getType() throws SQLException;
#InputStream getUnicodeStream(int index)
     throws SQLException;
#InputStream getUnicodeStream(String cname)
     throws SQLException;
SQLWarning getWarnings() throws SQLException;
void insertRow() throws SQLException;
boolean isAfterLast() throws SQLException;
boolean isBeforeFirst() throws SQLException;
boolean isFirst() throws SQLException;
boolean isLast() throws SQLException;
boolean last() throws SQLException;
void moveToCurrentRow() throws SQLException;
void moveToInsertRow() throws SQLException;
boolean next() throws SQLException;
boolean previous() throws SQLException;
void refreshRow() throws SQLException;
boolean relative(int rows) throws SQLException;
boolean rowDeleted() throws SQLException;
boolean rowInserted() throws SQLException;
boolean rowUpdated() throws SQLException;
void setFetchDirection(int dir) throws SQLException;
void setFetchSize(int rows) throws SQLException;
void updateAsciiStream(int index, InputStream is,
     int length) throws SQLException;
void updateAsciiStream(String cname, InputStream is,
     int length) throws SQLException;
void updateBigDecimal(int index, BigDecimal d)
     throws SQLException;
void updateBigDecimal(String cname, BigDecimal d)
     throws SQLException;
void updateBinaryStream(int index, InputStream is)
     throws SQLException;
void updateBinaryStream(String cname, InputStream is)
     throws SQLException;
void updateBoolean(int index, boolean b)
```

```
        throws SQLException;
void updateBoolean(String cname, boolean b)
        throws SQLException;
void updateByte(int index, byte b)
        throws SQLException;
void updateByte(String cname, byte b)
        throws SQLException;
void updateBytes(int index, byte[] bts)
        throws SQLException;
void updateBytes(String cname, byte[] bts)
        throws SQLException;
void updateCharacterStream(int index, Reader rdr,
        int length) throws SQLException;
void updateCharacterStream(String cname, Reader rdr,
        int length) throws SQLException;
void updateDate(int index, Date d)
        throws SQLException;
void updateDate(String cname, Date d)
        throws SQLException;
void updateDouble(int index, double d)
        throws SQLException;
void updateDouble(String cname, double d)
        throws SQLException;
void updateFloat(int index, float f)
        throws SQLException;
void updateFloat(String cname, float f)
        throws SQLException;
void updateInt(int index, int x) throws SQLException;
void updateInt(String cname, int x)
        throws SQLException;
void updateLong(int index, long x)
        throws SQLException;
void updateLong(String cname, long x)
        throws SQLException;
void updateNull(int index) throws SQLException;
void updateNull(String cname) throws SQLException;
void updateObject(int index, Object ob)
        throws SQLException;
void updateObject(int index, Object ob, int scale)
void updateObject(String cname, Object ob)
        throws SQLException;
void updateObject(String cname, Object ob, int scale)
        throws SQLException;
void updateRow() throws SQLException;
void updateShort(int index, short s)
        throws SQLException;
void updateShort(String cname, short s)
        throws SQLException;
void updateString(int index, String str)
        throws SQLException;
void updateString(String cname, String str)
        throws SQLException;
void updateTime(int index, Time t)
        throws SQLException;
```

```
        void updateTime(String cname, Time t)
            throws SQLException;
        void updateTimestamp(int index, Timestamp ts)
            throws SQLException;
        void updateTimestamp(String cname, Timestamp ts)
            throws SQLException;
        boolean wasNull() throws SQLException;
}
```

Class Attributes

CONCUR_READ_ONLY

```
        static public final int CONCUR_READ_ONLY
```

Description: The concurrency mode that specifies that a result set may not be updated.

CONCUR_UPDATABLE

```
        static public final int CONCUR_UPDATABLE
```

Description: The concurrency mode that specifies that a result set is updatable.

FETCH_FORWARD

```
        static public final int FETCH_FORWARD
```

Description: This value specifies that a result set's fetch direction is in the forward direction, from first to last.

FETCH_REVERSE

```
        static public final int FETCH_REVERSE
```

Description: This value specifies that a result set's fetch direction is in the reverse direction, from last to first.

FETCH_UNKNOWN

```
        static public final int FETCH_UNKNOWN
```

Description: This value specifies that the order of result set processing is unknown.

TYPE_FORWARD_ONLY

```
        static public final int TYPE_FORWARD_ONLY
```

Description: This result set type specifies that a result set can only be navigated in the forward direction.

TYPE_SCROLL_INSENSITIVE

```
        static public final int TYPE_SCROLL_INSENSITIVE
```

Description: This result set type specifies that a result set may be navigated in any direction, but it is not sensitive to changes made by others.

TYPE_SCROLL_SENSITIVE

```
        static public final int TYPE_SCROLL_SENSITIVE
```

Description: This result set type specifies that a result set may be navigated in any direction and that changes made by others will be seen in the result set.

Object Methods

absolute()

```
public boolean absolute(int row) throws SQLException
```

Description: This method moves the cursor to the specified row number starting from the beginning for a positive number or from the end for a negative number.

afterLast()

```
public void afterLast() throws SQLException
```

Description: This method moves the cursor to the end of the result set, after the last row.

beforeFirst()

```
public void beforeFirst() throws SQLException
```

Description: Moves the cursor to the beginning of the result set, before the first row.

cancelRowUpdates()

```
public void cancelRowUpdates() throws SQLException
```

Description: Cancels any updates made to this row.

clearWarnings()

```
public void clearWarnings() throws SQLException
```

Description: Clears all warnings from the **SQLWarning** chain. Subsequent calls to **getWarnings()** then returns **null** until another warning occurs.

close()

```
public void close() throws SQLException
```

Description: Performs an immediate, manual close of the **ResultSet**. This is generally never required, as the closure of the **Statement** associated with the **ResultSet** will automatically close the **ResultSet**.

deleteRow()

```
public void deleteRow() throws SQLException
```

Description: Deletes the current row from this result set and from the database.

findColumn()

```
public int findColumn(String cname) throws SQLException
```

Description: For the specified column name, this method will return the column number associated with it.

first()

```
public boolean first() throws SQLException
```

Description: Moves the cursor to the first row of a result set.

getAsciiStream(), getBinaryStream(), getCharacterStream(), and getUnicodeStream()

```
public InputStream getAsciiStream(int index)
    throws SQLException
public InputStream getAsciiStream(String cname)
    throws SQLException
public InputStream getBinaryStream(int index)
    throws SQLException
public InputStream getBinaryStream(String cname)
    throws SQLException
public Reader getCharacterStream(int index)
    throws SQLException
public Reader getCharacterStream(String cname)
    throws SQLException
#public InputStream getUnicodeStream(int index)
    throws SQLException
#public InputStream getUnicodeStream(String cname)
    throws SQLException
```

Description: In some cases, it may make sense to retrieve large pieces of data from the database as a Java **InputStream**. These methods allow an application to retrieve the specified column from the current row in this manner. You should notice that the **getUnicodeStream()** method has been deprecated in favor of the new **getCharacterStream()** method.

getArray(), getBlob(), getBoolean(), getByte(), getBytes(), getClob(), getDate(), getDouble(), getFloat(), getInt(), getLong(), getRef(), getShort(), getString(), getTime(), and getTimestamp()

```
public Array getArray(int index) throws SQLException
public Array getArray(String cname) throws SQLException
public Blob getBlob(int index) throws SQLException
public Blob getBlob(String cname) throws SQLException
public boolean getBoolean(int index) throws SQLException
public boolean getBoolean(String cname) throws SQLException
public byte getByte(int index) throws SQLException
public byte getByte(String cname) throws SQLException
public byte[] getBytes(int index) throws SQLException
public byte[] getBytes(String cname) throws SQLException
public Clob getClob(int index) throws SQLException
public Clob getClob(String cname) throws SQLException
public Date getDate(int index) throws SQLException
public Date getDate(String cname) throws SQLException
public double getDouble(int index) throws SQLException
public double getDouble(String cname) throws SQLException
public float getFloat(int index) throws SQLException
public float getFloat(String cname) throws SQLException
public int getInt(int index) throws SQLException
public int getInt(String cname) throws SQLException
public long getLong(int index) throws SQLException
public long getLong(String cname) throws SQLException
public Ref getRef(int index) throws SQLException
public Ref getRef(String cname) throws SQLException
public short getShort(int index) throws SQLException
public short getShort(String cname) throws SQLException
```

```
public String getString(int index) throws SQLException
public String getString(String cname) throws SQLException
public Time getTime(int index) throws SQLException
public Time getTime(String cname) throws SQLException
public Timestamp getTimestamp(int index)
    throws SQLException
public Timestamp getTimestamp(String cname)
    throws SQLException
```

Description: These methods return the specified column value for the current row as the Java datatype that matches the method name.

getConcurrency(), and setConcurrency()

```
public int getConcurrency() throws SQLException
```

Description: These methods access the result set concurrency mode. It initially takes its value from the statement that generated this result set.

getCursorName()

```
public String getCursorName() throws SQLException
```

Description: Because some databases allow positioned updates, an application needs the cursor name associated with a `ResultSet` in order to perform those positioned updates. This method provides the cursor name.

getMetaData()

```
public ResultSetMetaData getMetaData() throws SQLException
```

Description: Provides the meta-data object for this `ResultSet`.

getFetchDirection(), setFetchDirection(), getFetchSize(), and setFetchSize()

```
public int getFetchDirection() throws SQLException
public void setFetchDirection(int dir) throws SQLException
public int getFetchSize() throws SQLException
public void setFetchSize(int rows) throws SQLException
```

Description: These methods provide optimization hints for the driver. The driver is free to ignore these hints. The fetch size is the suggested number of rows the driver should prefetch for each time it grabs data from the database. The direction is a hint to the driver about the direction in which you intend to work.

getObject()

```
public Object getObject(int index) throws SQLException
public Object getObject(int index, Map map)
    throws SQLException
public Object getObject(String cname) throws SQLException
public Object getObject(String cname, Map map)
    throws SQLException
```

Description: Returns the specified column value for the current row as a Java object. The type returned will be the Java object that most closely matches the SQL type for the column. It is also useful for columns with database-specific datatypes.

getRow()

```
public int getRow() throws SQLException
```

Description: Returns the current row number.

getStatement()

```
public Statement getStatement() throws SQLException
```

Description: Returns the **Statement** instance that generated this result set.

getType()

```
public int getType() throws SQLException
```

Description: Returns the result set type for this result set.

getWarnings()

```
public SQLWarning getWarnings() throws SQLException
```

Description: Returns the first **SQLWarning** object in the warning chain.

insertRow()

```
public void insertRow() throws SQLException
```

Description: Inserts the contents of the insert row into the result set and into the database.

isAfterLast()

```
public boolean isAfterLast() throws SQLException
```

Description: Returns true if this result set is positioned after the last row in the result set.

isBeforeLast()

```
public boolean isBeforeFirst() throws SQLException
```

Description: Returns true if this result set is positioned before the first row in the result set.

isFirst()

```
public boolean isFirst() throws SQLException
```

Description: Returns true if the result set is positioned on the first row of the result set.

isLast()

```
public boolean isLast() throws SQLException
```

Description: Returns true if result set is positioned after the last row in the result set.

last()

```
public boolean last() throws SQLException
```

Description: Moves the cursor to the last row in the result set.

moveToCurrentRow()

```
public void moveToCurrentRow() throws SQLException
```

Description: Moves the result set to the current row. This is used after you are done inserting a row.

moveToInsertRow()

```
public void moveToInsertRow() throws SQLException
```

Description: Moves the result to a new insert row. You need to call `moveToCurrentRow()` to get back.

next() and previous()

```
public boolean next() throws SQLException
public boolean previous() throws SQLException
```

Description: These methods navigate one row forward or one row backward in the `ResultSet`. Under a newly created result set, the result set is positioned before the first row. The first call to next() would thus move the result set to the first row. These methods return **true** as long as there is a row to move to. If there are no further rows to process, it returns **false**. If an **InputStream** from the previous row is still open, it is closed. The **SQLWarning** chain is also cleared.

refreshRow()

```
public void refreshRow() throws SQLException
```

Description: Refreshes the current row with its most recent value from the database.

relative()

```
public boolean relative(int rows) throws SQLException
```

Description: Moves the cursor the specified number of rows forwards or backwards. A positive number indicates that the cursor should be moved forwards and a negative number indicates it should be moved backwards.

rowDeleted(), rowInserted(), and rowUpdated()

```
public boolean rowDeleted() throws SQLException
public boolean rowInserted() throws SQLException
public boolean rowUpdated() throws SQLException
```

Description: Returns true if the current row has been deleted, inserted, or updated.

updateAsciiStream(), updateBigDecimal(), updateBinaryStream(), updateBoolean(), updateByte(), updateBytes(), updateCharacterStream(), updateDate(), updateDouble(), updateFloat(), updateInt(), updateLong(), updateNull(), updateObject(), updateShort(), updateString(), updateTime(), and updateTimestamp()

```
public void updateAsciiStream(int index, InputStream is,
    int length) throws SQLException
public void updateAsciiStream(String cname, InputStream is,
    int length) throws SQLException
public void updateBigDecimal(int index, BigDecimal d)
    throws SQLException
public void updateBigDecimal(String cname, BigDecimal d)
```

```
        throws SQLException
public void updateBinaryStream(int index, InputStream is)
        throws SQLException
public void updateBinaryStream(String cname, InputStream is)
        throws SQLException
public void updateBoolean(int index, boolean b)
        throws SQLException
public void updateBoolean(String cname, boolean b)
        throws SQLException
public void updateByte(int index, byte b)
        throws SQLException
public void updateByte(String cname, byte b)
        throws SQLException
public void updateBytes(int index, byte[] bts)
        throws SQLException
public void updateBytes(String cname, byte[] bts)
        throws SQLException
public void updateCharacterStream(int index, Reader rdr,
        int length) throws SQLException
public void updateCharacterStream(String cname, Reader rdr,
        int length) throws SQLException
public void updateDate(int index, Date d)
        throws SQLException
public void updateDate(String cname, Date d)
        throws SQLException
public void updateDouble(int index, double d)
        throws SQLException
public void updateDouble(String cname, double d)
        throws SQLException
public void updateFloat(int index, float f)
        throws SQLException
public void updateFloat(String cname, float f)
        throws SQLException
public void updateInt(int index, int x)
        throws SQLException
public void updateInt(String cname, int x)
        throws SQLException
public void updateLong(int index, long x)
        throws SQLException
public void updateLong(String cname, long x)
        throws SQLException
public void updateNull(int index) throws SQLException
public void updateNull(String cname) throws SQLException
public void updateObject(int index, Object ob)
        throws SQLException
public void updateObject(int index, Object ob, int scale)
        throws SQLException
public void updateObject(String cname, Object ob)
        throws SQLException
public void updateObject(String cname, Object ob, int scale)
        throws SQLException
public void updateShort(int index, short s)
        throws SQLException
public void updateShort(String cname, short s)
```

```
        throws SQLException
public void updateString(int index, String str)
        throws SQLException
public void updateString(String cname, String str)
        throws SQLException
public void updateTime(int index, Time t)
        throws SQLException
public void updateTime(String cname, Time t)
        throws SQLException
public void updateTimestamp(int index, Timestamp ts)
        throws SQLException
public void updateTimestamp(String cname, Timestamp ts)
        throws SQLException
```

Description: These methods update column by column in the current row of your result set as long as your result set supports updating. Once you are done modifying the row, you can call **insertRow()** or **updateRow()** to save the changes to the database.

updateRow()

```
public void updateRow() throws SQLException
```

Description: Updates any changes made to the current row to the database.

wasNull()

```
public boolean wasNull() throws SQLException
```

Description: This method returns **true** if the last column read was **null**; otherwise it returns **false**.

ResultSetMetaData

Synopsis

Class Name:**java.sql.ResultSetMetaData**
Superclass:None
Immediate Subclasses:None
Interfaces Implemented:None
Availability:JDK 1.1

Description

This class provides meta-information about the types and properties of the columns in a **ResultSet** instance.

Class Summary

```
public interface ResultSetMetaData {
    static public final int columnNoNulls;
    static public final int columnNullable;
    static public final int columnNullableUnknown;
    String getCatalogName(int index)
        throws SQLException;
```

```
String getColumnClassName(int index)
    throws SQLException;
public int getColumnCount() throws SQLException;
public int getColumnDisplaySize(int index)
    throws SQLException;
public String getColumnLabel(int index)
    throws SQLException;
public String getColumnName(int index)
    throws SQLException;
public int getColumnType(int index) throws SQLException;
public String getColumnTypeName(int index)
    throws SQLException;
public int getPrecision(int index) throws SQLException;
public int getScale(int index) throws SQLException;
public String getSchemaName(int index)
    throws SQLException;
public String getTableName(int index)
    throws SQLException;
public boolean isAutoIncrement(int index)
    throws SQLException;
public isCaseSensitive(int index)
    throws SQLException;
public boolean isCurrency(int index)
    throws SQLException;
public boolean isDefinitelyWritable(int index)
    throws SQLException;
public int isNullable(int index) throws SQLException;
public boolean isReadOnly(int index)
    throws SQLException;
public boolean isSearchable(int index)
    throws SQLException;
public boolean isSigned(int index) throws SQLException;
public boolean isWritable(int index)
    throws SQLException;
}
```

Class Attributes

columnNoNulls

```
static public final int columnNoNulls
```

Description: The column in question does not allow NULL values.

columnNullable

```
static public final int columnNullable
```

Description: The column in question allows NULL values.

columnNullableUnknown

```
static public final int columnNullableUnknown
```

Description: It is not known if the column in question can accept NULL values.

Object Methods

getCatalogName( )

```
public String getCatalogName(int index) throws SQLException
```

Description: Provides the catalog name associated with the specified column's table.

getColumnClassName( )

```
public String getColumnClassName(int index)
    throws SQLException
```

Description: Provides the fully-qualified name of the Java class that will be instantiated by a call to `ResultSet.getObject()` for this column.

getColumnCount( )

```
public int getColumnCount() throws SQLException
```

Description: Returns the number of columns in the result set.

getColumnDisplaySize( )

```
public int getColumnDisplaySize(int column)
    throws SQLException
```

Description: Returns the maximum width for displaying the column's values.

getColumnLabel( )

```
public String getColumnLabel(int column) throws SQLException
```

Description: Returns the display name for the column.

getColumnName( )

```
public String getcname(int column) throws SQLException
```

Description: Returns the database name for the column.

getColumnType( )

```
public int getColumnType(int column) throws SQLException
```

Description: Returns the SQL type for the specified column as a value from `java.sql.Types`.

getColumnTypeName( )

```
public String getColumnTypeName(int column)
    throws SQLException
```

Description: Returns the name of the SQL type for the specified column.

getPrecision( )

```
public int getPrecision(int column) throws SQLException
```

Description: Returns the number of decimal digits for the specified column.

getScale( )

```
public int getScale(int column) throws SQLException
```

Description: Returns the number of digits to the right of the decimal for this column.

getSchemaName()

```
public String getSchemaName(int column) throws SQLException
```

Description: Returns the schema for the table for the specified column.

getTableName()

```
public String getTableName(int column) throws SQLException
```

Description: Returns the name of the table for the specified column.

isAutoIncrement()

```
public boolean isAutoIncrement(int column) throws SQLException
```

Description: Returns **true** if the column is automatically numbered and there-fore read-only.

isCaseSensitive()

```
public boolean isCaseSensitive(int column) throws SQLException
```

Description: Returns **true** if the column's case is important.

isCurrency()

```
public boolean isCurrency(int column) throws SQLException
```

Description: Returns **true** if the value for the specified column represents a currency value.

isDefinitelyWritable()

```
public boolean isDefinitelyWritable(int column)
    throws SQLException
```

Description: Returns **true** if a write operation on the column will definitely succeed.

isNullable()

```
public int isNullable(int column) throws SQLException
```

Description: Returns **true** if **null** values are allowed for the column.

isReadOnly()

```
public boolean isReadOnly(int column) throws SQLException
```

Description: Returns **true** if the column is read-only.

isSearchable()

```
public boolean isSearchable(int column) throws SQLException
```

Description: Returns **true** if the column may be used in a WHERE clause.

isSigned()

```
public boolean isSigned(int column) throws SQLException
```

Description: Returns **true** if the column contains a signed number.

isWritable()

```
public boolean isWritable(int column) throws SQLException
```

Description: Returns **true** if it is possible for a write on a column to succeed.

Statement

Synopsis

Class Name:`java.sql.Statement`
Superclass:None
Immediate Subclasses:`java.sql.PreparedStatement`
Interfaces Implemented:None
Availability:JDK 1.1

Description

This class represents an embedded SQL statement and is used by an application to perform database access. The closing of a `Statement` automatically closes any open `ResultSet` associated with the `Statement`.

Class Summary

```
public interface Statement {
    void addBatch(String sql) throws SQLException;
    void cancel() throws SQLException;
    void clearBatch() throws SQLException;
    void clearWarnings() throws SQLException;
    void close() throws SQLException;
    boolean execute(String sql) throws SQLException;
    int[] executeBatch() throws SQLException;
    ResultSet executeQuery(String sql)
        throws SQLException;
    int executeUpdate(String sql) throws SQLException;
    Connection getConnection() throws SQLException;
    int getFetchDirection() throws SQLException;
    int getFetchSize() throws SQLException;
    int getMaxFieldSize() throws SQLException;
    int getMaxRows() throws SQLException;
    boolean getMoreResults() throws SQLException;
    int getQueryTimeout() throws SQLException;
    ResultSet getResultSet() throws SQLException;
    int getResultSetConcurrency() throws SQLException;
    int getResultSetType() throws SQLException;
    int getUpdateCount() throws SQLException;
    SQLWarning getWarnings() throws SQLException;
    void setCursorName(String name) throws SQLException;
    void setEscapeProcessing(boolean enable)
        throws SQLException;
    void setFetchDirection(int dir) throws SQLException;
    void setFetchSize(int rows) throws SQLException;
    void setMaxFieldSize(int max) throws SQLException;
    void setMaxRows(int max) throws SQLException;
    void setQueryTimeout(int seconds)
        throws SQLException;
}
```

Object Methods

addBatch( )

```
public void addBatch(String sql) throws SQLException
```

Description: Adds the specified SQL statement to the current set of batch commands.

cancel( )

```
public void cancel() throws SQLException
```

Description: In a multithreaded environment, you can use this method to indicate that any processing for this `Statement` should be canceled. In this respect, it is similar to the `stop()` method for `Thread` objects.

clearBatch( )

```
public void clearBatch() throws SQLException
```

Description: Clears out any batch statements.

clearWarnings( ) and getWarnings( )

```
public void clearWarnings() throws SQLException
public SQLWarning getWarnings() throws SQLException
```

Description: The `clearWarnings()` method allows you to clear all warnings from the warning chain associated with this class. The `getWarnings()` method retrieves the first warning on the chain. You can retrieve any subsequent warnings on the chain using that first warning.

close( )

```
public void close() throws SQLException
```

Description: Manually closes the `Statement`. This is generally not required because a `Statement` is automatically closed whenever the `Connection` associated with it is closed.

execute( ), executeQuery( ), and executeUpdate( )

```
public boolean execute(String sql) throws SQLException
public ResultSet executeQuery(String sql) throws SQLException
public int executeUpdate(String sql) throws SQLException
```

Description: Executes the `Statement` by passing the specified SQL to the database. The first method, `execute()`, allows you to execute the `Statement` when you do not know if it is a query or an update. It will return `true` if the statement has result sets to process.

The `executeQuery()` method is used for executing queries. It returns a result set for processing.

The `executeUpdate()` statement is used for executing updates. It returns the number of rows affected by the update.

executeBatch( )

```
public int[] executeBatch(String sql) throws SQLException
```

Description: Submits the batched list of SQL statements to the database for execution. The return value is an array of numbers that describe the number of rows affected by each SQL statement.

getConnection()

```
public Connection getConnection() throws SQLException
```

Description: Returns the **Connection** object associated with this **Statement**.

getFetchDirection(), setFetchDirection(), getFetchSize(), and setFetchSize()

```
public int getFetchDirection() throws SQLException
public void setFetchDirection(int dir) throws SQLException
public int getFetchSize() throws SQLException
public void setFetchSize(int rows) throws SQLException
```

Description: These methods provide optimization hints for the driver. The driver is free to ignore these hints. The fetch size is the suggested number of rows the driver should prefetch for each time it grabs data from the database. The direction is a hint to the driver about the direction in which you intend to work.

getMaxFieldSize() and setMaxFieldize()

```
public int getMaxFieldSize() throws SQLException
public void setMaxFieldSize(int max) throws SQLException
```

Description: These methods support the maximum field size attribute that determines the maximum amount of data for any BINARY, VARBINARY, LONGVARBINARY, CHAR, VARCHAR, and LONGVARCHAR column value. If the limit is exceeded, the excess is silently discarded.

getMaxRows() and setMaxRows()

```
public int getMaxRows() throws SQLException
public void setMaxRows(int max) throws SQLException
```

Description: This attribute represents the maximum number of rows a **ResultSet** can contain. If this number is exceeded, then any excess rows are silently discarded.

getMoreResults()

```
public boolean getMoreResults() throws SQLException
```

Description: This method moves to the next result and returns **true** if that result is a **ResultSet**. Any previously open **ResultSet** for this **Statement** is then implicitly closed. If the next result is not a **ResultSet** or if there are no more results, this method will return **false**. You can test explicitly for no more results using:

```
(!getMoreResults() && (getUpdateCount() == -1)
```

getQueryTimeout() and setQueryTimeout()

```
public int getQueryTimeout() throws SQLException
public void setQueryTimeout(int seconds) throws SQLException
```

Description: This attribute is the amount of time a driver will wait for a `Statement` to execute. If the limit is exceeded, an `SQLException` is thrown.

getResultSet( )

```
public ResultSet getResultSet() throws SQLException
```

Description: This method returns the current `ResultSet`. You should call this only once per result. You never need to call this for `executeQuery()` calls that return a single result.

getResultSetConcurrency( )

```
public int getResultSetConcurrency() throws SQLException
```

Description: Returns the concurrency for the result sets generated by this `Statement`.

getResultSetType( )

```
public int getResultSetType() throws SQLException
```

Description: Returns the result set type for any result sets generated by this `Statement`.

getUpdateCount( )

```
public int getUpdateCount() throws SQLException
```

Description: If the current result was an update, this method returns the number of rows affected by the update. If the result is a `ResultSet` or if there are no more results, –1 is returned. As with `getResultSet()`, this method should only be called once per result.

getWarnings( )

```
public SQLWarning getWarnings() throws SQLException
```

Description: Retrieves the first warning associated with this object.

setCursorName( )

```
public void setCursorName(String name) throws SQLException
```

Description: This method specifies the cursor name to be used by subsequent `Statement` executions. For databases that support positioned updates and deletes, you can then use this cursor name in coordination with any `ResultSet` objects returned by your `execute()` or `executeQuery()` calls to identify the current row for a positioned update or delete. You must use a different `Statement` object to perform those updates or deletes. This method does nothing for databases that do not support positioned updates or deletes.

setEscapeProcessing( )

```
public void setEscapeProcessing(boolean enable)
        throws SQLException
```

Description: Escape processing is on by default. When enabled, the driver will perform escape substitution before sending SQL to the database.

Struct

Synopsis

Class Name:`java.sql.Struct`
Superclass:`None`
Immediate Subclasses:None
Interfaces Implemented:None
Availability:New as of JDK 1.2

Description

This class maps to a SQL3 structured type. A `Struct` instance has values that map to each of the attributes in its associated structured value in the database.

Class Summary

```
public interface Struct {
    Object[] getAttributes() throws SQLException;
    Object[] getAttributes(Map map) throws SQLException;
    String getSQLTypeName() throws SQLException;
}
```

Object Methods

getAttributes( )

```
public Object[] getAttributes() throws SQLException
public Object[] getAttributes(Map map) throws SQLException
```

Description: Provides the values for the attributes in the SQL structured type in order. If you pass a type map, it will use that type map to construct the Java values.

getSQLTypeName( )

```
public String getSQLTypeName() throws SQLException
```

Description: Provides the SQL type name for this structured type.

Time

Synopsis

Class Name:`java.sql.Time`
Superclass:`java.util.Date`
Immediate Subclasses:None
Interfaces Implemented:None
Availability:JDK 1.1

Description

This version of the java.util.Date class maps to an SQL TIME datatype.

Class Summary

```
public class Time extends java.util.Date {
    static public Time valueOf(String s);
    public Time(int hour, int minute, int second);
    public Time(long time);
    #public int getDate();
    #public int getDay();
    #public int getMonth();
    #public int getYear();
    #public int setDate(int i);
    #public int setMonth(int i);
    public void setTime(long time);
    #public void setYear(int i);
    public String toString();
}
```

Object Constructors

Time( )

```
public Timestamp(int hour, int minute, intsecond)
public Timestamp(long time)
```

Description: Constructs a new **Time** object. The first prototype constructs a **Time** for the hour, minute, and seconds specified. The second constructs one based on the number of seconds since 12:00:00 January 1, 1970 GMT.

Object Methods

getDate( ), setDate( ), getDay( ), getMonth( ), setMonth( ), getYear( ), and setYear( )

```
#public int getDate()
#public int getDay()
#public int getMonth()
#public int getYear()
#public int setDate(int i)
#public int setMonth(int i)
#public void setYear(int i)
```

Description: These attributes represent the individual segments of a **Time** object.

setTime( )

```
public void setTime(long time)
```

Description: This method sets the **Time** object to the specified time as the number of seconds since 12:00:00 January 1, 1970 GMT.

toString( )

```
public String toString()
```

Description: Formats the **Time** into a **String** in the form of **hh:mm:ss**.

valueOf( )

```
static public Timestamp valueOf(String s)
```

Description: Create a new **Time** based on a **String** in the form of **hh:mm:ss**.

Timestamp

Synopsis

Class Name:`java.sql.Timestamp`
Superclass:`java.util.Date`
Immediate Subclasses:None
Interfaces Implemented:None
Availability:JDK 1.1

Description

This class serves as an SQL representation of the Java `Date` class specifically designed to serve as an SQL TIMESTAMP. It also provides the ability to hold nanoseconds as required by SQL TIMESTAMP values. You should keep in mind that this class uses the `java.util.Date` version of `hashcode()`. This means that two timestamps that differ only by nanoseconds will have identical `hashcode()` return values.

Class Summary

```
public class Timestamp extends java.util.Date {
    static public Timestamp valueOf(String s);
    #public Timestamp(int year, int month, int date,
        int hour, int minute, int second, int nano);
    public Timestamp(long time);
    public boolean after(Timestamp t);
    public boolean before(Timestamp t);
    public boolean equals(Timestamp t);
    public int getNanos();
    public void setNanos(int n);
    public String toString();
}
```

Object Constructors

Timestamp()

```
#public Timestamp(int year, int month, int date, int hour, int minute,
        int second, int nano)
public Timestamp(long time)
```

Description: Constructs a new **Timestamp** object. The first prototype constructs a **Timestamp** for the year, month, date, hour, minute, seconds, and nanoseconds specified. The second prototype constructs one based on the number of seconds since 12:00:00 January 1, 1970 GMT.

Object Methods

after()

```
public boolean after(Timestamp t)
```

Description: Returns **true** if this **Timestamp** is later than the argument.

before()

```
public boolean before(Timestamp t)
```

Description: Returns `true` if this `Timestamp` is earlier than the argument.

equals()

```
public boolean equals(Timestamp t)
```

Description: Returns `true` if the two timestamps are equivalent.

getNanos() and setNanos()

```
public int getNanos()
public void setNanos(int n)
```

Description: This attribute represents the number of nanoseconds for this `Timestamp`.

toString()

```
public String toString()
```

Description: Formats the `Timestamp` into a `String` in the form of `yyyy-mm-dd hh:mm:ss.fffffffff`.

valueOf()

```
static public Timestamp valueOf(String s)
```

Description: Creates a new `Timestamp` based on a `String` in the form of `yyyy-mm-dd hh:mm:ss.fffffffff`.

Types

Synopsis

Class Name:`java.sql.Types`
Superclass:`java.lang.Object`
Immediate Subclasses:None
Interfaces Implemented:None
Availability:JDK 1.1

Description

This class holds static attributes representing SQL data types. These values are the actual constant values defined in the XOPEN specification.

Class Summary

```
public class Types {
    static public final int ARRAY;
    static public final int BIGINT;
    static public final int BINARY;
    static public final int BIT;
    static public final int BLOB;
    static public final int CHAR;
    static public final int CLOB;
```

```
        static public final int DATE;
        static public final int DECIMAL;
        static public final int DISTINCT;
        static public final int DOUBLE;
        static public final int FLOAT;
        static public final int INTEGER;
        static public final int JAVA_OBJECT;
        static public final int LONGVARBINARY;
        static public final int LONGVARCHAR;
        static public final int NULL;
        static public final int NUMERIC;
        static public final int OTHER;
        static public final int REAL;
        static public final int REF;
        static public final int SMALLINT;
        static public final int STRUCT;
        static public final int TIME;
        static public final int TIMESTAMP;
        static public final int TINYINT;
        static public final int VARBINARY;
        static public final int VARCHAR;
}
```

Index

About the Author

Randy Jay Yarger is a senior solution developer at US Web/CKS in Southfield, Michigan. He combines expertise in database construction and interaction with extensive knowledge of the Internet to create world-class web applications. Randy has an uncanny knack of growing attached to computer systems that quickly become defunct. His first computer was a VIC-20, after which he moved on to the Commodore 64, then to several Amigas, and finally to a NeXTStation. He plans for his next box to be an Intel-based Linux system, but he's considering going Microsoft to save everyone some trouble. Randy lives in Ann Arbor, Michigan with his fiancée Stacie and cat Baci.

George Reese has taken an unusual path into business software development. After earning a B.A. in Philosophy from Bates College in Lewiston, Maine, George went off to Hollywood where he worked on television shows such as *The People's Court* and ESPN's *Up Close*. The L.A. riots convinced him to return to Maine where he finally became involved with software development and the Internet. George has since specialized in the development of Internet-oriented Java enterprise systems. He is the author of O'Reilly's *Database Programming with JDBC and Java* and the world's first JDBC driver, the mSQL-JDBC driver for mSQL. He currently works as a enterprise systems architect in Minneapolis, Minnesota.

Tim King has been working with computers since the early 1980s, when he programmed games on his Commodore 64 computer and founded a computer club in his high school. He earned a bachelor's degree in computer science from the University of Minnesota Institute of Technology in 1991. While there, he taught Unix and *vi* classes and was the leader of a rag-tag group of *vi* devotees called the "VI Zombies." Presently, Tim is a software consultant in San Francisco, CA, specializing in database and web technologies. His favorite activity is snowboarding, but he also enjoys photography and reading.

Colophon

Our look is the result of reader comments, our own experimentation, and feedback from distribution channels. Distinctive covers complement our distinctive approach to technical topics, breathing personality and life into potentially dry subjects.

The animals featured on the cover of *MySQL and mSQL* are kingfishers. This type of bird can be found all over the world, including North America, Europe, Africa, and New Zealand, with the greatest numbers being found in southeast Asia. There are over 80 species of kingfishers, which range in size from five to eighteen inches and which cover a broad spectrum of color.

These typically long-billed birds pair for life and are considered to be very territorial. Their nests are long and tunnel-shaped, and are often found in exposed tree roots or water banks.

Most kingfishers live along the banks of rivers or lakes, as the primary staple of their diet is fish. To catch its prey, a kingfisher will perch on a branch above water, watch for a fish, hover for a moment, and then dive headfirst into the water, grabbing the fish in its beak, and heading back up to the surface. The process takes about a third of a second. The kingfisher's diet also consists of spiders, insects, and small amphibians.

Jeffrey Liggett was the production editor for *MySQL and mSQL*. Robert Romano and Rhon Porter created the illustrations using Adobe Photoshop 5.0 and Macromedia Freehand 8.0. Mike Sierra provided FrameMaker technical support. Claire Cloutier LeBlanc provided quality control. Editorial and production services were provided by Rashelle Perez and David Leiser at Electro-Publishing. Becky Peveler was the copyeditor. The index was written by Electro-Publishing, with assistance from Seth Maislin.

Edie Freedman designed the cover of this book, using a 19th-century engraving from the Dover Pictorial Archive. The cover layout was produced by Kathleen Wilson with QuarkXPress 3.32 using the ITC Garamond font. Whenever possible, our books use RepKover™, a durable and flexible lay-flat binding. If the page count exceeds RepKover's limit, perfect binding is used.

The inside layout was designed by Alicia Cech based on a series design by Nancy Priest. The layout was implemented in FrameMaker 5.5.6 by Mike Sierra. The text and heading fonts are ITC Garamond Light and Garamond Book. This colophon was written by Nicole Arigo.

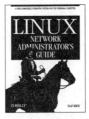

Linux

Using Samba

By Peter Kelly, Perry Donham &
David Collier-Brown
1st Edition October 1999 (est.)
300 pages (est.), includes CD-ROM
ISBN 1-56592-449-5

Samba turns a UNIX or Linux system into a
file and print server for Microsoft Windows
network clients. This complete guide to
Samba administration covers basic 2.0
configuration, security, logging, and troubleshooting. Whether
you're playing on one note or a full three-octave range, this book
will help you maintain an efficient and secure server. Includes a
CD-ROM of sources and ready-to-install binaries.

UNIX Tools

lex & yacc, 2nd Edition

By John Levine, Tony Mason & Doug Brown
2nd Edition October 1992
366 pages, ISBN 1-56592-000-7

This book shows programmers how to use
two UNIX utilities, lex and yacc, in program
development. The second edition contains
completely revised tutorial sections for novice
users and reference sections for advanced
users. This edition is twice the size of the
first, has an expanded index, and covers Bison and Flex.

sed & awk, 2nd Edition

By Dale Dougherty & Arnold Robbins
2nd Edition March 1997
432 pages, ISBN 1-56592-225-5

sed & awk describes two text manipulation
programs that are mainstays of the UNIX
programmer's toolbox. This new edition
covers the sed and awk programs as they are
now mandated by the POSIX standard and
includes discussion of the GNU versions of these programs.

UNIX Tools (continued)

The UNIX CD Bookshelf

By O'Reilly & Associates, Inc.
1st Edition November 1998
444 pages, includes CD-ROM & book
ISBN 1-56592-406-1

The UNIX CD Bookshelf contains six books
from O'Reilly plus the software from UNIX
Power Tools—all on a convenient CD-ROM.
A bonus hardcopy book, UNIX in a Nutshell:
System V Edition, is also included. The CD-
ROM contains UNIX in a Nutshell: System V Edition; UNIX Power
Tools, 2nd Edition. (with software); Learning the UNIX Operating
System, 4th Edition; Learning the vi Editor, 6th Edition; sed &
awk, 2nd Edition; and Learning the Korn Shell.

Managing Projects with make, 2nd Edition

By Andrew Oram & Steve Talbott
2nd Edition October 1991
152 pages, ISBN 0-937175-90-0

make is one of UNIX's greatest contributions
to software development, and this book is the
clearest description of make ever written. It
describes all the basic features of make and
provides guidelines on meeting the needs
of large, modern projects. Also contains a
description of free products that contain major enhancements
to make.

UNIX Power Tools, 2nd Edition

By Jerry Peek, Tim O'Reilly & Mike Loukides
2nd Edition August 1997
1120 pages, includes CD-ROM
ISBN 1-56592-260-3

Loaded with even more practical
advice about almost every aspect
of UNIX, this new second edition
of UNIX Power Tools addresses the
technology that UNIX users face
today. You'll find increased coverage
of POSIX utilities, including GNU versions, greater bash and tcsh
shell coverage, more emphasis on Perl, and a CD-ROM that
contains the best freeware available.

UNIX Tools *(continued)*

Writing GNU Emacs Extensions

By Bob Glickstein
1st Edition April 1997
236 pages, ISBN 1-56592-261-1

This book introduces Emacs Lisp and tells you how to make the editor do whatever you want, whether it's altering the way text scrolls or inventing a whole new "major mode." Topics progress from simple to complex, from lists, symbols, and keyboard commands to syntax tables, macro templates, and error recovery.

Perl

Perl in a Nutshell

By Stephen Spainhour, Ellen Siever & Nathan Patwardhan
1st Edition January 1999
674 pages, ISBN 1-56592-286-7

The perfect companion for working programmers, *Perl in a Nutshell* is a comprehensive reference guide to the world of Perl. It contains everything you need to know for all but the most obscure Perl questions.This wealth of information is packed into an efficient, extraordinarily usable format.

The Perl Cookbook

By Tom Christiansen & Nathan Torkington
1st Edition August 1998
794 pages, ISBN 1-56592-243-3

This collection of problems, solutions, and examples for anyone programming in Perl covers everything from beginner questions to techniques that even the most experienced Perl programmers might learn from. It contains hundreds of Perl "recipes," including recipes for parsing strings, doing matrix multiplication, working with arrays and hashes, and performing complex regular expressions.

Perl *(continued)*

Learning Perl, 2nd Edition

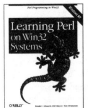

By Randal L. Schwartz & Tom Christiansen
Foreword by Larry Wall
2nd Edition July 1997
302 pages, ISBN 1-56592-284-0

In this update of a bestseller, two leading Perl trainers teach you to use the most universal scripting language in the age of the World Wide Web. Now current for Perl version 5.004, this hands-on tutorial includes a lengthy new chapter on CGI programming, while touching also on the use of library modules, references, and Perl's object-oriented constructs.

Learning Perl on Win32 Systems

By Randal L. Schwartz, Erik Olson & Tom Christiansen
1st Edition August 1997
306 pages, ISBN 1-56592-324-3

In this carefully paced course, leading Perl trainers and a Windows NT practitioner teach you to program in the language that promises to emerge as the scripting language of choice on NT. Based on the "llama" book, this book features tips for PC users and new, NT-specific examples, along with a foreword by Larry Wall, the creator of Perl, and Dick Hardt, the creator of Perl for Win32.

Mastering Regular Expressions

By Jeffrey E. F. Friedl
1st Edition January 1997
368 pages, ISBN 1-56592-257-3

Regular expressions, a powerful tool for manipulating text and data, are found in scripting languages, editors, programming environments, and pecialized tools. In this book, author Jeffrey Friedl leads you through the steps of crafting a regular expression that gets the job done. He examines a variety of tools and uses them in an extensive array of examples, with a major focus on Perl.

O'REILLY®

TO ORDER: **800-998-9938** • **order@oreilly.com** • **http://www.oreilly.com/**
OUR PRODUCTS ARE AVAILABLE AT A BOOKSTORE OR SOFTWARE STORE NEAR YOU.
FOR INFORMATION: **800-998-9938** • **707-829-0515** • **info@oreilly.com**

Perl Resource Kit—UNIX Edition

By Larry Wall, Nate Patwardhan,
Ellen Siever, David Futato & Brian Jepson
1st Edition November 1997
1812 pages, ISBN 1-56592-370-7

The *Perl Resource Kit—UNIX Edition* gives
you the most comprehensive collection
of Perl documentation and commercially
enhanced software tools available today.
Developed in association with Larry Wall,
the creator of Perl, it's the definitive Perl distribution for webmasters, programmers, and system administrators.

The *Perl Resource Kit* provides:

- Over 1800 pages of tutorial and in-depth reference
  documentation for Perl utilities and extensions, in 4 volumes.
- A CD-ROM containing the complete Perl distribution,
  plus hundreds of freeware Perl extensions and utilities—
  a complete snapshot of the Comprehensive Perl Archive
  Network (CPAN)—as well as new software written by Larry
  Wall just for the Kit.

Perl Software Tools All on One Convenient CD-ROM
Experienced Perl hackers know when to create their own, and
when they can find what they need on CPAN. Now all the power
of CPAN—and more—is at your fingertips. The *Perl Resource Kit*
includes:

- A complete snapshot of CPAN, with an install program for
  Solaris and Linux that ensures that all necessary modules are
  installed together. Also includes an easy-to-use search tool
  and a web-aware interface that allows you to get the latest
  version of each module.
- A new Java/Perl interface that allows programmers to write
  Java classes with Perl implementations. This new tool was
  written specially for the Kit by Larry Wall.

Experience the power of Perl modules in areas such as CGI,
web spidering, database interfaces, managing mail and USENET
news, user interfaces, security, graphics, math and statistics, and
much more.

Perl Resource Kit—Win32 Edition

By Dick Hardt, Erik Olson,
David Futato & Brian Jepson
1st Edition August 1998
1,832 pages, includes 4 books & CD-ROM
ISBN 1-56592-409-6

The *Perl Resource Kit—Win32 Edition* is
an essential tool for Perl programmers who
are expanding their platform expertise to
include Win32 and for Win32 webmasters
and system administrators who have discovered the power and
flexibility of Perl. The Kit contains some of the latest commercial
Win32 Perl software from Dick Hardt's ActiveState company, along
with a collection of hundreds of Perl modules that run on Win32,
and a definitive documentation set from O'Reilly.

Programming Perl, 2nd Edition

By Larry Wall, Tom Christiansen &
Randal L. Schwartz
2nd Edition September 1996
670 pages, ISBN 1-56592-149-6

Coauthored by Larry Wall, the creator of
Perl, the second edition of this authoritative
guide contains a full explanation of Perl
version 5.003 features. It covers Perl
language and syntax, functions, library
modules, references, and object-oriented features, and also
explores invocation options, debugging, common mistakes,
and much more.

Learning Perl/Tk

By Nancy Walsh
1st Edition January 1999
376 pages, ISBN 1-56592-314-6

This tutorial for Perl/Tk, the extension
to Perl for creating graphical user interfaces,
shows how to use Perl/Tk to build graphical,
event-driven applications for both Windows
and UNIX. Rife with illustrations, it teaches
how to implement and configure each
Perl/Tk graphical element.

O'REILLY®

TO ORDER: **800-998-9938** • *order@oreilly.com* • *http://www.oreilly.com/*
OUR PRODUCTS ARE AVAILABLE AT A BOOKSTORE OR SOFTWARE STORE NEAR YOU.
FOR INFORMATION: **800-998-9938** • **707-829-0515** • *info@oreilly.com*

How to stay in touch with O'Reilly

1. Visit Our Award-Winning Web Site

http://www.oreilly.com/

★ "Top 100 Sites on the Web" —*PC Magazine*
★ "Top 5% Web sites" —*Point Communications*
★ "3-Star site" —*The McKinley Group*

Our web site contains a library of comprehensive product information (including book excerpts and tables of contents), downloadable software, background articles, interviews with technology leaders, links to relevant sites, book cover art, and more. File us in your Bookmarks or Hotlist!

2. Join Our Email Mailing Lists

New Product Releases

To receive automatic email with brief descriptions of all new O'Reilly products as they are released, send email to:
listproc@online.oreilly.com
Put the following information in the first line of your message (*not* in the Subject field):
subscribe oreilly-news

O'Reilly Events

If you'd also like us to send information about trade show events, special promotions, and other O'Reilly events, send email to:
listproc@online.oreilly.com
Put the following information in the first line of your message (*not* in the Subject field):
subscribe oreilly-events

3. Get Examples from Our Books via FTP

There are two ways to access an archive of example files from our books:

Regular FTP

- ftp to:
  ftp.oreilly.com
  (login: anonymous
  password: your email address)
- Point your web browser to:
  ftp://ftp.oreilly.com/

FTPMAIL

- Send an email message to:
  ftpmail@online.oreilly.com
  (Write "help" in the message body)

4. Contact Us via Email

order@oreilly.com
To place a book or software order online. Good for North American and international customers.

subscriptions@oreilly.com
To place an order for any of our newsletters or periodicals.

books@oreilly.com
General questions about any of our books.

software@oreilly.com
For general questions and product information about our software. Check out O'Reilly Software Online at **http://software.oreilly.com/** for software and technical support information. Registered O'Reilly software users send your questions to: **website-support@oreilly.com**

cs@oreilly.com
For answers to problems regarding your order or our products.

booktech@oreilly.com
For book content technical questions or corrections.

proposals@oreilly.com
To submit new book or software proposals to our editors and product managers.

international@oreilly.com
For information about our international distributors or translation queries. For a list of our distributors outside of North America check out:
http://www.oreilly.com/www/order/country.html

O'Reilly & Associates, Inc.
101 Morris Street, Sebastopol, CA 95472 USA
TEL   707-829-0515 or 800-998-9938
             (6am to 5pm PST)
FAX   707-829-0104

International Distributors

UK, EUROPE, MIDDLE EAST AND AFRICA (EXCEPT FRANCE, GERMANY, AUSTRIA, SWITZERLAND, LUXEMBOURG, LIECHTENSTEIN, AND EASTERN EUROPE)

INQUIRIES
O'Reilly UK Limited
4 Castle Street
Farnham
Surrey, GU9 7HS
United Kingdom
Telephone: 44-1252-711776
Fax: 44-1252-734211
Email: josette@oreilly.com

ORDERS
Wiley Distribution Services Ltd.
1 Oldlands Way
Bognor Regis
West Sussex PO22 9SA
United Kingdom
Telephone: 44-1243-779777
Fax: 44-1243-820250
Email: cs-books@wiley.co.uk

FRANCE

ORDERS
GEODIF
61, Bd Saint-Germain
75240 Paris Cedex 05, France
Tel: 33-1-44-41-46-16 (French books)
Tel: 33-1-44-41-11-87 (English books)
Fax: 33-1-44-41-11-44
Email: distribution@eyrolles.com

INQUIRIES
Éditions O'Reilly
18 rue Séguier
75006 Paris, France
Tel: 33-1-40-51-52-30
Fax: 33-1-40-51-52-31
Email: france@editions-oreilly.fr

GERMANY, SWITZERLAND, AUSTRIA, EASTERN EUROPE, LUXEMBOURG, AND LIECHTENSTEIN

INQUIRIES & ORDERS
O'Reilly Verlag
Balthasarstr. 81
D-50670 Köln
Germany
Telephone: 49-221-973160-91
Fax: 49-221-973160-8
Email: anfragen@oreilly.de (inquiries)
Email: order@oreilly.de (orders)

CANADA (FRENCH LANGUAGE BOOKS)
Les Éditions Flammarion ltée
375, Avenue Laurier Ouest
Montréal (Québec) H2V 2K3
Tel: 00-1-514-277-8807
Fax: 00-1-514-278-2085
Email: info@flammarion.qc.ca

HONG KONG
City Discount Subscription Service, Ltd.
Unit D, 3rd Floor, Yan's Tower
27 Wong Chuk Hang Road
Aberdeen, Hong Kong
Tel: 852-2580-3539
Fax: 852-2580-6463
Email: citydis@ppn.com.hk

KOREA
Hanbit Media, Inc.
Sonyoung Bldg. 202
Yeksam-dong 736-36
Kangnam-ku
Seoul, Korea
Tel: 822-554-9610
Fax: 822-556-0363
Email: hant93@chollian.dacom.co.kr

PHILIPPINES
Mutual Books, Inc.
429-D Shaw Boulevard
Mandaluyong City, Metro
Manila, Philippines
Tel: 632-725-7538
Fax: 632-721-3056
Email: mbikikog@mnl.sequel.net

TAIWAN
O'Reilly Taiwan
No. 3, Lane 131
Hang-Chow South Road
Section 1, Taipei, Taiwan
Tel: 886-2-23968990
Fax: 886-2-23968916
Email: benh@oreilly.com

CHINA
O'Reilly Beijing
Room 2410
160, FuXingMenNeiDaJie
XiCheng District
Beijing, China PR 100031
Tel: 86-10-86631006
Fax: 86-10-86631007
Email: frederic@oreilly.com

INDIA
Computer Bookshop (India) Pvt. Ltd.
190 Dr. D.N. Road, Fort
Bombay 400 001 India
Tel: 91-22-207-0989
Fax: 91-22-262-3551
Email: cbsbom@giasbm01.vsnl.net.in

JAPAN
O'Reilly Japan, Inc.
Kiyoshige Building 2F
12-Bancho, Sanei-cho
Shinjuku-ku
Tokyo 160-0008 Japan
Tel: 81-3-3356-5227
Fax: 81-3-3356-5261
Email: japan@oreilly.com

ALL OTHER ASIAN COUNTRIES
O'Reilly & Associates, Inc.
101 Morris Street
Sebastopol, CA 95472 USA
Tel: 707-829-0515
Fax: 707-829-0104
Email: order@oreilly.com

AUSTRALIA
WoodsLane Pty., Ltd.
7/5 Vuko Place
Warriewood NSW 2102
Australia
Tel: 61-2-9970-5111
Fax: 61-2-9970-5002
Email: info@woodslane.com.au

NEW ZEALAND
Woodslane New Zealand, Ltd.
21 Cooks Street (P.O. Box 575)
Waganui, New Zealand
Tel: 64-6-347-6543
Fax: 64-6-345-4840
Email: info@woodslane.com.au

LATIN AMERICA
McGraw-Hill Interamericana
Editores, S.A. de C.V.
Cedro No. 512
Col. Atlampa
06450, Mexico, D.F.
Tel: 52-5-547-6777
Fax: 52-5-547-3336
Email: mcgraw-hill@infosel.net.mx

O'REILLY®